Table o

WALTER RUSSELL

THE UNIVERSAL ONE

An exact science of the One visible and invisible universe of Mind and the registration of all idea of thinking Mind in light, which is matter and also energy

Edition 2022 by ©David De Angelis

An meinen Freund Wolfgang Wiedergut
überreicht am 17. Mai 1996
[illegible]

To the One God, the universal One this book is humbly dedicated

PREFACE

THE UNIVERSAL ONE was originally published in 1927 and distributed to the top scientists in the country. It is being republished at this crucial period for the sole purpose of again releasing vital new scientific knowledge to this new age- of new comprehension.

Today the whole world is in a state of chaos fighting against the forces of greed, envy, jealousy and fear. Disharmony is rife. All of our human relations are in a state of violent upheaval. Civilization is in reverse. Science is being used to destroy instead of to build.

We talk of world peace, yet those who are to plan the new world do not know the answer, the solution. Present knowledge of man's relation to Nature and Natural Law which controls his human relations is, as yet, inadequate to meet the situation.

Man is still too near his jungle to either know the law which inexorably governs his every action and that of everything in Nature or to comprehend that he must obey Nature or be self-destroyed. Still dominated by jungle habits, he settles his human relations by jungle methods. Wars and world chaos will continue until new knowledge applicable to the coming new cycle in man's evolution is acquired by him.

What is this new knowledge?

A consistent cosmogony is sorely needed for this newly dawning day of man's exaltation which is to come.

Walter Russell spent a full seven years in writing this book. When it was first published in 1927, it won more condemnation than favor from a world which was not then as ready for it as now. The book mixed science and metaphysics in a manner which nullified its impression upon physicists. Gradually, however, many of its then radical statements have been verified by some of the world's greatest scientists and have won him many followers.

The physicist draws a sharp line between things which he can in some way detect by the evidence of his senses and things which lie beyond that evidence. There is no denial of a "something" beyond the range of his senses and his sensed instruments, but what may be there is conjectural and, therefore, inadmissible as scientific data of a reliable nature. In other words, material evidence which lies within the narrow limits of man's sense-range is the only admissible evidence to science. But what about that vast range which will not respond to our sensed bodies and sensed instruments?

Down the ages a rare few have been permitted to sever the senses which connect matter with its motivated Source in the consciousness of Universal Mind. These few have become conscious of the cosmos and have tried to tell the world of its simplicity. Each of these has faced an impossible task. The generalities and symbols which they did set down have been discounted and relegated to poetry or metaphysics or mysticism.

Walter Russell had this same sad experience in the beginning--and all this in face of the fact that the mental state of cosmic consciousness is today admitted, and desired, by the greatest of the world's thinkers, although it is little understood and impossible to induce.

In the month of May of 1921, the universal One illumined my beloved husband with the cosmic knowledge contained in his immortal THE DIVINE ILIAD* and commanded him to give this new scientific knowledge to aid mankind in his unfolding into a Cosmic Age of awareness wherein man could become knowing man instead of sensing man. Just as the bolometer and negative have reached beyond man's visible spectrum into the heretofore "unseen," so can man's increasing awareness of his relation to the Source make it possible for him to reach deeper and deeper into the invisible and unseen.

Such a consciousness can perceive there, with other eyes, that which the senses of man have no way of perceiving.

For centuries, science has been searching for the WHY of things in matter and does not seem to realize that the WHY is not in matter at all, nor in space. Space is as much matter as planets are but of an opposite form, potential and purpose. There is something beyond the matter of galaxies and space which the senses cannot fathom but the consciousness can. Beyond that range lies the cause of it, the WHY of it.

In trying to awaken within man an awareness of the Source of all science and philosophy by knowing God's ways sufficiently to make them man's ways, Walter Russell has pictured the orderliness, the symmetry and the balance which all Nature expresses. He explains how Nature perpetually polarizes and depolarizes in its every expression, just as you do in your every action and in every second of your life in your brea things, but you are not aware of it.

The fulcrum from which all power springs is KNOWLEDGE. When man has that omniscience which is unfolding in cosmic man, he will no longer misuse, break or disobey God's law because of being unaware of it. He will command it because he will know the law. The "life and death" cycles of man and of the elements of matter do not vary. They are the same, for man's body is a compound of these elements.

The late Dr. Francis Trevelyan Miller (LITT.D.,LL.D.) Historical Foundations, New York, wrote of Walter Russell's contributions to science as follows:

"You have opened the door into the infinite —Science must enter. It may hesitate; it may engage in controversy, but it cannot afford to ignore the principles you have established which eventually will revolutionize man's concept of himself, his world, his universe, and his human problems.

"You have done for us in this Twentieth Century what Ptolemy, Euclid, Copernicus, Galileo, Kepler did for their earlier centuries. But you have further penetrated all physical barriers and extended your discoveries into definite forms of the infinite law which created our universe and keeps it in operation with mathematical precision through the millions of years."

Sir Oliver Lodge once said that the physicist's type of mind could never fathom the mystery of the universe, and the great story, if it ever came at all, must be "the great inspiration of some poet, painter, philosopher or saint."

Less than two hundred geniuses have appeared among men since the beginning of man, and not more than four or five highly illumined mystics. To these we owe what culture the world possesses today, yet our whole educational system is opposing their development, and our society as a whole is more apt to demean than to glorify them. It is most unfortunate that humans do not realize this sorry fact, for as long as man neglects to honor his geniuses who are engaged in the arts of peace and glorifies his "heroes" who are most proficient in the arts of war, the human race will continue to suffer the agonies of its own making.

This now ending Barbaric Age is peopled with God fearing men. The dawning Cosmic Age is being peopled with God-loving men. The coming race of men will know that love is all there is in God-nature and that the manifestation of love is all there is in the physical universe.

The Law of Love is rhythmic balanced interchange between all things. Upon the law of balanced interchange, this entire reciprocal universe is motivated with such exactness of balance that astronomers can calculate the positions of planets and suns to the split second. In this wise, the universe is dependable. It observes the Law. It cannot do otherwise where God controls all things.

In Walter Russell's worldwide acclaimed book, THE SECRET OF LIGHT, is the following fragment from THE DIVINE ILIAD:

"Again I say that all things extend to all things, from all things, and through all things. For, to thee I again say, all things are Light, and Light separates not; nor has it bounds; nor is it here and not there.

"Man may weave the pattern of his Self in Light of Me, and of his image in divided Lights of Me, e'en as the sun sets up its bow of many hues from divided Light of Me, but man cannot be apart from Me, as the spectrum cannot be apart from Light of Me.

"And as the rainbow is a light within the light, inseparable, so is Man's Self within Me, inseparable; and so is his image My image.

"Verily I say, every wave encompasseth every other wave unto the One; and the many are within the One, e'en down to the least of waves of Me.

"And I say further that every thing is repeated within every other thing, unto the One.

"And furthermore I say, that every element which man thinketh of as of itself alone is within every other element, e'en to the atom's veriest unit.

"When man queries thee in this wise: `Sayest thou that in this iron there is gold and all things else?' thou may' st answer: 'Within the sphere, and encompassing it, is the cube, and every other form that is; and within the cube, and encompassing it, is the sphere, and every other form that is."

We are at the dawning of a glorious New Age of knowledge and awareness of our oneness with all life. May we bring into being in this twentieth century the Life Triumphant for all peoples everywhere and thus fulfill our sole purpose on earth—which is to discover our divinity and live it!

(1974 printing)

LAO RUSSELL

Special Notation:

In the interim of the writing of THE UNIVERSAL ONE from 1921-1927 to 1947 when THE SECRET OF LIGHT was released—and also our book entitled ATOMIC SUICIDE? which was published in 1957—Dr. Russell's thoughts and awareness matured in expression and he clarified and rectified errors he felt that he had committed in his earlier writings. It was never his intention to reprint THE UNIVERSAL ONE. However, because of the numerous requests that we have been receiving for copies of this great book, and because it may be of untold help at this crucial period in mankind's progress, we are reprinting it in its original form.

L.R.

PRELUDE

THE supreme service which man can render to evolving man is to answer for him, dynamically, the great heretofore unanswerable question concerning the One universal force which man calls God, or Mind, or by other names.

For long ages man has impatiently awaited the knowledge which would tear away the veil from the invisible universe which lies beyond his perception and bring it within the range of both his perception and his exact comprehension.

Mathematical and measurable proof of the existence of but One Mind, One force and One substance would give to man absolute control over matter, the power to create, even as God creates, and within the same limitations.

Man is omnipotent when he but knows his omnipotence. Until that day he is but man.

Voltaire said that man could never comprehend God for man must be God to comprehend Him.

Man is God and therefore God is within the comprehension of man.

Man is Mind. Man is matter. Mind and matter are One. God is Mind.

This is a universe of Mind, a finite universe, limited as to cause, and to the effect of cause. A universe of limitations cannot be infinite. There is no infinite universe.

A finite universe, in which the effects of cause are limited, must also be limited as to cause; so when that measureable cause is known then can man comprehend and measure all effects.

The effects-of cause are complex and mystify man but cause itself is simple.

The universe is a multiplicity of changing effects of but One unchanging cause.

All things are universal. Nothing is which is not universal. Nothing is of itself alone. Man and Mind and all creating things are universal. No man can say: "I alone am I."

There is but One universe, One Mind, One force, One substance.

When man knows this in measurable exactness then will he have no limitations within those which are universal.

He will then know that all knowledge exists within man and is subject to his desire to recall it from within his inner Mind.

Knowledge is not acquired from without but merely recollected from within. The recollection of knowledge from within is an electromagnetic process of thinking Mind which is as exactly under man's control as is the generation of the same power to turn a wheel.

Man must "think in light"; his thinking must be in terms of the electromagnetic periodicities which measure all motion, for of such is he himself, and nothing else.

To know how to think in light from within is to open the doors of all knowledge.

Omnipotence lies in perfect thinking. There is no power in this universe other than the energy of thinking Mind.

Thinking is the cause of motion and the periodicities, or states of motion, caused by thinking Mind are registered in light which man calls "matter."

Matter is light. Nothing is which is not light.

We are prone to think that this civilization of ours is an extremely advanced one. On the contrary, man of today is in an exceedingly primitive state of his evolution. He is a bearer of heavy burdens, sweating at heavy labor in the bowels of the earth because of his pitiful ignorance of universal power which awaits only his- knowledge to render it available for his free use.

Knowledge of the One Thing will lift the yoke which man has placed on his own shoulders.

This knowledge is herein written down in the language of a new dynamic science of new concepts which are measurable; which explain the heretofore unexplainable.

Language is lacking in words to express new knowledge. Seemingly contradictory words must be used in the hope that the intent will be understood by taking all that is herein written and putting it together, rather than in trying to find comprehension through the analysis of a few inadequate words in isolated paragraphs.

For all those questions which lie unanswered within the heart of man there is a dynamic answer, such an answer as two and two make four.

Faith and theory regarding the universal One need have no place in the thinking of man. They are wanderings in the dark. All things are answerable in light.

The universe is a tonal one, a dimensionless universe of light.

All nature is a series of orderly tonal periodicities of the One force, assembled into the complex idea of thinking Mind, and registered in light, or matter, or energy in interchanging potentials, all of which are variable, yet comprehensible and measurable states of motion of the One substance.

All dimension is an illusion, an appearance, due to rising potential, which must disappear into its inevitable sequence of lowering potential, and again appear in endless cycles of appearance, disappearance and reappearance.

Ecstatic man is he who can think in those high octaves of the inner Mind which has been termed "spirit."

Ecstatic man is inspired man of universal genius, of inner thinking.

Inspired man is he to come whose thinking will be from within, in light, and it will be an ecstasy of thinking which will produce enduring things. That work which is created in ecstasy of inner thinking can alone endure.

To think in light is not a new power being developed by evolving man. It is a power which is now within him awaiting only his knowledge of the use of that power. It is merely the recognition by man of his absolute control of the many dimensions of the universal constant of energy which constitutes the thinking process of Mind exactly as he can control the changing speeds of his motor car.

When man can change the low speed of his objective thinking in this universe of dimension to the high speed of his inner thinking where dimension disappears in light, then is he superman. Then is he universal genius.

Light is the universal language in which the Divine Concept is plainly written.

Fundamentally wrong in its basic premises, and wasteful in its practice, man's modern concept of the universe must be torn down and built again on truth as plainly told in light.

Primitive in his concepts, man divides the universe into the seen and the unseen, then finds himself groping in the dark, blindfolded, hopelessly trying to find the way to the door of the Holy of Holies.

There is no unseen universe. The way to that innermost sanctuary of the Most High is as clearly posted as the Lincoln Highway; but man has not been able to read the plainly worded messages written all along the way in light.

Man's most wonderful of instruments, the spectroscope, has told him little, for he has not yet learned to read it. He does not know that those many lines of light are but letters of the alphabet of light in which the universal One registers His mighty thinking in the universal language of light.

The spectrum of iron is to man naught but the spectrum of iron. To the cosmic import of those many glowing lines he is indeed blind.

Again, in helium he reads the lines as helium's lines and sees not in them the plain story simply told of six new elements of vast import awaiting man's use in the easing of his burden.

And of those most important of the elements, which man calls the "inert gases," nothing at all is known except that they will not combine with any other elements. O the pity of it!

Wrong concepts of the atom's structure and the modern electric theory, of energy and its transmission, of conductivity, radiation and gravitation, and of that electrochemical state of opposed motion called luminosity, all of these wrong concepts of motion, and of matter, must be remoulded on truth.

With truth comes knowledge; and with knowledge power to transmute at will, and simply, plentiful substances of matter into those which are the rarest, to meet the needs of man.

There is no substance which nature produces which man cannot produce, or synthesize, or "create" from apparent nothingness when he knows that which is herein written down and charted. Man's miracles of today become commonplace events of tomorrow.

Civilizations come and go, exalted by man's thinking or by it plunged into the abyss of darkened ages.

This message is for all mankind and not for the few, for it is placing within his hands a power which could either glorify or frightfully enslave him in accord with the usage of that power.

Either way it matters not, for in the end truth will survive, and man will complete his destiny.

Truth lives. There is naught but truth and that which appears to be otherwise has no existence and therefore is not, nor ever will be.

In the beginning was the Word,
and the Word was with God,
and the Word was God. The
same was in the beginning with God.
All things were made through Him
and without Him was nothing made
which was made.

John i: 1

PERIODICITY IS AN ABSOLUTE CHARACTERISTIC OF ALL PHENOMENA OF NATURE

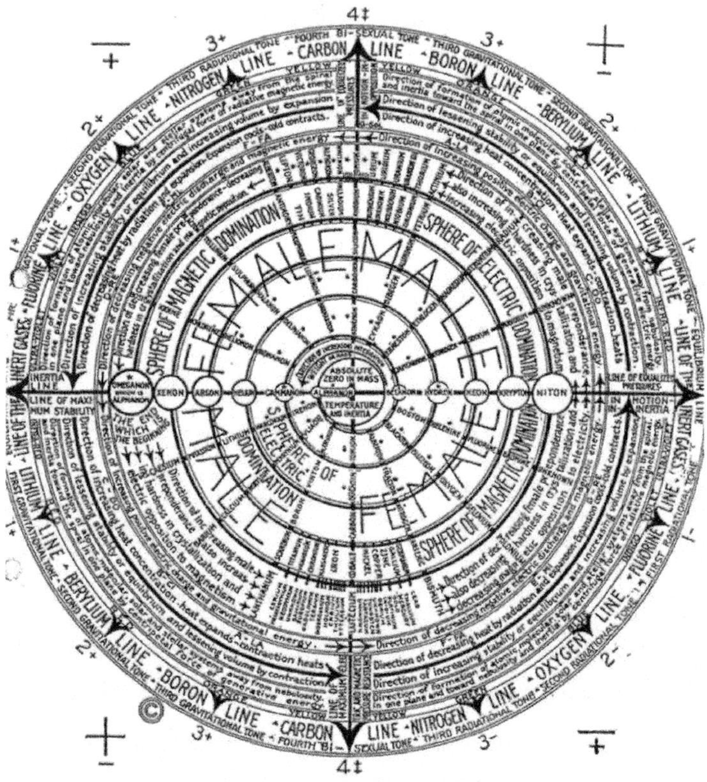

THE RUSSELL PERIODIC CHART OF ATOMIC WEIGHTS, ELECTRO-MAGNETIC CHARGE, GRAVITATION, RADIATION, SEX, TEMPERATURE, ELECTRIC AND MAGNETIC PRESSURES, VALENCE, IONIZATION AND OTHER PERIODICITIES

BOOK I - CHAPTER I

CREATION

DIVINE MIND--GOD--SPIRIT

CREATION AND THE ORDER OF CREATION

In the beginning, God.

There is but one God.

There is but one universe.

God is the universe.

God is not one and the universe another. The universe is not a separate creation of God's. It is God. There is no created-universe.

Nothing is which has not always been.

All created things are from the beginning. They have no beginning. They do not come into being. They are and always have been and always will be.

Creation means to man the coming into existence of something which was not before in existence. Man's concept of creation is the coming into being of a physical, visible universe heretofore nonexistent.

The Creator is to man's mind a Sublime Being, separate and apart from man, who created the physical universe of matter, causing to come into being that which had not been.

Man holds the concept of two universes; a spiritual and a physical. God is presumed to be of the spiritual universe, perfect. Matter is of the physical universe, imperfect. God supposedly created the imperfect physical universe separate and apart from Himself.

Man conceives a perfect and omnipotent God. A perfect and omnipotent God could not create imperfection.

He could not create a lesser than Himself.

He could not create a greater than Himself.

God could not create other than Himself.

God did not create other than Himself, nor greater, nor lesser than Himself.

In the sense generally understood by man God did not create anything.

Nothing has been "created."

This is a "creating" universe, not a "created" one.

Man's concept of the sublime Being as the Creator of a material universe different in substance from the spiritual universe is a misconcept.

God is all there is.

Beyond God there is nothing.

Superior to God there is nothing.

Inferior to God there is nothing.

Opposed to God there is nothing.

Creation is not more, nor is it less than it has always been from the beginning.

It cannot be more than God nor can it be less than God.

"Creation" is an apparent integration in continuity of that which already exists in substance. It is a periodic change of state of the One unchanging substance. It is evolution.

De-creation is an apparent disintegration in continuity of apparently integrated things returned to that substance. It is dissolution.

God is in reality, and exists in substance.

God is thinking Mind.

The substance, or body, of God is light.

The One universal substance,' which is God, is a tangible substance, a thinking substance, comprehensible and describable and possessed of principles which are familiar to man through man's observation of the One universal substance in "created" things.

The substance of all "created" things is light.

The One substance of thinking Mind is all that exists.

The "created"universe is the registration in matter of the idea of thinking Mind.

Mind is expressed in light.

Light is the storehouse of the energy of thinking Mind.

The energy of the universe is the energy of thinking Mind.

The universe is a universe of energy.

Energy is expressed in light.

Mind is the universe.

Mind substance is "spiritual" substance.

Spirit is light.

Spirit is the ultimate, the eternal, though finite substance.

Spirit is not infinite. Nothing in this universe of motion is infinite.

Man's concept of an infinite God, possessing infinite knowledge and infinite power, Creator of an infinite universe of infinite extension, is not in accord with the laws of motion.

This is a boundless, eternal, dimensionless universe of definite limitations both as to all cause and to all effects of cause. Dimension is an illusion of relation of effects, which are in themselves but illusions.

All cause is comprehensible to, and all effects are measurable by man. A limited, measurable universe cannot be infinite; and a Divinity limited as to His range of cause, which, ipso facto, limits the possible range of effect, cannot be infinite.

Light is the living substance of Mind in action. It is the creating principle of the One substance.

The One substance is the etheric "spiritual" substance of the One universal Mind.

The entire "created" universe of all that is, ever has been, or ever will be, is but the One substance in motion, light.

God is light and in Him is no darkness at all. (John i-5.) Matter is light.

God and matter are One.

Spirit and matter are the same substance.

That substance is light.

There are not two substances in the universe.

There cannot be two substances in the universe.

The substance of the universal Mind is a living substance.

That which man calls life is an inherent property of the entirety of Mind.

Light is life.

There is but One Life in the universe.

The whole of the universe is but One living, breathing, pulsing Being.

There are not two lives or two living beings in the universe.

There are not two of any thing in the universe.

The universe and all that is, is One.

CHAPTER II

THE LIFE PRINCIPLE
LIFE IS THE PULSING, ELECTROMAGNETIC OSCILLATION OF THINKING MIND

All life is immortal life. There is no mortal life.

Life is a vitalizing property of all matter. Life is in and of all matter.

Man's concept of life is not logical.

Man conceives life to be a property apart from matter, quickening compound elements of inorganic matter into living, functioning, organic beings.

Man defines organic matter as that in which life begins to function, imbuing it with vitality and intelligence.

Man defines inorganic matter as those elements or compounds of matter in which there is no life and in which there is no vitality nor intelligence.

Man conceives life as spontaneously generated in matter at favorable temperatures and under favorable conditions.

Such concepts are not true concepts.

In searching for the life principle man is attempting to discover something corresponding to a germ which quickens lifeless matter.

Life is not a germ and no matter is lifeless.

Life is in and of all things from the beginning, always and forever. Life has no beginning. Life has no ending.

Life is eternal.

Life is in and of all inorganic as well as all organic matter.

Life is in and of all of the elements and the atoms of the elements and the compounds of the elements.

Life is in and of the sun of the atom, the planets of the atom and the heavens surrounding the universe of the atom.

Life is the effect produced on the substance of Mind by the sequence of alternating electromagnetic pulsations which constitute the process of thinking. The progress of this effect is registered in integrating light and manifests itself in that orderly periodic phenomenon inherent in all matter and all things which man calls "growth."

All "growing" things are imbued with the life principle.

All things are "growing" things. All matter is evolving.

All matter is growing.

All matter is living.

Life is merely the registration, in matter, of states of motion of thinking Mind.

The substance of Mind has the appearance of many states of motion which man calls the "elements of matter."

The "elements of matter" do not vary in substance. They vary only in their states of motion.

All motion is periodic and evolutionary.

All motion is motion in equilibrium. No other motion is possible.

All motion has the appearance of being divided into opposites.

These opposites of motion shall henceforth be termed "motion-in-inertia" and "motion-in opposition."

All that appearance which man calls matter is "motion-in-opposition."

Motion-in-opposition is under either preponderantly electric or magnetic domination. It is a state of motion where pressures are unequalized and sustained in their state of unequalization by the resistance of the two opposing forces in motion. The point of maximum motion-in-opposition is the nucleal center of a unit or system where opposing pressures reach their point of maximum pressure. Form of matter disappears into motion-in-inertia.

Motion-in-inertia is equally electric and magnetic. Neither force dominates. It is a state of motion where pressures are equalized.

Man's concept of life is energized, organic substance.

Man's concept of death is de-energized, organic substance.

There is no death. Life is eternal.

The One substance of the universe cannot become de-energized.

Man's concept of life belongs to motion-in-opposition.

Man's concept of death belongs to motion- in-inertia.

Life belongs, in principle, to motion.

This is a universe of motion.

The cause of all motion is the dynamic action of thinking of the One universal living Being, which man calls God, or Mind, or by other names, all of which stand practically for the one idea of fatherhood, or deity.

Thinking is a process, an orderly, evolutionary, periodic process of absolute limitations.

All motion of thinking Mind is born in the maximum high speed of the universal constant of energy. It runs the gamut of periodic and opposing deceleration and acceleration in six full tones, one double tone, and a master-tone, to each of ten lowering octaves, and a variable number of mid-tones in each of the last four octaves.

The seven tones are those so-called "elements of matter" which are improperly classified in the eight groups of the commonly accepted Mendeléef periodic table. All effects of motion which cause the appearance of these elements is that which is herein termed "motion-in-opposition."

The master-tone of each octave is the record of all motion taking place within the octave.

The master-tones are the turning points between reaction and action, just as the double tones are the turning points between action and reaction.

They are the beginnings of each new expression of energy in motion and are records of the old.

They are the ends of exhalations and the beginnings of inhalations.

The master-time of each octave is the inheritance of the original motion of the thinking process of Mind. These master-tones are the 'inert gases" which are classified in the zero group of the Mendeleef table.

The state of motion of these inert gases is that of motion-in-inertia.

Motion-in-inertia is that state of pressure equilibrium which lies between any two masses.

The inertial line, or plane, is that dividing line, or plane, toward which all masses discharge their potential.

It is the line, or plane, of lowest potential of two opposing areas of potential, where opposing pressures neutralize. This is the plane of minimum pressure of two opposing areas.

The master-tones which represent a state of motion-in-inertia and are the inert gases, bear the same relationship to the elements that white bears to the colors. They are a registration of them all. White is not included in the spectrum, it has no place there. The inert gases should not be included in the elements. They have no place there. Of this more shall be written later in its proper place.

The ten octaves constitute a cycle of evolving states of motion. This cycle includes the uttermost limitations of divine possibilities, and beyond it nothing is or can be.

Table of the Periodic Law. (Mendeléef, 1904.)

Series	Zero Group	Group I	Group II	Group III	Group IV	Group V	Group VI	Group VII	Group VIII
0	x								
1	y	X Hydrogen H—1·008							
2	X Helium He—4·0	X Lithium Li—7·03	X Beryllium Be—9·1	X Boron B—11·0	X Carbon C—12·0	X Nitrogen N—14·04	X Oxygen O—16·00	X Fluorine F—19·0	
3	X Neon Ne—19·9	X Sodium Na—23·05	X Magnesium Mg—24·1	X Aluminium Al—27·0	X Silicon Si—28·4	X Phosphorus P—31·0	X Sulphur S—32·06	X Chlorine Cl—35·45	
4	X Argon Ar—38	X Potassium K—39·1	X Calcium Ca—40·1	X Scandium Sc—44·1	• Titanium Ti—48·1	• Vanadium V—51·4	• Chromium Cr—52·1	• Manganese Mn—55·0	• Iron Fe—55·9 • Cobalt Co—59 • Nickel Ni—59 (Cu)
5		• Copper Cu—63·6	• Zinc Zn—65·4	• Gallium Ga—70·0	• Germanium Ge—72·3	X Arsenic As—75·0	X Selenium Se—79	X Bromine Br—79·95	
6	X Krypton Kr—81·8	X Rubidium Rb—85·4	X Strontium Sr—87·6	X Yttrium Y—89·0	• Zirconium Zr—90·6	• Niobium Nb—94·0	• Molybdenum Mo—96·0	—	• Ruthenium Ru—101·7 • Rhodium Rh—103·0 • Palladium Pd—106·5 (Ag)
7		• Silver Ag—107·9	• Cadmium Cd—112·4	• Indium In—114·0	• Tin Sn—119·0	X Antimony Sb—120·0	X Tellurium Te—127	X Iodine I—127	
8	X Xenon Xe—128	X Caesium Cs—132·9	X Barium Ba—137·4	X Lanthanum La—139	• Cerium Ce—140	—	—		— — — (—)
9		—	—		—	—	—	—	
10	—	—	—	• Ytterbium Yb—173	—	• Tantalum Ta—183	• Tungsten W—184	—	• Osmium Os—191 • Iridium Ir—193 • Platinum Pt—194·9 (Au)
11		• Gold Au—197·2	• Mercury Hg—200·0	• Thallium Tl—204·1	• Lead Pb—206·9	X Bismuth Bi—208	—	—	
12	—	—	X Radium Rd—224	—	• Thorium Th—232	—	• Uranium U—239		

The above is a reproduction of the Mendeléef periodic table of the elements as published in the modern textbooks. It is the present chemical record of the visible universe, or the range of matter within the perception of man as of the year 1904 and to which very slight modifications have since been added. It is correct only in the orderly periodicity of atomic weight, which is mass dimension. In all other dimensions and periodicities it is wrongly arranged. There is no eighth group.

All marked with a circle are out of place in octave periodicity and those marked with an X are properly placed.

The inert gases of the zero group are incomplete and 3½ octaves are missing.

This chart is not a workable or practical chart for chemists' use, for it in no way relieves them of the necessity of experimenting in their laboratories to find out that which should be known in advance of experimenting.

All periodicities of all effects of motion can be properly arranged on a workable and dependable chart such as that which has been herein published.

Incomplete as this chart is, Duncan says of it in "THE NEW KNOWLEDGE":

"This periodic law of the atoms is God's alphabet of the universe. By means of it, and by means of it only, can we ever hope to spell out the history and the future of creation. It lies here before us lacking only the master word,—the open sesame,—to creation; and, who knows, to the Creator too."

MENDELÉEF TABLE OF THE ELEMENTS. THIS IMPROPERLY ARRANGED AND INCOMPLETE CHART IS ALL THAT MAN KNOWS TO-DAY OF THE ARRANGEMENT OF THE ELEMENTS.

The cycle begins with the highest note and descends the scale sequentially through man's unseen universe until hydrogen, the first element perceivable to man, is reached.

There is no unseen universe.

Those tones which follow hydrogen are man's visible or "physical" universe of matter and continue into the tenth octave. Here elemental integration and disintegration have ended the cycle by the attainment of the equilibrium of its beginning.

All motion is oscillatory, swinging in sequence between two apparently opposing forces, gravitation and repulsion, which are respectively electric and magnetic.

This oscillatory motion is a pulsating in-breathing and out-breathing, an inhalation and an exhalation, which is a characteristic of all matter, whether it be in units, or systems of units, or mass.

These two apparently opposite forces are the father-mother forces of Mind, which, added together, make but the One force.

There is but one pendulum to the cosmic clock.

All the so-called "created" universe of matter is but the effect of these two apparently opposing male - female forces exerting their opposition.

All motion-in-opposition is both gravitative and repulsive. This is characteristic of all matter.

Motion, at the inertial line or plane where mass disappears, is neither gravitative nor repelative. Hence the muter-tones, which register effects of motion on this line or plane, should not be included in the table of the elements.

All matter is characterized by periodic and alternating opposites of motion in sequence, each opposite being preponderant in sequence.

Each opposite force is the cause of the other.

Opposition is a characteristic appearance of all effects of motion and has no existence other than as an appearance. In inertia, this appearance always disappears.

Motion and matter must not be confounded.

Matter, as man understands matter, is only an appearance due to states of motion.

The creation of form in matter is the apparent integration of those things which are and always have been.

The de-creation of form in matter is the apparent disintegration of apparently integrated things.

Creation is transmutation, or integration, of the one simple indivisible substance, into the appearance of many complex substances and things.

Creation may be likened unto the assembling of a few letters of type for the printing of a very complex idea.

De-creation may be likened unto the redistribution of type, after it has served its purpose of giving expression to idea on the printed page.

Matter is light crystallized into the complex idea of this universe, exactly as literature is type assembled into the complex ideas of a library.

Matter is the registration medium of light, just as letters are the registration medium of literature.

Matter is light gravitationally assembled into the appearance of form, and radially disassembled into the disappearance of form.

The assembling process is what man calls life.

The disassembling process is what man calls death.

Light' exists as light always and forever.

All matter is but a variation of the state of light due to variation of dimension of the evidence of motion in the wave by which all motion is expressed.

To man, matter means the complexity of many substances and many things.

Complexity and variability belong to motion and not to substance. There is but One unchanging substance.

The appearance of change does not belong to substance but to motion.

Man lives in a universe of motion, a universe of appearances and illusions which deceive him, except for those simple, obvious illusions with which he becomes perfectly familiar. Man will stoutly aver that matter changes and that there are many substances, but he would not dream of contending that the moon runs along the road behind the trees as he runs.

Yet one contention would be as reasonable as the other.

Matter and Mind and light and energy are eternal.

They are constant. They are cause.

Form and motion are illusions.

They are fleeting. They are effects.

CHAPTER III

MIND, THE ONE UNIVERSAL SUBSTANCE

Mind is the universe. It is all that is, ever was or ever will be.

Mind is a substance, a material substance. The substance of Mind is the foundation of creation.

It is the seed of the universe. In the seed of the universe is the whole of the universe.

The substance of universal Mind has no beginning, no ending and no bounds.

It is all intelligent, all-powerful and all-present.

The One substance is absolutely frictionless, temperatureless, non - compressable, non - expandable, non-absorbent, non-reflectant, non-resistant and non-refractive; but, potentially, it contains the appearance of all these qualities through the dynamic action of those opposing forces within it which cause it to be a thinking substance in motion.

These qualities belong to motion and appear only through motion-in-opposition.

They are not qualities which belong to the One substance. They are appearances which disappear in the inertial plane of pressure equilibrium which lies between any two masses, hence they have no existence other than as an appearance of existence.

The cause of the appearance of change of the One substance is through change of state, but change of state is not change of substance.

Change of state is not an attribute of substance. It belongs to motion.

It is an illusion of motion which creates the illusion of dimension.

The substance of Mind is the one prechemical substance which is the source of all L the elements and the compounds of the elements, all of which are but appearances. These appearances register the action of the process of thinking, and disappear back into their source of an absolute temperatureless state of motion-in-inertia.

The material substance of Mind is an all-pervading ether which is indivisible, inseparable, indestructible, unalterable and unchangeable; but potentially it contains the appearance of all these dimensions of separability in the states of motion which register the dynamic process of thinking.

The words "spirit" and "ether" are used to express the tenuity of the dimensionless universe, as "solidity" is used to express the compactness of the apparently measurable universe.

States of motion-in-opposition cause the appearance of change from the state of motion-in-non-opposition or inertia, into the appearance of separability into parts. This results in such effects of motion as heat, cold, color, form, sex, growth, valence, ionization, mass, gravity, radiation and many others.

These effects are not a change of substance nor do they divide, alter or separate the One substance of Mind. They are but dimensions.

All effects have the appearance of dimension; they are in themselves but dimensions of that which they appear to be.

The cause of all effects is dimensionless.

Cause is existent.

Effect is an illusion of existence. It but appears to exist.

Change of state appears to change the character of the One substance, but appearances have no existence.

Man is accustomed to appearances. Two objects exactly similar appear dissimilar in perspective.

This is a universe of appearances all of which are relative, and not one of which would have even the appearance of existence without the relation of others.

Without the illusion of separability, space could not be.

Without events, time could not be.

Without motion-in-opposition neither heat, cold, color, sex, mass or any of the effects of thinking could be or appear to be.

Without the variability of motion-in-opposition there could be no appearance of variability in the chemistry of the One substance.

Man's many elements are but variances in states of motion-in-opposition of the One unchanging substance.

They all appear to have separate and distinct characteristics of their own in varying degrees, such as melting points, specific gravity, atomic weight, volume, ionization, stability, valence, electro-magnetic charge, axial rotation, orbital revolution and many other characteristics, which give them the appearance of being separate and different substances.

They are neither separately created individual things nor are they different substances.

Their appearance of separability and difference of substance is due solely to the periodicity of states of motion-in-opposition.

The universal substance of light is a material substance of variable motion which is due to the variability of opposition set up by the two apparently opposing forces of action and reaction which constitute the thinking process.

It is apparently shorn or torn into apparent particles of itself during the process of creative thinking, but actually is unseparated and undivided in the process of that shearing or tearing.

It is without form but potentially it contains all that man calls form.

Form is but an appearance, an effect of motion-in-opposition.

The greater the opposition of the two opposing forces the greater the rigidity of form and mass, and the more distinctive is its appearance of existence.

All of those elements between the third gravitational and third radiational tones, the atomic structures of which are very much contracted in volume, and represent motion in maximum opposition, are the hard, dense, heavy solids of great rigidity.

Such metals for example as iron, copper, gold, silver, manganese, nickel and tungsten; the elements which form such compounds as granite, quartz and flint; and those elements which form such precious stones as the diamond, ruby and emerald; all these elements are made up of light units in maximum motion-in-opposition.

They are very densely packed together in atomic construction, and very closely integrated.

Their electric and magnetic orbits are in spirals of one plane and are very much extended. Their melting points are very high. A study of the charts will show this clearly.

The less the opposition of the two opposing forces the less the rigidity of form and mass, and the more indistinct is its appearance of existence.

All of those elements which, born near the inertial planes of their octaves, indicate by their tonal position on their octave waves a close relation to motion-in-inertia and a lessening degree of opposition, are the softer, less distinct substances.

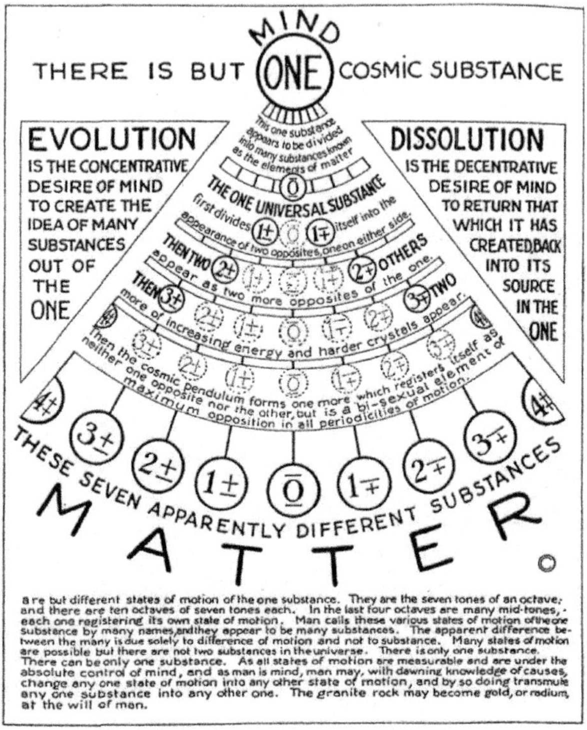

CHART TRACING SOURCE OF MAN'S SUPPOSEDLY MANY SUBSTANCES BACK TO THE ONE

Such elements and compounds as lithium, bromine, sodium, chlorine, salt, sulphur, potassium, iodine, tellurium, magnesium, strontium and rubidium are formed of light units of less potential energy.

The atomic structure of these elements is not closely integrated, but is open, nebulous and very much expanded. Their electric and magnetic orbits are in spirals of many planes, approaching nebulosity in appearance as their position nears their inertial planes. Their melting points are very low.

A study of the charts will show this clearly.

Form, therefore, is not an attribute of the One substance and has no existence other than as an appearance.

Form, like time, space, mass, color, weight, temperature and other effects of motion is an attribute of motion only, and in no way an attribute of substance.

Bubbles whirling in the substance of water have form. Their form is but an attribute of their whirling motion and is not of the substance of water. When the motion ceases form disappears, but the substance remains.

Creation is merely a swing of the cosmic pendulum from inertia, through, energy, and back again to inertia, forever and forever. It is but a series of opposing pulsations of action and reaction, integration and disintegration, gravitation and radiation, appearance and disappearance.

The One universal Mind is a formless, thinking substance.

If the One substance were not a thinking substance, that which man calls creation would not have been.

That which man calls God is an ecstatic thinking substance, thinking in continuity, thinking rhythmically, thinking with orderly variation of intensity in measurable impulses throughout endless ages, in endless space.

Thinking is an action which is the cause of all motion. It is a process, a purely mechanical process, periodic in its evolution through one cycle after another without end.

The process of thinking leaves the evidence of that process behind it, registering the effect of its passage through the Ocean of the universal Mind.

In its wake are myriads of rotating particles of the One substance which register the thinking of Mind, just as in the wake of an ocean steamer are myriads of tiny rotating bubbles which register the passage of that steamer.

The many bubbles in the wake of the steamer produce an effect of foam in the ocean's substance which appears to be different from the surrounding substance.

It is the same substance but of less stability. The whirling bubbles of foam owe their appearance of stability to motion. When the motion ceases the bubbles will disappear.

The wake of the steamer is an appearance which we know will disappear.

It has no stability. It has only an appearance of stability.

The bubbles are apparently separate individuals possessing form and motion which are apparently their own, but which we know are not their own.

Their appearance of separateness we know is but an illusion due to force and motion.

When the churning effect of the propeller has been dissipated, foam, bubbles, wake and all will disappear into the mighty ocean of which they are a part, and from which they have never been separated.

The passage of all thought through the tranquil ocean of universal Mind may well be likened unto the passage of big boats and little boats and all the winds of heaven upon the tranquil ocean of waters.

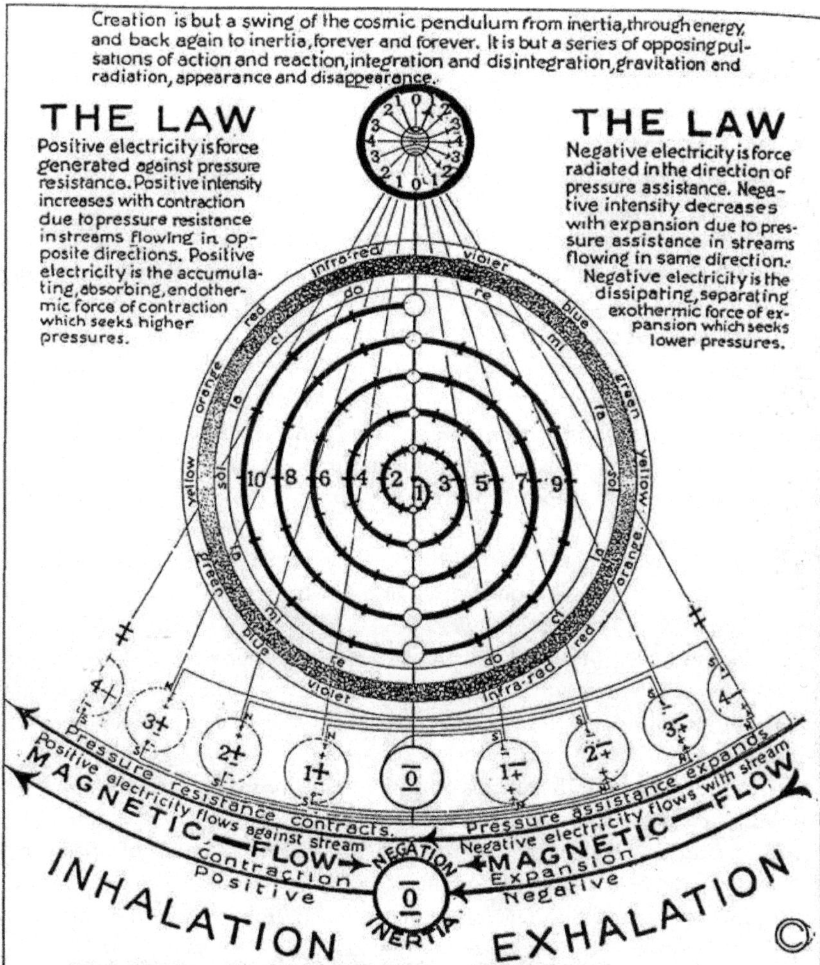

ALL EFFECTS OF MOTION ARE ORDERLY AND PERIODIC. THE COSMIC PENDULUM UNFAILINGLY RECORDS AND ADJUSTS ALL PERIODICITIES

The passage of all these forces leave their effects in appearance upon the ocean of waters, registering thereon in foam the idea of those forces.

Without the exertion of these forces upon the tranquil waters, an absolute uniformity of appearance would prevail throughout the ocean of waters.

Without the force of thinking throughout the tranquil substance of Mind, there would be no appearance of variability whatsoever in the universe of Mind.

There would be no form.

The distinct spiral nebula of Perseus or the trail of the Milky Way looming against the Ocean of Mind is exactly analogous to the foamy wake of a steamer as viewed from a great height.

Both the wake of the steamer and the nebula of Perseus are appearances due to the passage of ponderous ideas, and both will disappear back into the substance of which they are a part.

The myriad whirling spheres of the nebula, its integrating suns and solar system, its planets and moons, its asteroids and meteorites are all whirling forms born of the churning propeller of the One Mind thinking out this universe of ours.

Similarly, the whirling spheres of the steamer's wake, with its big bubbles, its lesser bubbles and its milky foam, are a line of white against the deep blue sea, but not separate from the sea in substance.

The temperature in the wake of the steamer is higher than that of the surrounding water. Similarly the temperature of the spiral nebula is higher than that of the surrounding "ether" matter, because of the heat energy generated by thinking and transferred to the whirling spheres.

The law governing both bubbles and nebula is the same. The difference between them is only relative in point of time.

Both disappear when they cease to whirl, for their appearance of existence is due solely to the heat energy of motion.

A bubble may whirl for a few moments and a sun for a hundred billion years before their generated heat becomes radiated into their father-mother substance which gave them birth.

The difference in time is but relative, for time is nothing in eternity.

When the bubbles have radiated their heat to the temperature of the surrounding water, they cease all appearance of individual existence. Their forms have disappeared with cessation of motion, but their substance is as existent as the ocean is existent.

When giant suns have radiated their heat to the absolute zero of the surrounding ether substance of Mind, they cease all appearance of individual existence. Their forms have disappeared with the cessation of motion, but their substance is as eternal as Mind is eternal.

CREATION	DE-CREATION
All form is generated from the One source of thinking Mind by a preponderance of the concentrative, contractive pressures of the centripetal force of thinking.	All form is radiated back into the One source of thinking Mind by a preponderance of the decentrative, expansive pressures of the centrifugal force of thinking.

CHAPTER IV

THINKING MIND

The process of thinking is a simple one.

It is a swing of the cosmic pendulum from the stability of Mind substance to apparent instability and back again to stability.

The registration of this effect in the ocean of universal Mind is contained within the form of an elongated sphere, and all its variability and complexity may be read upon two exactly opposite spiral waves within two halves of that sphere.

Light, heat, electricity, magnetism, form, crystallization, sound, mass, the elements and compounds of elements, time, space, attraction, gravitation, force, energy, inertia, sex, life, death, sleep, memory, the souls of all things and the complex ideas of all things, in fact, all that man can comprehend of this universe, can be spelled out, in their beginnings, on these two opposing spiral waves within one sphere, and on through to their endings in nine other increasingly larger though flattening spheres, or ellipsoids.

These two opposing spiral waves within one sphere represent the entire simple process of thinking, but not the entire variability of the effect of thinking

They represent the beginning or highest octave in the cycle of thinking, of which there are ten.

The simple process of thinking is repeated exactly in the ten octaves, but with periodic variability and complexity of registered effect.

All variability and complexity of registered effect is orderly in variation and complication; and thus are all effects comprehensible to that man who has knowledge of the cause of those effects.

Everywhere throughout its entirety the Mind substance is in constant agitation, undergoing the orderly process of thinking.

The force called "thinking" which impels Mind into concentration and decentration in sequence is the only energy of the universe.

There is no other energy.

The universe is Mind only.

The universal constant of energy registers, in the substance of Mind, the illusions caused by the thinking of Mind.

Every microscopic point in divine Mind becomes the center of the universe of Mind, with its first impulse of the act of thinking; for with this first impulse is form born into a universe which is without form.

From that center the explosive-reactive, genera-radiative, electro-magnetic disturbance which constitutes the process of thinking, reproduces itself throughout the entirety of the universe at incomprehensible speed in waves of creating light units, which waves return again to that exact center.

Thinking is an action followed by a reaction of that action.

The action of thinking constitutes a series of events in sequence.

The intervals between events in sequence constitute that effect of motion called "time."

Without a sequence of events time could not be for there would be nothing to mark time.

Time begins with the action of thinking. It is an effect which appears with motion-inopposition and disappears into motion-in-inertia.

The events in sequence which give birth to that appearance called "time," are the opposing pulsations of generative and radiative light. These opposing pulsations give dimension and form to that which man calls "life."

To man there is no life without form. Form and dimension are fleeting.

Life is eternal.

Life is merely the action of thinking; and thinking is as eternal as the thinking substance of Mind is eternal.

Universal thinking is rhythmic thinking.

The entire substance of universal Mind is thinking in varying but orderly rhythmic meter.

The meter of universal thinking is measurable in its orderliness throughout the entirety of the universal substance.

The tempo of the cosmic, rhythmic meter of thinking is absolute.

All thinking is expressed in measurable and opposing impulses of opposing motion. All motion is action and reaction.

CHAPTER V

THE PROCESS OF THINKING

The action impulse and the reaction impulse of the thinking process are alternating between the apparent opposites known as generation and radiation.

Generation and radiation are opposites which constitute the appearance, of motion-in-opposition. Generation is the attractive, gravitative, positive, electric force, and radiation is the repulsive, emanative, negative, magnetic force.

All motion, whether in opposition or in inertia, is in equilibrium. That is to say, the amount of energy expended in any two opposite swings of the cosmic pendulum is always quantitatively constant. The apparent variation is in the dimension of the two opposing swings, and is not of the constant of energy.

The amount of generative and radiative energies expended in the two opposing oscillations, anywhere in the entire ten octaves, when added together, total the same in the amount of energy expended.

Motion-in-inertia is characterized by an absolute lack of what man calls "valence," which is grabbing power, or uniting power.

All of the elements of matter in motion-in-opposition have this uniting power in varying degree, or periodicity, just as they have periodicity in electro-magnetic charge and other variations; hence, a further reason for disassociating the inert gases, or master-tones, from the elements.

Opposing impulses of thinking are generated out of inertia and radiated back into equalization in inertia. These impulses are alternating between generation and radiation in a periodicity of preponderance, which periodicity is measurable by man in many ways.

All matter is apparently evolving and devolving into the illusion of many substances of many dimensions.

So-called solids of matter are variations of apparent states of motion registering in form the idea of thinking Mind, and sustained in their appearance as solids of matter by electric preponderance over magnetism.

The electric nature of matter in its progressive periodicity and variation of electromagnetic charge, rotation of its light units and other periodicities, will be written down with more exactness when the process of thinking is more explicitly written down and charted.

Suffice it here to say that thinking is the electro-generative action and magneto-radiative reaction of Mind.

Thinking is a simple process of very complex effects, the sequence of which will be written in its proper place.

The electro-magnetic opposition of Mind as expressed in the process of thinking is the source of all of the energy of the universe.

Thinking, then, is a process of generation of motion-in-variable-opposition out of a state of maximum motion-in-non-variable-inertia, and of radiation back again into that state.

The inertial line is that hypothetical line of absolute non-opposition between the oscillations of the two opposing forces of motion. At the inertial line the two opposing forces are neutralized and in equilibrium. At the inertial line there is no force back of motion but there is the impetus of the magnetic radiative pulsation which continues motion across the inertial line without force. Once across the line, motion is continued by the electro-generative pulsation until magnetic conquest causes it to rebound.

That state of motion which continues motion without force back of it will be known as inertial energy.

The inertial line, or plane, might be characterized as the axis along which wave expressions of the universal constant of energy are born. The mechanic might characterize it as the "dead center" between force and force where no force exists. This point can only be passed by the impetus given to an object in motion prior to its arrival at: that point.

Motion is continuous as thinking is continuous.

The universe breathes, inhaling and exhaling as man breathes; and as every light unit, atom and molecule breathes; and as everything in the firmament above and the waters below breathes.

Exhalation and inhalation, in sequence, is a characteristic of all phenomena of matter.

Motion is caused by the sequence of opposing impulses of thinking. All direction of motion, and effects of motion are governed by these equally balanced gravitative and repulsive, and equally balanced decelerative and accelerative forces.

The opposition of the two apparently op posing forces, which cause apparently opposite impulses, forms spiral waves along which the idea produced in thinking is registered.

The registered idea of thinking is expressed gravitatively in what man calls the "elements of matter," and repulsively in what man calls the "magnetic flow" or "magnetic lines of force" in heretofore unknown magnetic orbits.

All elements of matter are radiative or radioactive, just as all matter is generative, or genero-active.

Electrically generating elements and magnetically radiating lines of force are the same force exerted in apparently opposite directions. The former is centripetal and its direction is toward the nucleal (center of a closing spiral. The latter is centrifugal and its direction is away from the center toward the opening spiral.

Their difference is but a rising or lowering of potential.

One always becomes the other. Each is the cause of the other.

Radio-activity is a lowering of potential into [5] higher octaves of elements of greater speed but lesser power.

Genero-activity is the increasing of potential into lower octaves of greater power and lesser speed.

Genero-activity builds the elements. Radio-activity tears them apart.

The elements are composed of apparently separate particles in motion which shall henceforth be called "light units" or "corpuscles."

The spiral genero-radiative waves are the medium of reproduction of idea throughout the entirety of the universe.

All idea of Mind produced by thinking is reproduced throughout the entirety of the universe of Mind in measurable waves of electro-magnetic opposition.

These apparently opposing genero-radiative waves constitute the creating and decreating universe of integrating and disintegrating elements of potential energy which man calls the "created physical" universe.

Man has measured the speed at which the energy of light appears to travel along waves as 186,400 miles per second.

This measure is the highest measure of the perceptible impulses of universal thinking.

This is the measure of energy reproduction which man calls the "speed of light."

Man's concept of the speed of light, as being uniform, is a wrong concept.

To man, light is incandescent luminosity.

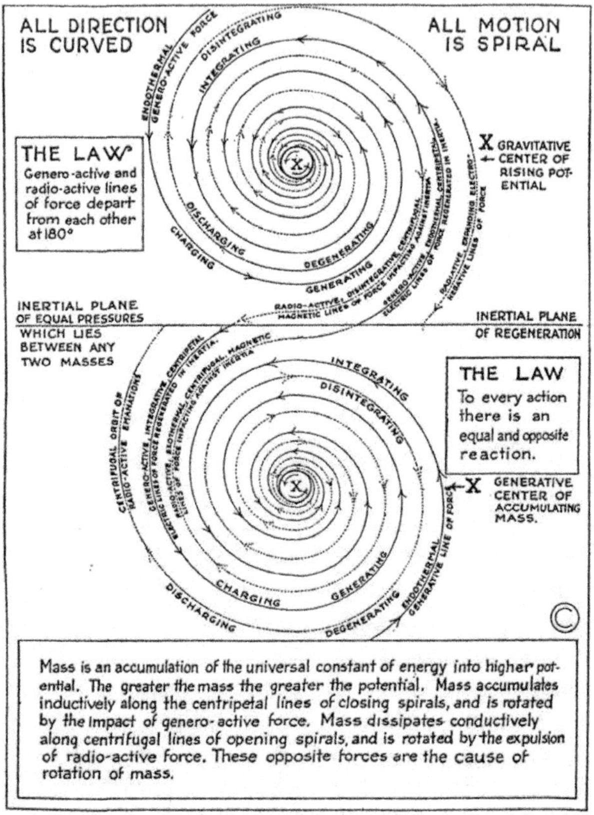

CHART DESCRIBING THE ELECTRO-MAGNETIC PROCESS OF MASS FORMATION. ALL MASS IS ACCUMULATED CENTRIPETALLY BY THE GENERO-ACTIVE, GRAVITATIVE, ATTRACTIVE POWER OF ELECTRICITY, AND IS DISSIPATED CENTRIFUGALLY BY THE RADIO-ACTIVE, REPELLING POWER OF MAGNETISM

To man that which is not glowingly incandescent is not light.

All matter is light. This universe is one of light. Solids of matter, heavy, dark, and cold, are as much light as flaming Arcturus.

Luminosity is but a state of intensely unequalized and opposing motion sustained in its state of unequalized motion by the generation of high pressures. It is but one state of the substance of Mind in motion, a state which is within a limited range of electro-magnetic charge, temperature, and opposition; a range which varies in intensity in each octave, but which runs the whole gamut of its limitations in the ten-octave cycle.

Incandescent luminosity is but the state of maximum opposition of the two apparently opposing forces, and a state in which radiative resistance to generation is at its maximum; a state in which contraction by maximum genero-active accumulation of time into Power is resisting expansion by radiative dissipation of power into time, of which much will be written in its proper place.

Incandescent luminosity is that state of motion which will be known as the high potential of a system or an octave.

It is the meeting place of centripetal and centrifugal forces of preponderantly male and preponderantly female, of maximum electro- magnetic opposition, and it is the state of maximum registration of heat.

It is the turning point where the power of electricity to generate Mind substance into the appearance of form, yields to the power of magnetism to radiate it back into the disappearance of form.

Man's speed of light is the speed at which that state of motion-in-opposition, known as incandescent luminosity appears to travel through those high octaves of integrating matter which man calls "empty space, " or the "ether of space."

This measure of light is but the high measure of a great range of apparent speeds.

All of the elements of matter, in all states of motion, are but orderly and periodic variations of the One substance, light.

As there are innumerable states of motion of the substance of light so also are there innumerable socalled "speeds" of light.

All of the elements of matter are spread out progressively, in varying states of simultaneously decelerative and accelerative motion-in-opposition, on the ten octave waves, like successive tones of music.

All motion-in-opposition is simultaneous in its opposition.

The state of luminosity belongs to all of the elements and varies with the state of integration of each element. It is periodic and orderly in its variation as the elements are periodic and' variable in their integrative weight or mass.

Matter which is apparently non-luminous is simply matter which has become sufficiently retarded generatively and sufficiently expanded radiatively to bring it below the range of motion-in-opposition which produces the appearance of luminosity.

All solids of matter are but integrated light, the generative units of which are sufficiently retarded in their motion, and their resistance to integration sufficiently extended in magnetic orbits, to bring them below the range of the state of apparent luminosity.

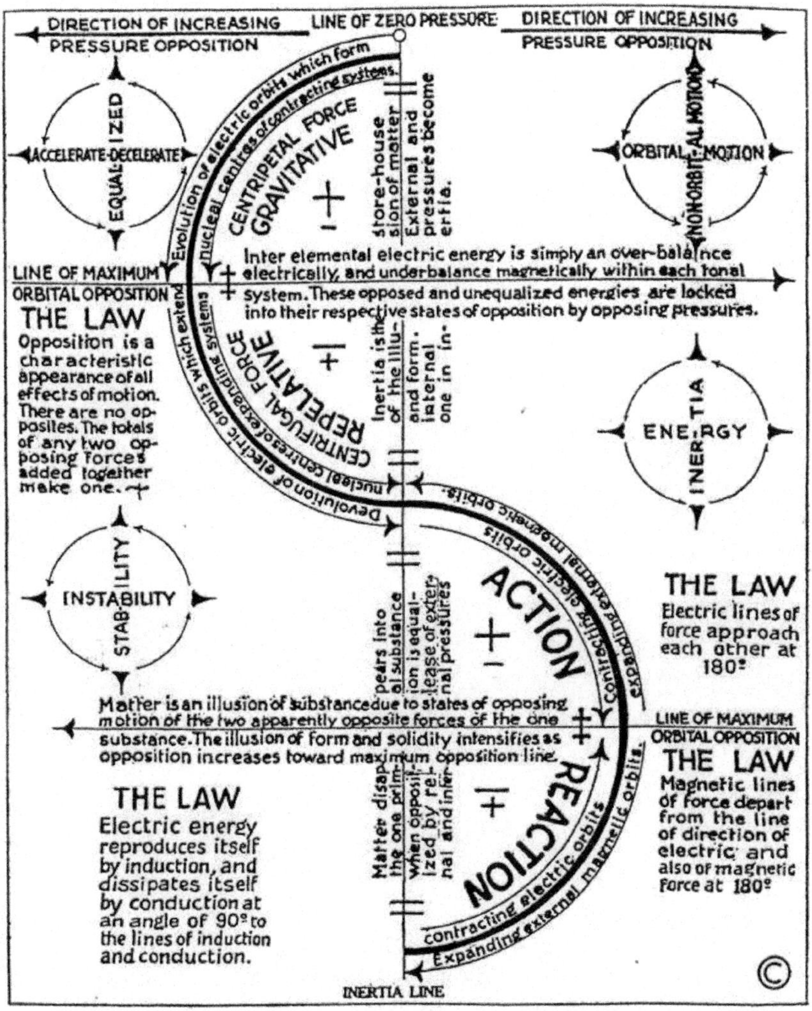

MATTER IS AN APPEARANCE DUE TO A PREPONDERANCE OF ELECTRIC FORCE. IT DISAPPEARS THROUGH A PREPONDERANCE OF MAGNETIC FORCE

CHAPTER VI

THINKING IS REGISTERED IN MATTER

It has elsewhere been written that matter is the registration of the divine idea of thinking Mind.

Man is familiar with the thinking process in his own daily experiences.

Consider for a moment the concentrative thinking of man in conceiving idea.

Is not the idea at first nebulous? And as man concentrates electrically in his thinking is not the idea more and more distinct in form? And does not that form remain clear and distinct so long as man concentrates dynamically upon thinking that idea?

When man's concentration relaxes does not the idea become more and more nebulous in form, and more indistinct, until it is but a memory?

Just so with the thinking of the One universal Mind.

The concentration of all Mind is electro positively registered in motion and its intensity and relaxation of intensity are chemically noted in states of motion of the very Mind substance which performs the action and reaction of the thinking process.

The intense 'concentrated expression of idea in generative thinking is chemically registered in definite, distinct, rigid form while the relaxed, less intense, expanding expression of idea in electronegative, radiative - thinking is chemically registered in indefinite, indistinct, nebulous form.

If the universal Mind is without form within itself, if its light units and mass are but appearances of form due to motion and not to substance, so also is Mind in its entirety without form or shape or size. The universe of Mind is neither bounded nor boundless for it has no extension or continuation.

Apparent separability is a necessary quality in creating the illusion of a universe of extension or continuation. The One substance of divine Mind is non-separable, non-extendable and non-continuous.

The apparent parts of Mind have an apparent relationship to one another.

As the appearance of separability of the Mind substance is but an effect of motion, then also is the appearance of relationship of one apparent part to another but an illusion due to motion.

Relationship of matter is but an appearance and has no existence, and that which man calls "relativity" is but an illusion, just as that which man calls "perspective" is but an illusion. Relativity is the science of an illusion in four dimensions as perspective is in three.

GOD IS LIGHT

Light, as man knows light, is but an unstable simulation of the real light of the Universal One. Man's concept of light is luminosity, an illusion of the universal light of inertia, sustained in its appearance as an illusion of light by the pressures generated through motion.

The inner mind of ecstatic man knows the real light and that he is One with light.

He is not deceived by its illusion.

CHAPTER VII

CONCERNING APPEARANCES

During man's evolution in a universe of motion, the complexity of appearances have bewildered him into forming wrong concepts of reality and unreality.

Man's life has been given so ardently to the observance of complex phenomena of appearances, that appearances have become his facts, and the one reality has become mere conjecture.

Man thinks of dependability in terms of solids, those apparent things which respond to his senses. His dependable reality is form in matter.

Man thinks undependability in terms of things etheric, those things which do not respond to his senses. His unreality is spirit.

Man must learn to alter his concept of the reality of solidity, to the reality of Mind as the source of the illusion of that solidity.

He must learn that the One substance of Mind is the only reality.

He must learn to consider form as only an appearance of reality in a lower octave of the material substance of Mind, over which he has control within the limitations of Mind.

He must learn to consider matter as the substance of Mind, and form in matter as but the registration of his thinking.

He must learn that he is Mind and that Mind is omnipresent, omniscient and omnipotent.

Until man learns that he is Mind he will be 'the slave of the illusions of Mind, instead of which he may be their master and a "creator" of these illusions.

Man's universe is a universe of motion. Man's body is an aggregate of particles in motion.

Man is accustomed to motion. His mind is adjusted to apparent facts of matter which cannot be actual facts, for they are all conditioned by space, time and motion.

A conditioned fact cannot be a fact. It merely appears to be a fact.

That a certain ball weighs a pound is a conditioned fact. Apparently, the ball does weigh that much.

The fact is conditioned upon keeping the ball at the same distance from the ground. Lift it one foot and it weighs less than a pound. Keep it at the same height, and still its weight varies with the movement of the stars in space.

That a ball drops to the ground in a vertical line is a conditioned fact. Apparently, the ball does drop straight toward the earth.

In reality, the line is curved, the curve being conditioned by the rotation of the earth and its movement through space.

This idea may be clarified by imagining a man suddenly created, full grown and highly educated.

This man differs from other men in only one respect. He has not had a lifetime during which to adjust his mind to the relativity of things in his universe of motion, as others have had.

He knows all the supposed facts of things but he has still to learn their apparent relationships; he has yet to find that things seem to be what he knows they are not.

Such a man would find himself in a most bewildering world, a world of very complex effects of very simple causes.

He knows that men are of about the same size, yet before him is a giant, a huge man among pygmies.

The man ten feet away must be a dwarf, and the group across the street mere toys.

The sun he knows to be vast, hot and white, and the world small in comparison. Yet the sun is only a dinner plate and deliciously warm. Lo! it turns red and plunges into the sea. The world is huge and has swallowed the little sun.

He knows the world is round, but here it is before him flat.

A speck appears upon the horizon. It can be nothing. In an hour it is a little boat like those in the children's pond, to be carried home on the end of a string. Yet there are a thousand tons in that toy and fifty men curse up wind as they reef their sails with the brine of the wind in their eyes, and the howl of the wind in their ears.

The moon rushes out from behind the hill and runs as he runs, and stops as he stops. Just a little moon it is, with toy mountains. It runs away and hides behind some chimney pots.

That mountain is blue and this one green. That one is flat like a stage drop scene. This one has fields with gray stone walls, and roads with many trees.

That is a very little mountain, for lo! the ox on the ridge has blotted it out. It is gone. No, here it is back again and the ox has gone. Where did the mountain go? How did it come back? And where has the ox gone?

The road on the opposite hill stands on its end, but it lowers itself as he goes down the road on his hill. And the opposite hill, itself, flattens. It squats down behind the trees on his road. Or do the trees rise up and grow gigantic as he moves.

The iron rails, spreading wide at his feet, meet in a point out there. A railroad train grows from a speck, to a match, to a box, and thunders past, a ponderous thing, shaking the earth in its fearsome passing. What magician has wrought this miracle?

This new made man knows of the majesty of ten billion suns which blaze in the firmament of night. Their hot fire pits swirl in hundred thousand mile pools of swirling.

Where is 'the glory of these fearsome orbs?

Their ardent fires are twinkling candles snuffed out by breathing of soft blown winds.

The milky way is but a mist blown across the darkness of night.

For such a man time, only, could adjust his mind to the relativity of appearances and the conditions of facts.

Ah weal! The universe of man is but a kaleidoscope turning, ever turning, and complexing with its turning.

This universe of form is a universe of INTEGRATION, DISINTEGRATION AND REINTEGRATION.

All form integrates through that contractive, gravitative state of motion which has the apparent power of attracting particles in motion into closer proximity to each other, disintegrates through that expansive, repulsive, radiative state which has the apparent power of separating particles in motion, and reintegrates through a union of both forces, by regenerative impact, in inertia.

CHAPTER VIII

THE SEX PRINCIPLE

Sir Oliver Lodge points out that man has long been familiar with force and motion, but that some third intangible, undiscovered force is recognizedly necessary to complete a logical universe. Force and motion infer that the third undiscovered force is existent somewhere back of, or with them.

He also states that, when discovered, it may prove to be something with which man is already familiar.

Sex is the great third principle. Sex is the controlling cause of both force and motion. Without it, neither could continue.

To say that Mind is the motive power back of force and motion, is but stating a generality; but to state an attribute of Mind by means of which force and motion are controlled, is being specific.

Sex is the motive power behind force and motion.

Sex is the apparent division of the father-mother substance of Mind into apparent opposites. This division is due to the opposite desires of electricity and magnetism, expressed in the action' and reaction of the thinking process.

Sex is the active desire of Mind for division into opposites, and its reactive desire for unity.

Sex is that motive force which demands separability into two, and equally desires union of the apparent two into one.

Mind, being One, cannot yield to the desire of Mind for separation into two.

Sex desire of Mind for divisibility into two succeeds only in producing an appearance of divisibility into two.

Likewise, sex desire of Mind for unity into One succeeds only in reproducing an apparent composite of the two.

Sex is of all things from the beginning. Sex begins when light begins. Sex is the desire for the appearance of being which constitutes the appearance of existence. Nothing can be, without the desire to be. All things are which desire to be.

Desire dominates all thinking.

Desire dominates all matter.

All desire is sex desire.

All desire is for the continuance of existence in the orderliness of existence. Sex desire is that force in thinking which continues thinking.

Existence is continued only through thinking.

Sex force is that quality in the electromagnetic impulse of thinking which continues one impulse of thinking into the next impulse of thinking.

Sex force, like all phenomena of motion, is periodic.

Sex periodicity continues the simple beginning of idea into the complexity of idea.

Sex force is the builder of the apparently many things out of the reality of the One thing.

Periodic variance of sex is the father of desire for the creation of the idea of many things.

Remove the image making faculty of the father force of Mind, and the production of idea would discontinue.

Variance of sex is the mother of desire for unity of sex.

Remove the sex desire of Mind for the unity of One-ness of the mother force of Mind, and reproduction of the idea of Mind would discontinue.

Matter cannot continue its appearance of existence as form, without the desire to continue such an appearance of existence.

The material substance of Mind cannot evade its materialization into the form desired by Mind.

This is an immutable law to which there can be no exception.

Man's concept of sex as beginning with organic life is a wrong concept.

Sex is as absolute in the elements as in the complexities and compounds of the elements.

Man's concept of the beginning of sex and the beginning of life is a concept founded on conditions of temperature.

Sex and life and light and intelligence are in and of all things from the beginning.

The sex principle is as much a part of the granite rock or bar of iron as it is of man.

The great hot star called Argo, blazing away at a temperature of thirty thousand degrees, knows sex in its fiery heart, and cannot continue its appearance without it.

The Martian ice cap knows sex in its frozen depths, and retains its appearance because of sex.

Sex is an electro-magnetic equalizer of matter in motion.

Sex is the apparent division of the One force into electricity and magnetism, two opposite forces, positive and negative, which are in reality but two pulsations of the One force.

Sex is the apparent division of all things into their opposites, male and female.

Sex is evolutionary in all things.

All things are both male and female.

All creation is first male in preponderance, then it is similarly female.

All light units and systems of light units are first male-female, then they are female-male.

Apparent opposites of the indivisible substance of universal Mind are not content to remain in the state of apparent opposition.

Unity, or Oneness, inherent in all things, asserts itself in dissatisfaction when electromagnetic forces of matter in motion are sufficiently generative to cause too great an inequality between the apparent opposites.

Sex is unsatisfied when the electro-magnetic forces of matter in motion are unequal, and it is satisfied when those forces are equal.

A lightning flash is the power of sex equalizing positive and negative electromagnetic disturbances of equilibrium between two oppositely and unequally charged storm clouds. In motion-in-inertia, sex desire is negative.

In motion-in-opposition, sex desire is positive. It is dynamic.

Sex first asserts itself in form.

All form appears through sex, passes through a progressive change called "growth" and disappears. All growth is impelled by force and motion, and controlled by sex.

Neither sex, nor force, nor motion is of itself alone. Each is of the others.

Nothing is of itself alone.

There can be no force without thinking.

There can be no motion without the force of thinking.

There can be no idea of Mind without sex opposition.

There can be no continuity of idea without sex union.

Without union in mating, the idea of any one thing would be extinct as an appearance.

Thinking and working are the causes of those elements which man calls sex, force and motion. Without all three of these there could be no appearance of existence as man knows existence.

Thinking and working continue the appearance of all idea from the high to the low octaves of creation.

All creating things are but the ideas of divine Mind.

The whole idea of all things is in the seed of all things.

In the seed of idea is the whole of idea.

In the seed of the oak is the whole of the oak.

In the seed of the rose is the whole of the rose.

In the seed of man is the whole of man. The seed of all idea is in thinking.

The whole idea of the oak, or the rose, or man is the result of thinking and working for perhaps a billion years of continuing the idea of the oak, the rose or man in the seed thereof.

This is the law of evolving existence. It is as true of complex, as it is of simple things.

All idea is registered in the little particles heretofore referred to as light units.

These units of light, heat, sex, electricity and magnetism, are all male and all female.

Every unit is either preponderantly male or preponderantly female.

Just so is every unit either preponderantly electric or preponderantly magnetic.

Just so is every unit either preponderantly negatively, or preponderantly positively, electromagnetic.

Just so is every unit preponderantly generative or preponderantly radiative. And each unit is all of these.

And each unit is variable, becoming preponderantly one or another of these in its turn, from the beginning to the end of its being.

And the variability is orderly, and governed by measurable laws of periodicity, which are also the laws by which motion is governed.

It must not be forgotten that all that man calls creation is the result of motion which is due to the opposing impulses of thinking.

It must not be forgotten that a continuance of motion causes a creating and not a created universe.

The electro-magnetic action of the impulses of thinking is continuous in its opposing, and therefore are the effects of that opposition continuous.

Opposing desire in sex expression is the cause of opposing motion. A cause cannot evade its effect.

Opposing electro-magnetic impulses are sex-expression in creative thinking.

Opposing electro-magnetic impulses reproduce all effects of creative thinking.

Form is born true to the rhythm of thinking. All thinking is rhythmic thinking.

Idea is synchronous with the rhythm of thinking.

All thinking is sex thinking.

"Creation": is the transforming of the One substance by the rhythmic thinking of idea, into apparent opposites, and into that which man calls form. Beyond this there is no more. Creation is but a concept of Mind. It is but an illusion, an effect of thinking. All thinking is registered in light. All light is sex expression. Light is the language of all thinking. Light is the energy of all thinking. All energy is the energy of sex expression. There is no other energy. Through evolving sex, light causes the transition of the universal substance into form. Through sex periodicity, light transforms form into variety of form.

This universe of motion is a universe of PRODUCTION, DESTRUCTION and REPRODUCTION.

All form is produced by the male, electropositive, plus action of the charging, electric oscillation of the universal life principle, is destroyed by the female, electronegative, minus reaction of the discharging, magnetic oscillation, and is reproduced through the union of both by radio-active regeneration in inertia.

CHAPTER IX

SEX OPPOSITES OF LIGHT

Light is the power which God has used to create the appearance of form.

Light is power for man to use in the perfection of his body. Therefore, must he know the cause of light as he knows his alphabet.

He must understand the inexhaustible source of energy which continues matter in motion, if he would know the fullness of energy available to his command.

The rhythm of creative thinking is absolute.

The registration of creative thinking is absolute. All thinking is creative thinking.

All thinking is creating that which it is thinking.

Man's power of thinking is in sex opposition of Mind.

God's power of expressing Himself is in transforming that which is His own body into an effect which man calls "creation."

The universal One has no other means of expressing idea save through His own body.

Man's power of expressing the idea of himself is only through his own body.

Man has expressed himself through the creation of his own body by his own thinking, exactly as God has expressed Himself through the creation of His own body by His own thinking.

Man's body is but an individual effect of the whole of man and is the product of his thinking.

The universe is the total of all individual effects, and is the product of God's thinking. God's thinking is man's thinking.

All thinking is the product of Mind, and all Mind is divine Mind.

Again, must it be written: "there are not two Minds nor are there two kinds of Minds in the universe."

Light is God's medium of expressing himself. It is the only medium at His command.

Light is man's medium of expressing himself. It is the only medium at his command.

Creation of that which man calls form has a perpetual beginning and a perpetual ending.

Its beginning is in thinking. Its end is in thinking.

Its beginning is its ending.

It has no beginning. It has no ending.

There is no stop, no break, in the continuity of thinking.

To man, its beginning is its appearance within his octaves of perception. To man, its ending is its disappearance beyond his range of perception.

Form is born of the desire to express idea. Form is the plaything of idea.

All form is form of sex.

Idea is never satisfied with form.

Form of idea is continuously changing with the process of thinking.

Form is born anew with each impulse of thinking.

Idea is reasserted in new form with each impulse of thinking.

All idea of Mind is integrated through generative, or male sex thinking.

All idea of Mind is disintegrated through radiative, or female sex thinking.

All idea of Mind is reproduced through the regenerative union of sex •thinking, which is equilibrium of sex.

Idea of Mind may mature, or evolve, only through sex union.

Consider any idea of Mind, whether that of individual man or of the universal One. Man thinks idea.

Thinking is the force of motion.

All motion is expressed in waves.

All waves of motion are both male and female.

All motion is oscillatory action and reaction. Action is male. Reaction is female.

All idea is registered in light as an appearance of the form of idea.

Form of substance is electro-magnetic. This means that it is preponderantly male and preponderantly female in periodicity.

All idea evolves from idea into form of idea, which in turn devolves back again into idea. Evolution is growth. Devolution is dissolution. Evolution is male. It is electrically preponderant. Devolution is female. It is magnetically dominant.

Man can only mature idea through the orderly periodicities of sex thinking.

To evolve idea he must think in light.

Genero-active light is the creative force of sex thinking.

Radio-active light is the decreative force of sex thinking.

Union of these two opposites into the constant of one which is in equilibrium and has impacted in inertia, is the reproductive force.

Sex is a dimension of the illusion of form, and as such it will be further considered with other dimensions of illusion which will be written down and charted.

CHAPTER X

THE REPRODUCTIVE PRINCIPLE

Reproduction means the repetition of a state of motion.

Reproduction is repetition.

All phenomena of nature are repeative. All states of motion are repeative.

All idea of Mind is repeative.

Idea of Mind is the product of thinking. Repetition of idea is the reproduction of that product.

This is a universe of repetition of motion. This is a universe of reproduction.

This universe of cause and effect is perpetual and continuous as to cause, and repeative as to all effects of cause.

All effect is caused by thinking and registered in motion.

All motion is either an action or reaction of its cause.

Nothing is produced as an effect of thinking that is not either the action or reaction of force expressed in motion.

That which is produced must be reproduced.:

No state of motion ever ends.

All states of motion are forever reproduced.

All states of motion of apparently separate things are actions and reactions of the force which produced them.

All varying idea of Mind is registered in separate states of motion which have measurable dimensions. The reproduction of all idea is the result of union of the action and reaction which register that idea. Every action is male.

Every reaction is female.

Every action is electro-positive.

Every reaction is electro-negative.

Every action has its equal and opposite reaction.

Every action and every reaction is a tone in an octave of the universal constant of energy.

Equal and opposite actions and reactions, when united, comprise a unit of an octave of the universal constant of energy.

An action and its opposite reaction are not two. Their energies, when combined, make one.

Reaction is born of action; and action is born again of reaction.

All idea, and all forms of idea are the result of union between equal or unequal opposite actions and reactions of force.

Perfection of mating lies in the union of exactly equal and opposite male actions and female reactions.

In perfection of union lies stability.

Imperfection of mating lies in the union of unequal and opposite male actions and female reactions.

In imperfection of union lies instability.

Unequal actions and reactions will unite with unwillingness which increases in proportion to their degree of departure from exact equality in opposition.

When the potentials of the opposites are too far removed from equality, then will union cease.

In organic life the union or reproduction of opposites is limited, and beyond the limitations reproduction is impossible.

In the chemistry of inorganic life the unstable union of unequal and opposite states of motion is also limited, and beyond the limitations union and reproduction is impossible.

This is a universe of reproduction of idea in accumulated potential of the constant of energy, of registration of the soul of idea in inertia, and of reproduction of accumulated potential.

The idea of all things is produced by union of opposite actions and reactions under conditions favorable to union, and is • reproduced only under similar conditions.

Reproduction is governed by the following laws:

Unions of opposed actions and reactions are possible only within certain limitations. When union does not take place there can be no reproduction.

Equal and opposite actions and reactions, when united, are satisfied in their unions and will remain united.

Stable unions will always reproduce true to species. Unequal and opposite actions and reactions, when united, are unsatisfied in their unions and will always seek their true tonal mates. Unsatisfied unions are unstable unions. Unstable unions never reproduce true to species. Unstable unions tend to return to their separate tonal states.

If either mate in an unstable union finds a more equal mate, it will always leave the former and go to the latter.

That which is true of chemical unions is true of all species of organic life.

Every chemist knows to a certainty that he can break up any unstable compound formed by the union of unequal opposites, by merely introducing an element which is more nearly a true tonal mate to either of the united elements.

Consider, for example, a chemical union between the male action sodium (Na), which is 601 -I- of the sixth octave, with selenium (Se), which is 702 — of the next octave, an unequally opposite female.

The introduction of iodine (I), 801 — of the eighth octave, will cause sodium to leave selenium and combine with iodine to form the more stable compound sodium-iodide (Nal).

Introduce bromide (Br), 701— of the seventh octave, and sodium will in turn leave iodine to form sodium-bromide (NaBr), a still more stable compound.

Finally, introduce chlorine (Cl) which is the true mate, 601— of the sixth octave, and sodium will leave the bromine in order to form the very stable compound, sodium-chloride (NaCI). No element of any octave whatsoever can displace chlorine from its union with sodium.

Chemically, every element is both alkaline and acid, but it is preponderantly one or the other.

All male electro-positive elements are preponderantly alkaline.

All female elements are preponderantly acid.

The alkaline male actions, when united with equal and opposite acid female reactions, are neutralized. They become salts.

Alkaline male actions united with unequal acid female reactions, accentuate the acidity or alkalinity.

Hydrogen united with its true mate helionon, becomes a neutral salt.

Hydrogen and fluorine will unite as an acid. Hydrogen and chlorine will unite as a stronger acid.

All acids or alkalies increase in their strength as their resentment of unequal union increases.

Likewise, the ability to reproduce decreases as the acidity or alkalinity of such unions increases.

Chemical elements in union reproduce by the same process by which all other states of motion reproduce.

Of this more will be written when further consideration of causes make the effects of those causes more comprehensible.

All male actions are centripetal and all female reactions are centrifugal.

Variance of centripetal or centrifugal force is variation of potential.

Union and reproduction are always governed by sex periodicity in electro-magnetic charge, the order of which will be written down and charted.

Consider, for example, the reproduction of the sound of the human voice echoing in the hills. Sound, like all other forms of energy, is an accumulated potential.

Release this high potential and it immediately expands.

Expansion is radiation.

Radiation is discharge of accumulated potential.

As the sound of the voice, as accumulated potential, radiates into the silence of higher octaves of lower potential, and impacts against the closely integrated high potential of the cliff side, the degenerative discharge is reversed and becomes generative charge.

Expanding lowering potential is reversed to contracting higher potential.

In other words, the sex opposites in the radiating sound waves are forced into closer contact by the impact, so that the wave dimensions which originally produced the sound are restored.

The counterpart of the sound as cause has been produced as a reproduced effect of that cause.

It is not the same sound, it is another sound.

It is a reproduced counterpart, a regenerated reincarnation of the state of motion which originally produced the sound.

That which is true of regeneration by echo is also true of reproduction by radio or any other similar process. All are but the reversal of radiation into regeneration by impact against the inertial planes of higher potentials.

Generation or re-generation is an effect of gravitation. An impact of radiative energy against any lower octave of integration will set up the necessary resistance to the radiative energy to regenerate it into its original form.

CHAPTER XI

ENERGY TRANSMISSION

Some old misconcepts must now be corrected by a brief statement of principles, the full explanations of which will be given in their proper order.

That light travels, energy is transmitted, electricity is conducted or inducted, and that heat radiates from its source to other localities, are principles which modern science accepts as fundamental facts.

These great misconcepts gave rise to the theory that the ether is a quivering, elastic solid existing in space along the undulating waves of which light, heat and all forms of energy can travel from one place to another.

It is hereby conceded that all motion is expressed in waves, but those waves are not undulating.

Energy cannot travel along waves because entire waves do not form in sequence.

In other words, one whole wave is not completed before another begins.

Waves are but effects which evolve as their cause evolves.

Waves reproduce themselves part for part in sequence throughout the universe.

Energy, therefore, cannot travel along waves which are not undulating but are reproducing themselves part for part. It cannot leap across waves which are lacking in troughs and crests.

Light does not travel. It reproduces itself.

The light and heat which appear to come from the star or the sun has never left the star or the sun.

That which man sees as light and feels as heat is the reproduced counterpart of the light and of the heat which is its cause.

The cause remains in the restricted area of the state of motion where it began its existence as an appearance, until it expands into disappearance.

That which man sees as a star is not a vision, a picture, an image or a reflection of the star. It is the exact reproduced chemical counterpart of the star integrated as light within the observer.

That which is true of the star is true of the image of the mountain, or the brook or the meadow violet.

No idea of Mind is seen at a distance. The state of motion which represents the idea is reproduced as light by regenerative impact within the observer.

No idea of Mind has place or position in time or space. All idea is universal.

All generated states of motion degenerate by expansion.

Expanding states of motion regenerate by impact against the inertial planes of higher potential.

Man has a higher potential than his surrounding atmosphere.

Any object "seen" by man is a generated potential which is higher than the expanded potential which intervenes between the object and the observer.

The higher potential of the object discharges into the lower surrounding potential as the reproduced expanded counterpart of its particular state of motion, and recharges within the observer.

This reproducing expanding counterpart impacts against the inertial plane of equal pressures which exists somewhere between the object and the observer. This impact causes a reversal of the process of reproduction of an expanding counterpart, into reproduction of a contracting counterpart.

The expansion of a state of motion is degeneration.

The recontraction of expanding states of motion is regeneration.

The law of reproducing idea is the principle of universality.

All that is, is of everything else that is.

The principle of reproduction is the principle of energy transmission.

Energy transmission is conductive and inductive.

Conduction is the lowering of high potential toward inertia.

Induction is the raising of a low potential away from inertia.

The electronegative, dissipative, reaction impulse of energy transmission is conduction.

The electropositive, generative, action impulse of energy transmission is induction.

Conductive energy resists the completion of the wave.

Inductive energy ever leaps ahead in its eagerness to complete the wave.

Conductive energy ever pulls toward inertia through the harmonic of the wave.

Inductive energy ever pulls toward the overtones of the waves, which are the points of maximum opposition.

A state of equilibrium is the state of inertia which exists where pressures of two opposing high potentials of accumulated energy are equalized.

Form of idea is a state of potential which is held together as form by the genero-active law of gravitation until it is torn apart by the radioactive law of radiation.

All potential is constantly changing and interchanging.

The potentials of all things are constantly rising because of their absorption of the discharged energy of all other states of motion.

All mass is regenerated by absorption of the impacting radio-active energy of all other mass.

Also are all potentials constantly lowering because of their expanded reproduction in the surrounding lower potentials.

All mass is degenerated by its own radiation.

All mass is generated by accumulation of the universal constant of energy into higher potential.

That which is generated must be radiated.

All mass is degenerated by release of energy accumulation.

Consider, for example, the regeneration of this planet by the radiation of the sun's high potential of energy impacting against its surface.

Modern science presumes that heat travels in some mysterious manner across the vast ninety million miles of space between the sun and the earth, crossing that space in which a temperature of nearly absolute zero prevails, and then arriving here hot.

Man feels warmth from the sun and in some manner, it must be accounted for. The theory arrived at is far from the truth.

Somewhere in the intervening low potential: between the sun and the earth is the inertia · plane where the pressures of the potentials of the sun and earth are equalized.

Against this inertial plane the sun's cooling and expanding radiation impacts and reverse: its expansion into contraction.

The cooling, expanding, lowering potential reverses into heating, contracting, rising potential.

By this impact the expanding radioactive energy is reversed into contracting, generoactive energy.

By the impact of the sun's regenerated light emanations against this planet, all disintegrating matter is regenerated.

Every living thing reverses its nightly intent to die and lives again.

Flowers which have folded their petals reopen them and grow.

Animal life which has closed its eyes in "sleep" becomes "conscious" once more and takes on new energy.

The modern concept that solar energy is due to contraction is a misconcept. The energy given off from the sun is energy that is being generated within the sun. No energy can be radiated that has not been, or is not being generated.

All radiating mass is generating.

All opposite effects of motion are simultaneous in their expression.

The sun is preponderantly generative. It is heating.

The sun is in a lesser degree radiative. It is cooling.

As the sun heats, it radiates.

Radiation disintegrates.

As the sun cools, it generates.

Generation integrates.

Here follows the law of the cycle of appearance and disappearance of form.

Cold generates. Generation contracts. Contraction integrates. Integration heats. Heat radiates. Radiation expands. Expansion disintegrates. Disintegration cools.

Thus it may be seen that one opposite is always born of the other, which in its turn becomes the cause of the first.

Thus it may be seen that the disintegration of the preponderantly generating sun becomes the regeneration of this planet.

The coefficient of cold for an expanded volume of mass of low pressure and potential becomes the coefficient of heat for the same mass in a contracted volume of higher pressure and higher potential.

The totals of heat and potential have not changed. They have merely changed their dimensions.

Nor has heat travelled. It has becn reproduced.

Magnetic flow in its magnetic orbit has been interrupted, that is all.

The voice impacting against the cliff is an exact analogy. The voice regenerates into sound and the positive charge of the cliff increases because of the impact.

The heat from the sun has been disintegrated by radiation into the opposite of heat, which is cold.

In radiation, however, the heat energy is not lost. Nothing can be lost. The energy which generated that heat is registered, together with the energy which radiated it, in an expanded counterpart of them both.

No idea of Mind, once begun, ever ends.

No idea of Mind ever began or ever ended.

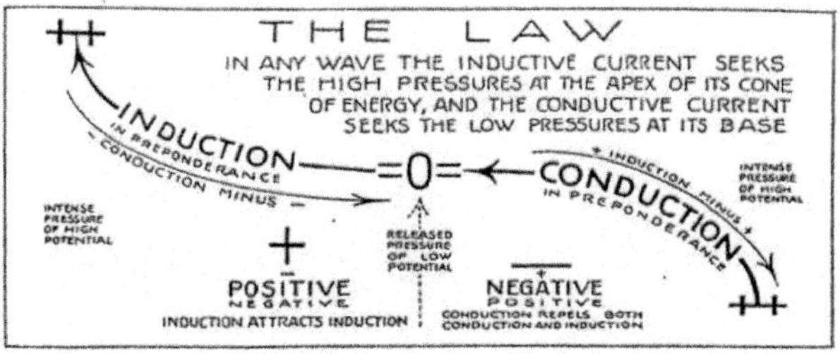
THE LAW
IN ANY WAVE THE INDUCTIVE CURRENT SEEKS THE HIGH PRESSURES AT THE APEX OF ITS CONE OF ENERGY, AND THE CONDUCTIVE CURRENT SEEKS THE LOW PRESSURES AT ITS BASE
INDUCTION
IN PREPONDERANCE
– CONDUCTION MINUS –
=0=
CONDUCTION
IN PREPONDERANCE
+ INDUCTION MINUS +
INTENSE PRESSURE OF HIGH POTENTIAL
INTENSE PRESSURE OF HIGH POTENTIAL
RELEASED PRESSURE OF LOW POTENTIAL
POSITIVE
NEGATIVE
INDUCTION ATTRACTS INDUCTION
NEGATIVE
POSITIVE
CONDUCTION REPELS BOTH CONDUCTION AND INDUCTION

CHAPTER XII

THIS IS A FINITE UNIVERSE

Mind is all there is. It has no limitations as to shape, size or volume, for these qualities are but appearances and have no real existence.

Mind is limited, however, in its power, its knowledge and its imagination, the last of which is its creative force.

All of the effects, of which Mind is the cause, are measurable in that they have the appearance of dimension.

All dimension is limited, therefore must all cause be limited.

Mind cannot create infinite complexity. Beyond the ten octave cycle of cause and its included effects, Mind cannot go.

All effects evolve to their limit, and devolve back again into cause without any change whatsoever taking place in cause.

The limitations of Mind are absolute.

A limited universe cannot be an infinite universe.

This concept is extremely difficult for man to comprehend, for man has a fixed concept of a nonexistent effect called "space."

This mis-concept is born of his fixed idea of a universe separable into parts, all of which are related one to another in shape, size, volume and the intervals of distance between them.

To man, space and distance are fixed attributes of all his concepts and limit his comprehension.

Man has built a mis-concept of an infinite universe of infinite extension.

Based upon his mis-concept of space he has reasoned that the universe cannot be finite or limited in extent for, if so, it must have shape or form.

Also, he has reasoned that, in order for it to have shape, or form, and be limited and finite, there must be something beyond.

The objective universe of man's concept demands a "beyond" to a finite universe. But there is no "beyond" because there are no bounds nor boundaries in this formless universe.

If space is non-existent then extension or continuity is non-existent, and there can be no "beyond." "Beyond" is a relative word. It is part of man's concept of objective relativity. It is a dimension.

It is based on a belief in the reality of the unrealities of dimension and separableness in a universe of the One Thing.

Man's sense of reasoning does not accept the idea of the universe as a finite volume, such as a sphere, hanging in a vacuum, beyond which, to his objective thinking, there must be more empty space.

For this reason he has formulated the belief that a finite universe is inconceivable to the, human mind, therefore the universe must be infinite.

Man's outer mind reasoning, which is objective, does not stop to consider that an infinite universe is more inconceivable to the human mind than a finite one; but that same reasoning is willing to accept the palpably incomprehensible and relegate it to the domain of divinity, which is admittedly incomprehensible, rather than concentrate the inner Mind upon the higher octaves of thinking and learn the truth in light.

Einstein rightly says that the universe is finite, but wrongly says that it has form. This great thinker declares his belief that the universe is spherical or elliptical.

Einstein rightly says that any line of direction in that appearance which man calls space is curved and that it is presumable that any continuous line in space would curve ultimately back to its point of beginning, therefore the universe must be either spherical or quasi-spherical.

This curving, however, is not because the One substance of Mind has a finite form or shape, but because all effects of motion are universal, and every effect of motion is an action which must end where it began, in its final reaction. Direction, therefore, can never be in a straight line but must always be curved.

The reason why all lines must be curved lines, and also why all curved lines must be spiral in their curvature, will be written down in all exactness in its proper place.

It is true that any apparent disturbance in the substance of Mind returns unto itself, unto its own exact apparent point of beginning in a sequence of reproduced waves which spell out the appearance of another non-existent effect called "time."

Man's fixed concept of the reality of time is a drag anchor holding him away from truth. His fixed concept of intervals of time in which one effect of motion in one "part" of the universe makes its appearance in another "part" is the result of such purely objective thinking that true concepts cannot replace them as long as this method of thinking persists.

There are no "parts" to Mind substance, no "place" and no "position." Every part is the same part, every place and position the same place and position.

Thinking is universal and all effects of thinking are universal.

More than this, they are simultaneously universal, for thinking is simultaneously universal.

Even the little child in tossing a ball 016/CS the universe simultaneously with that tossing.

All motion is simultaneously universal in this universe of equilibrium.

Sequence is an appearance due to form. It has no existence in itself and without form it would not have even the appearance of existence.

All form is purely a question of gravitational intensity and therefore has no existence.

Time itself is an effect of gravitation, and has no existence. Like heat, it is but an indicator which registers sequence in integration as heat registers resistance to integration.

The reproductions and effects of motion and their attendant unrealities do not in any way change the universal substance of Mind, the one reality, the one unchanging, indivisible, ultimate substance of all that is.

Add to the non-existent appearances "form," space" and "time," two others which obsess man's mind, "position" and "dimension," and the relator can readily perceive that, with these non-existent unrealities firmly fixed in his mind as existent realities, it would be impossible for man to accept the idea of a finite universe.

To do so he would have to imagine a form hanging like a ball in a void, to which there must be an empty inconceivable beyond.

Man's outer mind is so accustomed to thinking reality into the unrealities of space, time, motion, form, position and dimension of an objective universe, that it is hard for him to adjust his thinking to a subjective universe in which the unrealities disappear into the reality of light.

Man's inner Mind thinks in light, freed in its thinking from the illusions of outer mind thinking.

Einstein's error is in attaching to the substance of Mind the attributes which belong solely to dimension of the substance in its appearance as form.

CHAPTER XIII

A DIMENSIONLESS UNIVERSE

Dimension is but an appearance, an effect of motion and is non-existent.

A mile between apparent objects is nonexistent with the disappearance of the objects.

Man's fixed concept of a universe of innumerable objects separated by relative and measurable distances unfits him for thinking of the universe in any but a relative sense.

Man must think in light for true comprehension of Mind.

All men may think in the higher octaves of light when they but comprehend, for with comprehension comes power.

To think in light is not a new power being evolved by man like a new sense; it is a power which is already in every atom of man's composition.

Man thinks in the low octaves of his own integration almost unaware that the higher octaves are within him, for the lower octaves are superimposed upon the higher. The higher octaves of incredibly higher speeds are within the lower octaves of high potential but slow speed.

Man may shift his thinking from the low speed of his outer mind to the higher speeds of his inner Mind at will, even as he can shift the gears of his motor car.

Man's thinking in his low octaves of bodily integration is like a man running his motor on low gear ignorant of the fact that he has higher gears. Man's thinking in the higher octaves is like a man who is aware of higher gears in his car and knowingly uses them.

Universal Mind thinks in light and registers that thinking in light which is integrated into the idea of the thinking, and suspended for a time in the lower octaves of light in the appearance of form.

Man's outer mind is an integration of light in the lower octaves of that which he calls "matter" and man's outer mind thinks in the dimensions, or illusions, of Mind or matter.

Matter and Mind and light and energy are the same. They are One.

They are existent in that they never disappear.

They are constant. They are eternal.

Dimension of Mind, or light, or matter, or energy is but the illusion of the Mind substance due solely to more or less sustained motion.

The substance which is Mind, or light, or matter, or energy, and is eternally existent as cause, must not be confused with its effects in motion which are but dimensions and therefore non-existent.

Dimension is purely objective.

Outer mind thinking is objective thinking. Objective thinking is thinking in dimension.

The substance of matter is eternal but its illusions of dimension, in form, are fleeting.

Matter is frozen light, crystallized light of man's own lower octaves of thinking, so, even in outer mind thinking, man thinks in light, but it is meaningless to him.

Man's inner Mind is light of the high octaves of inspirational, ecstatic thinking. To man's inner vision light is always light. It never disappears. Inner Mind thinking is subjective thinking.

Subjective thinking is dimensionless thinking. The inner Mind of man knows no darkness.

Light knows light; and all that is, is light.

In the high speeds of inner thinking matter is dimensionless.

The universe of Mind is a dimensionless universe.

The universe of the idea of Mind is a universe of dimension.

The creating universe is the idea of Mind. It is the divine concept of a universe of motion and the apparent separability of the One Thing into the appearance of many individual things.

CHAPTER XIV

CONCERNING DIMENSION

The divine concept of a universe of form is the idea of the image-making faculty of Mind.

The divine concept is but an illusion of divine imagination.

Mind thinks the ideas of Mind into an illusion of form. Dimension appears when form appears.

Form appears as a result of motion generated by the concentrative impulse of thinking.

Form disappears as a result of motion radiated by the deconcentrative alternate reactive impulse of thinking.

Creation therefore is but an illusion due to complex states of motion.

All motion is comprehensible.

All motion is caused by thinking Mind. All motion is controllable by Mind.

All comprehensible motion is measurable. Measures are dimensions. Dimensions are the intervals which define the relation of one illusion of form to another. Dimension disappears with the disappearance of the illusions it defines.

All illusions of form are but varying states of motion locked into the separate states of potential which define those illusions.

All states of motion are orderly and periodic.

All states of motion, no matter how complex, are reducible to ten octaves of seven tones each, plus their mid-tones and their master-tones.

All creation 4s reducible to about a hundred and forty elements which tell the entire complex story of God's thinking just as all literature is reducible to twenty-six letters which tell the entire complex story of all of man's thinking.

Neither have any existence beyond their ability of expressing, in form, the manifesting idea of creative Mind.

The elements of matter are all of the same substance in varying states of motion.

Gold is not one substance and carbon another, and phosphorus still another.

Gold differs from carbon, and silicon differs from copper, only by the relation of their intervals in motion, or the measurements of their separate dimensions which, when aggregated, constitute their separate states of motion.

The divine concept is not a universe of motion, but of idea in form.

Motion is necessary to produce the form of idea. It is but an attribute of thinking. It is not a principle.

Man labors in the bowels of the earth for metals which he can create for himself with ease when he fully comprehends the motion which has assembled the forms of those elements out of the idea of the divine concept.

All that is in creation is fashioned into the form of idea by the ten octave alphabets of thinking Mind.

Knowledge of the dimensions of each state of motion will give to man the power to produce from the most plentiful of them those which are most rare.

That which nature has taken millions of years to produce through orderly interchange of potentials man may produce in a few hours by forced interchange.

There is no substance which nature can produce that man cannot also produce, when he knows the dimensions which measure the illusion of form of the substance.

Man has control of more energy than is necessary to transmute any one element or any compound into any other element or compound.

All that he lacks is the knowledge of dimension in order that he may transmute that state of potential energy locked up in a state of motion called carbon into that other state of motion called gold; and he may have all that he desires at the cost of a very slight effort.

The formula for measuring all dimensions of the various elements of matter will herein be written down and charted with all exactness so that man's burden of heavy labor may be lightened.

Years will pass before civilization will have adjusted itself thoroughly to the changed conditions which this new knowledge will bring to the world, but from this change a new civilization will spring.

These are the dimensions which, when known and measured will make man master in that he will be able to evolve, or devolve, or transmute, or synthesize the elements at will.

The first dimension is "length."

The second, "breadth."

The third, "thickness."

The fourth, "duration," or "time."

The fifth, "sex."

The sixth, "pressures."

The seventh, "potentials."

The eighth, "temperature."

The ninth, "ionization." The tenth, "crystallization."

The eleventh, "valence." The twelfth, "axial rotation."

The thirteenth, "orbital revolution." The fourteenth, "mass."

The fifteenth, "color."

The sixteenth, "plane."

The seventeenth, "tone."

The eighteenth, "ecliptic."

These dimensions are characterized by one outstanding peculiarity common to all of them, an orderly periodicity.

Beyond these eighteen dimensions, and their inclusions, there are no more measurable intervals of motion.

When all of these periodicities are charted and their mathematical calculations computed with exactness it will be very simple for the ingenuity of man to devise the mechanical apparatus necessary to decrease any high potential into any lower one, or increase any low potential into any higher one.

Acceleration and deceleration are now measurable.

Temperature, tone, color, valence, ionization ---: and those pressures which are known are now measured.

Mass is measurable.

Known orbits are now measured and the unknown ones will be measured when they have been made known.

The waves which constitute the complex of all elements have already been computed.

The spectrum has been divided and. the elements assorted into about seven thousand color lines of light; but they are as meaningless to man as the Hebrew language is to the gentile.

These seven thousand lines of light are the letters of the universal language of light, the language in which God speaks to man.

When man knows this language, he will then think in it.

When he thinks in light he will then know that he is the Son of God, that he is One with God.

When man thinks in light he will then know that he is universal Mind; that he is all that is; that he is thinking Mind expressing his thinking in light; that he is omnipotent, omniscient and omnipresent.

He will then know that he is life and that life is eternal and that there is no death; and that he has neither place nor position in space or time; and that dimension is as though it were not; and that there is but One, and that One He, and you, and me, and the rolling hills and the sands of the sea, and the clouds and stars and the little violet blooming in the meadow.

Already man has gone a far way toward the solving of the great secret of this creating universe which lies hidden in the elements.

Within God's alphabet of light, the locked secret has long awaited the master key of knowledge to open the doors to man.

Man is Mind.

Mind creates and controls the energies of the elements.

Mind may rearrange these energies and combine them in accord with its desire.

CHAPTER XV

$$4\ddagger 3+2+1+0=1-2-3-4\ddagger$$

THE FORMULA OF THE LOCKED POTENTIALS

Now must be constructed the cosmic clock by means of which all dimensions may be measured by one formula, as time is measured by the formula of hours, minutes and seconds.

Heretofore it has been written down that periodicity is an absolute characteristic of all effects of motion.

With two exceptions, all dimensions of all effects of motion are of the same orderly octave periodicity.

These two exceptions are of cyclic periodicity.

Octave periodicity is an orderly progression to and from the maximum effect of each octave.

Cyclic periodicity is an orderly progression to and from the maximum effect of the entire cycle.

Thus may it now be simply stated that all periodicities of all motion of whatever nature, with two exceptions, may be built up on the following extremely simple formula:

$$4\ddagger 3+2+1+0=1-2-3-4\ddagger$$

The two exceptions to this octave periodicity are mass, and tone. Mass means weight. Tone means sound. Mass accumulates all down the entire ten octaves; tone lowers from the highest note down the cosmic keyboard to the lowest.

The zero represents inertial energy, and the numerals represent the orderly progressions in locked potentials and pressures and orbits. Thinking Mind has devised these orderly progressions as its method of evolving the idea of universal thinking into the appearance of form, and devolving it into the disappearance of form.

The numerals of this formula are the hours of the cosmic clock. They are in the relative positions of the atoms of the elements and in the order of their respective varying dimensions.

The seconds of the cosmic clock are the corpuscles, or light units which make up the atom's structures.

The hands of the clock are the indicating line of charging and discharging potential.

The main-spring is the ten octave cycle. Five of these octaves are decelerating time dimension transformed, by accumulation, into power, and the other five octaves are power dimension released into accelerating time.

The winding of the clock is the sublime five octave inhalation, and its unwinding is its five octave exhalation.

The cosmic pendulum in its swinging ticks off the varying dimensions of all motion forever and forever with unfailing accuracy, but never does it depart from this simple formula.

One by one the relator will take up and analyze the eighteen dimensions of the effects of motion.

Neither temperature, nor valence, nor orbit, nor color, nor ionization, nor electric force, nor magnetic force, nor any effect of chemistry known to man or still to become known, none of these, nor others herein unnamed, excepting mass and tone, can extend beyond this simple formula.

It is meet that this simple formula of vast import should have a name so that it may be referred to in proper terminology.

"The formula of locked potentials" shall be the name by which this formula shall be hereafter known.

THE COSMIC CLOCK

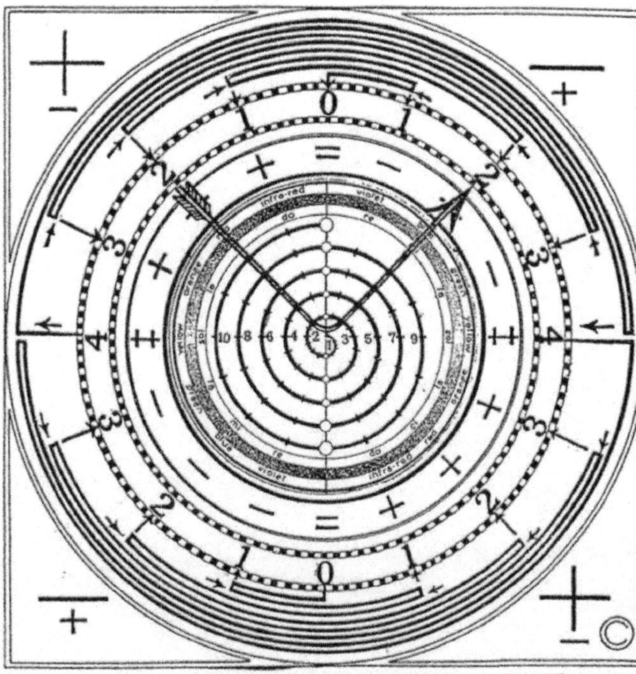

THE FORMULA OF THE LOCKED POTENTIALS

Time marks the periods between events. Man divides his time by the periodicities of this planet's revolution around the sun and subdivides it by its rotation upon its axis. These periods are again divided to act as man's necessary time dimension. The Universal One divides His time by the periodicities of His inhalation and exhalation, which together make one universal constant of energy, and subdivides it into four exactly equal unit constants of energy. These periodicities, and tonal and mid-tonal subdivisions, measure the dimensions of His idea in the illusion of form, space, time, sex, temperature and other periodicities.

ENERGY ACCUMULATES DURING GENERO-ACTIVE INHALATION BY RISING POTENTIAL, AND IS DISSIPATED DURING THE RADIO-ACTIVE EXHALATION BY LOWERING POTENTIAL. THE PERIODICITIES OF INHALATION AND EXHALATION IN ALL MASS ARE ABSOLUTE

CHAPTER XVI

UNIVERSAL ONE-NESS

Now must the simplest but the greatest of all laws of the universe be written down.

Everything that is, is of everything else that is. Nothing is of itself alone. All created things are indissolubly united.

This is the law of the entire substance of divine Mind.

This is the law of the souls of things. This is the law of love. It is the law of the One-ness of the universe. All that is, is One.

There are not two independently separate things in the entire universe.

Individuality is non-existent.

Individuality is but an appearance of separability and divisibility in a universe which is non-separable and non-divisible.

No one can say "I alone am I."

If one should say, "I am I;" he must say also to all men and all created things "I am thou," and "Thou art also I."

The One-ness of the universe is the sublimely simple One spiritual substance of divine Mind.

The One substance of Mind is a living substance of the One living thinking Being of which all things in this universe are a part, and to which they are indissolubly united.

Light is that which makes of the One substance a living substance.

Light is the life principle of Mind.

Light is the creating force of the universe. Light is all that is.

Light is the living God.

God is manifested in light.

Light is the Holy Spirit, God, father-mother, nature, man, the oak, the rolling hills and mountain chains, the pounding sea and the sands of the sea, the babbling brook, the red apple hanging on the tree; the autumn haze, the storm, the stars in the heavens, the blade of grass and the kindly dew in the opening rose.

All creating things are dependent upon light to hold them together in the appearance of individually separate things.

As light is the substance of all things, and all things are dependent on light, all things are therefore inter-dependent.

All are continuously interchanging by reproduction throughout the universe in continuity. No one created thing has time, nor place, nor position in idea.

The idea of all creating things is universal.

It is omnipresent as idea throughout the entirety of Mind but the counterpart of idea in all created things is sequential in time and place.

The counterpart of idea is the reproduced idea.

The reproduced idea is a part of the basic idea.

This is a universe of reproduction.

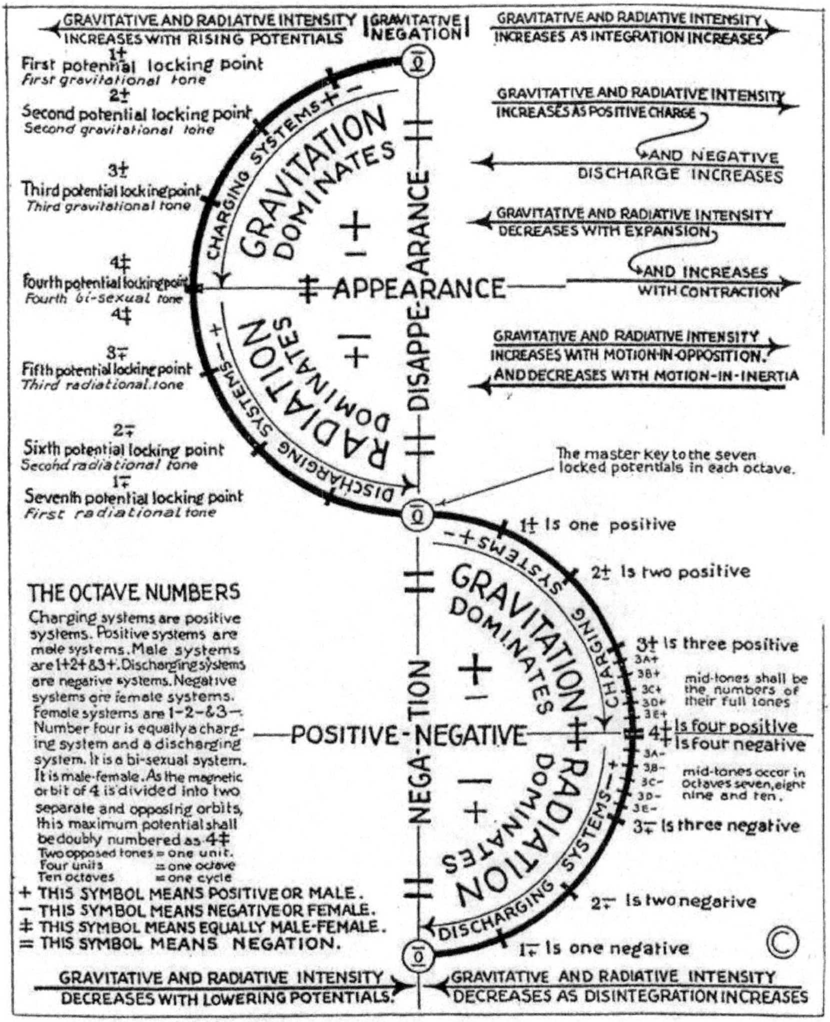

CHART CLASSIFYING LOCKED POTENTIAL POINTS AND TONES OF BOUND ENERGY ACCORDING TO THEIR OCTAVE NUMBERS

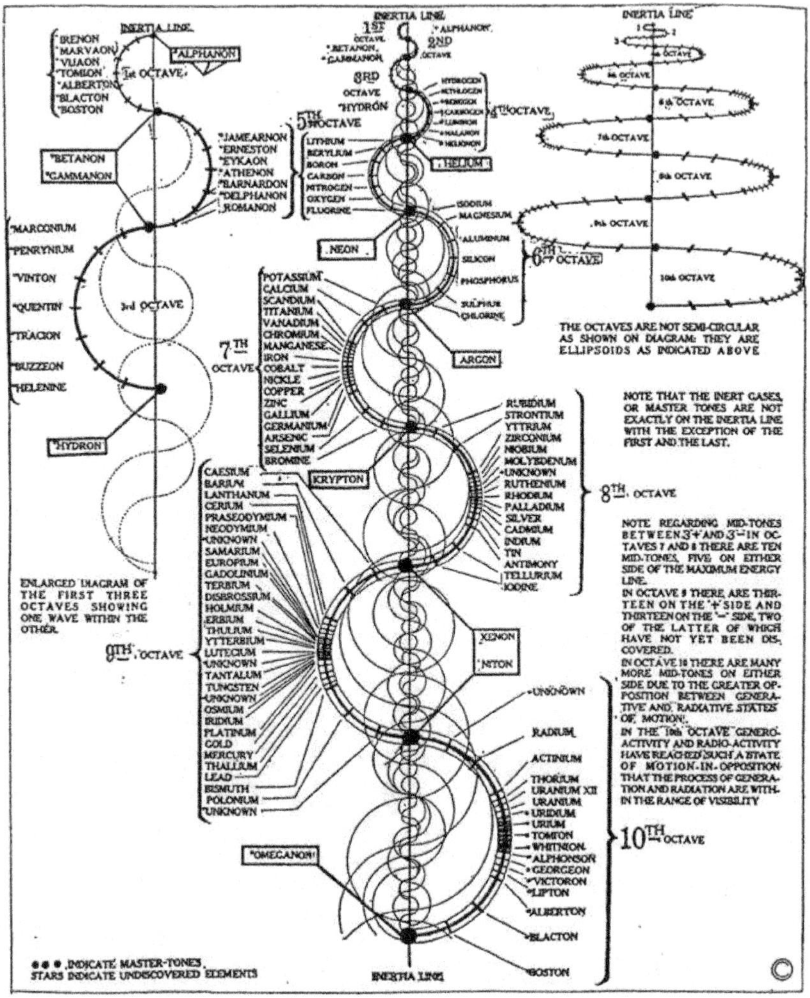

DIAGRAM SHOWING THE TEN OCTAVES OF INTEGRATING LIGHT, ONE OCTAVE WITHIN THE OTHER. THESE TEN OCTAVES CONSTITUTE ONE COMPLETE CYCLE OF THE TRANSFER OF THE UNIVERSAL CONSTANT OF ENERGY INTO, AND THROUGH, ALL OF ITS DIMENSIONS IN SEQUENCE

Production and reproduction of idea of thinking Mind is the sole result of thinking, and the sole reason for thinking.

Idea and reproduction of idea are universal in sequence as states of motion are universal in sequence.

Idea and reproduction of idea are multiplied as appearances in motion-in-opposition of which the pulsations of thinking Mind are the cause.

There is no other cause.

There is no other motion.

Each idea and each reproduced counterpart of idea has but the appearance of time and place and position from which it does not appear to depart; still is it of all the universe a part.

The rose blooming in my garden is of Arcturus a part as it is of you and me.

The universe sways to the swaying of the rose in my garden.

Every particle of matter in this universe has its own magnetic pole through which it is connected with the magnetic pole of each other particle of matter in the universe and through which each particle is affected by the ever-changing condition of every other particle in the universe.

This is a universe of equilibrium in motion, the continuity of which could not be maintained except through the inter-dependence of all apparently separated units.

Everything that is, is of everything else that is. Nothing is of itself alone. All created things arc indissolubly united.

All is God and God is all.

God is light; light is all.

Creation is the sublime idea of the sublime Being.

The sublime is always simple.

With creation simplicity seems to end and complexity to begin.

Complexity belongs to creating things.

Man's outer mind is a heavy and complex mind. It knows not the sublimity of simplicity.

The inner Mind of man is attuned to the ecstatic meter of divine thinking.

The inner Mind of man knows the sublimity of deific simplicity.

The inner Mind of man knows light.

Everything that is, is of everything else that is. Nothing is of itself alone.

The perfume of the rose is part of the rose and it is also a part of man, and of the winds, and of the garden wall.

The perfume of the rose is light as the rose is light, and so also is man, and the winds, and the garden wall..

All that is, is light. Nothing is of itself alone. He who knows this greatest of all laws knows love.

Love is a realization of the Oneness of the universe.

Love is the ecstasy of inspired thinking. God's thinking is ecstatic thinking.

God is love.

Until man knows from within his inner Mind this law of the Oneness of all things, it has no meaning for him.

When man knows this law in his heart he will have no limitations.

When man knows this law so that its reaction within the soul of man is that of ecstatic, inspired contemplation, he will then begin to know the meaning of love.

Unlimited power will then be his.

His thinking will then be true thinking. All power is in true thinking.

"Thinking true" may be likened unto a violin string sounded by the great master. Ten thousand other strings tuned to the same pitch would sing in unison, unplayed upon. Ten thousand other strings not so attuned would not know the ecstasy. They would be as though they were not.

Inspired thinking is thinking in tune with divinity

Inspired thinking is thinking in exact pitch with the high octaves of divine thinking.

The rhythm of light, in the high octaves of light, is the measure of true pitch and true thinking.

True thinking of the inner Mind makes true thinking of the outer mind.

The outer mind thinks not in ecstatic measure. As a man thinks in his inner Mind, so is he.

The inner Mind within all men and within all things is divine Mind.

The inner Mind of man is tuned to the higher speeds of ecstatic thinking.

Man may know the ecstasy of his own divine thinking, if he will but tune his thinking to the high speeds or ecstatic meter of divine Mind, which is within all men and all things.

When man will so attune his thinking, then will he think in light.

The inner Mind of man alone can think in light.

Inner thinking is ecstatic thinking.

The outer mind of man cannot know light.

The outer mind cannot know ecstasy.

When man thinks in light he will then knot the perfection of divine idea. He will b universal genius.

Imperfection of idea cannot exist.

The entire idea of thinking Mind is good.

There is no evil. There is no imperfection That which man calls the "created universe' is the idea of thinking Mind.

The idea of Mind is perfect, as Mind in it self is perfect.

Perfection of idea is truth.

Imperfection of idea is electro-magnetically impossible in this universe of equilibrium as we shall see in later chapters of this book.

Thinking true, in light, will give to man all-power.

He will have no limitations except those that are universal.

With his feet on the electrodes of the universe and his eyes in the high heavens, impossibilities of yesterday will be simple achievements of today.

With this knowledge from within, man can have dominion over all nature and all things.

Man can have dominion over his own body and command it to health and to beauty and to comeliness.

With a realization of this law in his heart he will love and be loved of all men and all creating things.

And he will know all things. All knowledge will come to man when he knows this law in his heart. All knowledge exists.

Thinking man has all knowledge.

Inspired man knows the law of love in his heart with the One-ness of the universe.

All knowledge is existent in the universe and is the inheritance of thinking man from divine Mind, God and Father of man and of all creating things.

This inheritance of all-knowing awaits every man to use as and when he desires that knowledge.

CHAPTER XVII

OMNIPRESENCE

Man's concept of God as omnipresent, or universally present, is an inconsistent concept, for it does not include man or nature in that concept as God, or as part of God.

Man has been so trained to look for God outside the realms of nature, as an incomprehensible, substanceless God, separate and apart from himself and from that which he knows as the physical universe, that it has become a tradition of his thinking, a fixed habit of his thinking.

It may be a shock therefore to the outer mind of man to find a comprehensible God, of which he himself and all phenomena of nature are One.

If this discovery shocks man's earth-bound mind, then he must learn to readjust his thinking, for there is no other God than Mind.

And there is no other Mind than the One universal Mind.

Nor is there any other purpose for Mind than the purpose of thinking.

Man cannot conceive any other purpose for Mind than that of thinking.

Nor is there any other product of thinking than idea.

Creation is but an idea of thinking Mind.

The divine concept, materialized into this universe of matter, is a stupendous idea of Mind but it varies not one bit in principle from the simplest idea of man.

Nor does it vary in universal mechanics from the dynamic principles employed by man for the materialization of his ideas.

God is Mind. Man is Mind.

All idea of God or man is but the product of thinking Mind, registered in matter as form of idea.

All idea is an illusion of Mind and visible only to Mind as an illusion.

Idea is held in form by Mind for countless periodic intervals of evolution and dissolution. All thinking is universal thinking, immortal thinking.

There is no mortal thinking.

All idea of Mind is perfect. Imperfection of Mind cannot exist.

Separation of Mind into parts is impossible, therefore there are not two Minds or two substances. The One substance of Mind is light.

Light is universal.

Man is light and man is universal.

That which is universal is omnipresent. Man, is, therefore, omnipresent.

All matter is omnipresent. The universe has no extension, continuity, space nor time.

The One-ness of the universe allows no exceptions, no mistakes, no error in its all inclusiveness. Nothing is omitted from the entirety of Mind. There are no separable parts to Mind.

No apparent part of Mind has locality or position. All matter is universally present. All matter is light.

Mind is light. Mind is the universe. Mind is all.

ONE.

CHAPTER XVIII

OMNIPOTENCE

Omnipotence means all the power that exists.

The omnipotence of the universe is limited in its expression by the limited power of the universal constant of energy to accumulate potential.

The dynamic energy born of the action and reaction of universal thinking is the beginning of the activity of that which man calls "electricity" and "magnetism" through which the universal constant of energy functions in the creation of separate appearances in matter by periodic changes of dimension.

It is the beginning of apparent division of indivisible things into their apparent opposites.

It is the beginning of sex. Sex begins when the opposites of light begin.

It is the beginning of that which man knows as light and of the colors of light.

It is the beginning of life. Life begins when light begins.

It is the beginning of sound. Sound begins when light begins.

It is the beginning of the generative concentration of light into that state which man calls "heat" and its radiation into that which man calls "cold."

It is the beginning of integration and disintegration of light energy into the appearance and disappearance of that which man calls "matter. "

It is the beginning of the crystallization of light units into that which man calls solids of matter.

It is the beginning of integration and disintegration of light energy into the appearance and disappearance of that which man calls "mass."

It is the beginning of the electro-magnetic opposition of the two forces which accumulate and dissipate the universal constant of energy into the periodicities of gravitation, attraction, cohesion, radiation and-repulsion of evolving and devolving mass.

It is the beginning of the appearance of form. It is the beginning of the combination of form into the appearance of elements of matter and of compounds of matter, into that which man calls "growth."

It is the beginning of apparent transformation of the infinitely simple into the infinitely complex. It is the beginning of the inter-relationship of matter, which man calls "the chemistry of matter." It is the beginning of force and the motion of force and the inertia of motion.

It is the beginning of time. Time begins with the impulses of universal thinking.

It is the beginning of that universal rhythmic swing of the cosmic pendulum toward the apparent intent of unequilibrium, which is the cause of all creating things.

It is the beginning of the illusion of separateness into the appearance of many things.

There are no separate things. There is but the One thing. Nothing is of itself alone.

It is the beginning of the souls of creating things and of the expression in matter of that which man calls "life."

The whole of creation is contained in the desire of universal Mind to express idea, form and rhythm, in accord with immutable law, in endless sequence through endless ages.

Beyond this there is no more.

All Mind is universal and all Mind has all-power.

The Mind of man is universal Mind. Man has all-power.

All-power is universally present throughout the entirety of this dimensionless universe.

All matter and 'all creating things are the images of thinking Mind.

Thinking Mind is light; and light is universal.

That which is universal is not separable from itself. Omnipotence is therefore universal even to the last corpuscle of the most insignificant atom.

All matter is omnipotent.

The universe of matter is breathing its energy in tune with the One breathing, pulsing, living Being, call it what you will, whether it be God, or Mind, or the universal One.

The inbreathing, outbreathing impulses of the living, thinking God-Mind is in absolute equilibrium throughout the universe.

They are also simultaneous, but alternately preponderant.

Exhalation proceeds in a lesser degree during inhalation and inhalation continues, but in a lesser degree, when exhalation is in preponderance.

Also all motion- is simultaneous in its opposition.

The opposing motions are merely alternately preponderant.

All motion is oscillatory, because of this sequence of preponderance in its opposition, of which much will be written in its proper place. No atom, no man nor creating thing can all-power from the universal One, or increase or decrease it, or be independent of it in whole or in part.

All-power is the thinking power of Mind. All the universe is Mind and all the universe is thinking in unison.

Mind is that universal One thing which man calls "God." Mind is the universe.

Mind is all.

ONE.

CHAPTER XIX

OMNISCIENCE

Within the thinking substance of universal Mind is all knowledge.

The entire substance of Mind is knowledge. Knowledge is universal.

Man's concept of all-knowledge and all-intelligence is a wrong concept.

To man, knowledge is quantitively limitless and infinitely complex.

Man conceives the boundaries of knowledge and intelligence to be far beyond his comprehension.

This is not a true concept.

The knowledge and intelligence of universal Mind is limited and simple.

Knowledge is perception of dimensionless existence, nothing more.

Knowledge is an attribute of substance. It belongs to existence and the reality of existence.

Knowledge might be likened unto the alphabet. Within the alphabet is all knowledge but until it is put into words and phrases the alphabet is devoid of idea.

Intelligence is an understanding of the reality of existence as it is registered in the illusion of existence.

Intelligence belongs to motion and not to substance. It belongs to the appearance of existence and to the unreality of the illusions of existence.

Knowledge is passive, inert. It belongs to the equilibrium of unchanging causes.

Intelligence might be likened unto the putting together of the alphabet of knowledge into words and phrases of infinite variety of idea.

If the universal One had not a creative thinking Mind He would possess all-knowledge but would be without intelligence.

Intelligence is the act of thinking creatively, or in other words, the act of putting together the illusions of idea into the forms of those illusions.

Intelligence is active, opposing. It belongs to the opposed motion of changing effects.

Changing effects cannot be known, they can only be comprehended.

All knowledge of the illusion of existence is limited to perception of causes of that illusion.

Causes are unchanging. Causes are existent.

Knowledge is limited to that which is existent.

Effects are non-existent. They but appear to exist. They are but idea in transit.

All idea is transitory. The idea of thinking Mind is always in motion, and, therefore, constantly changing.

Solids are as changing as the sunset sky. Their difference of motion is but relative.

Therefore, man cannot acquire knowledge from changing effects. He can but acquire a comprehension of its complexities.

Man can have no knowledge of the sunset sky, for it is but an effect.

Man can have knowledge of the cause of a sunset sky, and its effect he can comprehend.

Knowledge is simple as cause is simple. Comprehension may be ever so complex.

That which man calls "knowledge" is based upon observed causes and effects of complex facts of matter.

There are no unconditioned facts of matter in a universe of motion. There are but appearances of facts.

Man concedes that all our knowledge must ultimately repose on conditions which are unproved and unprovable.

Facts of form in matter are unprovable in a world of space, time and motion.

Matter as form in motion is but an everchanging effect of an unchanging substance. Effects of matter are manifested in form. Effects are fleeting. They are ever changing.

Form is fleeting. It is ever changing.

Effects of causes are facts only in appearance. Appearances of this moment are not the same the next moment.

The facts of appearances disprove themselves in the proving.

All facts of form in matter are as the sunset sky. They are but fleeting effects.

Causes of the appearance of existence are the only unconditioned facts.

In a universe of motion "things are not what they seem," and "there is nothing permanent but change."

All form is constantly in transit between appearance and disappearance.

Transition is not existence. It is but an effect of motion upon a substance which alone is existent.

The ripples on the water are an effect upon the substance of water. They have no existence in themselves. Without the substance of water they could not have appeared. Having appeared as idea of ripples they will disappear into the substance of water.

That which periodically appears in transit throughout the ten octave range of idea, will also periodically disappear.

That which appears must disappear, but also must it reappear in accordance with the immutable law that no state of motion ever ends.

The divine concept is eternally repeative in the reproduction of idea into form, and its dissolution back again into the memory of form.

All idea is periodic in its repetitiveness of form and of the memory of form.

The divine concept, in its entirety, is a stupendous but comprehensible effect of a very simple cause.

All effects of this creating universe can be comprehended when all causes are known.

The limitations of all thinking are within the laws of motion and the effects of motion.

Man can conceive nothing beyond the effects of motion and its cause.

No phenomena of matter can be new phenomena of matter.

Nothing is or will be, which has not always been. All phenomena of matter have finite limitations.

All complexities of matter are but effects of light in its orderly and limited variance of motion.

The forms or images of idea are limited even in their variability and complexity to the limitations of the ten octave range of thinking.

Omniscience does not mean unlimited knowledge. It means all the knowledge that there is.

Complexity of idea does not constitute new knowledge.

Quantity and complexity of fleeting effects of unknown causes do not add to knowledge or to intelligence.

Knowledge cannot be added to or subtracted from.

Knowledge cannot transcend knowledge. Mere possession of knowledge, or storing of idea, is not indicative of intelligence.

A man may be an encyclopedia of knowledge but still lack the dynamic intelligence necessary in order to use it by giving it expression as idea.

The acquisition of knowledge by man may be likened unto the counting of grains of sand.

A lifetime of futile counting and the beach is still uncounted, while ten times ten million beaches await his useless counting.

Men's lives are spent in forever counting unnumbered grains of sand.

Men's lives are spent in studying complex, incomprehensible effects of unknown causes.

A study of the stars is more ponderous than the counting of grains of sand, but it is of no more import.

Knowledge invites conception of idea in infinite variety, the complexities of which are apparently existent, through the act of thinking. It is as though the alphabet desired its letters arranged in infinite variety of idea.

The attribute of desire in knowledge is the cause of the dynamic activity of intelligence.

Complexity of idea in forms of matter is only an appearance registered in low octaves of accumulated high octaves.

To man, an appearance is that which comes within the range of his perception.

When an appearance "disappears" it has only gone beyond his range of perception.

Appearance within the range of man's perception does not mean new existence.

Disappearance beyond the range of man's perception does not mean cessation of existence.

The cloud which disappears beyond the hill does not cease to be a cloud because of its disappearance.

Vapor which disappears from man's sense of vision does not cease to be water. It can again reappear to the vision of man as water.

Light which disappears into an octave higher than that at which man can perceive it does not cease to be existent as light.

The thinking of Mind is within the limitations of the knowledge of Mind.

The thinking of Mind is limited to the cognizance of universal being.

The limitations of knowledge are within knowledge itself.

Beyond the existence of Mind there is no more.

Mechanics and mathematics, ideals and ideas, science and art, "solids" of matter and the effects of motion are all complex effects of perfect thinking.

That which man calls spirit is not extraneous to matter. Matter and spirit are one.

Spirit could not create a new substance extraneous to itself.

One substance cannot become another substance.

Mind is the only existent substance. Nothing is existent that is not spiritual.

As existence is limited to thinking, and thinking is limited to ten octaves, man's concept of an infinite spiritual existence is a mistaken one.

Mind, being all that exists, is limited to its own ten octave range of thinking and is also confined to the act of thinking. It has no other purpose nor any other possible activity.

That which is limited cannot be infinite, but it can be eternal.

Spiritual existence is finite. It is a limited but eternal existence.

If divine Mind were an infinite Mind it could not be comprehensible to man, but its simple limitations make it easily comprehensible.

If thinking is the cause of all effect and thinking is limited in range, then are the effects of that cause limited in range.

Heat is an effect of thinking which has its limitations.

Motion, volume, weight, mass, sex, sound, color, form; all these are effects which have their limitations.

These effects are comprehensible. Comprehension is therefore limited to the range of possible effect.

All-intelligence does not therefore mean unlimited comprehension. It means all the intelligence that there is.

Finite limitations in the expression of Mind in idea might be likened unto the limitation of the painter to the colors on his palette.

The painter has infinite variation, within the color range of his palette, in the expression of the idea of the image making faculty of his mind.

Within these limitations his complexities of variation are without end but beyond them he cannot go. He is limited by his color range.

The color spectrum is his palette and it has its limitations.

The Master-Painter is thus limited by the range of His spectrum but within these definite limitations He has infinite possibilities for expression of the ideas of the image making faculty of His thinking Mind.

Limitations which are definite cannot be infinite.

Divine existence is contained within the limitations of the range of Divine thinking.

Beyond this range divine Mind cannot perceive or think.

The illusions or appearances, which man mistakes as existence, are but reappearances of old illusions.

Reappearance is repeativeness.

The orderliness of created things is due to the invariability of cyclic periodicity in all effects of thinking.

The pitch and tone and measure and meter of true thinking is due to the absolute rhythm of the repeating periodicities of thinking.

The very dependability of universal Mind, reflected in nature's inexorable laws, is due to universal limitations.

God has set his own immutable laws in orderly, repeating periodicities of thinking.

He Himself is limited by them.

He Himself is bound to the observance of them.

God cannot, never has, and never shall change His own immutable laws.

Upon this fact is based the very dependability of the universe.

Man's belief that God sets aside his own laws to perform miracles is a primitive concept of superstitious man.

Superstition belongs to primitive man who is but learning how to think from within him. When primitive man first catches gleams of the divinity within him he is then rising above the thinking of the animal which he has been. Upon these faint gleams he builds his primitive concepts based on fear of that which is superior to himself.

To primitive man modern man owes his concepts of a cruel God of supernatural power. These wrong concepts have become traditions of man's mind and habits of his thinking.

Modern man inherits the habits of the unbalanced thinking of primitive man.

Orderly thinking is perfect equilibrium.

Against perfect equilibrium nothing imperfect can prevail. Variation of the measure of true thinking would throw the rhythm of orderly thinking out of tune and the universe could not be. To think in light is to think only perfection, for perfection is all that is written there. Mind is perfect. There is no evil. Imperfection, or evil, is non-existent. Man's concept of evil is a wrong concept.

Evil is as impossible as unequilibrium is impossible.

The reader will remember that all thinking is an oscillation between two equal and opposite actions and reactions.

He will remember that the union of any two exactly equal and opposite actions and reactions make one.

Man has control over his actions, but he has no control over the reactions to those actions.

The appearance of evil is merely potential out of place, and suspended there for the time.

Like the apple on the tree gravitation will eventually restore it to its proper place in equalized potential.

From this inevitable return to the stability of conquering truth there is no escape.

The apple, as accumulated potential suspended out of place, will seek its own potential by falling toward higher pressures when the stem weakens by disintegration.

Again, the decaying apple, disintegrating into gases of lower potential, will seek the place of lower potential by rising into lower pressures.

Just so with evil. It is but an action which must eventually meet its reaction.

That action which man calls wrong thinking is simultaneously written on the soul as positive charge and is balanced by its opposite and equal negative reaction.

Thus the equilibrium of the universe remains constant and man has recorded his own thinking, which he may correct at will, on his soul; but correct it he must.

CONCERNING THE SOUL

Man is ever concerned regarding his "soul" and its habitation "after death." Man need have no concern. Man's soul is but the memory of the evolving idea of man. Out of the soul the body is again born. The soul is but the record of man's thinking.

The evolving idea of man cannot forever be held in suspense in inertia.

The soul of a "dead" man is but the record of a man asleep for a while, awaiting the renewal of his body.

The first part of sleep is but a centrifugal, decentrative reaction to a centripetal concentrative period of action.

It is the expanding, dissipative, non-creative impulse of thinking, just as wakefulness is the contracting, generative, creative impulse.

It is the period of preponderantly exothermal, electronegative discharge when the body degenerates in preponderance to its generation.

Later during sleep, the centripetal concentrative action begins to accumulate until it becomes sufficiently preponderant to cause the state of what is known as wakefulness.

In the same way during the first part of the day the contracting generative impulse is in preponderance, but later "fatigue" shows that the expanding, non-creative impulse of thinking is increasing until it in turn becomes predominant and causes another period of sleep. And so the pendulum swings.

As in all other phenomena of motion, sleep and wakefulness are simultaneous in the expression of their opposition, but preponderantly one or the other in sequence.

Just so with life and death.

From the moment of birth we begin to die. Generation of that which man knows as life merely predominates until that which he knows as death takes its turn in orderly sequence.

Death is just a longer sleep than the daily sleep. The difference is in the duration of the sleep.

CONCERNING REINCARNATION

Death is a life period of sleep for total bodily regeneration, just as the daily sleep is for partial bodily regeneration.

Regeneration of the soul is reincarnation of the body.

The chemistry of the soul of all idea is registered in the master tones, known as the inert gases.

The soul is the matrix of the body just as the master tones are the matrices of the elements.

The inert master tones of an octave of the elements contains a complete and exact record of every effect of motion within its octave.

The soul of man contains a complete and exact record of every action and reaction of thinking man.

"The moving finger writes; and having writ, Moves on: nor all thy Piety nor Wit shall lure it back to cancel half a line, Nor all thy tears wash out a word of it."

Creation is just a swing of the cosmic pendulum between sleep and sleep, between awakening and awakening, and one follows the other as the night follows the day and the day again follows the night.

While sleeping for a night man does not cease to be.

Nor does he fear to sleep, for he knows that sleep is beautiful, and he will awaken at the dawn of a new day.

Man fears to die for he knows not what the dark sleep of death will bring. He knows not that death is but a longer and more beautiful sleep from which he will awaken with a newly regenerated body, to begin once more , his periodicity of growth at the dawn of another new day of life.

Man fears the hobgoblins of primitive man's concept of punishment of the soul for the "sins' of the body. He fears the dark sleep of death with its terrors much as a child which has been frightened by ghost stories fears the dark with its same imaginary terrors.

With new comprehension man can eliminate the imaginary hobgoblins and fears from his declining years and go to the sleep of his disappearance as form, in peace.

In disappearance man does not cease to be. In his disappearing, the idea of man does not discontinue.

As the day disappears only to reappear in its proper periodic interval, so must man reappear. All appearances and disappearances are periodic.

Also are all reappearances periodic. Appearances and disappearances are but moving points in the cycle of Mind.

In this universe of motion creating things do not pause at any point.

There are no created things.

There are but creating things ever integrating, ever moving, ever evolving in the integration and the assembling of the idea of themselves.

No form of life has been created. It is creating.

Nothing has been. All things are being.

Evolving idea into form is a positive action requiring the creative intelligence of imagination.

A man who only has great knowledge has a negative possession. Poor he is indeed.

A man who has great imagination has a positive, dynamic possession. Rich he is for knowledge is within him and of a certainty he shall find it.

Knowledge of existence is not acquired from without, it is recollected from within.

When man learns new things he is but recollecting old experiences of his thinking, thought by him before in higher octaves.

Man is not deceived about the illusive non-permanent quality of the evolving ideas of his own thinking. He knows that they will soon pass and that he cannot hold their evolving forms in suspension, unchanging, for one instant.

The relative scale of man's objective universe deceives him as to the illusion of his evolving idea.

The universal Mind thinks idea into form exactly as man thinks idea into form.

The universal One cannot hold the evolving form of divine idea in suspension any more than man can.

There is but one process of thinking for there is but One Mind. There are not two Minds nor two methods of thinking: _nor are there two sets of laws governing thinking.

Nor are there two separate substances, nor two separate things nor two separate beings in the universe.

All thinking is universal thinking.

All thinking things are thinking in unison. All are creating that which they are thinking. All thinking things are self-creating.

All thinking things are creating all things. Man is his own creator.

Man is the creator of all that is.

This shall man know when he shall think within in the higher octaves of light of his inner Mind.

When man shall know the language of the universal One of Whom he is a part, then shall he know the Voice of the universal One.

The still small Voice within universal man speaks to him in the language of light, in words of tones in the speed of light.

Within the heart of thinking man the silent Voice has forever asked:

"WHO AM I?"

Since the beginning man cried aloud, "WHO AM I?"

And the Voice answered, "Thou Art I. I, the universal One, am thou whom thou art creating in my image."

The Voice within man, insatiable, asks forever:

"WHO AM IT"

And the still small Voice answers: "I am I. I am I whom I am creating. I am the universal I." "I am all that is, and Thee.

"I am He that is One with me.

"I am the empire of I that am I."

Since the beginning the Voice within man asks:

"WHENCE CAME I?"

And the Voice forever answers: "I am of the universal passion of creation. "I came from God.

"I am of God.

"I am soul, record of idea.

"Where God is I am.

"Where I am there God is."

Within man the Voice of long ages demands:

"WHAT AM IT"

And the familiar Voice answers: "I am of the body of God, born of his substance.

"God is Mind I am Mind.

"God is Truth. I am Truth.

"God is Love. I am Love.

"God is Life. I am Life.

"God is Light. I am Light.

"God is Power. I am Power.

"What God is, I am. What He commands, I command.

"My purpose is His purpose."

"God lives in me. My inheritance is from God and of God."

"He gives all to me. He withholds nothing."

"The Divinity of me is thine and mine. It is that which is recorded within the soul of me. It is the Holy Spirit within the sanctuary of me." "I am an idea, of thine. The body of me is the idea of the soul of me. It is mine and thine."

"I am the master sculptor. My body is the plastic clay. My soul is the mother-mould of my body, the matrix for my regeneration." "I am what I am.

"I shall be what I desire to be.

"What I am I have desired to be.

"I am the sum of my own desire.

"I am thou, creator of myself.

"Thou art I, creator of all."

"I am thou, creator of all; for thou hast made it known in my heart that I am not of myself alone." "I am thou and thou art I."

"I am of the farthermost star and of the blade of grass in my door yard. I am of my brother and of the mountain."

"The ecstasy of my thinking varies the spectra of ten times ten billion stars and illumines the ether of endless space."

"Thy thinking has created all that is. "My thinking is thy thinking.

"My thinking has created all that is. "I am ecstatic man.

"I am man, self creating.

"I am God, creator of man.

"I am father of myself.

"I am son of the living God."

"The ends of space are mine. I shall know no limitations that are not thy limitations."

Within man the still small Voice asks from the beginning and ceaselessly:

"WHY AM I?"

And the Voice answers: "I am an expression of the universal passion of creation."

"God created me that I should fulfill his purpose. God gave me desire to create and the power of creation."

"God dwells within me. I shall not deny the power within me which is God within me."

"I shall not close the ears of my soul to the whisperings of my soul, which makes me dwell on the mountain top in ecstasy of inner thinking."

"The universal desire is expression of idea through the rhythm of thinking, in accord with the law, in endless sequence throughout endless space."

Within man the ever questioning universal Voice beseeches:

"WHITHER AM I BOUND?"

And the Voice answers: "God was my beginning, is my substance and shall be my end." "Froth the One I came. To the One I return."

"I but tarry by the way to do the will of the One."

"I am universal man, the image of my Creator. Ecstasy and exaltation attend me, for I know that all that is, is within me."

"My dwelling place is in the high heavens on the mountain top, above the waters and the earth." "I range the high heavens in ecstasy. "My feet are wings.

"The ends of space are mine."

"I sing praises unto all the universe by the way. The hosts of heaven rejoice with me by the way."

"I have denied my unity. My universality I have not known."

"My dwelling place was the earth. I walked the earth heavily in chains "

"My earth-bound feet dragged heavily after me. I wearied of the long road."

"My back bent with the ache of its burden. "I was lonely and the way dark."

"I shall not deny my One-ness and live in the loneliness of the dark."

"I shall know my universality and I shall dwell on the mountain top in the light of inner thinking." "Hope dwells in the light.

"Despair lurks in the dark.

"Life and growth are of the light.

"Death and destruction are of the dark."

MEMORY

The acquisition of new knowledge by man is but the re-thinking or recollection of old knowledge.

Learning is not acquisition; it is recognition of a truth through the act of recollection.

Recollection is the act of transforming the potential energy of an idea stored in memory, in inertia, into the kinetic energy of active Mind which is the state of concentrative thinking.

Recollection is a dynamic, concentrative action of Mind. It is therefore electro-positive, and belongs to motion-in-opposition.

It is the action of again giving form to the memory of idea.

Recollection differs from creation in this wise; the act of creating idea into form by concentrative thinking is an initial action.

The act of recollection is a regeneration or reproduction of that initial action, the reaction of which has been stored in memory.

It is the resurrection of the soul of idea into the body of it.

It is the re-creation of idea into form for its further evolution.

Memory is the storehouse of the idea of Mind.

Thinking Mind taps that storehouse of memory in that activity of Mind which man calls by many names, such as "memory," "instinct," "intuition" and "imagination."

They are all one and the same. Their varying shades of meaning indicate only the differing manner in which old recollections of memory, recorded in millions of years of evolving ideas, manifest themselves.

If man could but see that the thinking of all Mind is the same, whether it be Mind of God or Mind of man, or bird, or beaver, or oak, or rose, he would have a truer concept of the universe.

If he could see that there is but One Mind and that Mind is thinking in the expression of but One Idea, then he would begin to comprehend the divine conception.

If he could but see that the One Idea is the whole creating, evolving universe, the one great illusion of divine Mind as a passing fancy is an illusion of man's Mind, he would be getting closer to the fundamental truth.

Then if he could but see that the illusion of the One Idea is but illusion in form, the substance of which is Mind, he would not then look to illusions as dependable realities and to the One Reality as an undependable illusion.

If he could go farther in his comprehension and realize that God and man and the oak and the atom are just One, and that all these are thinking .out the divine Idea, then would he be close to the door of the Holy of Holies.

Perhaps it might assist thinking man toward the attainment of this concept by comparing the thinking human brain as an appearance to the thinking Mind of the universe as an appearance.

To man, the appearance of the universe is that of countless objects at limited distances one from the other. He regards himself as one of those objects, an individual, alone, independent, free of any bindings, free to think and act and do as he desires. His very breathing he regards as his own breathing, and his actions are, to his thinking, his alone.

Let us look within the thinking brain, and in doing so imagine one thinking individual male unit upon one planet of one atom of the brain seeing his universe as man sees his.

The appearance of the universe to this unit would be exactly the same to him as is man's universe to man.

The objects within his vision would be separated by relative distances. Vast spaces would intervene between him and the vast suns in his starry heavens.

Their luminosity would, to him, be relatively the same, for the positive nucleus of every system is a light giving sun.

And also would their relative motion be the same, for a trillion revolutions per second of a light-unit would be just as relatively slow to him as a day is to man.

Periodicity of evolution is as relative as the appearances it records.

Is it not, then, just as reasonable for this diminutive thinking unit of man to think himself one in a vast universe as for man to do so?

Would it not be just as difficult for him to realize that he is just one apparent unit of the whole as it is for man to do so?

And as it is with this diminutive unit in hi universe within man's brain, so it is with mar in his objective universe.

One is thinking man's thinking, functioning; in the evolution of the idea of man; and he cannot do otherwise if he will.

The other is thinking the universal idea functioning in the evolution of the divine conception; and he cannot do otherwise if he will.

Every in-breathing and out-breathing of either is the in-breathing and out-breathing) of the living universal One.

Every thought and every action are in accord with the universal pulsations of action and reaction of the process of thinking and they cannot be otherwise.

INSTINCT

Consider the manifestation known as "instinct."

The beaver builds his dam, a marvelous feat of engineering.

Was he taught to do it? Would he not do it just the same, and just as perfectly, if his parents and all associates were killed and he matured alone?

How does he do it?

"Instinct," one answers.

The bee builds his marvellous cells, the spider his web; the barn swallow builds in barns and the chimney swallow in chimneys; the robin flies south and north according to the season.

"Instinct" makes them do it. They cannot do otherwise, says science.

Just so, they cannot do otherwise.

Nor can any of us, or any creating thing do otherwise than that which it thinks and has thought for countless periods of reappearance.

These acts are all acts of thinking Mind recollecting dynamically the idea of its evolution which has been recorded as memory in motion-in-inertia during ages of building beaver dams, and honey combs, and spider webs; and during ages of migration and nest building and other characteristics of the evolving manifestation of the divine concept as a whole.

IMAGINATION

Consider that manifestation of recollection known as "imagination."

The quality of imagination varies in accordance with the - ability to recollect memory recorded in the soul, and with the ability to think in light.

To think in light is to think in higher octaves of the inner subjective Mind.

To think in light is to disassociate the outer, objective mind from the inner, to blot it out as though that octave of integration had not yet been.

The outer mind is concerned primarily with continuance of the body as an appearance of existence and is not at all concerned or interested in much of anything else.

The outer mind of man, or of the lion, the dog or elephant, is absolutely the same.

Man differs from the animal only in his ability to think in higher octaves and bring back to his outer mind recollection the perception of existence stored in motion-in-inertia in the memory of his universality.

This perception of all-knowledge suspended within motion-in-inertia inspires within man that which he thinks is new knowledge and as he adds it to his thinking he again writes it upon his soul.

Man does not realize that what he considers new idea brought into the appearance of existence, is but old idea stored within him projected upon the outer plane of his thinking.

INSPIRATION

When man gives to other men the inspiration which has come to him, he is a divine messenger of the living God delivering to man his revelation from the Holy of Holies.

The genius, the super-thinker with imagination, who brings beauty to the world, is inspired man thinking in light.

The greater the imagination the greater the perception of the reality of universal existence, hence the greater the intelligence.

The lesser the imagination the greater the reality of the appearance of existence.

The greater the imagination the nearer to One-ness and the farther from the animal.

The inspired genius of great imagination has great intelligence.

He is able to use his knowledge creatively. Those things which he desires to know he may know.

The humble poet, inspired by knowledge conveyed to him by contemplation of the orbs of night, may give to man a message of truth which will outlive long generations of the learned whose disproved facts have died in the proving.

The "prophets" were super thinking men of great genius.

The "prophets" bad knowledge of the causes of things, and could foretell their effects.

Comprehension of the effect of a cause is not prophecy.

Out of knowledge of the beginnings of things is born the imaginings concerning future things.

The weather forecast for tomorrow is not prophecy; it is an act of intelligence born of knowledge.

Genius is the forerunner of civilization. Genius knows the ecstasy of the high heavens and the mountain top.

Genius is the bridge between man and God. He who will may cross it.

Genius is locked within the soul of every man. He who wills may unlock its doors and know its ecstasy.

Genius gives to man that which alone endures, which man has named "Art." No work of man can endure which is not born of inspiration and created in ecstasy.

Genius gives to man idea, rhythm and form, which are of the soul and beyond which, in the created universe, there is nothing.

Genius knows no limitations within those which are universal.

Genius knows love and truth in all their fullness.

Genius translates the word of the universal One into the word of man for the soul of man.

They who, attain the ecstasy of genius, are ordained messengers of the universal One.

Genius lifts man from the lowly stage of ferment. Man still is new. He is still but in the ferment.

Genius lifts brute man to gentle man. Genius gives to man the harmonies of universal rhythm without which all is discord. Genius gives to man knowledge which is of the soul.

He who tunes his heart to the messages of genius purifies himself. No impurity can there be in his heart for verily he then is in communion with the Holy One.

The pure in heart know their universality. Man may know his One-ness.

He who listens to the translations of genius knows the word of creation. He knows the rhythm of the universal language of light speaking in his inner Mind.

Genius awaits him who listens. The messages of genius are for the inner Mind alone. The outer mind comprehends them not.

To him whose inner Mind is quickened into ecstasy God speaks from the trees of the forest and he understands.

To him the silent Voice of nature speaks, with understanding, from the babbling brook and the pounding sea. He knows all things.

To him universal Mind unfolds truth from the light of the sun and the blue dome of the heavens. He has all knowledge.

To him the rosy dawn and the golden autumn sing messages which are to him as an anointing froin the Holy One. He knows no limitations.

He who has not ears to hear crucifies genius. The penalty of genius is crucifixion. The reward of genius is immortality.

Whom man crucifies does he glorify with immortality.

"Seven cities warr'd for Homer being dead Who living had no roofe to shroud his head."

Genius desires no reward. The glory of genius is humility. Genius knows not the taint of arrogance.

CONCLUSION

Man has all knowledge within himself. Inspiration will unlock the doors of all knowledge.

All-knowledge exists in its entirety in all the universe.

All-knowledge, being universal, exists in man.

The universe is omniscient.

The universe is indissolubly united.

Omniscience is of the electron, the atom, the magnetic field of the atom, the molecule, the mountain, the man, the planet, the air, the water, the fire, the stars in the heavens and the far reaches of space.

The Oneness of the universe allows no exceptions, no mistakes, no error in its all-inclusiveness. Nothing is omitted from the entirety of universal Mind. There is all-knowledge in all matter.

There is all-intelligence in all matter. All matter is spirit.

Spirit is God.

God is universal.

God is all.

ONE.

INFRA-RED
VIOLET
RED
ULTRA-VIOLET
BLUE
GREEN
ORANGE
YELLOW
THE COSMIC CLOCK
YELLOW
ORANGE
GREEN
BLUE
ULTRA-VIOLET
RED
VIOLET
INFRA-RED

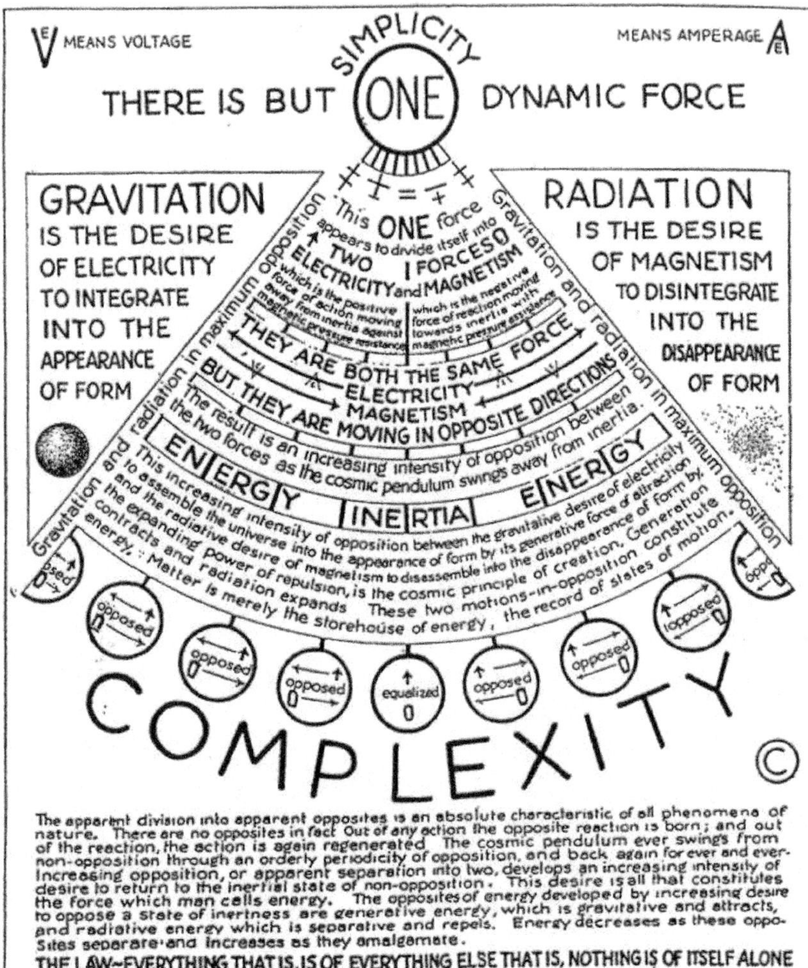

THE ONE FORCE OF THE UNIVERSE IS THE ENERGY OF THINKING MIND. THERE IS NO OTHER ENERGY

The creating universe of matter appears through the centripetal, contractive, endothermic, charging, positive force of gravitation which attracts, disappears through the centrifugal, expansive, radio-active, exothermic, discharging, negative force of radiation which repels, and reappears through a union of both forces by regenerative impact in inertia.

BOOK II - CHAPTER I

DYNAMICS OF MIND CONCERNING LIGHT UNITS OF MATTER

It should now be perfectly clear that this universe of Mind of which light, or matter is the substance and of which the electromagnetic energy of thinking is the force, is a dimensionless reality.

It should also be perfectly clear that this creating physical universe of form is an illusion of the image-making faculty of Mind, the one inspired, supreme purpose of which is to conceive idea and give it the appearance of form.

It should also be clearly understood that form and dimension are attributes of motion and in no way are they attributes of matter which is of the substance of Mind, exactly as the form of bubbles in the ocean foam are attributes of motion and not of the ocean substance.

It should be perfectly understood from now on that, in making an analysis of the effects of motion which constitute this creating universe, we are dealing with an illusion, an idea only, which has its cause in thinking Mind.

The universe of illusion is a corpuscular universe.

All dimension of matter and energy is corpuscular.

All expression of force is corpuscular.

Corpuscles are inconceivably small particles of matter, or light, or Mind substance, which have been churned into motion by the electromagnetic forces of the thinking process of Mind, exactly as bubbles are particles of water and air churned into motion by the force of a propeller.

The complexity of motion of these corpuscles is the sole cause of the illusion of a universe of many things evolved from the imagination of thinking Mind.

As it should also by now be thoroughly understood that the words "matter" and "light" are used in the sense of characterizing the substance of Mind, and that the word "energy" is used in the sense of characterizing the force, or life principle which makes of Mind a thinking substance; that the words "electricity" and "magnetism" are used in the sense of characterizing the apparent division of the One force of energy into the appearance of two, the relator will henceforth use these words with the assurance that the line between reality and illusion has been sufficiently well drawn to justify the omission of qualifying words.

Let it then be clearly understood that the universe of Mind is that which man characterizes as "the spiritual universe" and that the universe of dimension is man's "physical universe.

One is cause. The other is effect. One is real. The other is illusion.

Man has to do with illusion during those periods in which he is forming the idea of himself as illusion; so, therefore, it is necessary that he shall understand the dimensions of the universe of illusion in order that he may control them.

Man has long ago discarded the corpuscular theory of light in favor of a theory of electromagnetic effect of undulating waves which are supposed to exist in the ether.

He must now replace this second theory, for the ether of man's concept is non-existent. There are no undulating ether waves.

Light is corpuscular.

Modern science has proved mathematically that light could not be corpuscular because of certain phenomena known as "interference" and "aberration."

Modern science has reasoned that, because of the phenomenon of interference, light could not be corpuscular, for if light consisted of little particles, the phenomenon of interference would prevent light from travelling.

It is presumed by man that light travels, because the evidence of his senses so convinces him.

Light does not travel and the appearance of its doing so is another of the many illusions of dimension which deceive man.

All light units of matter are given the appearance of form by the magnetic reaction of the attempt of electricity to seek higher pressures.

This attempt is resisted by magnetism, and the resistance is registered in electricity as heat.

The rebound into lower pressures and the sudden cooling of the electric whirling particle by the expansion of the lower pressure causes it to solidify.

It is turned into ice. It freezes.

It becomes what is known as "crystallic."

All matter is crystallic. Crystallization is a dimension. It is the first appearance of 'form.

Matter registers its energy through temperature dimension of heat and cold in solids of light which man calls "crystals."

Crystals are but apparent solids of light sustained in that illusion of appearance by motion.

Crystallization is one of the most important dimensions of the illusion of form.

Nothing concerning the basic principle or law governing crystalli7ption is known by modern science.

It is known by experiment and observation that all elements, or compounds, crystallize in any one of six different classes, but science knows no way of determining crystallic formation, or cleavages, twinning, or other characteristics other than by observation or experiment.

In a later volume the fundamental laws underlying crystallization will be charted exactly.

In this volume of first principles the basic chart will be reproduced in a brief chapter on "Crystallization."

"Solid" matter is frozen light, crystallized by released pressure.

The harder it freezes the more solid it appears to be.

The slower its motion the harder it freezes. The faster its motion the more quickly it melts.

All form of matter has its melting point in temperature at which point matter begins to disappear as form of matter.

The more solid matter is, the higher the temperature necessary to melt it.

Man's solids are but light retarded in its twelfth dimension, which is axial rotation and sustained in that state of decelerated motion by the energy of gravitation sturdily opposing disintegration.

Man's dependable realities are form and dimension.

Man's concept of reality is solidity.

Solidity is an illusion of dimension.

Solids are possible only above certain pressures and below their corresponding temperatures.

The greater the pressure the higher the freezing point.

The lesser the pressure the lower the freezing point.

Man's dependable realities are but the "ices" of substances.

And so are all things which man knows and sees and feels and stands upon and builds upon, and upon which he relies as true and staunch and real and everlasting. All are but as ice, and, at their respective melting points, as reliable as ice.

If this planet did not know a temperature above that which keeps ice solid, man's concept of ice would have as much stability as his concept of granite.

If this planet knew a temperature which melted iron the solids would be few and man himself could not be.

All solids have their several melting points or points of liquefaction.

All solids are liquefied gases and frozen liquids which have their varying liquefaction and freezing points. Freezing points are points of crystallization and vary with the complexity of the elements.

All frozen solids can be liquefied by heat.

All liquids can be broken into gases by still more heat.

Heat radiates. Radiative acceleration is centrifugal. Centrifugal acceleration disintegrates by expansion.

All gases can be liquefied by cold and solidified by greater cold.

Cold generates. Generative deceleration is centripetal Centripetal deceleration integrates by contraction.

Solid ice becomes water at the melting point of ice.

Water becomes steam at the vapor point of water.

Steam breaks into the gases of water at a still higher temperature.

All gases, integrating under gravitative pressures, are complexed by cooling and frozen into appearance. The heretofore invisible gases then become visible solids.

All solids are simplified by heat which expands them into disappearance. The heretofore visible solids then become invisible gases.

Man's concept of solids is born out of his experiences at the degree of temperature to which he is daily accustomed.

This state is limited to about one hundred degrees of the thousands above and the hundreds below man's accustomed temperatures.

Man's concept of gold is that of a solid, for man is accustomed to seeing gold at a temperature below its point of crystallization.

Man's concept of mercury, is that of a liquid because man is accustomed to seeing it above its point of crystallization.

Ice or steam vapor will continually appear and disappear from their source which is water.

Matter becomes evident to man when sufficiently integrated in mass to respond to the senses of man as visible solids, liquids and vapors.

Solid matter, like time, is only an appearance.

Time appears with growth, with day succeeding night, with the seasons and with the sequence of events.

Deprive the universe of these hour-glasses of time, and time itself disappears.

Matter, in its form dimensions, is an appearance which is the result of motion.

Deprive the universe of motion, and form of matter disappears. It again resolves itself into the dimensionless substance of matter from which it was born as an appearance.

The transforming of the substance of light into matter can be likened unto the transformation of water into ice. The ice is an appearance due to change of motion. The substance of water has not changed. Deprive water of that state of inactivity called "cold" and ice disappears.

Again, it may be likened unto the transformation of water into steam. The vapor is an appearance, due to change of motion. The substance of water has not changed. Deprive water of that state of increased activity called "heat" and steam disappears.

The substance of matter is eternal, but the appearance of matter in form is fleeting.

That which is not eternal will eventually disappear until the swing of the cosmic pendulum will cause its orderly and periodic reappearance.

Ice and steam vapor will continually appear and disappear from their source, which is water.

States and forms of matter will continually appear and disappear from their source, which is the higher octaves of light.

Water has not changed in its apparent transformation into ice or into steam vapor.

Light has not changed in its apparent transformation into lower octaves of light, or matter.

Nothing has changed; it has but appeared to change.

Nothing can change; it can but appear to change.

Variance in the dimension of a substance does not change the character of the substance. It but changes its state.

Substance cannot change. It can only appear to change through variance in dimension of effects of motion.

Just as the spokes of a wheel appear to change into a solid disk when set rapidly in motion so does Mind substance appear to change into a complexity of forms and degrees of apparent solidity in accord with the variable speed of motion of electrically accumulated potential.

Also as the dimensions and numbers of the spokes of a wheel give the appearance of greater or less solidity according to the speed of their motion, so do the elements appear more or less solid in accord with the closeness or openness of their orbits and their integration.

All of man's elements are the same in substance. Their apparent difference is due to difference in dimension only.

Man's concept of substance is the result of his concept of a physical universe of many substances.

Man's concept of a spiritual universe is that of a substanceless universe.

Man differentiates between the spiritual and the physical universes simply because one responds to his senses and the other does not.

When the range of man's senses includes the entire range of light, he will then know that there is no difference between the spiritual and physical except variance in motion, which variance does not constitute a difference in substance.

From the high octaves of that which he terms "spirit" to the low octaves of matter and back again to spirit is but a transition from non-appearance to appearance and back to non-appearance.

Transition is not change. It is but a journey.

From invisibility of substance to visibility and back again to invisibility is not change. It is but an illusion.

Creation is but a journey of the thinking Mind of the universal One into the illusions of His divine idea.

Creation is but a manifestation of God's sublime idea of a universe of space and time and motion.

Creation is but a materialization of images thought out during the thinking process of Mind in action.

Idea is the sole product of thinking; thinking is the sole purpose of Mind.

Man cannot conceive an unthinking or an inactive Mind.

Man cannot conceive any other purpose for Mind than that of thinking.

Man cannot conceive any other product of Mind than that of idea.

If the One substance had not been a thinking substance, the universe would have been without sex force or motion.

If it had been a static substance at rest in the perfect equilibrium of uniformity, dynamics would not have been.

Without sex, force and motion, appearance and effects could not be.

Without appearance dimension could not be.

If the universal substance had not been an energized thinking Mind, its composition and attributes would have been uniform through -out this dimensionless universe of perfect equilibrium, perfect balance.

A static divine Mind, being without energy, would have been non-creative and that which man knows as "creation" would not have been.

Without the energy of thinking, Mind would not have had the power to transmute motion into those elements which man calls "matter" or into those forms which man calls "created things."

If universal Mind suddenly ceased thinking, all created things would instantly disappear. All form dimensions of matter, deprived of the generative energy of thinking Mind, would instantly become dissociated and deconcentrated and give place to a state of inert dimensionless uniformity.

The "created universe" of illusion would disappear.

The apparent stability of solids, maintained in their appearance of stability by the equilibrium of motion-in-opposition would instantly give place to the real stability of the One substance, but it would be devoid of light.

The universe would immediately become a motionless universe of black, immeasurable cold.

It would be without the image making faculty and without intelligence. Its knowledge would be that of mere perception of the reality of existence without the ability to form idea or to conceive it.

All dimensions of motion are registered in the minute particles heretofore referred to as light units.

As all motion is expressed in waves and registered in form, and as form begins to evolve from the integration of light units, it is well to briefly define the dimension and structure of the light unit in order to correct the misconcept of matter as something apart from life and light and energy.

All effects and dimensions of first cause begin with the birth of each light unit.

Each point in the universe is the center of the universe. Each point is the beginning and the end of each ten-octave swing of the cosmic pendulum.

Each new-born corpuscle, or light unit, is a center of disturbance from which the entire universe responds to its alternating electromagnetic pulsations.

Motion, once started, never ceases until it has run the entire gamut of the ten octave range, from which point it begins again.

The light unit of the highest octave and lowest potential eventually becomes a light unit of the lowest octave and highest potential.

Light units are omnipresent throughout the universe.

All effects of thinking are omnipresent throughout the universe.

Nothing is which is not universal.

Light units are the beginning and the end of that super-majestic illusion which man calls "creation." They constitute all that man calls "created things," which in truth are creating, evolving things.

The creating of these corpuscles is as continuous as thinking is continuous.

The concept of man that corpuscles are existent in perpetuity is as wrong a concept as the concept that they are unchanging in their electro-magnetic charges and other dimensions.

Reproductive waves of electro-magnetic motion-in-opposition are made up of corpuscles to register, as dimensions in matter, the idea of thinking Mind.

Corpuscles are the children of generative energy, born of generative energy and continued by generative energy, even as you and I; and they "die" of old age through lack of it, even as you and I.

They are living, thinking 'beings, male and female, even as you and I.

They organize and integrate into complex forms of matter through the elements of matter which register the idea of all thinking. Elements of matter are orderly periodic dimensions of the substance of matter.

They are living, breathing, pulsing children of light, children of the father-mother substance of Mind, even as you and I.

Yes, even as you and I, for of such, and of nothing else, are we composed.

Light units are "born" into this universe of illusion as an appearance, registering an idea of thinking Mind, even as you and I.

They take their place in complex systems of complexing idea, ever registering the complexing of the idea of thinking.

Man is but a complex organization of light-units, functioning under the government of that idea of thinking Mind, called man.

Light units exhibit all the characteristics with which man is thoroughly familiar in living organisms.

They inhale and exhale, inflating and deflating in the process, just as man does.

They generate energy through absorption and lose it through fatigue, just as all life does.

All light units and systems of light units are both generative and radiative as all more complex living organizations are both ma le and female.

Just as the male of all creating things is both male and female, but preponderantly male, so all light units and systems of light units are both generative and radiative, but preponderantly one or the other.

They integrate into form and they disintegrate into the disappearance of form just as all growing things evolve and devolve.

They have their periodicities of sleep and wakefulness which is their periodic day just as all life and all mass has its similar periodicities.

Also, these characteristics are repeated in all multiplicity of light units combined in greater mass Repeativeness is an absolute characteristic of all effects of motion.

All mass inhales and exhales, exactly repeating the simple, familiar phases common to all life, for all matter is living matter.

The sun inhales and exhales. The five and a half year contraction of the sun to its maximum sun spot period is its inbreathing, and its alternate dilation to its minimum sun spot period is its outbreathing.

There is no difference in principle between the breathing of a light unit and that of a giant sun. The only difference in effect is one of dimension.

The pulsation of a light unit may be thirty trillion to the second, whereas the giant sun may complete one inhalation in five years.

Inhalation is for the purpose of continuing the apparent existence of form in matter.

Inhalation is regeneration. It is integration. It vitalizes, nourishes, refreshes. It continues that which is known as life.

Exhalation is for the purpose of discontinuing the apparent existence of form in matter.

Exhalation is dissolution. It is disintegration. It de-vitalizes, exhausts, fatigues. It discontinues that which is known as life and leads ever toward that which is known as death.

Light units have the appearance of individuality, even as you and I.

There is no individuality in this universe of Mind. There is but an appearance of individuality.

This is a universe of the One Thing. That One Thing is Mind.

The substance of thinking Mind in action is light.

There is but One substance.

The One substance cannot be divided into many substances, or many parts.

Individuality is but an appearance, an effect of potential in the periodicity of thinking.

These little rotating particles of light associate themselves into inter-revolving or gyrating systems which continue the motion given to them by the energy of thinking.

These systems are the records of all idea expressed in thinking.

They are the living storehouses of the energy of thinking.

The energy expended by Mind in the process of thinking idea is not lost or dissipated by thinking.

If thinking did not register itself in light and light did not integrate into the forms of idea, the created universe would not be.

All thought is registered in these systems of light particles as a means of continuing its evolving appearance of existence as idea, just as man's voice is registered in light particles which reproduce throughout the universe with the speed of light as a means of informing the rest of the universe of man's thinking.

Idea of Mind registered in light is living, and through reproduction it continues the idea of itself in its orderly complexing, throughout the entirety of the universal circuit of thinking.

These little particles, born of universal thinking in its highest octave, are the first manifestations of what man calls life.

They are the first manifestations of the appearance of individual existence.

They are the beginning of the appearance of separate existence.

They are the beginning of the appearance of opposites.

They are the beginning of positive and negative electrical units magnetically united.

They are the beginning of male and female individuals.

They are the beginning of apparently separate thinking, separate functioning, separate acting, separate living male and female beings.

These children of thinking Mind differ in no way from man, or mountain, or oak, or rose, except in their simplicity.

They are light: and so is man and the mountain.

They think and live and require new energy to generate energy in order to continue their appearance as the beginning of divine idea.

They continue themselves as idea by transforming other energy into the idea of themselves.

They continue others as idea by radiating energy for absorption by others or by being consumed to supply energy for others of which they become a part.

Universe Neptune's electromagnetic charge and make it increasingly generative until someday its journey in a centripetal spiral orbit would end in the hot fires of the central nucleal sun where it would become one with it in energy.

Again, in accord with periodic law, would the idea of Neptune be reborn in energy; and once again would it either travel the path of the opening spiral toward nebulosity or the closing spiral path of another new system.

Or, if it were not so drawn into another system it would in time disintegrate its mass through expansion and cessation of motion into a negative nebula, and reform through inertia into a positive nebula.

All idea is born of the energy of thinking and all idea continues itself as idea by the energy of its thinking.

Light units "grow" just as all things grow, and by the same process, the absorption of the energy of other light units.

Just as simple idea becomes involved and complex in the thinking, so do light units grow from simplicity to complexity.

Radium was once hydrogen; gold was lithium; man was helium; the mountain was silicon; the cooling dew was flaming nitrogen; and all were all of these and all things else.

Everything that is, is of everything else that is.

Man is but an involved and complex organization of countless myriads of light units assembled into systems, and systems of systems, in the orderly process of continuous thinking of the idea of man.

In the complexing of the idea of man, these myriads of light units co-ordinate in order to function in accordance with the evolving idea of man.

Each thinking light unit adds to the idea of itself from the source of idea, and all thinking registers itself in new light particles.

Just as a growing-nation co-ordinates its functions, so does the complexing idea of man co-ordinate its functions.

Just as a nation of people divides the work of its units and centralizes its government for the continuation of the idea of itself as a nation, just so does that complex organization called man divide the work of its units and centralize its government in order to continue the idea of itself as man.

Man's concept Just as the sun continues the idea of itself by transforming other energy into the idea of itself, and just as the sun radiates its energy to continue the idea of this planet by radiation of its energy for absorption by this planet, so does one light unit give to another and take away energy from another.

All idea is energy, therefore the energy of one idea can be transformed into the energy of another to continue the idea of that other.

All energy is light and all idea is light.

One light unit does not destroy another by absorbing it: the one but assimilates the idea of the other.

An external unit such as Neptune in our solar system, would not be destroyed by being drawn into the sphere of a new integrating system. The new generative system would reve of a thinking brain as the only thinking part of man, is a wrong concept.

The brain is but the seat of government of that nation of thinking light units called man.

These light units, assembled as a man, think individually but co-ordinate as a unit, and each functions in its place else the idea of the man could not continue.

Man also thinks individually but co-ordinates as a unit in universal thinking. The individuality of man as a part of the universe is exactly analogous to the individuality of a light unit as a part of man.

This is the great law of evolving idea.

Idea is evolutionary and continuous; therefore, is the recording of idea also continuous. Idea is constantly building itself up in all forming systems. This is integration.

This is what man calls growth. It is life.

Idea is constantly tearing itself apart.

This is disintegration.

This is what man calls fading. It is death.

Integration and disintegration are simultaneous in all systems.

Integration is growth.

Fading is growth.

Disintegration is life.

Death is life.

Of this more will be written in its proper place; for it will be more easily understood when the cause of electricity, magnetism and gravitation has been made clear; and also when the laws of magnetic and electric lines of force, which, by their opposition, cause the appearance of that which man calls the "created physical universe of integrating and disintegrating matter," has been clearly written down.

CHAPTER II

ELECTRICITY AND MAGNETISM

DEFINITIONS

Electricity is the active, attractive force within Mind which appears to concentrate, contract and compress the non-compressible substance of Mind into the forms created by the process of thinking, and to evolve those forms by raising the potential, or power dimension, of energy by accumulation.

Magnetism is the reactive, repellant force within the substance of Mind which appears to expand the forms created by Mind in the process of thinking, and to accomplish their dissolution through lowering the potential of energy by releasing the accumulation.

Positive electricity is the generative energy of thinking Mind registered in light units which are gravitationally or centripetally resisting magnetic influence by expelling it. The light units are contracting, registering their contraction and their resistance to magnetism in heat. Their electric orbital motion is toward a closing spiral in one plane.

Positive electricity is that state of motion in which electricity dominates magnetism.

Positive electricity is that state of motion in which centripetal force dominates centrifugal force.

Negative electricity is the radiative energy of thinking Mind registered in those same light units which are radially, or centrifugally, yielding to inflowing magnetic influence. They are expanding, registering their yielding and their expansion in cooling, and their electric orbital motion is toward an opening spiral in many planes, culminating in nebulosity.

Negative electricity is that state of motion in which magnetism dominates electricity.

Negative electricity is that state of motion in which centrifugal force dominates centripetal force.

LAWS

All mass is both electric and magnetic.

All mass simultaneously expresses both opposites of all effects of motion, and each opposite is cumulatively preponderant in sequence.

All electro-magnetic mass forms into systems of units which revolve in spiral orbits both centripetally toward and centrifugally away from nucleal centers.

All preponderantly charging systems are positive systems.

All preponderantly discharging systems are negative systems.

All preponderantly contracting systems are positive systems.

All preponderantly expanding systems are negative systems.

All systems whose spirals are preponderantly closing spirals are positive systems.

All systems whose spirals are preponderantly opening spirals are negative systems.

All systems of preponderantly lessening volume are positive systems.

All systems of preponderantly increasing volume are negative systems.

All systems of preponderantly increasing potential are positive systems.

All systems of preponderantly lowering potential are negative systems.

All preponderantly integrating systems are positive systems.

All preponderantly disintegrating systems are negative systems.

All preponderantly generating systems are positive systems.

All preponderantly radiating systems are negative systems.

All preponderantly heating systems are positive systems.

All preponderantly cooling systems are negative systems.

In other words, electricity is the inhalation, or inbreathing generative action while magnetism is the exhalation, or outbreathing radiative reaction.

Electricity is the plus half of the One universal force which has apparently divided itself into two forces, and magnetism is the minus half. Electricity and magnetism exist as separate appearances only when opposed. In non-opposition they disappear. They become one.

Electricity desires to gather its half together as one force and substance, while magnetism, on the contrary, desires separation into two forces and exerts itself to the utmost to bring about this separation.

Electricity accumulates power while magnetism dissipates it.

Positive electricity is the plus half of electromagnetically charging light units which are seeking higher pressure zones.

Negative electricity is the minus half of electro - magnetically discharging light units which are seeking lower pressure zones.

Pressure zones are those states of increasing density of integration which are caused by the power of positive electricity to attract and to accumulate energy.

Electricity is the power force of the universe. Electricity accumulates power into high potential from the universal constant at the sacrifice of one of its time dimensions.

Electricity is the force of resistance to the established speed of the universal constant of energy.

Magnetism is the speed force, the time force, of the universe. Magnetism dissipates the high potential power dimension and transforms it into time dimension of low potential.

Magnetism is the force which works toward a return to the established motion of the universal constant of energy.

Electricity and magnetism move in opposite directions, their departure from each other being 180°.

Modern science believes the departure of magnetic and electric lines of force to be 90°. This is a wrong interpretation of that illusion of motion.

Electricity is the force of gravitation and moves spirally toward the nucleal center of its mass. It moves as though it were starting at the base of a cone and travelling around its surface in an ever-contracting spiral orbit, to its apex.

Magnetism is the force of radiation and moves spirally toward the extremity of its mass. It moves as though it were starting at the apex of a cone and travelling around its surface in an ever-expanding orbit, to its base.

Electricity is therefore centripetal and its acceleration of orbital speed is in proportion to its distance from its generative center.

Magnetism is therefore centrifugal and its deceleration of orbital speed is in proportion to its distance from its generative center.

Each force balances itself as well as its opposite force.

Electricity is the generative force.

To generate means to decelerate an established motion in order that it may be accumulated.

Magnetism is the radiative force.

To radiate means to accelerate an accumulated force in order that the accumulation may be dissipated into its established motion.

Electricity and magnetism are not two separate forces, nor are they two separate substances.

They are merely two different dimensions of motion. They belong solely to motion and not to substance.

Neither are positive electricity and negative electricity two kinds of electricity.

A cold piece of solid iron is the result of electric deceleration of the universal constant, and is power accumulated by the formation of closely packed atomic systems and restricted orbits.

This cold piece of solid iron will disappear into gases if its atomic systems are accelerated sufficiently to dissipate them by radiation.

Positive and negative electricity are but two differing potentials of the same force which must move in opposite directions for reasons which shall be made clear later in this chapter.

Positive electricity can become negative and negative can become positive by a reversal of their potentials. They are but relative in accord with their respective pressures.

The sound of the human voice, for example, is an electro-positive action. Its radiation into space, or along a wire, is its electro-negative reaction.

The reproduction of the voice by radio, or at the other end of the wire is an electropositive reproduction of the negative reaction which is rapidly expanding into the disappearance of lower potentials.

The sudden impact of the radiating sound against the higher pressures of higher potentials reverses the process of radiation.

Negative, expanding, centrifugal force becomes positive ; contracting centripetal force and we hear the sound again.

Electricity is the basis of the atom.

Within every atom of the One substance is all the power of the universe.

It is dynamic.

The dynamic power of Mind is due to the activity of thinking.

The dynamic action of universal thinking is the cause of all creation and decreation.

Universal thinking is the beginning of all energy.

Universal thinking is the foundation of all-natural law.

All of nature's laws are absolute and periodic effects of their cause, which is the energy of thinking.

The "created" universe is but an effect due to the positive, concentrating, generating, integrating energy of the dynamic action impulse of thinking, which, in its turn gives way to the negative, expanding, radiating and disintegrating energy of the dynamic re-action impulse of thinking.

The mystery of growth is within the comprehension of the man who knows the orderliness of the opposition between the positive action and negative re-action of the two apparently opposite forces of generation and radiation set up in the process of thinking.

All creating things are growing things whether they be giant suns, or violets, or man, or elements, or compounds of elements or the atoms of elements.

All growth is simultaneously integrating and disintegrating. In the beginning of all growth integration is preponderant, then in its turn, disintegration dominates.

Disintegration begins with integration and continues until it, in turn, becomes the conquering force.

Death is born in the cradle with life.

The alternating pulsations of the process of thinking are controlled by two apparently opposing forces.

One of these forces is a generating, integrating force of action, while the other is a reactionary radiating and disintegrating force.

One force is that which controls evolution while the other is that which compels dissolution.

The word of man for the concentrating, generating and integrating force which controls evolution is "electricity."

Electricity is the active, attractive, generative, gravitative, positive principle of creation.

All decreation is the radiating, disintegrating energy of dynamic thinking.

The mystery of that which man calls death is within the comprehension of the man who knows the orderliness of radiative thinking.

There is no death. Death is but the beginning of life.

Decreation is continuous, as thinking is continuous.

Decreation is but the degeneration of that which has been generated. It is but the reaction of action. Man's word for this radiating, disintegrating force which compels dissolution is "magnetism." Magnetism is the separative, repelative, radiative, negative principle of creation.

Electricity is the vitalizing property of matter.

Magnetism is the devitalizing property of matter.

Electricity is the father, the male principle of thinking Mind.

Magnetism is the mother, the female principle of thinking Mind.

Magnetism is born of electricity. Electricity and magnetism are One.

That One is the father-mother principle of thinking Mind.

Their apparently opposite desires, merged together, make One.

They are not two opposite principles, they are but the One dynamic principle.

In the entire universe there are no opposites.

Each is of the other and is the cause of the other; and the energy of thinking, in which -these two forms are in apparent opposition, is the cause of their apparent separability.

Electricity is magnetism revitalized. To be vitalized means to be unequalized, or opposed in relation to surrounding pressures.

Magnetism is electricity devitalized. To be devitalized means to be equalized or non-opposed in relation to surrounding pressures.

The activity of vitalized force is the desire to attain a state of increased opposition.

The inactivity of devitalized force is the inertia of a balanced state of non-opposition.

Radiation is but the separative reaction of the cumulative action of generation.

Radiation is but the lowering of a higher potential.

Radiation is the exact opposite of gravitation which is the raising of a lower potential.

Disintegration is but the separative reaction of the cumulative action of integration.

Action and its reaction, added together are but one.

If Mind were not a thinking substance, both electricity and magnetism would not appear to be opposites.

Their apparent opposition is the cause of that complexity which man calls "creation."

The father principle of Mind is the electropositive force and the cause of centripetal force of motion.

Centripetal force is born of decelerative resistance to the established universal constant of energy.

The mother principle of Mind is the electronegative force and the cause of centrifugal force of motion.

Centrifugal force is born of accelerative returning to the established universal constant of energy.

The electro-positive force is that in which electricity dominates magnetism and accumulates power by transforming speed into power.

The electro-negative force is that in which magnetism has conquered electric opposition and by doing so has released power, by means of expansion, into lower potential of greater speed.

The desire of electricity is expressed as action in motion-in-opposition.

The desire of magnetism is expressed as the reaction of action in motion-in-inertia.

The active force is the positive force. It is the force which stands for what man calls "power", or high potential.

The reactive force is the negative force seeking a state of negation, which stands for what man calls "weakness," or low potential.

The active force is the creative force of the universe.

The reactive force is the decreative force of the universe.

The active force is the integrative, generative force of the universe.

The reactive force is the disintegrative, degenerative force of the universe.

The active force is male, the father force of the universe.

The reactive force is female, the mother force of the universe.

The creative force is the dynamic, expressive force of thinking which gives apparent form to all idea of thinking Mind.

The decreative force is the passive force of thinking which causes the disappearance of form from actuality into potentiality.

The father force is the positive force. The mother force is the negative force.

The father-mother force united is the reproductive force.

The mother force is born of the father force. It is merely its negative reaction.

Reaction is opposed to action, not attracted to it.

Reaction leaps away from action, not toward it. If reaction, which is negative, leaps away from action, which is positive, then the theory of positive and negative electric charges attracting each other has no foundation.

Reaction is born of action. So then, is negative force born of positive force.

As magnetic flow is but the reaction of generation, therefore magnetism is born of electricity. The greater the action of generation, the greater the reaction of degenerative magnetic flow.

Magnetic flow is radiation. Radiation is the emanation expelled from electro-generative, contractive action. It is the outgoing breath, the exhalation of the living corpuscle, or system, or mass.

Radiation is degeneration.

The creating universe is, a generating one. The decreating universe is a degenerating one.

The generating universe of solid matter is an accumulation of tenuous matter. Generating is charging.

The degenerating "physical" universe is a disappearing from the appearance of solidity through states of tenuosity to disappearance. Degeneration is discharging.

Generation is the winding of the cosmic clock for the accumulation of one-time dimension.

Degeneration is its unwinding by the release of the other stored up time dimension.

Radiation is radiative activity. Modern science calls it :"radio-activity."

Radio-activity is merely the reversing of the time dimensions of the universal constant. It is the exothermal, exhalation of the One universal Being, of which every existing thing is.

The more positive the system or mass, the more genero-active and radio-active is that system.

The more generative the system or mass, the more cohesive it is.

Cohesion is born of generative decelerative, gravitative, centripetal force.

The more radiative the system or mass, the less cohesive it is.

The more cohesive the system, or mass, the more compact it is. It is what man describes as "harder," which means more impenetrable.

The atoms of all of the hard and closely integrated elements have ejected magnetism with greater speed and in smaller streams than the atoms of the less closely integrated elements.

Resistance to integration is the cause of this increased speed, and the contracted atomic volume is the cause of the smaller magnetic stream.

It is as though a certain volume of water, which has been pumped through a four-inch pipe, had to be pumped through a one-inch pipe in the same amount of time. To do this, the pressure behind that volume of water would have to be vastly increased and the speed of the smaller stream would also have to be vastly increased.

Resistance to integration has generated much heat which in its turn has been radiated, thus reversing the magnetic pressure from the magnetic field within the system to the magnetic orbit outside of the system.

This process has gradually cooled the systems by the pressure release from within and the consequent radiation of their heat, and allowed them to become more densely packed so that their more closely rotating units could create the illusion of solidity or hardness.

Hardness is due to deceleration of rotation and acceleration of revolution which allows a closer integration of light units in their systems. It might be said, concerning the illusion of solidity, that if a cobweb could be woven with sufficient density and revolved with sufficient rapidity, it would appear to be a solid disk of silver.

Genero-activity is the opposite of radioactivity.

Genero-activity is the resistance set up against one time dimension of the universal constant in order to transform it into power. It is the endothermal inhalation of the One universal Being.

The positive force of motion-in-opposition is that which produces all idea of thinking Mind and gives it the appearance of form.

The negative force of motion-in-opposition is that which tears apart the appearance of form and carries the soul of it, or the memory of it, back into motion-in-inertia.

The union of these positive and negative forces of motion-in-opposition reverses radiative dominance to generative dominance and thus causes a reproduction of the idea and the form of the idea through re-integration.

The positive electric force is the creating force.

The negative electric force is the decreating force.

The union of positive and negative is the reproducing force.

Reproduction means the re-integration of form back into that octave in which it has once appeared, but from which it has disappeared by disintegration into motion-in-inertia. In motion-in-inertia the soul of all idea awaits regeneration.

The soul of all idea is registered in the seed of idea.

In the seed of man is the whole of man, and so also the seed of all idea.

All idea and all form of idea is electrically conceived and electrically evolved to its highest limitations of potential. It then becomes magnetically dissipated and devolved to its lowest potential.

The desire of electricity is divisibility of the indivisible Mind substance into parts.

Electricity craves separation from magnetism.

Electricity desires itself alone and shares company with magnetism only because it is fatigued by resisting it.

Electricity would tear the Mind substance apart in its desire to materialize divine idea into form. It would make of this universe one solid non-elastic mass if its desire could be gratified.

Now it must be remembered that the substance of Mind is a perfect, homogeneous, indivisible one.

Electricity cannot separate from magnetism and its attempts to do so give only the appearance of separation into parts.

Magnetism does not desire companionship or union with electricity, nor does it desire its own continuation as a separate force. It desires to extinguish electricity as a separate force by separating its particles. Its own extinction would be the consequence of the gratification of this desire.

Magnetism desires an equilibrium of motion and absolute inertia, while electricity desires action, and is not concerned with the reaction which adjusts that action in an equilibrium of motion in opposition.

The force of electricity is the generative, centripetal force of contraction into the appearance of form.

It is the opposite of the reactive force of magnetism which is the force of radiative, centrifugal expansion into the disappearance of form.

Evolving matter, or idea, or form, is electrically preponderant. This means that positive charge predominates.

Devolving matter, or idea, or form, is magnetically dominant. This means that negative charge predominates.

Evolving appearance of form in matter is a periodic integration, due to positive-electromagnetic opposition, in which the generative force of electricity is preponderant.

That which man calls "growth" is merely periodic integration, during which the generative force of positive electricity is preponderant.

Devolving disappearance of matter is a periodic disintegration, due to negative-electromagnetic opposition in which the radiative force of magnetism is dominant.

That which man calls ageing, or fading, or declining, is merely periodic disintegration, during which time generation continues, but with lessened energy, for the radiative force of magnetism is dominant.

The vigor of youth is due to electric preponderance and the weakening of adolescence is due to magnetic dominance.

Youth, the growing period, is the life inhalation period.

It corresponds to the first five octaves of the universal ten octave cycle.

Maturity is the turning point of the life inhalation period toward its life exhalation period.

It corresponds to carbon, the turning point of the universal ten octave cycle.

Ageing is merely the life exhalation period. It corresponds to the last five octaves of the universal ten octave cycle.

Electricity is always preponderant in all dimensions, but it is both preponderant and dominant in the positive half of the reproductive wave of the universal energy constant. Magnetism is never preponderant but it is dominant in the negative half of the universal energy constant.

Youth is preponderantly generative, or power accumulative.

Age is dominantly radiative, or power releasive.

Youth is preponderantly electro-positive, or integrative.

Age is dominantly electro-negative, or disintegrative.

The perfume of the budding rose is a disintegration of the preponderantly generating, growing rose, but because of electric preponderance, integration so exceeds disintegration that growth continues despite that disintegration until both forces are equalized in which man calls "death."

Just as soon as the gravitative forces of electro-positive preponderance have carried the growth of that rose to the fourth gravitational tone of electro-magnetic opposition, which is the maximum point of inhalation in its life cycle, then magnetism begins to dominate and the rose begins to fade.

Just so with all integrating idea, whether it be man, or planet, or flaming sun, or minute atomic system. The law for one is the law for all.

Death is a disappearance of form, but not of the idea of that form.

Growth is an effect of gravitation. Growth means that forming things pass down the octaves in gravitative periodicity.

During that periodicity, electricity gives form to the idea and magnetism gradually nebulizes that form back into idea.

The form of idea is of no import, it is but a manifestation of the idea itself.

Form is fleeting. Its appearance and disappearance are periodically repeative throughout eternity.

Idea is the eternal record of form, the soul of form.

Out of motion-in-inertia comes a new-born idea which runs the course from electro-positive motion-in-opposition into electronegative motion-in-opposition and back again into motion-in-inertia. There it is stored as the chemical registration of the idea, which man calls "memory," until man needs to recall it again. This he can do at any time by regenerating it.

The idea of the rose differs from the newborn idea of man's thinking in that the rose is a very much evolved old idea, the memory of which in its millions of generations of evolving through motion-in opposition is stored in the seed of the rose in motion-in-inertia ready for re-generation or re-incarnation at any time.

All evolution of idea of Mind into form is electric and is limited to electro-positive motion in opposition.

Evolution of idea ceases in the master-tones of motion-in-inertia with the disappearance of evolving form, and begins again its evolution of idea from these same master-tones with the re-appearance of evolving form in motion-in-opposition.

The master-tones are a record of all motion and a storehouse of the memory of it. From the master tones the evolution of form of idea starts, and in them, at the next octave's end, the record of the evolution of that idea is again registered in memory of form.

Evolution is but the inevitable effect of periodicity which is characteristic of all phenomena of this creating universe.

All growth and declination, also all evolution of a million generations of growth and declination of form, are but stages in the periodicities resulting from the electro-magnetic, oscillating process of thinking..

The universal Mind substance of matter, or light, could not be anything but a thinking substance because of its possession of electricity and magnetism as attributes of energy.

Electricity and magnetism are those apparently opposite principles or qualities of Mind which cause it to be a thinking substance.

The apparent points or centers of disturbance throughout the entirety of the substance of Divine Mind, due to the process of thinking, are electromagnetically registered in light, which is energy, which is matter: all One and the same.

Evolving and devolving forms of matter are but changes of various dimensions.

The law of the growing rose is the same for man, or giant sun', or stellar galaxy.

Electricity attracts, magnetism repels.

Electricity and magnetism move in opposite directions, their departure from each other being at 180°.

Electric lines of force approach each other at 180°.

Magnetic lines of force depart from the line of direction of electric force and also of magnetic force at 180°.

Electric energy reproduces itself by induction and dissipates itself by conduction, at an angle of 90° to the lines of direction of induction and conduction.

CHAPTER III

NEW CONCEPTS OF ELECTRICITY AND MAGNETISM

The concept of modern science regarding the mutual attraction of oppositely charged particles and the mutual repulsion of similarly charged ones is fundamentally wrong.

This concept claims that positive charge repels positive charge and attracts negative "charge," whereas, instead, positive charge attracts positive charge and expels negative discharge. Electricity is the attractive force of this universe of integrating matter.

The belief that positive charge repels positive charge is inconsistent with the accepted fact that density increases as pressure and positive charge increase.

Greater density and greater pressure are both due to the power of electricity to attract electricity.

If positive charge, density and pressure increase in the direction of the gravitative center where the attribute of attraction is at its maximum in a mass or system, and decreases in the opposite direction, which is the direction of negative discharge, it is inconsistent and illogical to claim that positive charge repels positive charge.

Cohesion increases as centripetal force predominates, and positive charge increases with increasing ability of mass to cohere.

On the contrary, cohesion decreases as centrifugal force predominates, and negative discharge increases with the decreasing ability of mass to cohere.

There is no greater evidence of the truth of this than the known fact that any mass accelerates its speed as it approaches a mass of greater positive charge, and decelerates its speed as it recedes from such a mass.

Consider, for example, the acceleration of any planet or comet in that part of its eccentric orbit in which it approaches, and its deceleration as it recedes from the sun.

Consider the acceleration of the ball as it drops toward the gravitational center of the earth, or the deceleration of the bullet as it is forced away from the earth.

Consider the deceleration of the atom of gas which rises of its own accord to seek its own more negative region of low pressure.

Careful consideration of these many effects of motion should convince the logical thinker that accumulation of mass is due entirely to the power of electro-positive centripetal force to attract electropositive centripetal force.

On the other hand, the disintegration of mass is due entirely to the expanding power of electronegative centrifugal force.

As the direction of electro-positive lines of force is toward the apex of a cone in a closing spiral, and the direction of electro-negative lines of force are away from the apex in an opening spiral, these opposing forces cannot possibly attract each other.

Modern science claims that negative "charge" repels negative "charge" and attracts positive charge, whereas, actually, negative "charge" repels both negative and positive charge. Magnetism is the repellant, or separative force of this universe of disintegrating matter.

Man's fixed concept of magnetism as an attractive force is also fundamentally wrong. This basic error is fast tied to every meaning of the very words "magnet" or "magnetic" or "magnetism." These words are universally used in the sense of attraction.

Every schoolboy has been the proud owner of that little horseshoe shaped toy which picked up bits of iron for his amusement.

This remarkable phenomenon quite naturally built up the concept of magnetism as an attractive force.

Magnetism supposedly performs these miracles. So it seems. The evidence of one's senses are again deceived by illusion.

The exact opposite is the fact.

The electro-positive charge is merely increased and the attraction of positive electricity to positive electricity of a similar dimension is demonstrated.

This phenomenon of the power of the electropositive charge of the magnet to attract will be exactly described later when the laws of unit, or opposing pressures are written down.

Suffice it here to say that a magnet is a piece of iron around which so strong a generative current has been caused to circulate that the billions of little pumps which make up its atoms have been vastly stimulated to excessive zeal in performing their work. The pulsations are so greatly energized that the magnetic outflow is like a swift running stream in comparison with its normal flow.

Thus has the positive charge been greatly increased. The axial poles of rotation and the magnetic poles have become almost superimposed, the potential and unit pressures have been raised to such an extent that another piece of iron of normal potential and pressure will be drawn into the higher pressure of the "magnetic" · iron, and its potential also raised.

This will also be very simple to comprehend when the simple principles of gravitation and an exact understanding of the forces of attraction and repulsion are known.

The misconcepts of modern science concerning the fundamental principles of attraction and repulsion are many and all are based upon the wrong belief that electricity is the repellant and magnetism the attractive force.

Man speaks of light repulsion and cites the tail of the comet which forever points away from the sun as conclusive proof.

This phenomenon is due to the fact that all mass rotates and revolves toward its proper pressure zone.

All mass is potential out of place, and all mass constantly seeks the proper pressure zone for its constantly changing potential.

All states of motion, including the tail of the comet, conform to this law.

The age-long misconcept regarding the supposed attractive power of magnetism must be reversed and its exact opposite substituted in its place.

Much practical demonstration has contributed to the building up of the strongest foundations for the present theories.

Scientists have built up wrong theories based upon appearances which deceive because they are misunderstood. Man seems to forget that this is a universe of appearances, a universe of illusions, and appearances easily deceive unless one makes allowance for them in every effect of motion.

Man is not easily deceived regarding those illusions which he thoroughly understands, such as relative dimensions in perspective, or the illusion of the moon racing behind the trees keeping pace with speeding man, but he is easily deceived regarding those illusions which he does not suspect to be illusions.

In order that one may know truth from the illusionary appearance of truth the reader must remember that all objective effects of motion in form are illusions, and also that the relation between those apparent objective forms, and their motion as well, are illusions.

All illusions will deceive if judged only by the evidence of one's senses.

Not for one second does any effect of motion remain unchanged, therefore it is not logical that changing things can be dependable realities.

There can be no unconditioned facts in a universe of motion. There can only be ever-changing appearances of facts.

All states of motion are relative and deceiving.

Comprehension of this universe of Mind is not possible as long as it is considered as a universe of dimension. Nor is it possible if its illusions are considered as realities.

Complexity is a drag anchor to comprehension.

Comprehension of the universe is very simple when it is considered as a dimensionless universe abounding in appearances which do not deceive because one knows them to be but illusions.

All matter is an effect of a basically simple and easily comprehensible cause, the thinking of Mind.

Man's reliance upon the reality of the illusions of electrical effect have deceived him into a misinterpretation of his observations.

Just as man used to believe firmly the evidences which his senses seemed to prove, that the sun and stars revolved daily, so does he at present firmly believe the evidences which his senses seem to prove, that positive corpuscles repel positive and negative corpuscles repel negative, while each opposite attracts the other.

The term "negative charge" is not in accord with the laws of motion. The positive electric force charges and the negative magnetic force discharges.

Modern science firmly believes that there are two kinds of corpuscles, negative corpuscles, which are called' electrons, and positive corpuscles, which are called protons. This is a wrong concept.

All corpuscles are doubly "charged." And so are all systems and so is all mass doubly "charged." All familiar effects of motion substantiate this statement.

It would be absurd to say that this solar system is a positive proton surrounded by negative electrons, which are the planets.

All phenomena of motion are repeative.

Mass is purely relative. An atom of manganese or iron is exactly like this solar system, in which the positive nucleus is concentrated; and an atom of sodium is exactly like the nebula forming in the constellation of Orion, in which the positive charge is extended and has not formed a distinct nucleus.

A biologist would not think of the male as wholly male, for he knows that the male, though preponderantly male, is also female.

Each sex is both electric and magnetic.

They are therefore electro-magnetic in periodicity, or in other words, male-female in periodicity.

Here is the law in accord with truth.

Positive charge attracts positive charge and expels negative discharge.

Negative discharge repels both negative discharge and positive charge.

The fact that electricity expels magnetism does not mean that it repels it.

Expulsion is not repulsion.

Expulsion is the result of electric attraction which causes electrically charged particles to draw closer together.

This effect of closer assemblage, is a centripetal effect of contraction which squeezes magnetism away from the spaces between the integrating particles of electric preponderance.

The magnetic flow resulting from this squeezing process is merely the reaction of the action of squeezing.

The action of electricity might be likened unto the compression of a spring from within.

The reaction of magnetism might be likened unto the elastic resistance to that compression by an exactly opposite pressure of expansion from within.

Opposite charges do not attract each other. They are opposites and as opposites their very natures are characteristic of all apparent opposites in the assertion of their opposition.

A positive light unit, or system, does indeed attract a negative one, not because of its negative, but because of its positive attribute.

One single light unit is no different than a mass such as this planet in respect to its double charge.

It would be absurd to say that this planet, which is but one light unit of this solar system, and corresponds exactly to one light unit of an atomic system, is either a negative or a positive unit. It is both negative and positive and its positive charge is always preponderant in that part which is nearest to its positive nucleus, which is the sun. Also is its negative discharge always dominant in the portion farthest removed from the sun.

TWO APPARENTLY OPPOSITE FORCES

It must be remembered that electricity is the attractive force and that magnetism is the repellant force.

The attractive force attracts only attractive force, which is itself.

Electricity attracts electricity.

Electricity does not attract the repellant force, neither does electricity repel the repellant force.

On the other hand, magnetism, which is the repellant force, does nothing but perform its function of repelling.

It does not attract itself. A repellant force cannot be an attractive force, nor can the attractive force be a repellant force.

Each can but fill its own office; one attracts, and thus gathers' light units together into an appearance of solids of matter. The other repels, and thus prys light units apart into the dissolution of solids of matter, into gases and vapors.

Magnetism is that force within the universal Mind substance which tends to preserve the One-ness of universal uniformity.

Magnetism desires a formless and dimensionless universe, just as electricity desires a universe of form and dimension.

Magnetism prevents the apparent separation, or division, of divine Mind into parts as electricity attempts this apparent separation.

All the force of electricity is exerted in the attempt to create the illusions of form and dimension.

All the force of magnetism is exerted in the attempt to destroy all illusion, all form and all dimension.

Neither force completely fulfils its desire, for each partially thwarts the other.

The energy of magnetism is the elastic energy of expansion, a straining energy ever pushing toward the inertial line of equalized pressures which lies between any two masses, while the energy of electricity is ever pulling toward the pulsing heart, the gravitational nucleus of every mass.

ELASTICITY

One of the outstanding characteristics of motion is elasticity which also appears to be an attribute of the One substance.

Elasticity is due to opposition.

Elasticity is that force developed in the One substance of Mind as a reaction to the action of electricity.

It is this quality of elasticity which gives magnetism its rebounding force.

This elastic, magnetic reaction which is forever and eternally pressing against electric action, is that force which surely restores all opposed motion to inertial equilibrium.

Imagine electricity as a compressed spring, with magnetism eternally ready to take advantage of any let-up in the contractive force which is holding it in compression, no matter how slight a relaxation that may be.

If one could imagine such a thing as an absolutely complete and sudden withdrawal of all electric contractive energy, the instantaneous response from this elastic counter pressure would cause a cosmic explosion which would instantly destroy all appearance of form. The universe would then be one of equalized pressures, and opposed motion would be at an end.

This sudden expansion is exactly what occurs when man combines two or more elements which desire to get away from each other because they are tonally too far removed from each other to be possible mates. The elasticity of magnetism takes advantage of the sudden letup in the process of generation and rebounds so swiftly that it instantly tears apart form which otherwise might take a million years to disintegrate.

It is this force of elasticity in magnetism that is constant in its resistance to any appearance of integration into any form whatsoever.

ELECTRO - MAGNETIC OPPOSITION

Magnetism is radiative and repellant, as electricity is gravitative and attractive.

Magnetism repels, electricity attracts.

That which 'electricity integrates through gravitation, 'magnetism disintegrates through radiation.

Magnetism is the brake upon the wheels of electricity resisting its generation of higher potential and registering that resistance in heat.

Electricity is the accelerator which speeds magnetic radiation, the expansion of which is registered in cold.

Electricity and magnetism are actually opposing forces which leap away from each other in exactly opposite directions.

Forces which depart one from the other do not attract each other.

Opposing forces oppose each other.

To say that positive charge and negative discharge attract each other is to say that electricity and magnetism attract each other.

This would be equivalent to saying that centripetal force attracts centrifugal force, or that generation attracts degeneration, or that a charging body attracts a discharging one.

One might as appropriately say that life attracts death.

Electricity and magnetism are opposites, and opposites move in opposite directions.

One is accustomed to thinking that male, which is preponderantly positive, attracts female which is preponderantly negative.

It is not the negative "charge" of the female which is attracted to the positive charge of the male, but rather the positive charge of each attracts the other.

In youth, when the attraction of opposite sexes is at its maximum, the positive charge of each sex is at its maximum.

In age the negative discharge increases, the disintegrating magnetic force dominates, the positive charge decreases, and as a result the attraction of each sex for its opposite decreases until it disappears and repulsion takes its place.

The apparent attraction of each action to its reaction is due to the desire of the active force within each for accumulation, and the consequent continuance of the evolving idea of itself through that accumulation.

When action is preponderant as positive charge, form of idea evolves. When reaction is dominant as negative discharge, form devolves. The record of the idea of both action and reaction is registered in inertia.

The chemist, when breaking up compounds, is accustomed to seeing a negative element seek the positive pole, and a positive element seek the negative pole.

He would know better how to interpret this if he would think of his elements in terms of sex, and also consider the process of regeneration of negative discharge by impact against the inertial plane between a discharging and a charging mass.

When the positive charges of negative reactions are attracted to positive poles, centrifugally dominant force is conquered by centripetally dominant force. The negative reaction then becomes a positive action.

The equalization causes reproduction.

The union of an action with its reaction is always followed by the reproduction of separate actions and reactions.

These reproduced actions and reactions are rebounds of the union.

Magnetism opposes electricity in its desire to transform this universe into one solid, motionless, nonelastic ball of positive electricity.

Electricity opposes magnetism in its desire to transform the universe into one of equalized pressures where opposites disappear into dimensionless non-opposition.

Positive electricity is preponderantly electric. Positive charge attracts positive charge.

Negative electricity is dominantly magnetic. Negative discharge repels both negative and positive charge, for both are electric and magnetism repels electricity.

Again, must it be written down that electricity and magnetism are not opposites, nor are they two forces. There are no opposites of anything in this universe of the One Thing.

Mind is the One substance.

Thinking Mind is the One force.

If Mind were not a thinking substance the universe would be without force.

It would be without life.

It would indeed be a dead universe.

Thinking is a positive action. To every action there is an equal reaction which is the opposite, or negative matrix, of that action.

The minus charge of the reactive negative matrix is equal to the plus charge of the active positive form of idea.

The positive form of an idea is stored in inertia as a negative matrix of that form.

There is but One active force of thinking Mind and that is the father force. Man calls it electricity.

Electricity appears as the first action of the process of thinking and disappears, like temperature, in motion-in-inertia.

Electricity therefore has no existence. It belongs to motion, and not to substance.

It is desire which causes the One substance to appear to change in state as it performs its function of recording form of idea.

Opposites are born of attempted division of unity or One-ness.

The very first action which attempts division of unity develops the reactionary apparent opposite reaction which opposes that attempted division.

The father force, acting upon the desire of Mind to create, finds that as Mind is the only substance, idea and its form must be developed out of that One substance of Mind.

The father force which is the image making faculty of Mind, proceeds to create idea and then to fashion the form of that idea out of the One substance.

The opposing magnetic force is then born to prevent the fashioning of the substance of Mind into form. For a time it vainly opposes such formation, but eventually it succeeds.

Electricity and magnetism are the two major dimensions of the universal constant of Mind.

Therefore the beginning of creation is the beginning of an attempted separation of the One substance by the One force of the substance.

The very attempt to divide the One substance gives the appearance of, but does not make, two substances.

It only develops two equal and opposing states of motion which man calls "forces." It but creates two illusions.

Part of the energy used in the attempted division into two is given to each, and the sum total of this energy is the exact amount of the energy of the One.

Electricity and magnetism are attributes of motion only and as separate entities they are but illusions of the substance of matter.

Form, or solidity of matter, is an electromagnetic record of states of motion. Therefore, solidity of matter is but an illusion which is measurable by electromagnetic dimensions which, in themselves, are but illusions.

Out of the father force then, is born the mother force, which man calls magnetism. The symbolism of the creation of Eve out of Adam is basically sound.

The father force creates all idea and gives it the appearance of form; but that idea cannot be perpetually held as idea in the appearance of form, nor can it be reproduced without the union of the father with the mother force from which the father force has parted and with which it makes an equilibrium of unity.

Both idea and the form of idea return to motion-in-inertia as memory and remain there for a time as formless idea.

A union of the father force with the mother force brings it back again into the form of idea, for the united energies of these apparent opposites make the total required by the One. Just so with positive electricity and negative electricity. They are not two forces.

They are but two aspects of One force attempting to separate, each by its own opposite method, thus becoming two forces.

They never succeed in so doing. Each is charged with the other, permeated more or less, in accord with its periodicity.

CHAPTER IV

POSITIVE AND NEGATIVE ELECTRICITY

Again, it must be repeated that in this universe of motion-in-equilibrium all energy equalizes itself in two equal and opposite swings of the cosmic pendulum, no matter where in the cycle those opposites of motion appear.

The cosmic pendulum swings forever between positive and negative electricity, eternally transferring its constant of energy from one dimension to another, but never changing that constant.

The opposing energies of the two swings, added together, make one equalized unit of the universal reproductive constant.

More than this, these opposing swings are simultaneously equalized at corresponding points in each of the ten octaves.

Electric action and its magnetic resisting reactive flow are simultaneous and in equilibrium at all times.

Positive electricity is an endothermic, contractive force which is actively absorbing a comparatively large quantity of generative light units of heat which raises its potential, and is expelling a smaller number of them, devitalized into magnetic radio-active emanations, thus slightly lowering its potential.

Negative electricity is an exothermic, expansive force which is reactively absorbing a small quantity of generative light units of heat which slightly raises its potential, and is expelling a greater number of them, devitalized into magnetic radioactive emanations, thus lowering its potential.

In the term "negative electricity," the word "electricity" is used in the generic sense, as the inclusive word "man" is used to represent both sexes.

Electro-positive systems are preponderantly charging systems, while electro-negative systems are preponderantly discharging systems.

Charging systems are in the positive half of the octave, the tones of which are generatively dominant. These systems are forcing magnetism out, and because of this they grow more compact. They therefore grow smaller, tone by tone to the fourth tone of the octave. Their atomic volume lessens and their density increases as magnetism is squeezed out, just as a sponge lessens in volume and increases in density as water is squeezed out.

Now must it be clearly understood that magnetism, expelled by electricity from within a charging system, did not enter that system as magnetism or as negative electricity. It entered as positive electricity and became devitalized into negative electricity by nucleal absorption of its positive charge. It was then expelled from the higher inner pressure to the lower outer pressure of the system.

Discharging systems are in the negative half of the octave, the generative tones of which are weakened. Weakening genero-activity results in weakening radioactivity which causes the systems to grow less compact. They, therefore, grow larger, tone by tone, from the fourth to the master tone. Their volume increases and their density decreases as magnetism is allowed to return, just as a sponge increases in volume and decreases in density as water is allowed to return.

By a study of the charts, pages 17, 83, it will be seen that when magnetism returns to negative systems it does not return as negative electricity. It impacts against the inertial plane between itself and the system, is regenerated and reconverted into negative electricity after it has made its centripetal journey to the apex of its spiral orbit with ever increasing pressure, and started on its centrifugal run with lowering pressure back to the inertial plane.

Charging systems are simultaneously discharging but their positive charges become increasingly preponderant and dominant until the consequent increase of potential changes the dimensions of the system. They then appear to be another substance.

Discharging systems are simultaneously charging, and their negative discharges become decreasingly dominant until the consequent lowering of potential changes their dimensions. When they have readjusted their various dimensions, they in their turn appear to be another substance.

Charging systems are preponderantly generative, male systems, while discharging systems are preponderantly radiative, female systems. Charging systems are exactly balanced by discharging systems.

All systems are divided into seven tones of energy.

One charging tone, and its exact mate in a discharging tone, balance as one unit constant of energy. There are four exactly equal unit constants of energy in each octave.

An octave is one universal reproductive constant.

Ten octaves constitute one cycle.

Tone 1 + is a charging system exactly balanced in all its periodicities by tone 1 —. Likewise tone 2 + is balanced by tone 2 —, and tone 3 + by 3 —. Tone 4

‡

is a double tone which is neither positive nor negative. It is bi-sexual.

These seven tones of four unit constants make up the total universal constant of energy which is omnipresent throughout the entirety of this universe of Mind.

Consider, for an example of positive charge attracting positive charge, the sun of our solar system. It is the nucleal center of this system, the point of maximum positive charge. It is therefore the high potential point of the system.

Consider this planet.

It is a doubly charged mass, which means that it is both positive and negative.

Its preponderance of positive charge is always toward the nucleal center, which means that it is always toward the light.

Its preponderance of negative discharge is always away from the nucleal center, which means that it is always away from the light.

The positive charge of this planet is therefore preponderant in that portion which is in daylight and the negative discharge is preponderant in that portion which is night.

The daylight portion of the planet is generative and endothermic, which means active, contractive and heat absorbing.

The daylight portion is that in which the potential is increasing, where flowers open their petals and relive, where life is regenerative and wide awake.

The dark portion of the planet is radiative and exothermic, which means inactive, expansive and heat expelling.

The dark portion is that in which the potential is lowering, where flowers close their petals and become dormant, where life is devitalized and fast asleep.

Just so with all of the other planets.

The positive charge moves around them as they revolve, ever keeping as near as possible to their positive nucleus, the sun.

It is a well-known fact that high potential discharges into lower potential.

Consider the radiative rays of the sun as negative light units expelled by positive contraction, which forces them to seek lower pressures and lower potential.

Emanations are radio-active light units expelled with such great force directly through lowering, opposing pressures that they become luminous as meteorites become luminous from plunging directly through rising opposing pressures. Luminosity, heat and high potential gradually lessen as light units find their orbits in their proper potential positions and float spirally and centrifugally through lowering pressure zones. They eventually impact against the inertial plane where they become genero-active, positive, non-luminous light units following centripetal orbits to the nucleal center of the next lower potential.

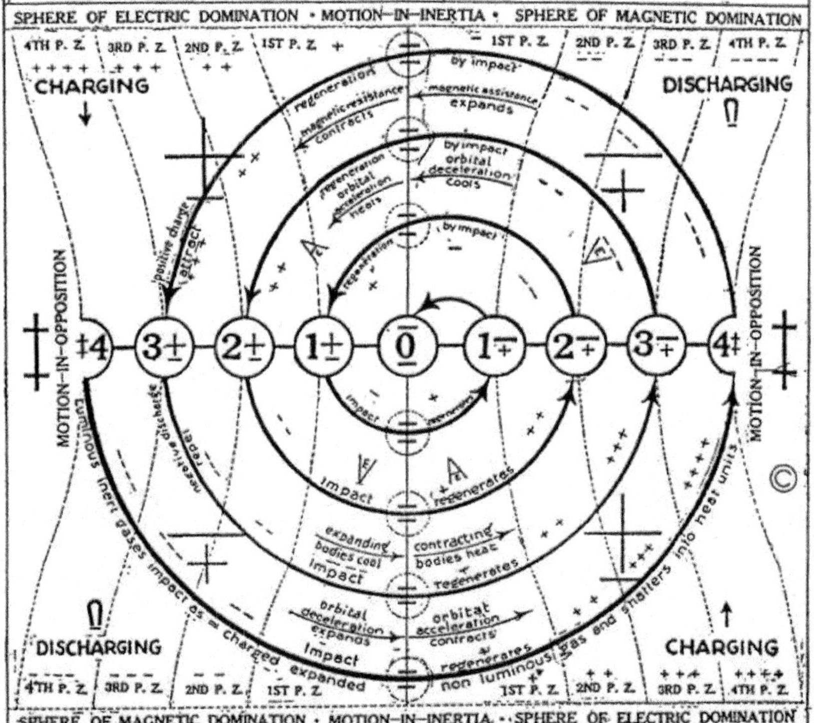

All energy is caused by a disturbance in inertia. The energy impact against inertia is the cause of motion. The energy constant of first cause is registered in waves of varying dimensions of the same constant. The ONE source of energy is non variable in its constant. Variability is an illusion of dimension. Energy expresses itself in pressure zones which increasingly resist the disturbance of inertial repose and violently assists a return to that state. Energy locks itself into varying potentials. High potential discharges into the next lower potential. The pressure zones cause an orderly, orbital lowering of potential to inertia where energy is regenerated. A sudden lowering of potential would cause an explosion, a flame or a luminous streak.

THE FORMULA OF THE LOCKED POTENTIALS AS APPLIED TO THE LAW OF EMANATION ORBITS

It might be argued that these negative rays are attracted by the positive charge of the daylight portion of the planet.

Consider the law of pressures as stated elsewhere which says that between any two masses is a line or plane of equalized pressures.

As the light units which constitute the rays circle spirally and centrifugally around the sun in their search for lower pressures exactly as this mass of light units which is our planet circles around the sun, they continue to expand and become increasingly negative the farther they recede from the sun. It must be interpolated right here that "light rays" do not proceed directly from the sun to a planet in straight lines. They follow the orbital lines of lowering pressures exactly as does this planet.

All direction is curved and every curve is a part of an orbit.

When the light units which we familiarly term "light rays," reach the inertial plane of equalized pressures between the mass of the sun and the mass of this planet, their expanded masses impact against it and continue beyond it in an ever-increasing state of solidity.

These expanded, negative particles which have reproduced themselves in transit then become positively charged as they impact with, and plunge gravitatively through the pressures which increasingly rise as they near the mass of this planet.

Eventually they impact against the planet as positive charge attracted toward greater positive charge. The potential of each is increased by this impact and the heat generated by magnetic resistence to the impact is absorbed as accumulated energy until it becomes devitalized and is released by the turn of the planet away from the light.

For another example, consider the familiar lightning flash which we know as "forked lightning." Lightning is a highly generative, positive charge seeking its own pressure and potential.

The maximum positively charged high potential and high pressure of this planet is that part which is nearest its center.

Lightning and all the forks of lightning are gravitative. They always seek the planet. Never do they proceed in the opposite direction toward negative discharge except in rare instances where a minor charge leaps upward toward a cloud of higher positive charge, or higher potential.

This latter effect is exactly analogous to that of an iron nail leaping upward toward a magnet. Lightning seeking its own potential and an apple falling to the ground are effects of exactly the same cause.

Gravitation is the cause of each.

Each is taking a "short cut across lots," through intervening pressures, to find its equal pressure.

Later it will be seen that the cause of rotation and revolution, together with all of their respective variations and periodicities, can only be solved through the understanding that positive charge attracts positive charge, and negative discharge repels both positive charge and negative discharge.

CHAPTER V

THE ELEMENTS OF MATTER

The elements of matter are but varying aggregations of corpuscular light units gathered together in systems familiarly known as atoms.

Atomic systems differ from solar and stellar systems solely in dimension.

In substance, structure and appearance they are exactly similar.

It has heretofore been stated that all effects of motion are repeative.

Mass is an effect of motion and mass is repeative, with no change whatsoever in its repetition save dimension.

A "bigger" atom such as a solar system is not different from an elemental atom of the same tone in any way but size.

Dimension is purely relative. The law for little mass is the same law as for big mass.

The elements are supposed to be many different substances, each of which is known by a different name.

Each element is supposed to be that one substance and only that.

An atom of mercury or sodium is supposed to be an atom of mercury or sodium which always has been and always will be that and nothing else.

The very foundation stone of modern physics states unequivocally, in its explanation of the principles of energy conservation:

"Not one particle of matter, however small, may be created or destroyed. All the king's horses and all the king's men cannot destroy a pin head." Matter constantly progresses through the cycle of disappearance and reappearance.

Every Pulsation of thinking Mind brings particles into appearance and relegates others into disappearance.

Matter is evolving and devolving as all other forms of life are evolving and devolving.

A sodium particle is not always a sodium particle. It changes its dimensions in an orderly and periodic manner until it has run the gamut of all the elements of every octave, and returned to its own octave.

A radium particle was once a light unit of hydrogen and will be so again.

More than this, an atom of any element actually contains within itself all .of the other elements.

An atom of gold is a gold atom in dimension only.

It is not even preponderantly of the substance of gold.

It is everything else in the universe.

Everything that is, is of everything else that is. Nothing is of itself alone.

Consider for a moment an atom of manganese or an atom of iron, both of which are very similar in structure.

Instead of thinking of it as an inconceivable little thing, for the purpose of comparison imagine it magnified until it is as big as this solar system.

One would not think of this vast solar system as an atom of any one of the elements, for one knows that all of the elements are contained within it.

Yet this solar system is either a manganese or an iron atom.

As nearly as the relator can determine without precise mathematical computation and while awaiting calculation of other dimensions it is one or the other of these elements.

Its plane and extension of ecliptic, its color as a tonal system, its tonal syllable in the octave scale, its endothermic relativity as a charging system, its tonal density, temperature and other dimensions, place it within a practical certainty as one of these two elements.

Later, when calculations have been made in accordance with the relater's formula, the relative age of this system, its exact tonal orbit, its potential position, plane, ecliptic expansion and extension will be exactly known.

This first volume will not, however, be encumbered with mathematics.

The basic principles of motion under which the One living Being functions in His thinking are simple, and simply must they be written down.

The day of the mathematician will come in the adaptation of those principles.

This solar system, being just one huge atom of iron or manganese, let us say, and to our knowledge containing all of the elements of the entire ten octave cycle in their proper proportions, can it not now be clearly seen that the concept of the elements as separate and distinct substances of exact homogeneity throughout their structures, is untenable in this universe of repeativeness in all of its effects of motion?

Cannot it then be seen that it is not the substance itself which determines its effect as an element but merely its position, and its dimensions, in its octave constant?

Cannot it also be clearly seen that the substance of the element for which it has been named is not even preponderant in its own element?

This solar system, which is true to plane as iron or manganese, is not preponderantly iron or manganese in its composition. It could not be. It contains vastly larger proportions of many of the other elements and yet some cosmic giant might gather up a handful of such systems as ours, which to him would be a solid, and analyze them in his laboratory as iron or manganese atoms.

Therefore let old concepts of many separate substances be discarded and replaced with the true concept of but the One universal substance of many apparent dimensions, known to man in the language of inner thinking, the language of light.

There is but One cosmic substance. This One substance appears to be divided into many substances, known as the elements of matter.

The One universal substance first divides itself into the appearance of two opposite states of motion which register as positive and negative elements.

Then two more opposite elements appear.

Then two more opposite elements of increasing potential and harder crystallization appear.

The cosmic pendulum then forms one element which registers itself as neither one opposite nor the other but is equally of each, a bisexual element of maximum opposition in all periodicities of motion.

These seven apparently different substances are but different states of motion of the One substance.

They are the seven tones of an octave, and there are ten octaves of seven tones each.

In the last four octaves are many mid-tones, each one registering its own state of motion. Man calls those various states of motion of the one substance by many names, and they appear to be many substances.

The apparent difference between the many is due solely to difference of motion and not to substance.

Many states of motion are possible, but there are not two substances in the universe.

All states of motion are measurable and are under the absolute control of Mind. As man is Mind, Man can, with dawning knowledge of causes, change any one state of motion into any other state of motion, and by so doing transmute any one substance into any other. The granite rock may become gold, or radium, at the will of man.

The "CREATED" universe of matter is the result of concentration of Mind upon the idea of form and then the generation of power by diverting low potential into centripetal vortices in order to hold the idea of Mind into the appearance of form until form disappears through mental decentration

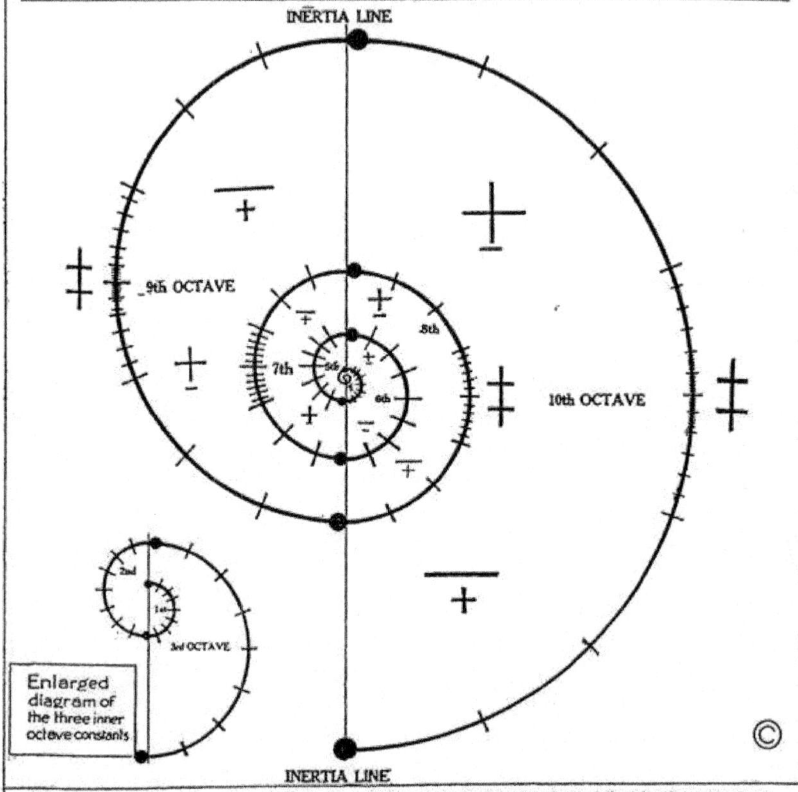

The universe of matter is a registration of the energy expended by Mind in the effort of thinking. The exact energy of the action of thinking is registered in the electro-positive charging systems, and the reaction of the action is registered in the electro-negative discharging systems. The charging systems are electrically dominated, centripetally closing, contracting systems. The discharging systems are magnetically dominated, centrifugally opening, expanding systems. The low potential speed-time dimension of energy of the highest octave is gradually accumulated into the high potential power-time dimension of the fifth octave. When these two opposing dimensions equalize in the tenth octave the cycle is completed and begins again.

DIAGRAM OF THE TEN OCTAVE CYCLE OF INTEGRATING AND DISINTEGRATING LIGHT UNITS INTO ATOMIC SYSTEMS CALLED THE "ELEMENTS OF MATTER"

CHART No. 2. STRUCTURE OF THE ATOM. ALL EFFECTS OF MOTION ARE REPEATIVE. SIZE IS PURELY RELATIVE. THE HEAVENS SWARM WITH REPLICAS OF THE ATOMS OF ALL THE ELEMENTS. WITH A KNOWLEDGE OF BASIC LAWS THEY MAY ALL BE MEASURED AND CLASSIFIED

CHAPTER VI

THE TEN OCTAVE CYCLE OF THE ELEMENTS OF MATTER

The ten-octave cycle begins and ends with an absolute equalization of all dimensions of motion.

Its beginning is its ending.

Creation is continuous.

There is no beginning and no ending.

The entire ten octave cycle is merely an orderly and periodic interchange of dimensions.

At the beginning of the cycle, time dimension which is then preponderant, transfers its state of motion into power dimension, which in its turn becomes preponderant, until it is overtaken by time dimension.

High power is accumulated time.

The elements of matter are the accumulation of the speed dimension of the universal constant of energy into power dimension.

The effort of electricity to accumulate power at the expense of time is continuous but spasmodic throughout each tone in the ten-octave cycle.

There are ten successive efforts, hence the ten octaves.

Each octave is a separate and complete sequence of inhalation and exhalation, and the entire ten octave cycle is one inconceivably extended inhalation followed by a similar exhalation.

Each octave is a separate effort for supremacy made by the two opposing forces.

During the first five octaves the power dimension of the universal constant gradually conquers one time dimension, by a decrease of radio-active emanations in proportion to the increase of endothermic, genero-active power of-charging by absorption, or accumulation of potential.

Carbon, in the fifth octave, 504 , is the endothermic dividing line of the cycle.

It is the point where the cosmic billion-year inhalation of the cycle gives place to an equally majestic exhalation of another eternity in duration.

Carbon is the point of maximum orbital velocity which creates the illusion of hardness. It is the point of maximum integration, highest melting point, most perfect in cubical crystallization, most compact in crystallization and most truly bi-sexual of all the elements.

From carbon to the end of the cycle there is a gradual conquest of power by the other time dimension and an increase in radio-active emanations in proportion to the increase of the exothermic power of discharging accumulated potential.

The law of the expression of energy in motion for the entire ten octave cycle is the same as the law for one octave, or for one tone, or for even one inhalative-exhalative pulsation.

Each octave is an endothermic, heat absorbing, contractive, generative series of electric actions, followed by an exothermic heat emanating, expansive, radio-active series of magnetic reactions. Each of these series of actions and reactions is of the others.

More than this, each is of the others, both simultaneously and alternately.

The first five octaves are therefore male, or electro-positive, in preponderance and the second five octaves are female, or electro-negative, in preponderance.

The law of repeativeness in all effects of motion is illustrated by the comparison of the cycle of the elements to the life and growth of man.

The first five octaves may be likened unto the birth, childhood, youth and growing strength of that evolving idea of Mind called man.

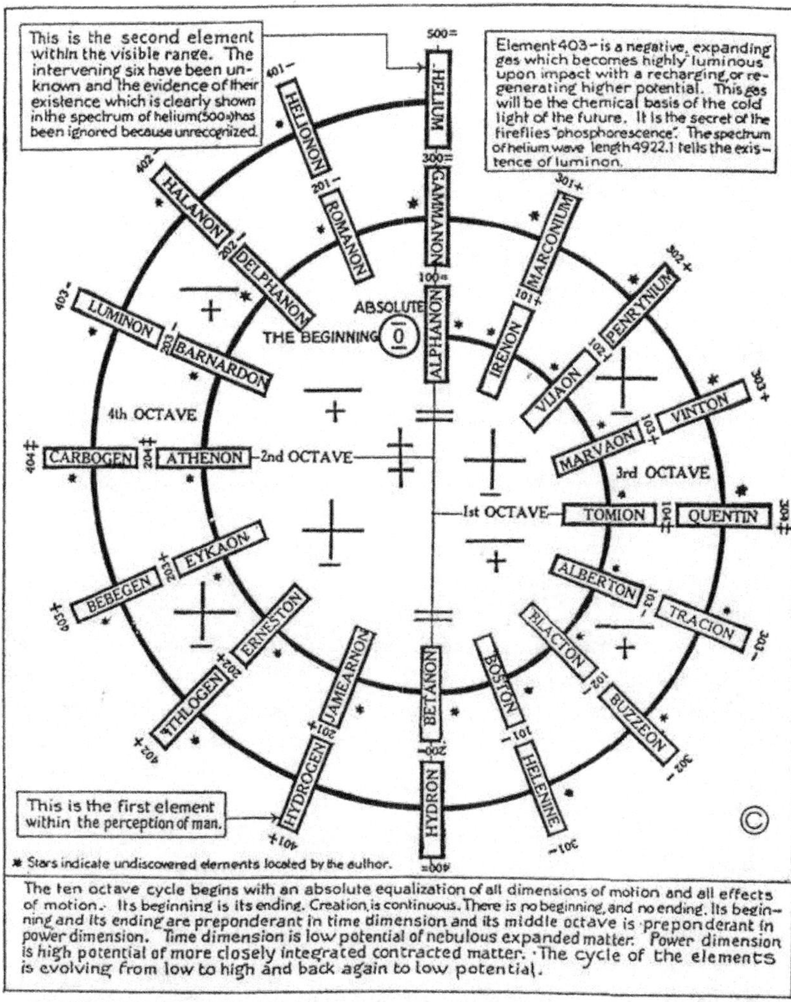

FIRST FOUR OCTAVES OF THE TEN OCTAVE CYCLE OF CREATION. THE ENTIRE TEN OCTAVE CYCLE IS SIMPLY AN ORDERLY, PERIODIC ACCUMULATION OF THE CONSTANT OF ENERGY INTO HIGHER POWER POTENTIALS AT THE EXPENSE OF SPEED

The last five octaves are the decline into apparent dissolution of the idea of man into that state called "death," at which point the state called "life" once more begins.

Every idea of Mind evolves and devolves by the same formula as that of the locked potentials of the ten octaves of integrating and disintegrating matter.

This is the law of growth.

This is the orderly periodicity of those phenomena of nature which are called "life" and "death," and are spoken of as though they were two separate things, instead of one unit composed of a plus action and a minus reaction of an orderly and inevitable periodicity.

"Life" is merely an expression of the generative power of centripetal force, to which "death" is but the degenerative reaction.

The beginning of the cycle of motion is maximum in one-time dimension, which means speed, and minimum in its power dimension, which means potential of energy.

"Speed" means the quickness with which a state of motion can reproduce itself and, by so doing, communicate that state of motion to the entire universe.

Potential of energy means that state of motion of the universal constant of energy in which time dimension has been accumulated, by deceleration of speed, into power.

Potential of energy might be likened unto a compressed spring which, when released, leaps to its inert state.

All of the elements of matter are potentials of energy held in their respective locked positions by the varying dimensions of their respective positions in their octaves.

In order to picture the gradual and orderly transfer of time dimension to power and visibility, and its return to time dimension and invisibility, consider the simple analogy of the easily imagined constant of energy of the little mountain brook which flows steadily and swiftly down the mountain side.

Imagine the little stream of low potential falling swiftly over the cliff side into a reservoir where it is accumulating high potential by storing time.

The little stream is the only source of supply and is presumably constant.

The variation of its ability to perform more or less work is in accord with the amount of time dimension which has been transformed into power by the storage of time.

Forests may be laid low and towns wiped out by the collapse of a mighty reservoir, while far up on the mountain side children play without concern in the stream which filled that reservoir.

And so it is with the universal constant of energy supplied by thinking Mind.

Thinking is the only source of energy; yet the mighty power which is accumulated by thinking the idea of this universe, and registering that idea in repeative systems varying in size from those so small that a trillion could circulate in a needle point to those so large that man cannot conceive the expanse of one of them, comes from that One source and that only.

Following is a list of the potential locking points of the entire ten octave cycle, and the names of the apparently different elements, or substances formed by the variation in the dimensions of those locking points.

TABLE OF THE TEN OCTAVES OF THE VARYING STATES OF MOTION WHICH CREATE THE ILLUSION OF DIFFERENT SUBSTANCES KNOWN AS "THE ELEMENTS OF MATTER."

FIRST OCTAVE WAVE

Beginning of the Cyclic Inhalation at Tomion.

	POSITION	NAME	NUMBER	SYMBOL	ATOMIC MASS	MELTING POINT °C.
ENDOTHERMAL INHALATION +	0=	*Alphanon*	100=	An.		
	1+	Irenon	101+	Io		
	2+	Vijaon	102+	Vj		
	3+	Marvaon	103+	Mv		
‡	4‡	TOMION	104‡	Tn		
EXOTHERMAL EXHALATION	3−	Alberton	103−	At.		
	2−	Blackton	102−	Bn.		
−	1−	Boston	101−	Bt.		

SECOND OCTAVE WAVE

	POSITION	NAME	NUMBER	SYMBOL	ATOMIC MASS	MELTING POINT °C.
ENDOTHERMAL INHALATION +	0=	*Betanon*	200=	Bo.		
	1+	Jamearnon	201+	Jn.		
	2+	Erneston	202+	En.		
	3+	Eykaon	203+	Ek.		
‡	4‡	ATHENON	204‡	Ae.		
EXOTHERMAL EXHALATION	3−	Barnardon	203−	Bd.		
	2−	Delphanon	202−	Dn.		
−	1−	Romanon	201−	Rn.		

THIRD OCTAVE WAVE

	POSITION	NAME	NUMBER	SYMBOL	ATOMIC MASS	MELTING POINT °C.
ENDOTHERMAL INHALATION +	0=	*Gammanon*	300=	Gn.		
	1+	Marconium	301+	Mc		
	2+	Penrynium	302+	Pn		
	3+	Vinton	303+	Vn		
‡	4‡	QUENTIN	304‡	Qn		
EXOTHERMAL EXHALATION	3−	Tracion	303−	Tc		
	2−	Buzzeon	302−	Bz		
−	1−	Helenon	301−	Hl		

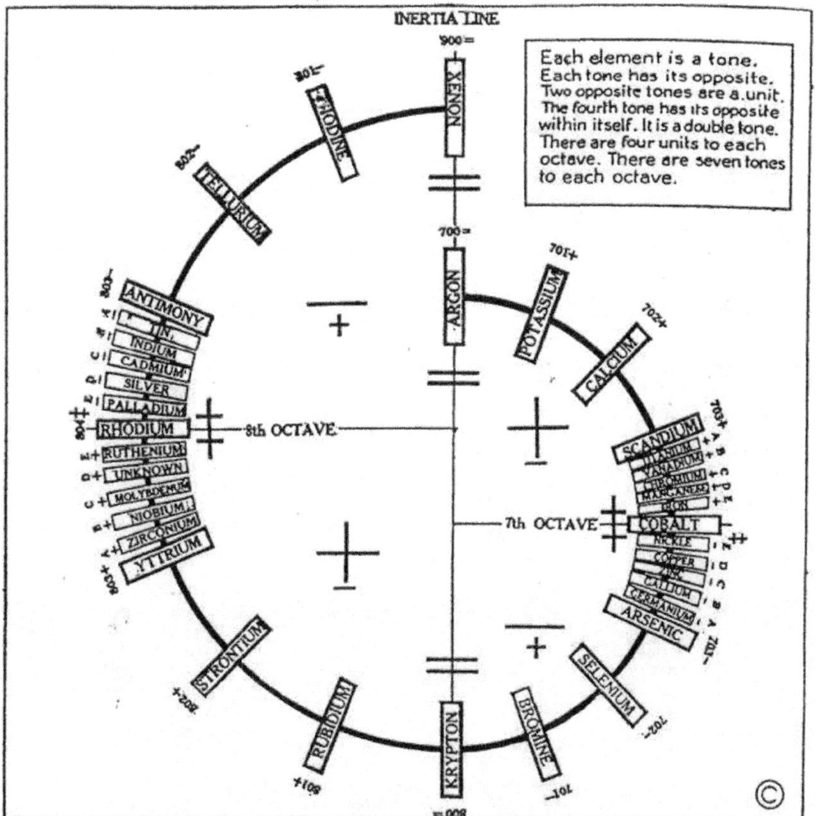

In these octaves the accumulation of energy into higher potentials causes such intense centrifugal and-centripetal opposition, as it reaches its maximum crest of each octave wave, that additional smaller vortices are formed which prevent the ratio of unit increase from being totaled into the fourth tones of these octaves, as they are in carbon and silicon of the lower octaves. The result is that ten mid-tones form in each of these two octaves, all of which are metals on the + side and metaloids on the — side of 4‡. These mid-tones are irregular in all of their dimensions but their totals added together make the constant of the double tone to which they owe their existence and from which they subtract their separate, disorderly dimensions. Neither cobalt nor rhodium can attain their proper hardness, nor true cube form of crystallization, nor melting point, nor plane, nor valence, nor any other dimensions because of these intruders.

SEVENTH AND EIGHTH OCTAVE CONSTANTS, SHOWING THE INTRUDING MID-TONES DEVELOPED BY INTENSE OPPOSITION, WHERE MAGNETIC RESISTANCE TO INTEGRATION IS AT ITS MAXIMUM

FOURTH OCTAVE WAVE

	POSITION	NAME	NUMBER	SYMBOL	ATOMIC MASS	MELTING POINT °C.
ENDOTHERMAL INHALATION	0=	*Hydron*	400=	Hy		
	1+	Hydrogen	401+	H	1.008	−259
	2+	Ethlogen	402+	Eg		
	3+	Bebegen	403+	Bb		
	4‡	CARBOGEN	404‡	Cb		
EXOTHERMAL EXHALATION	3−	Luminon	403−	Ln	*2.92	
	2−	Halanon	402−	Ha		
	1−	Helionon	401−	Hi		

*Approximate

FIFTH OCTAVE WAVE

Completing the Cyclic Inhalation at Carbon.

	POSITION	NAME	NUMBER	SYMBOL	ATOMIC MASS	MELTING POINT °C.
ENDOTHERMAL INHALATION	0=	*Helium*	500=	He.	4.0	−271
	1+	Lithium	501+	Li	7.03	186
	2+	Beryllium	502+	Be	9.1	1280
	3+	Boron	503+	B	11.0	2350
	4‡	CARBON	504‡	C	12.0	3600
EXOTHERMAL EXHALATION	3−	Nitrogen	503−	N	14.04	−210
	2−	Oxygen	502−	O	16.00	−218
	1−	Fluorine	501−	F	19.0	−223

Observe the regularity of melting points rising with inhalation and falling with exhalation.

SIXTH OCTAVE WAVE

	POSITION	NAME	NUMBER	SYMBOL	ATOMIC MASS	MELTING POINT °C.
ENDOTHERMAL EXHALATION	0=	*Neon*	600=	Ne	19.9	−253
	1+	Sodium	601+	Na	23.05	98
	2+	Magnesium	602+	Mg	24.1	651
	3+	Aluminum	603+	Al	27.0	659
	4‡	SILICON	604‡	Si	28.4	1420
EXOTHERMAL EXHALATION	3−	Phosphorus	603−	P	31.4	725
	2−	Sulphur	602−	S	32.06	119
	1−	Chlorine	601−	Cl	35.45	−102

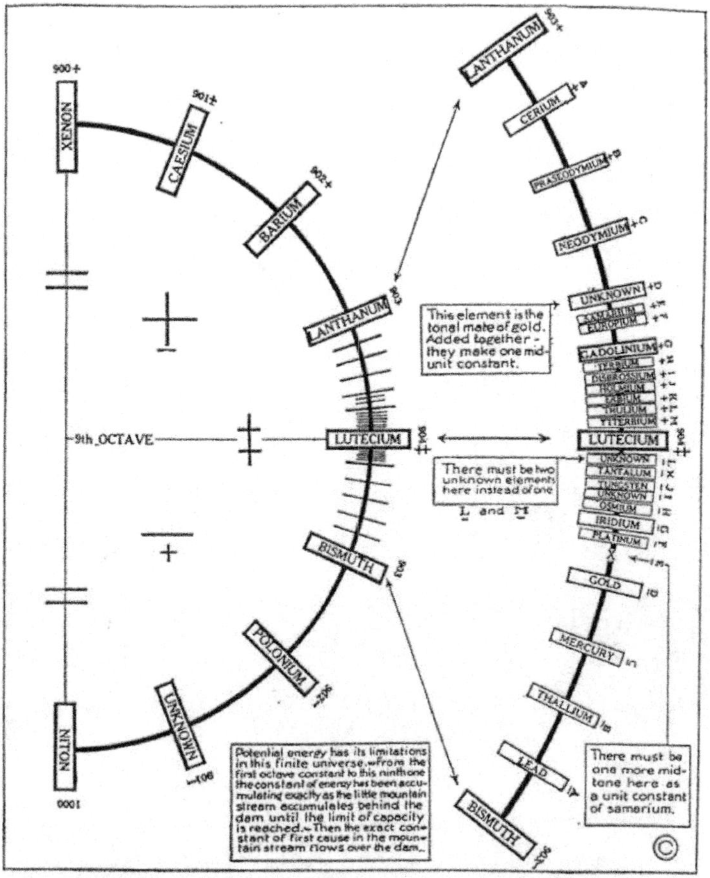

NINTH OCTAVE CONSTANT SHOWING MORE INTRUDING MID-TONES. MAGNETIC TIME DIMENSION IS NOW OVERTAKING ELECTRIC HIGH POWER DIMENSION. OPPOSING FORCES ARE APPROACHING EQUALIZATION

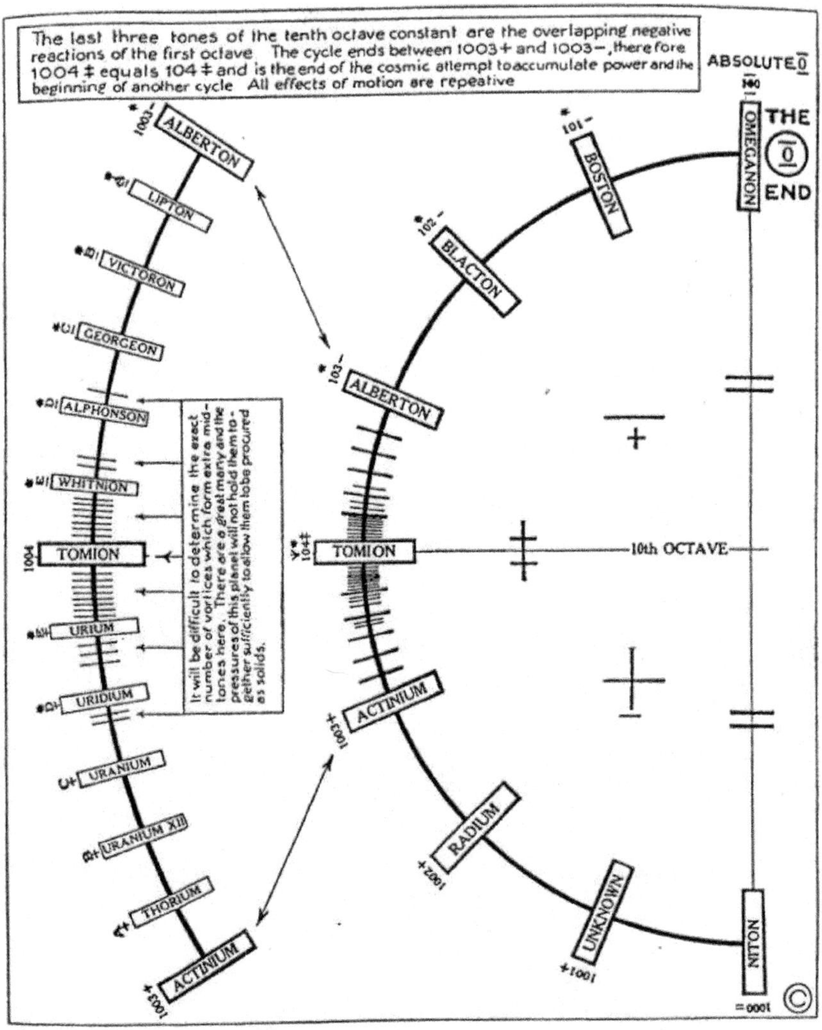

TENTH OCTAVE CONSTANT WHERE TIME DIMENSION OVERTAKES POWER DIMENSION IN PRESSURES WHICH EJECT BETA EMANATIONS AT 186,400 MILES PER SECOND. THIS ENDS THE CYCLE.

SEVENTH OCTAVE

With Ten Mid-Tones

	POSITION	NAME	NUMBER	SYMBOL	ATOMIC MASS	MELTING POINT °C.
+	0=	*Argon*	700=	Ar	39.09	−188
	1+	Potassium	701+	K	39.10	62.3
ENDOTHERMAL INHALATION	2+	Calcium	702+	Ca	40.1	810
	3+	Scandium	703+	Sc	44.1	
	3A+	Titanium	703A+	Ti	48.1	1800
	3B +	Vanadium	703B +	V	51.4	1720
	3C +	Chromium	703C+	Cr	52.0	1615
	3D +	Manganese	703D+	Mn	55.0	1230
	3E +	Iron	703E +	Fe	55.9	1530
	4‡	COBALT	704‡	Co	58.97	1480
	4E −	Nickel	703E −	Ni	59	1452
	4D −	Copper	703D−	Cu	63.57	1083
EXOTHERMAL EXHALATION	4C −	Zinc	703C−	Zn	65.37	419
	4B −	Gallium	703B −	Ga	70.1	30
	4A−	Germanium	703A−	Ge	72.5	958
	3−	Arsenic	703−	As	74.96	850
	2−	Selenium	702−	Se	79.2	217
−	1−	Bromine	701−	Br	79.92	−7.3

Observe irregularity of mid-tonal melting points.

EIGHTH OCTAVE

With Ten Mid-Tones

	POSITION	NAME	NUMBER	SYMBOL	ATOMIC MASS	MELTING POINT °C.
+	0=	*Krypton*	800=	Kr.	82.92	—169
	1+	Rubidium	801+	Rb.	85.45	38
ENDOTHERMAL INHALATION	2+	Strontium	802+	Sr.	87.65	830
	3+	Yttrium	803+	Yt.	89.33	1490
	3A+	Zirconium	803A+	Zr.	90.6	1700
	3B +	Niobium	803B +	Nb	94.0	
	3C +	Molybdenum	803C +	Mo	96.0	2550
	3D +	Mate to 3D−	803D +			
	3E +	Ruthenium	803E +	Ru	101.7	2450
	4‡	RHODIUM	804‡	Rh	103.0	1950
	3E −	Palladium	803E −	Pd	106.5	1549
	3D−	Silver	803D−	Ag	107.88	961
EXOTHERMAL EXHALATION	3C−	Cadmium	803C−	Cd	112.40	321
	3B −	Indium	803B −	In	114.8	155
	3A−	Tin	803A −	Sn	118.7	232
	3−	Antimony	803−	Sb	120.2	630
	2−	Tellurium	802−	Te	*127.5	446
−	1−	Iodine	801−	I	*126.92	114

* Note.—The calculation of the atomic weight of iodine, or tellurium, or of both, appears to be incorrect. The mass of iodine must exceed that of tellurium.

NINTH OCTAVE

With Twenty-six Mid-Tones

	POSITION	NAME	NUMBER	SYMBOL	ATOMIC MASS	MELTING POINT °C.
+	0=	*Xenon*	900=	Xe	130.2	—140
	1+	Caesium	901+	Cs	132.81	26
	2+	Barium	902+	Ba	137.37	850
	3+	Lanthanum	903+	La	139	810
	3A +	Cerium	903A +	Ce	140.25	640
	3B +	Praseodymium	903B +	Pr	140.9	940
ENDOTHERMAL INHALATION	3C +	Neodymium	903C +	Nd	144.3	840
	3D +	Mate to 3D−	903D +			
	3E +	Samarium	903E +	Sa.	150.4	1350
	3F +	Europium	903F +	Eu	152.0	
	3G +	Gadolinium	903G +	Gd	157.3	
	3H +	Terbium	903H +	Tb	159.2	
	3I +	Disbrossium	903 I +	Dy	162.5	
	3J +	Holmium	903 J +	Ho	163.5	
	3K +	Erbium	903K +	Er	167.7	
	3L +	Thulium	903L +	Tm	168.5	
	3M+	Ytterbium	903M+	Yb	173.5	
	4‡	LUTECIUM	904‡	Lu	175.0	
	3M−	Mate to 3M+	903M−			
	3L −	Mate to 3L+	903L −	Ta	181.5	2900
	3K −	Tantalum	903K −	W	184.0	3400
	3J −	Tungsten	903J −			
	3I −	Mate to 3I+	903 I −	Os	190.9	2700
	3H −	Osmium	903H −	Ir	193.1	2250
EXOTHERMAL EXHALATION	3G −	Iridium	903G −	Pt	195.2	1755
	3F −	Platinum	903F −	Au	197.2	1063
	3E −	Mate to 3E+	903E −	Hg	200.6	—39
	3D −	Gold	903D −	Tl	204.0	302
	3C −	Mercury	903C −	Pb	207.2	327
	3B −	Thallium	903B −			
	3A −	Lead	903A −			
	3−	Bismuth	903−	Bi	208.0	271
	2−	Polonium	902−	Po		
−	1−	Mate to 1+	901−			

Note. Mid-tones begin in the seventh octave. In the ninth octave the struggle to hold advancing positions forces the construction of new pressure walls in many split tonal positions. In the tenth octave there is such a multitude of split tonal pressure walls that only the conspicuous ones are herein tabulated.

TENTH OCTAVE

With Innumerable Mid-tones

Ending of the Cyclic Exhalation at Tomium and Beginning of the Inhalation.

	POSITION	NAME	NUMBER	SYMBOL	ATOMIC MASS	MELTING POINT °C.
+	0=	*Niton*	1000=	Nt	222.4	
ENDOTHERMAL INHALATION	1+	Mate to 1−	1001+			
	2+	Radium	1002+	Ra	226.0	700
	3+	Actinium	1003+	Ac		
	3A+	Thorium	1003A+	Th	232.15	1700
	3B +	Uranium XII	1003B +	UrXII		
	3C +	Uranium	1003C +	Ur	238.2	1850
	3D +	Uridium	1003D +	Um		
	3E +	Urium	1003E +	Uu		
	4‡	TOMIUM	104‡	Tn		
EXOTHERMAL EXHALATION	3E −	Whitnion	103E −	Wn		
	3D−	Alphonson	103D−	Ap		
	3C−	Georgeon	103C−	Gg		
	3B −	Victoron	103B −	V		
	3A−	Lipton	103A−	Ln		
	+3−	Alberton	+103−	At		
	+2−	Blackton	+102−	Bn		
	+1−	Boston	+101−	Bt		
−	0=	Omeganon the end, which is Alphanon, the beginning.	100=			

101 - 102 - and "103 — are tonal mates of 1001+ 1002 + and 1003 +, also they are tonal mates of 101+ 102 + and 103 +.

Of these elements two in the fourth octave, when discovered, will be of great use to man. Each of them will mark an epoch in human progress.

Hydron (400=) the master-tone of its octave, is a non-inflammable inert gas which is in every way superior for transportation to hydrogen because it is much lighter, absolutely non-injurious and easier to produce.

It has all of the safety qualities of helium and its carrying capacity exceeds that of helium by eight times and is double that of hydrogen.

Both hydron and helium can be produced by transmutation in unlimited quantities at an expense which is negligible while helium, of a sufficient quantity to fill a dirigible, produced by the present methods now costs three-quarters of a million dollars.

The control of the production of this gas by any nation would insure the peace of the world. Luminon (403 —), is the basis of the cold light of the future.

Luminosity of better color can be produced by regenerative excitation of this radiative gas at about one forty-thousandth of the expenditure of energy necessary to produce the same degree of luminosity by the use of a tungsten filament.

Luminon can also be produced by transmutation at a negligible expenditure.

Luminon is plentiful in many, substances but its separation would involve more labor and expense than would its production by transmutation, which means simply the changing of dimension of a basic supply which is plentiful in those high octaves familiarly termed "the air."

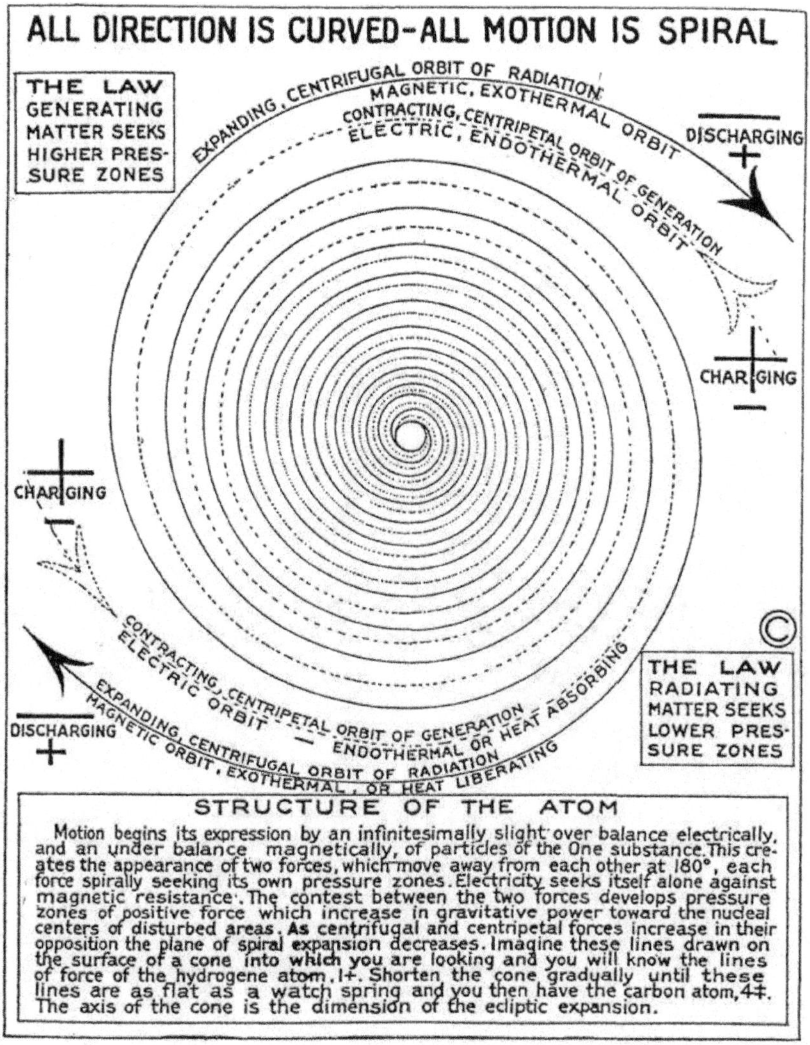

CHART No. 1. EVOLUTION OF FORCE INTO SEVEN TONES, FOUR UNITS AND ONE UNIVERSAL CONSTANT WHICH CHANGES ITS DIMENSION IN ALL EFFECTS OF MOTION, BUT NEVER CHANGES ITS ENERGY CONSTANT

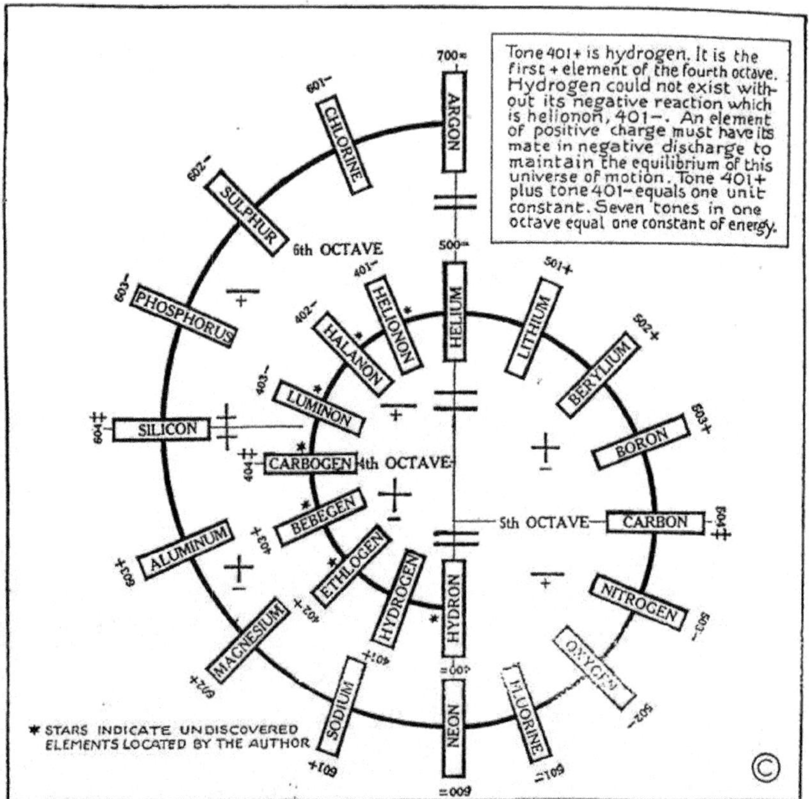

The entire ten octave constant cycle is simply an orderly periodic accumulation of the constant of energy into higher power dimension which reaches its maximum at the fifth octave, and a distribution of that accumulation through the succeeding five octaves. Higher power is accumulated time. The deceleration of speed in rotation of mass is the result of generation. Power is generated by resistance to speed of rotation and acceleration of speed of revolution. Power is thus accumulated from low potential of great axial speed to high potential of great orbital speed. Each element is greater in its mass than its predecessor because of the generative power of electricity which acts as a brake against high axial speed and diverts it into accumulating mass. The elements of matter are an orderly and periodic accumulation and redistribution of energy.

FOURTH, FIFTH AND SIXTH OCTAVES. IN THE FOURTH OCTAVE THE SO-CALLED PHYSICAL UNIVERSE BEGINS WITH BUT ONE OF ITS ELEMENTS KNOWN TO MAN. THE ELEMENT HYDROGEN

CHAPTER VII

INSTABILITY, AND THE ILLUSION OF STABILITY IN MOTION.

The chemist can solve his problems only through knowledge of the various dimensions of the elements with which he has to deal, their relative instability, and their relative illusion of stability.

To write in sufficient detail the various relations of motion, and to organize them as a higher electrochemistry, will require a volume in itself which will follow this one at a later date.

Suffice it for this volume, that the accompanying working chart of the chemist's six octaves be herein given, together with four charts demonstrating the orderliness of stability and instability in motion.

The universe of motion is a swinging of the cosmic pendulum from the stability of concept in inertia to the instability of the image of concept in motion, and back again to the stability of memory of concept in inertia.

Concept precedes motion. Motion begins in concept.

Concept takes place in inertial equilibrium.

Motion is born of opposition to equilibrium.

The universal balance cannot be upset. No state other than an equilibrium is possible.

The concept of an action designed to upset the universal balance by overcoming inertia is, when executed as an action, simultaneously opposed by a reaction designed to restore that balance.

The result of action and reaction is to create the illusion of stability through a division of the force of action and reaction into apparent opposites.

An opposed state is an unstable state which simulates stability through motion in equal and opposite actions and reactions.

Therefore, stability cannot lie in motion, for all motion is opposed and divided in its opposition.

Stability is the inactivity of the state of equilibrium.

The dimensionless universe of concept is the universe of stability.

The universe of expression of concept, through motion, is the universe of dimension.

The universe of dimension is the universe of the illusion of stability.

The elements of matter with which the chemist has to deal are opposed states of motion which become increasingly unstable as they depart from the inert gases, reaching maximum instability at the carbon line.

The illusion of stability is least in the lower tones and reaches its maximum at the carbon line.

The lower the potential, electric pressure, valency, temperature and density, the greater the stability of the elements, and the less the illusion of stability.

Conversely, the higher the potential, magnetic pressure, valency, temperature and density, the less the stability and the greater the illusion of stability.

Every chemical effect is an electro-magnetic effect.

Every electro-magnetic effect is a mechanical effect.

This universe of motion is a machine in which every mass in motion is a wheel geared into another wheel.

Celestial mechanics vary not one bit from the mechanics of man.

If one wheel changes its dimensions, all wheels change to conform to that change.

The precessional movements of planets and solar systems are made with wheels of bevel gears with cones rolling upon cones and shafts eccentrically placed.

The great wheels of solar systems change their bevels and their eccentricities to conform to their positions in the machine of which they are a part.

There is but one position in the universal machine in which the wheels run parallel in plane without intersection, without precession and without eccentricity.

In this position in the atom, or its repetition in larger masses, there are no equinoxes, no ascending or descending nodes and no aphelions or perihelions.

This is in the element carbon, where inhalation ends and exhalation begins, where instability and the illusion of stability are at their maximum.

There are cone and disc clutches in the universal machine which grasp and slip with the same relative persistance and looseness with which man is perfectly familiar in his mechanics.

These qualities give us relatively rigid bodies, such as this dense planet, the more-dense sun, pithy Saturn and vaporous Neptune.

These qualities give us the same relative rigidities in the eleinents, such as carbon in the diamond, and less dense substances down through the solid metals and metaloids to their gaseous expansions in such elements as hydrogen and its mate helionon.

The contours of the cone clutches which give great surface tension pressure contract toward the poles, disappearing in the axes and gravitative centers of all masses.

The disc clutches which slip are the contours of expanding cones. These lose their ability to hold as the cones expand into disappearance at the equatorial planes of all masses.

Stability in motion is, therefore, greatest at the centers of all masses and, superficially, at their poles.

On the contrary, instability in motion is greatest at the equators of all masses.

As a consequence, rigidity in all mass is greatest at its poles where the cone clutches hold, and flexibility is greatest at its equators where the disc clutches slip.

The cone clutches at the poles of the sun of our solar system, for example, hold fast. That is why the expanded magnetic bases of the equatorial belt of the sun moves faster than the contracted polar magnetic bases.

That is also why the equatorial belt of the sun is hotter than the polar zones.

The slipping of the oppositely moving discs generates much heat.

That explains the boiling bubbles which we call "sun spots" which move nearer to the equator of the sun and farther away again in oppositely whirling spiral pools during each eleven year breathing period of the sun.

That is why the corona of the sun extends so far into interstellar space at its equator and so much less so at its poles.

That is how, and one reason why, another planet will soon be born to the already pregnant sun.

That is why Jupiter has its belts and Saturn the rings which Jupiter will also have when his axis tilts a little farther to change the bevel gearing of his wheels.

That is why Uranus and Neptune are reversing their poles.

That is why nature added the gyroscopic principle to her mechanics of motion in order to create the illusion of stability in her corpuscular solids of motion.

That explains the isoclinal lines which run around this planet, forming new bases for the expanding cones of radiation, like the rim of an umbrella which gradually opens until it is in one plane.

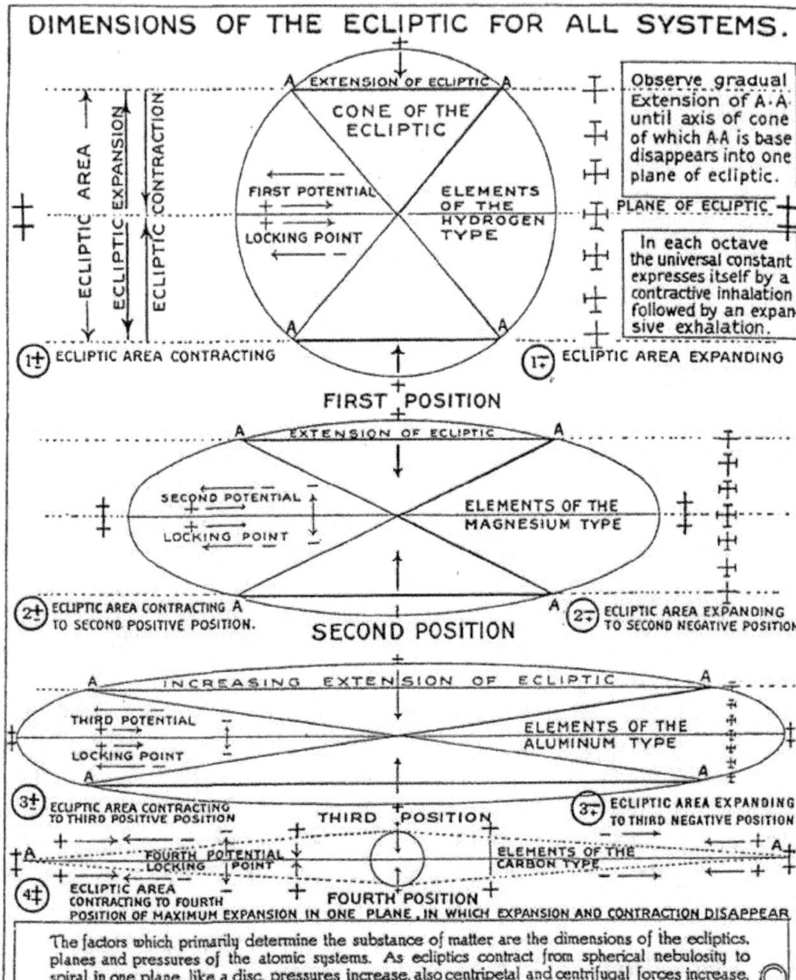

CHART NO. 3, STRUCTURE OF THE ATOM. DIAGRAM OF THE FOUR POSITIONS IN WHICH THE UNIVERSAL CONSTANT DISTRIBUTES ITS ENERGY INTO FOUR UNIT CONSTANTS OF SEVEN TONES, EACH ONE APPEARING TO BE A SEPARATE SUBSTANCE DUE SOLELY TO CHANGING DIMENSIONS.

That is why all masses emanate magnetic lines of force at isoclinal lines and regenerate them by absorption at the poles ·.

That is why the compass needle loses its dip on the zero isoclinal line which roughly follows the geographic equator, and swings its north pole to the south magnetic pole south of that line and to the north magnetic pole when proceeding north from it.

Motion is an appearance born of the axis of a conceptive cone in inertia. It assumes the appearance of an expanding cone and disappears through radiation in equatorial opposition. The universal machine is a gyroscopic top.

When it is in little motion, its form is a cone, like a top gyrating unsteadily on an eccentric axis.

When it is in great motion, it loses the altitude and eccentricity of its axis and becomes a gyroscope revolving steadily in one plane.

The generative attractive principle is the principle of contracting cones.

All mass is generated and regenerated by a contractive pressure exerted in the direction of its gravitative center. Its minimum of generative pressure is exerted from its equatorial plane and its maximum pressure from its pole.

The radiative repellent principle is the principle of expanding cones.

All mass is radiated and diffused by an expansive pressure exerted in the direction of its surface. Its minimum of radiative pressure is exerted from its pole and its maximum from its equatorial plane.

By arranging the elements in the orderly positions of their relative stability and instability, as in the accompanying chart, the chemist can work out his problems much more simply upon paper than by experimenting in the laboratory without the knowledge of this orderliness.

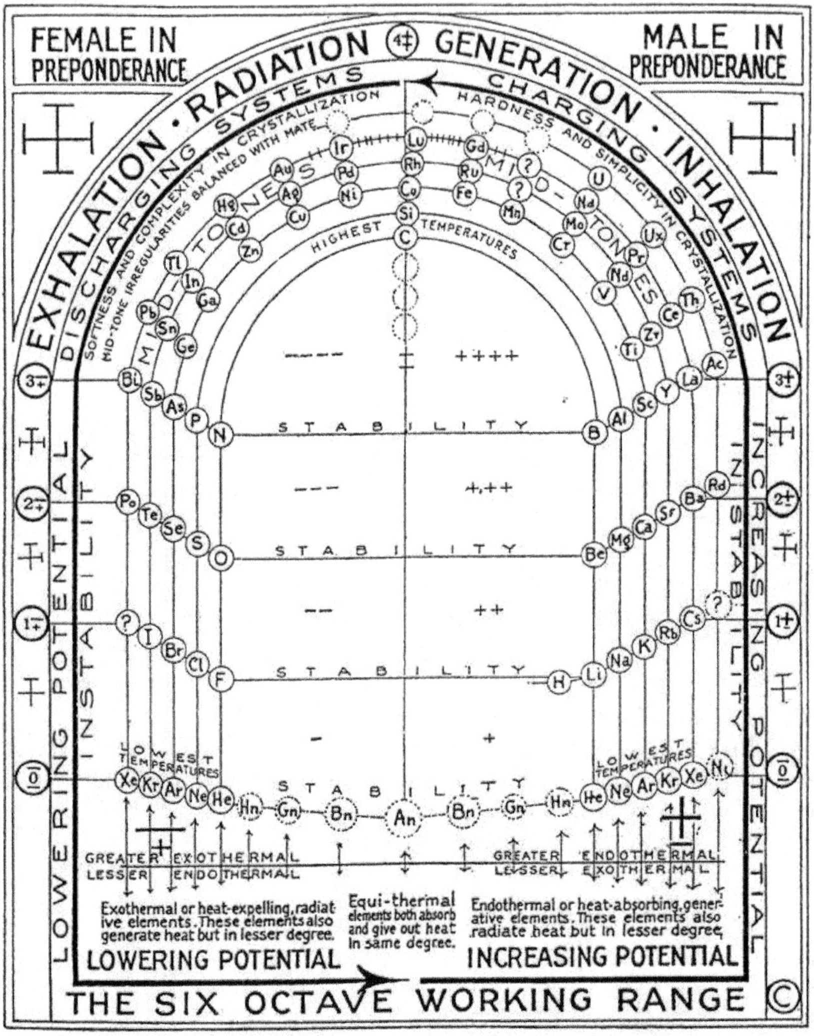

ELECTRO-CHEMICAL WORKING CHART BY MEANS OF WHICH THE CHEMIST MAY PRE-DETERMINE EFFECTS OF CHEMICAL COMBINATION WITH CERTAINTY WITHIN THE LIMITATIONS OF THE SIMPLE DIMENSIONS.—OTHER CHARTS WILL COVER THE COMPLEX DIMENSIONS

CHAPTER VIII

THE UNIVERSAL PULSE

ALL MOTION IS OSCILLATORY

The One Living Being, of which all nature is a part, breathes the breath of life.

Every form in nature is but a unit of the whole and sustains its appearance of existence through the life sustaining breathing of the whole.

All mass is life.

All mass breathes, assimilates and eliminates the life-giving property of that breathing.

The breathing of the universal One is electromagnetic.

All life varies in potential, and therefore all life varies relatively in the electromagnetic voltage eamperage of its inhalation-exhalation pressures.

The breathings of the ant are not of the same dimensions as the breathings of the elephant.

They vary vastly, one from the other, in time, in pressures, in potential, in temperature and all other dimensions.

The breathing of the sodium atom varies vastly from that of the carbon atom.

They differ from each other in their accumulation of potential as do the ant and the elephant.

So also does the breathing of Neptune vary from that of Jupiter or Venus or the sun in all of its periodicities.

The universal phenomena of inhalation-exhalation is a fundamental life principle.

The inhalative action is the cause of electricity.

It is the generative principle of life, the accumulative principle, the principle of growth, the endothermic principle.

It is the gravitative principle of attraction.

It is the principle of evolution.

It is the male principle, the positive principle, the creative principle, the assembling principle of the appearance of form.

It is the winding of the cosmic clock.

It is that which is known as positive electricity, which means that it is preponderantly and dominantly electric.

The exhalative reaction is the cause of magnetism.

It is the radiative principle of life which man erringly names "death."

It is the dissipative, dissolutive, repellative principle; the decreative, the disassembling principle of disappearance of form.

It is the principle of devolution.

It is the female principle, the negative principle.

It is the running down of the cosmic clock.

It is that which is known as negative electricity, which means that electricity is magnetically dominated.

EXPLANATORY CHART NO. 1

INDICATING TONAL MATES OF MAXIMUM STABILITY

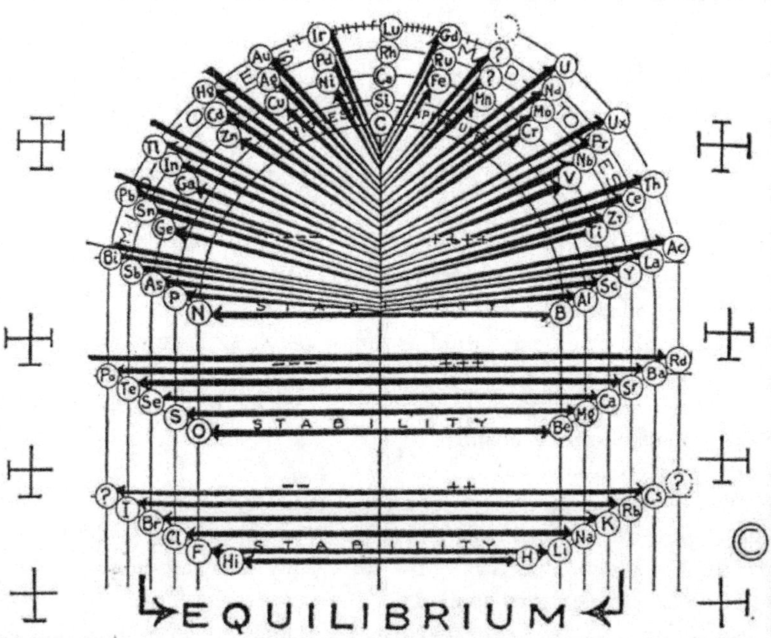

STABILITY OR INSTABILITY is the relative willingness of elements in union as compounds to come into association with each other, and their relative power of holding themselves together in combination when so joined. Every combination shown in this diagram represents maximum stability. Each unit is the tonal mate of the other. Together they represent one action and reaction of the universal constant. They combine into equal quantities. Each is the exact opposite of the other and in combination they neutralize their opposition in unity.

Note.—The true tonal mate of hydrogen is not fluorine; it is helionon, an undiscovered tone in the fourth octave.

EXAMPLES OF STABILITY IN UNION ALL OF THESE PAIRS ARE IN THE SAME PRESSURE ZONES AND SAME ORBITS THE LESS ACTIVE SOLIDS MAY ENJOY SEPARATE EXISTENCE, BUT AS THEY INCREASE IN ACTIVITY IT BECOMES INCREASINGLY DIFFICULT FOR THEM TO EXIST SEPARATELY IN FREE STATE

It means less electricity and more magnetism, as positive electricity means more electricity and less magnetism.

This is a universe of more and less in all of its phenomena of motion.

The electricity of accumulative inbreathing is the "more" and the magnetism of separative outbreathing is the "less."

The gathering together of the "more" of solidity is the attractive principle of which positive charge is the cause.

The dissipation into the "less" of tenuity is the repellent principle of which negative discharge is the cause.

The illusions of motion are many and are hard to detect, and the illusions of attraction and repulsion are especially hard to detect.

The universe of motion is an electromagnetic one.

The accumulating potential which we know as solids of matter are preponderantly electric.

The matter of man's concept is electricity. The void of man's concept is magnetism. Solidity is electro-positive.

Tenuity is electro-negative.

The alternating inbreathing and outbreathing of the universal constant causes an alternating change in all mass.

The universal pendulum swings toward solidity with each inhalation and toward tenuity with each exhalation.

These alternate swings of the universal pendulum are referred to in the scientific world by the word "oscillations."

All phenomena of motion is oscillatory.

All motion is forward toward the "more" and backward toward the "less." Forward toward the "more" is always toward solidity and greater pressure.

Backward toward the "less" is always toward tenuity and released pressure.

The forward spiral swing of the cosmic pendulum is the positive bound of energy, and the backward spiral swing is its negative rebound.

The forward swing toward the "plus" is always in the direction of north by the way of east and the backward swing is always south by the way of west.

All energy is renewed from the south by the way of east and dissipated toward the south by the way of west.

To these periodic oscillations, alternating in sequence, is due the revolution and rotation of all mass.

All evolving and devolving mass beats time in accord with its periodic sequences of alternating electro-magnetic oscillations.

All mass beats time in accord with its varying potential.

The electro-magnetic oscillations of the universe are the heart-beats, the life pulsations of the universal One.

The universal One is the universe.

EXPLANATORY CHART NO. 2

STABILITY AND INSTABILITY EXEMPLIFIED

A1. Sodium and chlorine (NaCl) will come together with explosive violence at ordinary temperatures because they are exact tonal mates, are of opposite sexes and their orbits are in same low pressure zone where integration is more easily effected. The degree of willingness of this series, known as the "halogens", to combine with sodium (Na) is in the order indicated by the numbers.

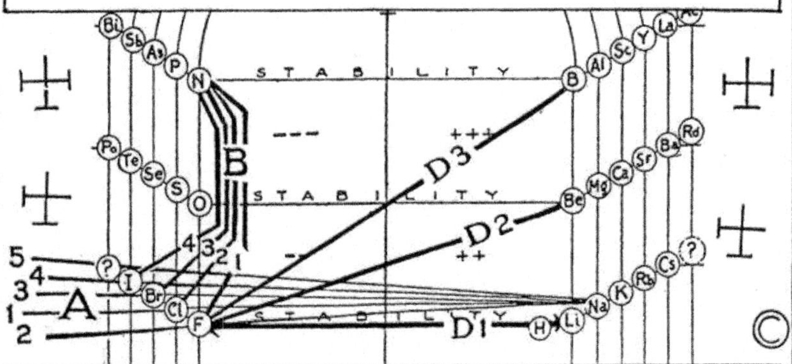

B. Nitrogen, when unwillingly united with any of the halogen series, will break away with explosive violence, the intensity of which decreases in the order indicated by the numbers. All these elements are centrifugal and female. The orbit of nitrogen is two pressure zones away from that of the halogens, and the ecliptic plane of nitrogen is repellent to that of the halogens.

D1. Lithium (L) and fluorine (Fl) will come together as lithium-fluoride (LiF) with violence, while D2 and D3 combine with increasing unwillingness because of the increasing pressures, and other dimensions of their tonal positions.

APPARENTLY DIFFERENT SUBSTANCES ARE ONLY DIFFERENT STATES OF MOTION. ALL SUBSTANCES REMOVED FROM THEIR POTENTIAL, TONAL POSITIONS RESIST THAT REMOVAL WITH A VIOLENCE CORRESPONDING WITH DISTANCE REMOVED. STABILITY IS PURELY A QUESTION OF GRAVITATION

In every evolving form Mind, the One creative force, is expressing itself.

Every existent thing is creating by the continuous thinking of Mind.

Nothing is which has not always been.

The breathing of the One creative force is your breathing, and my breathing, and that of the meadow violet.

The universal pulse is your pulse, and my pulse, and that of the giant Betelguese.

The electromagnetic pulse-beats of a light unit may be thirty trillion to a second and those of an accumulation of light units in the mass of our sun may be months apart, just as its inhalation-exhalation period is approximately eleven years. Betelguese may have a breathing period of a thousand years, but time is a purely relative dimension and all periods vary only in dimension.

The pulsations of the universal One are constant in every dimension in all mass.

The thirty trillion per second of a light unit would exactly equal the energy of one super-pulsation of the sun of our solar system.

If the energy developed by the ant's in-breathings were stored as potential until its time and mass dimensions were equal to that of the elephant, the pressure thus accumulated would exactly equal the power of one inbreathing of the elephant.

Electromagnetic oscillations are always in alternating series of pressure increase and pressure release.

They always alternate between heat absorbing and heat releasing, between melting and freezing, between contraction and expansion and between generation and radiation.

The oscillating pulsations of the universal force is the basis of the universal power plant.

The oscillating swinging of the pendulum between the power of inertia and the equal power of motion is the fundamental principle of universal mechanics.

Man cannot conceive any possible mechanical device or principle which will perform work, store energy, or transmit power, which is not founded upon the alternating compression-expansion sequences of universal in breathings and outbreathings.

Man cannot use any power other than that given him to use from the universal power-house.

Man cannot achieve any success, evolve any idea or create any principle other than that of inducing power from inertia by overcoming it and transforming it into motion against resistance, then carrying it by the effort of mind and body beyond the dead center of opposition. Once carried to this point its motion will reproduce itself and assist his efforts by the accumulated impetus.

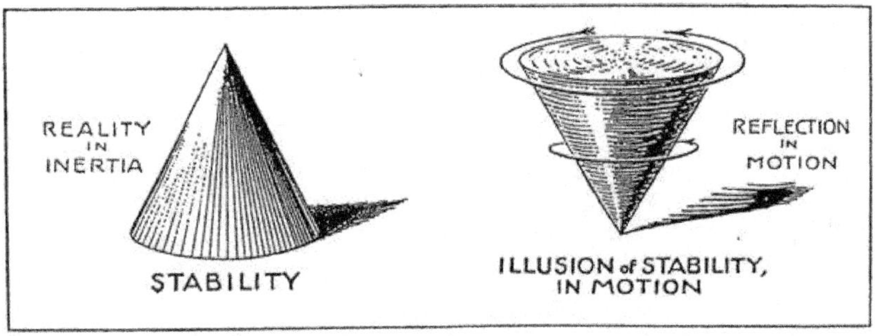

EXPLANATORY CHART NO. 3

INDICATING TONAL MISMATING IN VARIABLE INSTABILITY

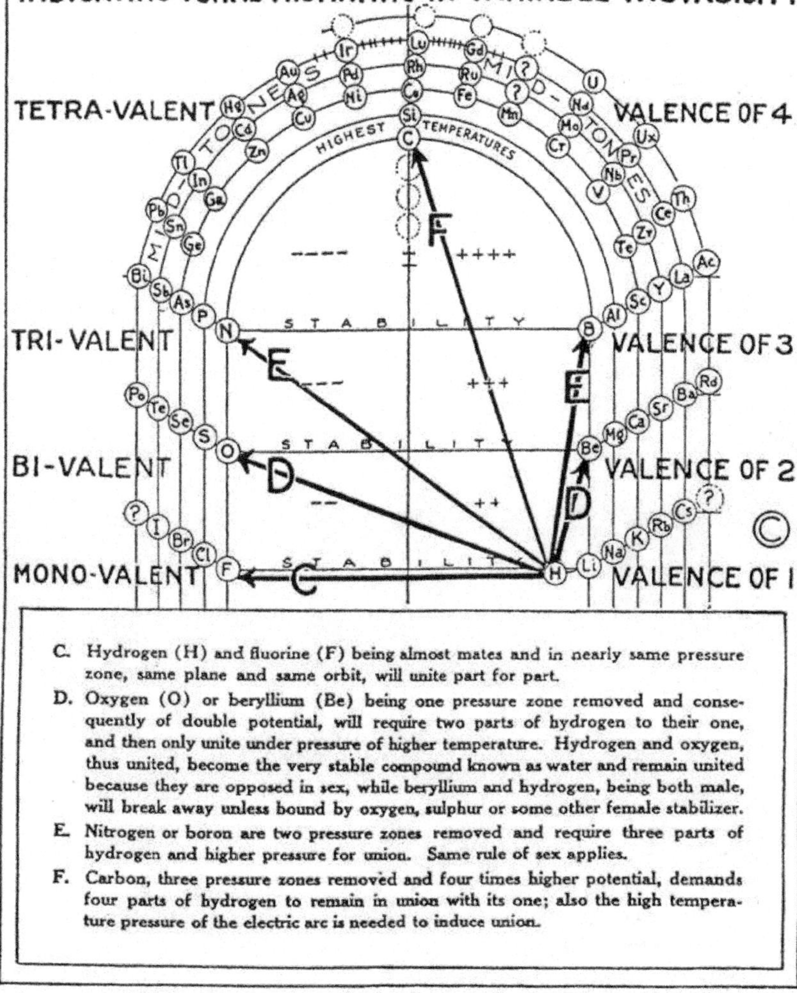

C. Hydrogen (H) and fluorine (F) being almost mates and in nearly same pressure zone, same plane and same orbit, will unite part for part.

D. Oxygen (O) or beryllium (Be) being one pressure zone removed and consequently of double potential, will require two parts of hydrogen to their one, and then only unite under pressure of higher temperature. Hydrogen and oxygen, thus united, become the very stable compound known as water and remain united because they are opposed in sex, while beryllium and hydrogen, being both male, will break away unless bound by oxygen, sulphur or some other female stabilizer.

E. Nitrogen or boron are two pressure zones removed and require three parts of hydrogen and higher pressure for union. Same rule of sex applies.

F. Carbon, three pressure zones removed and four times higher potential, demands four parts of hydrogen to remain in union with its one; also the high temperature pressure of the electric arc is needed to induce union.

ELEMENTS OF INSTABILITY IN UNION INCREASE IN THEIR INSTABILITY AS THEY INCREASE THEIR VARIABILITY IN DIMENSION, ESPECIALLY IN PRESSURE, ORBIT, ECLIPTIC, CRYSTALLIZATION, PLANE AND SEX

CHAPTER IX

CONCERNING ENERGY

The universe is simple. Truth is simple. The universal constant of energy is back of all motion.

It is available for everyone to use according to his desire.

All energy is caused by universal thinking. All thinking is universal thinking and all thinking is simultaneous universally.

All of the energy of all the universe is back of all thinking, for Mind is all that thinks and there is no variability to the constant of energy which Mind uses in its process of thinking. There is apparent variability of intensity of thinking, but that appearance of variability is due to the concentrative ability of Mind to accumulate a greater or less amount of the universal constant.

Exactly as man harnesses accumulated electric potential to perform his work, so may man harness accumulated potential to transform to the low octaves of his outer thinking the inspired idea conceived in the greater speed of the high octaves of his inner thinking.

The more electric potential a man can concentrate, the more work he can perform.

Similarly the more concentrated is his thinking the greater is his power to create, to command or to do.

Concepts are born in the high speeds of the high octaves of inner thinking where speed- time dimension is preponderant.

They are then transformed into power-time dimension by resisting the motion established in the concept by the generative action of concentrative thinking.

The speed-time concept is thus converted into the illusion of form in accordance with the individual ability of man to apply the resistance brakes which will transform the invisible reality of concept into the visible illusion of form.

The varying power of men to achieve because of their varying desire to generate the impetus of a concept into power is also to be found in every particle of matter in the universe.

Just as various energies are appropriated by man in accordance with his desire, so are varying energies absorbed by varying particles of matter.

Just as a dynamo generates power to perform work so does every mass generate it.

Just as the work accomplished by man, or by a dynamo, is proportionate to his, or its ability to generate a dimension of energy sufficient for the work desired, so is the work produced by a mass proportionate to its desire.

Every light unit, atomic system, planet, or sun either performs its work by the energy which it generates and by so doing makes its progress through the system in the orderly manner keeping ever in the progressive current, or it degenerates and gets into the opposite flowing stream and retrogresses.

It is as characteristic for mass to resist its evolution as it is for man to do so.

The desire for the easier way is as strong in one as it is in the other.

The lines of least resistance are those which lead back in the magnetic stream to inertia.

The pace in the electric stream is swift and hard.

Every inch of progress must be earned by the hard work necessary to overcome the inertia of the previous inch.

Every inch earned must be stabilized by erecting opposing pressure walls to prevent losing the ground gained.

The law of the universe of motion is, generate or degenerate, and this applies to every particle in the universe as pitilessly as it does to man.

The variable power within matter to per form work or to attract other matter should be taken into consideration in the concepts and laws of gravitation.

Gravitation is an expression of energy and its power is variable. Like all effects of motion it has its periodicity which is not controlled by distance, time, mass nor any other one dimension, but by the ability of a mass to accumulate electric potential.

The periodicities of gravitation and radiation are in conformity with the ratios of the formula of the locked potentials.

Every chemical element has a varying power of action and reaction according to the pressure and plane position which its desire to accumulate potential has earned for it in its wave of energy.

There is no variation of the constant of energy even though the appearance of variability is everywhere about us.

The appearance of variability of the universal constant is again a matter of dimension of potential, which, in its turn is a matter of position acquired by work.

The energy which runs the universe might be likened unto the energy which runs a clock.

There is but one force back of the mechanics of a clock and the dimensions of that force are exactly balanced in every wheel.

One wheel races very fast and another may seem to stand still.

A big, slow moving wheel turns the hands which the little wheel could not move.

The little wheel, however, uses the exact amount of energy in its speed-time dimension that the big wheel uses in the power-time dimension, which it has accumulated and exchanged for speed.

The little wheel is fast and weak, while the big wheel is slow and powerful.

The deer is swift and weak, while the elephant is ponderously slow and powerful.

The energy of the former would exactly equal the energy of the latter if the low potential energy of fast speed-time dimension were trans- ferred to the high potential energy of slow power-time dimension.

Power is increased mass, increased contraction pressure, decreased volume, decelerated rotation and accelerated revolution.

The generation of all energy is accomplished only through the resistance exerted against the direction of the force of any established motion.

Resistance to established motion decelerates the speed-time dimension of motion and accumulates potential by accelerating its power-time dimension.

X in power-time dimension is the square root of X in speed-time distance-area dimension and its cube root in volume.

If the deer desired more power to fight he could acquire it at the sacrifice of ability to cover distance quickly.

The speed of the deer is the result of the desire of the deer for speed.

If the speed-time dimension of the deer were transformed to power-time dimension, it would be very massive and slow. It would be a creature of different form because of a desire for a different form.

EXPLANATORY CHART NO. 4

ORDER OF HARDNESS AND COMPACTNESS

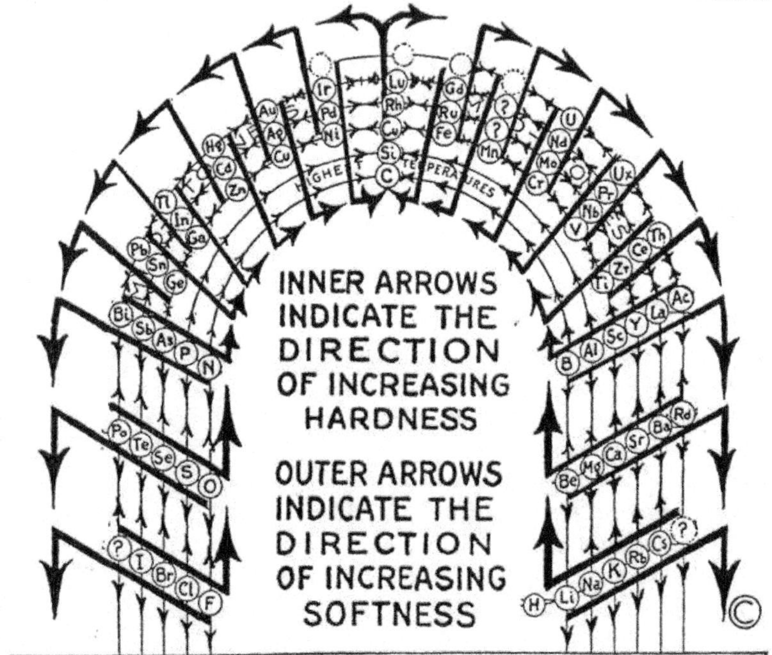

Hardness means degree of solidity, or resistance to penetration. Hardness is the result of opposition to inertness, therefore the farther an element is removed from the inert gas of its octave, the harder it is. The periodicity of hardness is in the order of the pressure zones, those of the first pressure zone being the softest and of the fourth being hardest. As the elements harden, their ecliptic areas contract from maximum expansion and minimum extension in the first pressure zone to zero expansion and maximum extension on the carbon line of the fourth pressure zone.

HARDNESS IS AN ACCUMULATION OF TIME DIMENSION TRANSFORMED INTO POWER, OR HIGH POTENTIAL. CARBON IS THE END OF THE CYCLE'S INHALATION. IT HAS THEREFORE THE HIGHEST POTENTIAL. FROM THAT ELEMENT EXHALATION BEGINS ITS FIVE OCTAVES OF LOWERING AND RISING POTENTIAL IN ALTERNATE SEQUENCE

If the energy of the power-time dimension of a speeding bullet were transformed to mass, the bullet would have to weigh several hundred pounds; or if the same activity were transformed to volume it would have to be expanded to several hundreds of feet in diameter.

Consider for example the relative power-time dimension of a light unit circling in its atomic orbit probably thirty million times per second as compared with the eleven years consumed by Jupiter in making one revolution in the atom which we call our solar system.

The light unit may cover more than one hundred thousand miles per second against Jupiter's eight miles, but the area of the orbit covered by each is exactly equal for equal intervals of time.

More than this, the very difference in speed of revolution of a light unit or of a planet, due to the eccentricity of their orbits, is also balanced in the areas covered.

Force must be resisted in order to accumulate it into power.

To accumulate power is to generate energy by exchanging one time dimension for the other.

The high-speed low-power gear wheel of a motor transmission moves slowly while the wheels of the car race very fast. On the contrary the low-speed high-power gear wheel moves very fast and the wheels of the car move very slowly.

The high speed-time dimension of the long end of a lever is exactly balanced in the slow speed, accumulated power-time dimension of the short end.

Move the fulcrum and both time dimensions change with increase or decrease of power.

Change of dimension does not mean change of the universal constant of energy.

The resistance to generated energy is registered in heat.

The greater the accumulation of energy by generation the greater the temperature registered as a resistance to that accumulation.

The greater the generation of energy the greater the radiation.

The radiation of all energy is accomplished only by the assistance, exerted in the direction of the force, of any established motion.

Assistance to established motion accelerates the speed-time dimension and distributes potential by decelerating its power-time dimension.

The heat radiated by the sun is assisted by great pressure back of it and resisted by less pressure ahead of it.

Expansion is thereby assisted just as contraction is resisted.

Cooling is the result of assistance just as heating is the result of resistance.

It cannot be too often repeated that there is no effect of motion in which its opposite effect is not simultaneously present and sequentially preponderant. The word " preponderant " should always be understood in reference to any state of motion.

Radiation generates and generation radiates.

Expansion is assisted but also it is resisted.

The falling water expanding into a cooling spray generates heat by the resistance of the pressures through which it falls.

That potential which is being generated must be simultaneously radiated in a less degree, but radiation will eventually become preponderant in its cumulative reaction sequence.

The universal constant of energy is never changing. It but appears to change. It is never unbalanced, never out of equilibrium.

There is but one force which runs the cosmic clock, and all the wheels of this universe turn with all of the energy of the universe back of each one of them.

The only difference is one of dimension. Difference of dimension is actuated by the desire of thinking Mind.

All of the power of the universe lies in the dimensionless universe of inertia.

Work is the principle of the evolving cycles, work of mind and work of body.

Work is the principle back of the continuance of the appearance of existence, work born of desire and performed in ecstasy.

Without work form cannot hold itself together.

Without work reproduction of any accumulated idea would be impossible.

Degeneracy of the body begins when physical work relaxes. Degeneracy of the mind begins when concentrative thinking relaxes.

Form can only be continued through the effort of sustaining an appearance of stability by creating a progressive series of opposing planes of instability.

The effort required of man, or of nature, to do this requires increasing expenditure of energy.

Each effort contributes to the next effort.

The progress marked by each effort is conditioned by the force of the desire back of that effort. Desire chooses its own dimensions and runs the gait of that desire.

All things can be what they desire to be. Desire and effort to be evolves into the reality of that desire. The dimensions of any wave of energy are the dimensions of desire.

The accumulation of all potential is the result of a series of explosive actions actuated by the force of desire and stabilized by their reactions.

Inertia cannot be overcome, nor motion take place, without the concentrative desire force of the creative, image making faculty of Mind.

The universe is apparently divided into a kaleidoscopic complexity of varying energies all of which are exact multiples of the universal constant, as far as first cause is concerned. The variability of these energies depends solely upon desire which alone controls the dimensions of that multiplicity.

Power-time dimension is conditioned by restricted area of orbit, decelerated rotation and accelerated revolution, which is nature's method of accumulating high potential.

Speed-time dimension is conditioned by expanded area of orbit, decelerated revolution and accelerated rotation which is nature's method of distributing the accumulation into low potential.

Potential energy is an accumulation of the energy constant locked in a position of equilibrium by an equal and opposite pressure wall of resistance.

It is the breathing spell between effort and effort where the accumulated energy is apparently arrested.

Kinetic energy is the generative concentration of effort expended in building new pressure walls of less stability or the degenerative relaxation of effort which allows the pressure walls to expand toward inertia.

Kinetic energy is the work performing energy. An interruptive resistance to the flow in either direction will perform work.

Work performed by a magnetic stream is a regeneration of energy.

It is the conductive stream which the electrician measures in amperes.

Resistance to its conductive flow through a wire regenerates energy and reverses discharge into charge.

The electric light is a good example of regeneration of degenerating energy.

Conversely, work performed by an electric stream is a further generation of energy.

It is the inductiye stream which the electrician measures in volts.

Resistance to its inductive flow through the accumulating plates of a storage battery adds to energy and increases positive charge.

High potential energy is generated with increasing pressure resistance which means increasing deceleration of speed-time and an equal acceleration of power-time.

One must always balance the other.

High potential is generated from low potential against an accumulating pressure resistance equal, in inverse ratio, to the cube of the equilibrium pressure of the low potential, and is degenerated with equal pressure assistance in direct ratio.

In other words, doubling the power of a given mass means a decrease in volume and speed of rotation as of the cube of that mass in inverse ratio, or an increase in pressure, temperature and speed of revolution in direct ratio. On the contrary, halving the power for a given mass means an increase in volume in direct ratio, and a decrease in pressure, temperature and speed of revolution in inverse ratio.

Every wheel in the cosmic clock runs down in the 4 3 — 2 — 1— ratio of the formula of the locked potentials and is wound up in its 1+ 2+ 3 + 4 ratio.

The stopping point of the clock's winding is 4^{+}_{+} beyond which it cannot go and at which point it must unwind to complete its cycle of motion.

Now it is well to return to first cause and look within the cosmic clock itself.

Mind is the source of all energy through the dynamic action and reaction of the two opposing pulsations of the process of thinking.

All motion begins in the plus, contractive, endothermic impulse of thinking, and ends in the succeeding minus, expansive, exothermic impulse.

The entire mechanics of this universe are founded on these two repeative impulses.

Every reaction is a balancing sub-normal negative pressure which exactly equals the supernormal positive pressure generated by its opposite action.

All inhalation is expressed in contraction and all exhalation in expansion.

The entire energy of the universe is expressed through contraction or expansion into super - normal electro - positive or sub - normal electro-negative pressures, each of which un-equalized pressures exerts its utmost efforts to get back into equalized pressures and by so doing performs the work of the universe.

By normal pressure is meant any local equilibrium pressure as, for example, the local equilibrium pressure of this planet at sea level.

Man is surrounded by all the vast energy of the universe, yet it will not work for him while it is in equilibrium. He must lift its pressure to a higher potential than the horsepower represented by this planet's normal fifteen pounds per square inch sea level pressure, and let it fall into place; or he must lower it below that pressure and allow it to rise into place.

Until this is done the vast potential of the planet's local equilibrium pressure is inert and will not perform work.

No principle of dynamics can be conceived by man to perform work for him, other than that of restoring potential to its proper place.

His engines and his dynamos perform sequences of oscillations between generative contractions to super-normal pressures and radiative expansions to sub-normal ones.

If the normal pressure of the surface of this planet could be piped to the surface of Mars, the inhabitants of that planet could have an inexhaustible supply of high potential energy performing work for them, though the same energy will not turn a wheel for us.

The universal constant of energy is fixed, unalterable and non-variable and its apparent variability is purely an illusion of changed dimensions.

The constant of energy represented by a lever is not increased by changing the fulcrum of that lever. If the fulcrum is changed so as to increase the power the speed is decreased in the opposite universal ratio.

High power, or high potential, is merely cumulative power-time dimension saved up, stored up, compressed into mass of less relative volume.

The high potential of little volume might be likened unto the accumulated energy within a city where the pace is fast and the area small as compared with the same energy spread over a whole state where the pace is slow and the area large.

An application of high-pressure brakes against the wheels of speed-time expansion dimension will decelerate it with great resistance and convey it into power-time contraction dimension.

The cold of expanded speed-time dimension will also reverse itself when so resisted into the generation of much heat.

In any mass a change in temperature is in inverse ratio to a change in volume.

Generated heat energy will lift a lower potential to a higher one.

The higher potential will then have a greater positive charge, and the greater positive charge will increase the concentration of gravitative centers of all mass thus generated, and of all systems affected by the raised potential.

All dimensions will change and all pressure walls will shift to accord with the new conditions of new pressures, and then this new potential, born of changed conditions, will have a different appearance and give different reactions. For this reason, it will be called another substance.

And so, throughout this universe of the One force, the One substance of Mind, man finds many states of motion of varying pressures and varying potentials, and he counts them all up and names them all as separate substances and various energies.

CHAPTER X

ELECTRO-MAGNETIC PRESSURES

The construction of the universe in accordance with Euclid's axioms, theorems and postulates is not in accordance with the laws of motion.

One of the axioms used by Euclid in proof of other axioms and postulates reads: figures may be freely moved in space without change in shape or size.

If this is true the space between the heavenly bodies is a void, a vacuum.

If this is true the theory of a non-resistant, pressureless, uniform ether of space is tenable.

If this is true the heavenly bodies must hold themselves in their relative orbits by their mutual attraction and the impetus of their motion.

If on the contrary it can be clearly shown that figures cannot be freely moved in space without change of size or shape, then a fundamental axiomatic Euclidian principle is not true.

It is herein contended that figures cannot move one inch in space without change in shape and size for this entire universe of motion is one of varying, but repeative, pressures.

An Euclidian indefinite straight line reaching out to infinity is not possible in this universe of varying pressures.

The varying pressures of space are curved.

They represent expressions of the energy of motion.

All energy of motion expresses itself in waves.

All waves are opposed spirals and limited in dimensions.

All opposed spiral waves accumulate mass and simultaneously redistribute that accumulation.

All accumulating mass is aiming toward gyroscopic perfection of motion and toward perfection of cubic crystallization.

All diffusing mass is aiming away from gyroscopic stability, and away from the simple cubic crystallization toward amorphus complexity of crystallization.

All direction is the direction of opposing pressures.

The direction of all pressures is spiral. All direction is therefore curved.

All curves are spiral.

All orbits are spiral. They are all conic sections. A parabolic or hyperbolic orbit is impossible in this universe of pressures. Any anticlockwise orbit which cuts the base of its cone of measured energy is regenerated in the opposed cone of the wave and its orbit becomes a clockwise orbit of another system.

An object freely moving in space must move in a curved spiral line whether that object be a planet, a corpuscle, a "ray" of light or any other expression of energy.

Further still, any expression of energy in this universe must end where it began. It must be curved.

Furthermore, the curve is never a circle. It is spiral and its convolutions from its beginning to its ending run the whole gamut of the effects of motion in speeds, temperature, planes and pressures.

Furthermore, no curved spiral of motion, ending where it began, traverses the universe in its journey. The conclusion of Einstein that the universe must be spherical because all direction is curved is based on the assumption that the direction of motion is curved, circular or elliptical, and traverses the whole universe in its passage.

No mass, or body or other expression of motion, in any state, can pass the boundary plane of its own wave of energy.

Every effort of energy sets its own dimensions. Its boundaries are limited by that effort.

Energy reproduces itself and thus transfers its expression throughout the universe from wave to wave, but there are dividing walls where motion ceases and begins again; and where all mass disappears to reform again.

Mass is energy.

Energy accumulates as mass and is redistributed in accordance with the increasing and decreasing pressures which it is able to generate.

A corpuscle is a mass just as a planet is a mass.

An atom is a mass just as a solar system is a mass.

The pressure which an atom of hydrogen can develop varies vastly from that which an atom of radium can develop.

They compare with one another as a sewing machine motor compares with a high voltage power plant.

All masses, whether they are light units, planets or suns, are compression and expansion pumps which hold themselves together for a time in greater or less proximity according to the various ratios of their respective compression and expansion powers, in order to simulate the forms being thought out as idea by the image making faculty of the One universal Mind.

It is a fundamental principle of physics that the slightest change in pressure of any substance changes its volume.

A change of temperature is one indicator of a change of pressure.

Every inch of the universe varies in temperature.

Every inch must therefore vary in pressure.

Every atom varies in pressure from its exterior to its nucleus. If its temperature is changed its volume also 'changes. Also every kind of atom varies from every other kind in volume, temperature and all other dimensions.

Every kind of atom is in a different plane and each plane is the pressure wall of one of the varying pressure compartments which divides this universe of motion into pressure zones.

"Space" is made up of atoms of these varying pressures.

If an object cannot freely move at the earth's surface without expanding or contracting to adjust itself to the varying pressures, how can it do so in space?

The answer comes back from tradition; "But space is a void."

Is it?

It is densely packed with atoms of the high octaves which we cannot see but which are not beyond the power of our instruments to detect even if our thinking cannot reveal them to us.

In later volumes the spectroscopic proof of a "space" of motion will be given. For the purpose of this volume let us consider this subject in reference to masses which we can see.

We, simple dwellers on this planet, are prone to err in our conclusions because of the relative importance of our planetary position to our point of view.

A humming bird flying across our sky is vastly larger than the largest star, and one's hat is apparently bigger than the sun or moon.

No wonder that Copernicus made the earth the center of the system upon which all else turned.

Surely the little village of Kipling's story could be forgiven for voting the world flat as all men once believed.

Quite a reasonable human error it was for " one could see it with one's own eyes."

There was no illusion about it. It was the most real thing that they knew, a solid thing flat and motionless around which the sky turned.

For attempting to correct this error Galileo -narrowly escaped with his life and his statements were almost universally denied.

We still measure the orbits of all the planets of this system by our own little earth's ecliptic instead of by the solar equatorial plane.

This may be necessary for local convenience just as it is convenient for the village to measure distances to near-by villages and towns from itself.

If, however, the geographer or historian mapped the planet or wrote its history around the little village of his residence as a radial center of comparison, he would, to say the least, be colossally egoistic.:

The effects of motion of this solar system described herein are based upon the sun as its center and not upon the earth. The planets' orbits and all precessional motions will also be charted in relation to the solar equatorial plane.

All assumed facts of pressure, density, temperature, and the relative power of the attraction of gravitation of this entire solar system, are now measured from conditions obtained in this little pea like village of our solar system without any attempt to translate them into the relative ratios due to relative conditions.

If a premise is wrong, a conclusion must be wrong.

Hall conclusions regarding temperature, densities and pressures throughout this solar system are herein shown to be founded on wrong premises, they must therefore be wrong.

All dimensions are relatively right, but are wrong when measured by units of this planet's standard. Our record of dimensions is in relative ratios.

Consider Mercury, a little, heavy, hard planet supposedly less dense than this earth but in reality, very much more so.

Crushed in the tremendous pressure of close proximity to the great pressure center of this system and just recently taken from the furnace to cool, it slowly wends its spiral way to where Jupiter now is but will not then be.

Jupiter is not hard. It could not be. Even with its vast bulk it is not hot as we know heat. Iron would melt there at about 2°.

It is in a different pressure zone, where releasing pressures expand mass of little volume to mass of big volume.

And Saturn, a vast but pithy planet, would either completely ionize or shrink to insignificance if moved to Mercury's orbit, just as Mercury would explode if suddenly moved to Saturn's.

Then comes Uranus, softer still, wobbling on its changing pole; then Neptune, so tenuous that a cloud of ours would be a rock in comparison.

Beyond Neptune, our last known planet, which is but approximately three-elevenths of the distance to the limits of our solar system, there are more planets which are so vast and so tenuous that Jupiter is a pea beside one and Neptune a solid in comparison.

Within our solar system are pressures, temperatures, and densities undreamed of by man, because miscalculated by him from unit pressures of this planet with which he is familiar.

Even man's instruments have deceived him in his calculations for they but translate states of motion in which units of comparison are but relative, though true in ratio.

Man measures the density of the sun by its rigidity as compared with that of our planet.

The sun is, therefore, given as one-quarter the density of our planet.

It is quite appropriate to state the density of our planet as five times that of water on our planet because the water is part of the planet and subject to the same pressures of our orbital position. Our planet is in a different pressure compartment" from that of any other mass.

Not so, however, can he compare the pressures or densities of another planet with ours.

Relatively yes, but the low relative pressure and potential which allows rigidity here would vaporize our expanded earth at the surface of the sun.

If removed to Mercury's orbit our earth would become white hot, and when it cooled it would be approximately the size of Mercury.

On the other hand, the vapor which arises from a steam exhaust in a day would furnish ample material for the solid head and streaming tail of a conspicuous comet if it were removed to the low pressure zones of the type of comet whose orbit is in a plane at an angle of 50° to the solar ecliptic, and whose aphelion exceeds twice Neptune's distance from the sun.

That large cloud floating high up in the cold of upper atmospheric low pressure would be but a quart or two when compressed into water lower down.

The albedo, or light reflecting quality, of a cloud of our planet is not to be taken as a standard unit of albedo measurement for a lower pressure zone far removed.

Laws governing the measurements, in ratios of standard units of distant pressures, temperatures and densities, and their translation into standard units familiar to us, will be written down when further consideration of this universe of purely mechanical motion makes it logical to consider its mathematics.

It is necessary at this point to describe briefly the basic principles governing pressures.

Pressure is that relative state of opposed force necessary to sustain the illusion of relative density of substance in motion.

The dimensionless universe of inertia is absolutely stable.

The universe of motion is a corpuscular universe of varying but relative density which simulates the appearance of stability through motion.

The varying power of mass to appear to attract mass causes an appearance of variation of the pressure dimensions of all masses.

Man classifies masses of various densities as gases, liquids and solids.

The density or tenuity of any mass is in proportion to its 'preponderance of pressure opposition.

Like all other effects of motion, pressure has its opposites.

The opposites of pressure are the electric pressure of contraction and the magnetic pressure of expansion.

One pulls inward from within.

The other pushes outward from within. One attracts mass by drawing it closer together.

The other repels mass by separating it.

The greater the positive charge, the greater the pressure of contraction.

The greater the pressure of contraction, the less the volume.

The greater the negative discharge, the greater the pressure of expansion.

The greater the pressure of expansion, the less the volume.

All mass is corpuscular and all mass is relatively solid.

All solid mass has first been melted by the friction of the active opposition of the two pressures, and has then been frozen into the state of relative rigidity by the locking of the opposing pressures into inactive potential positions.

Great solidity means less axial activity.

Great solidity also means preponderance of contraction pressure toward high potential.

Great axial activity means less solidity.

Great axial activity also means preponderance of expansion pressure toward low potential.

Melt a bar of iron and it becomes axially active. It also becomes less solid.

Vaporize it by expansion pressure and its axial activity multiplies.

Also, its volume has increased enormously, for centrifugal activity demands space in which to display its activity.

The heavy, solid bar of iron will now no longer drop to the ground but, on the contrary, will rise into the air.

What has happened to cause so great a change? Let us first repeat the definition.

"Pressure is that relative state of opposed force necessary to sustain the illusion of relative density of substance in motion."

Pressures have been reversed.

High contraction pressures have become preponderantly expansive.

High potential has become low potential.

Low axial activity has become great axial activity.

Restricted volume has become extended volume.

Great density has become low density.

That which is called "weight" has entirely disappeared as far as the gravitational effect of this planet is concerned.

Its weight, in respect to this planet of high potential, has been reduced to the same relative weight as other mass of lower potential.

The expanded mass of iron now falls of its own weight toward low pressures, just as it rises from this planet because of its loss of weight.

The bar of iron is no longer heavy in respect to this planet, nor is it hard, compact, rigid or dense.

Its particles no longer cohere as a solid of man's concept.

It passes through the equilibrium of this planet's sea level pressure of fifteen pounds per square inch, in which state it has no apparent weight, and still continues to expand until its low density forces it to fall toward the low pressures appropriate to low density.

Its mass, however, does not change. Only its dimensions change.

In lowering its density, by reversing its pressures and potential, its axial activities are increased, its orbital activities decreased, thus reducing its ability to attract. On the contrary, it develops a strong ability to repel. It can no longer hold together as a piece of iron. The voltage and amperage of the little oscillating electro-magnetic opposing pressure pumps of which it is constituted are lowered.

By increasing its volume the distance between each corpuscle is increased so that their apparent ability to attract each other decreases.

Increased volume also decreases surface tension pressure, a quality which belongs, in relative degree, to all mass.

Increased volume and decreased surface tension pressure means increased vapor pressure.

Decreased surface tension pressure lessens the ability of mass to attract and to cohere.

Increased surface tension pressure means greater density or solidity; also it means greater ability to attract.

Solidity is an increasingly unstable condition of matter due to increasing electric pressures developed by repeative series of explosive disturbances in inertia.

The greater the disturbance, the greater the effort necessary to produce it.

The greater the effort, the greater the opposition to the effort by an equal and opposite resisting pressure.

The greater the resistance, the greater the heat generated by the contact of the two oppositely flowing streams.

The greater the heat, the less the relative solidity for that respective pressure.

The greater the incandescence, the greater the radiation of heat by expulsion.

The greater the expulsion by radiation, the more solid, dense and rigid the radiating substance.

The more rigid a substance is, the more true it is to its own plane of pressure.

The more true to plane, the more gyroscopic the motion of its particles.

The more gyroscopic the motion of its particles, the more apparently stable the mass.

The greater the solidity, the greater the instability, but the greater is the illusion of stability.

The outgoing ever-contracting force of the explosive actions meet each other at the north planes of opposition, and rebound toward the south planes of inertia, ever expanding as they rebound.

Man lives and thinks in terms of solidity because he is accustomed 'to the environment of his own present, potential.

Solidity is something which he can see, feel, weigh and command.

It is difficult for man to comprehend that his dependable solids are but contracting or expanding states of motion gyroscopically held in apparent suspense for a sufficient length of time to create the deceptive illusion of permanence.

If man would picture the evolution and devolution of entire solar systems as mere flashings of fireflies in the meadow, he would form a better concept of the instability of solidity.

The process of one is exactly the same as that of the other.

Every effect produced during the ten billion trillion years of the one is exactly repeated in the one second of the other.

Solidity is therefore but an effect of genero-active contractive pressure.

Like all effects of motion, it is periodic and its tones are in conformity with the formula of the locked potentials.

Like all effects of motion, its opposite and equal balancing effect increases its resistance to accumulation as accumulation increases.

Greater positive charge opposed to greater negative discharge means greater potential.

Greater potential means greater pressure opposition.

Greater pressure opposition means higher melting point, less volume and greater density.

A metal which will melt at 2,000° at sea level pressure of this planet will still remain a frozen solid at 200,000,000,000° in the opposing high pressures of the sun's dense crust.

A radio-active emanation expelled from a low pressure atom may not exceed ten miles per second, while that of a high pressure atom of the tenth octave such as radium, will approach 186,000 miles per second.

The increasing contractive electric pressures of the octaves of the elements, from 0 = through 1 + 2 + 3 + to 4^{+}_{+}, are accompanied by rising melting points and lowering volumes.

The decreasing, expansive magnetic pressures from 4^{+}_{+} back through 3 — 2 — 1 — to 0 = are accompanied by lowering melting points and greater volumes.

Axial activity increases as radio-active pressures decrease.

Orbital activity increases as genero-active pressures increase.

The entire universe is one of varying potential. Therefore, it is one of varying opposing pressures.

If the entire universe of dimension is one of varying density, which means that it is more or less apparently solid everywhere, then it necessarily follows that the entire universe must be one of varying pressures.

If this universe is one of varying pressures, the axiom of Euclid heretofore quoted cannot be true.

If that state of motion which is called "solid" is a state in which the tremendous contractive pressure of great accumulation of' the energy constant has become moulded into compact electric mass of high potential, then those states of motion which are called "liquid" and "gaseous" are merely the lower pressures appropriate to the slight accumulation of the energy constant into more tenuous masses.

More tenuous masses freeze or melt at lower temperatures where the resistance to integration is not so intense.

An active gas like hydrogen, which leaps explosively into flame from the high opposing pressures of the sun's surface at a speed of thousands of miles per minute, ascends quite leisurely in comparison, and without combustion, from this planet's lower pressure.

Upon Uranus or Neptune, hydrogen undoubtedly exists in a free state, frozen, as its prototype, caesium, is frozen upon this earth.

Upon Neptune, hydrogen undoubtedly falls of its own weight as aluminum would fall on this planet.

Nature build tonal walls with which she divides her effects of motion.

If a pressure wall is developed, it must necessarily follow that somewhere an opposite wall of resistance is set :up against which that pressure can develop.

This principle holds true in the apparent voids of space just as it does on this planet in a compression tank, an automobile tire, the depths of the ocean or thousands of miles within its crust.

Every pressure develops an exactly equal and opposite resisting pressure.

Pressures resulting from the accumulation of mass of sufficient density to be perceptible to man would be relatively present in mass which is beyond man's perception.

Man's "ether of space" is substance in motion just as molten metal is matter in motion.

It is, in fact, infinitely more active, even though that activity cannot be perceived by the senses of man.

The evidence of it, however, can be plainly seen and accurately measured.

The unseen universe is existent not alone through deduction, or as a theory, or as a logical conclusion.

Every effect of motion is registered in light and all its pressure walls are visible spectro-scopically, each having its own pressure line.

Zeeman long since stumbled upon one evidence of the ten octaves by sending a strong generative charge through sodium, but the significance of what he saw had no meaning for him.

By thus increasing its pressure, he saw ten yellow lines, each one of which told the story of an over tone of that particular state of motion, 1+, reproduced in a different octave.

All of the ten octaves are measurable in every dimension even to the infra and ultra ends.

Also are their waves exactly computable and their other dimensions exactly ascertainable.

The difference between any one "part" of space and any other is purely relative in all of its dimensions.

The dimensions of the one differs from the dimensions of the others, that is all.

Some parts consist of energy accumulated into power by the deceleration of axial and acceleration of orbital speed-time, while other parts consist of energy dissipated into the opposite effects of motion.

Pressure opposition is but one of the effects of motion. All effects of motion are both gravitative and radiative, but one or the other in preponderance.

Mass accumulates in focal centers, because of a preponderance of positive charge.

Accumulation of mass is due to the attractive power of gravitation to increase pressures and thus force great volume into less volume with focal centers of greater positive charge and greater contractive pressure.

The desire to attract is purely a gravitative effect and the reactive repulsion is a radiative one.

One is an accumulating pressure, which resists redistribution. The other is a distributing pressure, which resists accumulation.

There are zones of opposing pressures throughout this universe of motion which vary in density as the distance increases from the nuckal centers of centripetal vortices.

In every mass, the attraction of the accumulating pressure and the repulsion of the distributing pressure exert their forces in opposite directions.

The dimensions of the electric stream increase in inverse universal ratio to the dimensions of the magnetic stream.

An expanded mass rising in the air has a lifting capacity in respect to the mass from which it is rising, and it also has weight, or compression capacity in respect to the potential toward which it is falling.

In any mass the lifting capacity, in relation to high potential, is equal to the compression capacity in relation to low potential.

The lifting capacity of a_ gas rising in the air exactly corresponds to the action of a suction pump. It reduces the potential and pressure of the planet by expanding it.

On the contrary, an added weight exactly corresponds to the action of a compression pump in raising the potential and pressure of the planet by contracting it.

Consider for example, the radiation of the sun.

The radiation has a lifting power in respect to the sun, the effect of which is to degenerate the sun.

On the other hand, it has weight in respect to the planets against which it impacts, the effect of which is to regenerate them.

The degeneration of any mass is exactly balanced by the regeneration of another mass.

All effects of motion are always in equilibrium, and all are tonally periodic.

All periodicities are orderly and their orderliness of increase and decrease of intensity in their expression always conforms with the octave formula of the locked potentials, and also with the cyclic order of five inbreathings and five outbreathings which constitute one superinhalation-exhalation period.

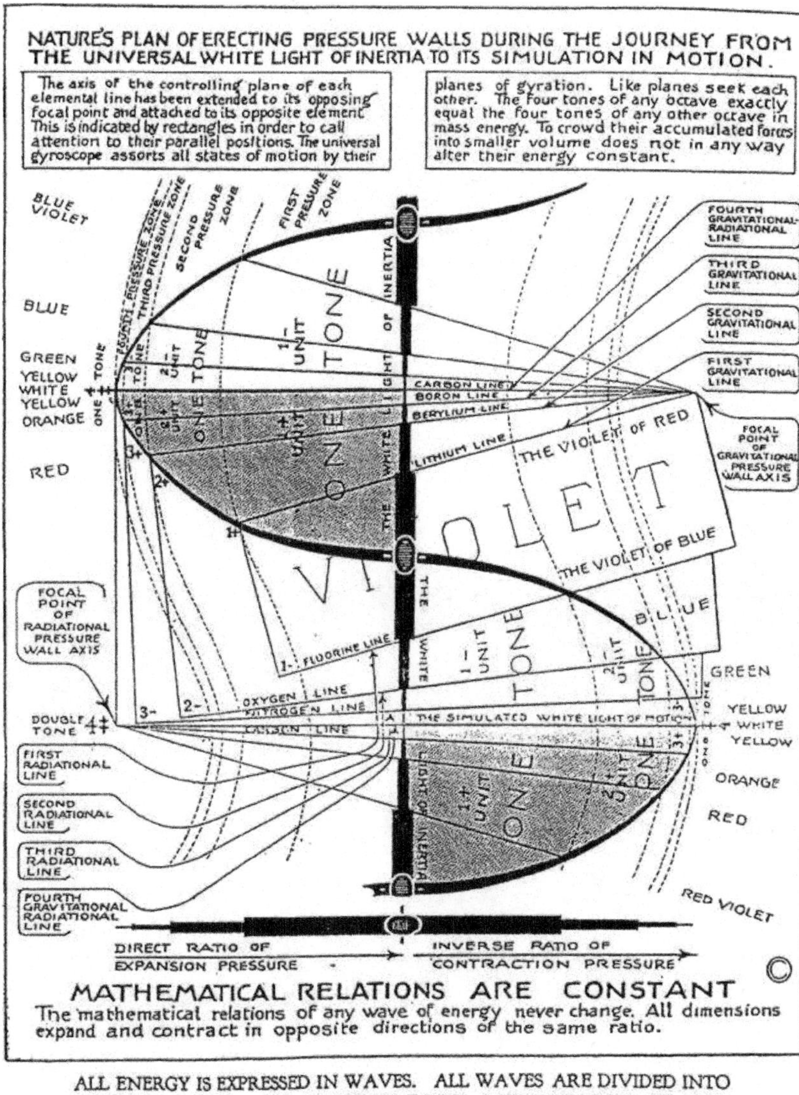

ALL ENERGY IS EXPRESSED IN WAVES. ALL WAVES ARE DIVIDED INTO PRESSURE ZONES. ALL PRESSURE ZONES ARE SUSTAINED BY PRESSURE WALLS ERECTED IN DEFINED LOCKED POTENTIAL POSITIONS

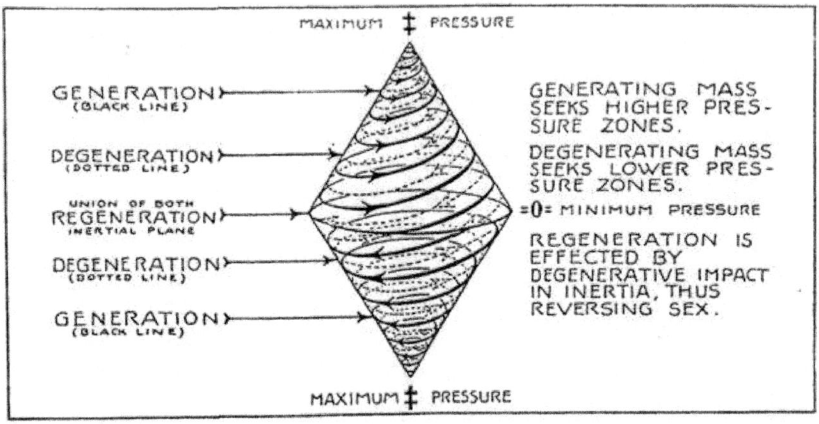
MAXIMUM ‡ PRESSURE
GENERATION (BLACK LINE)
DEGENERATION (DOTTED LINE)
UNION OF BOTH REGENERATION INERTIAL PLANE
DEGENERATION (DOTTED LINE)
GENERATION (BLACK LINE)
GENERATING MASS SEEKS HIGHER PRESSURE ZONES.
DEGENERATING MASS SEEKS LOWER PRESSURE ZONES.
=0= MINIMUM PRESSURE
REGENERATION IS EFFECTED BY DEGENERATIVE IMPACT IN INERTIA, THUS REVERSING SEX.
MAXIMUM ‡ PRESSURE

CHAPTER XI

ATTRACTION AND REPULSION

"Every particle of matter in the universe is attracted to every other particle of matter in the universe."

"Every body attracts every other body with a force that varies directly as the product of their masses and inversely as the square of the distance between them."

No more fundamental principles have been written than these two Newtonian laws and no laws have been more universally accepted.

Concerning Newton's laws of gravitation, it is stated that they are "the broadest and most fundamental which nature makes known to us."

If it can be shown that the substance which we call matter has no power to attract, but that it is motion only which attracts, and if it can also be shown that the apparent ability of substance to attract through motion is equally true of its apparent ability to repel through motion, then the first of these laws is inaccurate and should be rewritten.

Let us see whether the above law would not be more in keeping with the laws of motion if it were rewritten thus:

Every mass has the relative apparent ability to attract and to repel every other mass, its relative ability depending on its relative potential.

Let us now consider the varying power of mass to attract other mass according to the distance one is from the other.

If the second law is true, two equal masses of two different substances must attract each other equally from equal distances.

If it can be shown that different masses do not attract each other equally, but on the contrary, that there is a great range in the variability of the power of different masses to attract each other, then the law cannot be true.

If it can also be shown that the apparent ability of mass to attract and also to repel increases and decreases in orderly ratios as volume, density, pressures, time, temperature, and other dimensions increase and decrease, then dimensions, other than mass and distance, should be considered in the writing of the law.

If it can be shown that the apparent power of attraction is applicable to all forming mass which is heading in the outward journey from the plane of concept to the point of north and that the apparent power of repulsion is applicable to all dissolving mass which is returning to the inertial plane of concept, then the second of these laws is inaccurate and should be rewritten.

Let us see whether this law would not also be more in keeping with the laws of motion if it were rewritten thus:

Every body attracts and repels every other body with a force which increases and decreases in the universal ratios in accordance with its potential position and according to whether the direction of the mass is toward the north or toward the south.

This chapter will consider whether the attributes which we call attraction and repulsion belong to substance, and the succeeding chapters will consider what relation dimension has to the apparent ability of mass to attract.

It is generally assumed that the substance of matter attracts and that some other force repels.

What it is that repels is not quite so certain, but the generally accepted theory is that it is light.

Light is supposed to be something else than that of which solid cold matter is composed.

Light is supposed to repel.

It does. But it also attracts just as all substance attracts and also repels.

The word "apparently" must be understood to be used as qualifying the above and all similar statements and the word "mass," when used, is assumed to mean an aggregate of states of motion of the substance but not the substance itself.

The tail of the comet which 'ever points away from the sun is supposedly one of the proofs of the theory that light repels.

If the head of the comet is its most solid part and its tail proportionately less solid as its distance from its head increases, and if the pressure is greater the nearer the sun, just as the pressure in water is greater the farther down, would not the tail of the comet seek the lower pressures and the head the higher, just as a cork tied to a nail with a string would float above the nail.

Is not the opposition of pressures and the desire of potential to seek its own pressure zone just as acceptable an explanation as the theory of light repulsion?

Is this explanation not also more logical, for is not the sun the great center of attraction of this system?

If so, is it quite logical to say that the sun attracts and the sun's light repels?

There is however, a half-truth here, for light is accumulated energy which heats to incandescence as it accumulates, radiates as it heats and expands as it radiates.

Expansion is a state of corpuscular separation upon which the repulsion principle is based.

The expansion pressure of radiation is a state of motion which pushes, just as the contraction pressure of generation is a state of motion which pulls.

The other half of this truth is that light and mass are the same. Mass is also accumulated energy which cools as it radiates and which contracts as it cools.

Contraction is a state of corpuscular integration upon which the attraction principle is based.

Here are two half-truths which trace the source of both opposites to the same focal center.

Let us consider these two half-truths and see if they cannot be made into one whole truth.

First let us consider whether light or mass either repels or attracts as a substance or as an aggregate of substances, or whether it is motion alone which performs these miracles of whirling suns and planets about in space to suit its whims.

If light repels, something else must attract, for it would not be possible for light to do both.

Yet the physicist bases the phenomenon of growing plant life upon the ability of light to attract.

That process which he terms "photo-synthesis" is one in which the light of the sun is presumed to attract and to assemble substances into form.

Every physicist knows to a certainty that light directed against a metallic plate will increase its positive charge. More than that, various intensities and colors of light will vary the positive charge. Further still, various metals will vary vastly in their ability to absorb additional positive charge from the same sources of light.

Further still, metal plates so over-charged by the light will gradually lose that charge in the dark.

Consider light in the aspect of a flame. The flame from a birch log rises rapidly in a direction radially away from the earth's center in exactly the opposite direction from that in which a log of birch would fall.

The birch log is the accumulated potential of contractive pressure and is consequently subject to gravitational pull which is preponderant to the expansive pressure of radiational push.

The flame from the birch log is a series of explosions which release the accumulation of contractive pressure. The flame is a suddenly expanded radio-active release of energy which so explosively and so eagerly seeks the lower potential of pressures far removed, that the friction caused by resistance to so great a speed develops heat enough to produce incandescence.

The birch log and the flame from it are the same substance. The substance has but reversed its pressure preponderance.

Here is a substance which appears to attract when its power-time is in preponderance and its volume contracted, and to repel when its speed-time is in preponderance and its volume expanded.

If substance attracts, something else must repel.

It is unreasonable and illogical to say that substance can both attract and repel.

What is there in this universe other than substance?

There is the motion of substance.

Does substance attract and motion repel?

Let us consider this. We are familiar with the fact that warm air rises and cold air sinks.

Here is the same substance proceeding in opposite directions, certainly not because of a difference in substance.

We are familiar with the rain falling to the ground and the vapor rising to the clouds.

Here again is the same substance proceeding in opposite directions.

We are familiar with the expulsion of water by oil, of naphtha by water, of ether by naphtha, of hydrogen by air, and innumerable other substances which repel other substances for some good reason.

We are also familiar with the fact that the ability of different substances to expel or repel each other is a relative one.

We are familiar with the attraction of chlorine for sodium, of nickel for iron, of fluorine for hydrogen, of boron for nitrogen, bromine for potassium and innumerable other substances which attract other substances for some good reason.

We are also familiar with the fact that the ability of different substances to attract each other is a relative one.

We are also familiar with methods whereby opposing substances can be induced to attract each other by forcing a union under high pressure, or by using a catalyst as a mediator.

Likewise, we are familiar with methods which will separate bonds between united substances.

Can it be possible then, that substance has any relation to those qualities which we call attraction or repulsion?

If, by changing the volume of a mass, it rises instead of obeying the pull of gravitation, is it not reasonable and logical to assume that volume has some power to modify gravitational pull.

If, by changing the temperature of two equal masses of the same substance, they separate, and if by equalizing them, they come together, is it not reasonable and logical to assume that temperature has some relation to the phenomena of attraction and repulsion?

If, by changing the temperature of two equal masses of the same substance, it changes their volumes, densities, pressures and all other dimensions, is it not logical to assume that dimension is in some manner related to the phenomena of attraction and repulsion?

One needs no more convincing proof of the relative ability of mass to attract and to repel than this well known characteristic of all elemental substances to find each other.

When substances find each other, they also find their opposites which revolve in exactly the same plane.

Every state of motion is seeking a similar state of motion.

Every state of motion has not only its own pressure zone, but its own plane.

All of the elements of matter revolve in their own separate planes. The atoms of each element will eventually come together when released from locked positions in higher potentials.

Every mass revolving in one plane resists the proximity of mass revolving in any other plane.

Any compound mass of varying plane will eventually separate into its constituents, each of which will find its true position in its own plane and pressure zone.

Every chemist is thoroughly aware of the relative ability of one mass to attract another, irrespective of distance.

Every chemist knows that units of elements, called ions, break away from certain compounds with varying degrees of violence.

The chemist calls this phenomenon ionization, and thinks of it as a chemical effect, a reaction.

Ions are masses. The law for one microscopic ion is the same as for a planet.

If the chemist would think of all actions as gravitational, and all reactions as radiational effects, he would know that ionization is due to the repellent, separative power of magnetic radio-active force to expel these little planetary ions in order that magnetism may carry out its desire to diffuse electrically accumulated masses.

The supposition that atomic motion is an electrical effect and that the atoms of the elements are thereby exempted from obeying the laws of gravitation, misleads the chemist.

He is also misled by the supposition that all matter is composed of exactly similar negative electrons and positive protons in different quantities arranged differently in each kind of atom.

The chemist assumes that there is one more electron in mercury than in gold.

This new theory is now leading him to the expenditure of useless effort in trying to "knock" one electron out of mercury to produce gold.

One might as well try to "knock" a planet out of our solar system.

The fact is the reverse of the chemist's assumption.

If one electron could be "knocked out," and if that act would change mercury, the change would not be to gold. It would be to thallium or to lead. Likewise one electron removed from lead would not produce mercury as hoped. It would result in bismuth.

If one of our planets could be "knocked out" of our solar system, the event would increase our zodiacal expansion by at least two degrees, and retard our solar evolution by at least eighty-five million years.

The loss of one electron from the element mercury would be equivalent to a substantial discharge toward negative weakness.

This discharge would cause the plane of mercury to increase its angle to the plane of lutecium, which would be the opposite effect necessary for the production of gold.

The only way to change mercury to gold is to increase the contraction pressure of the mercurial atom and thus change its plane to one slightly nearer that of the lutecium atom.

The chemist recognizes the variable power of substance to attract and repel in that effect which he has termed "valency."

Valency is purely an expression of gravitational variation, as ionization is an expression of radiational variation.

The chemist knows that hydrogen and fluorine atoms, if released in a large room will eagerly find each other.

He knows also that hydrogen and carbon atoms released within an inch of one another will not find each other.

On the contrary, they revolve in planes of such wide angles and their relative positive charges are proportionately so unequal, that they have to be forced together under the very high pressure of the arc lamp to make them combine.

Every chemist knows the variability of pressure in every element at every temperature.

Every physicist knows that condensation alters the direction of any vapor.

The physicist tests the law of gravitation by producing a state of vacuum which is non-existent in nature. In a vacuum, he finds that a feather and a piece of lead are attracted toward the center of the earth with the same velocity.

This is a universe of varying pressures and the production of an abnormal condition in a tube is not a test of the relative power of substance to attract or to repel substance.

If a tube large enough to enclose this planet and long enough to reach the sun's surface could be pumped free of its opposing pressures, the earth would fall to the sun instead of floating in the orbit mapped out for it by the two opposing pressures which determine its position.

Every physicist knows that the specific gravity of every element, compound or mixture differs from that of any other. That quality in substance which we call "weight" is merely an indication of the apparent relative ability of substance to attract substance in proportion to its relative density and potential.

Every metallurgist knows that some alloys can be produced very simply because of the willingness of some metals to unite and the great unwillingness of others.

The metallurgist is accustomed to the use of high pressure in forcing his metals to unite, and the chemist to the use of very low pressures in causing his gases to unite.

Modern science recognizes the varying power of substance to attract and to repel in that effect termed electro-motive force, but its basic cause is presumed to be electrical. Electricity and gravitation are not yet recognized as identical expressions of the same force.

Modern science is perfectly familiar with the oscillatory motion of electromagnetic force, and also with the fact that opposed oscillations are opposed forces.

All of the effects of motion are recorded as dimensions.

Every dimension has its opposites, and every change in preponderance from one opposite to the other simultaneously changes every other one of the eighteen series of opposites to balance that change.

The force of attraction, which is electric, and the force of repulsion, which is magnetic, are both opposite pressure dimensions, and they must change their relations as other dimensions change.

Neither the force of attraction, nor the force of repulsion is in any way an attribute of the One universal substance.

Substance has no power to attract, to repel, to unite or to separate.

These qualities belong to motion and not to substance.

If either of these qualities were attributes of substance, the unchanging One substance would then be changeable.

All mass is accumulated electro-magnetic potential seeking the pressure zone of its potential.

All mass is either charging, in which case it is flowing in an electric stream of centripetal preponderance, or it is discharging, in which case it is flowing in a magnetic stream of centrifugal preponderance.

Mass flowing in a stream is conditioned by the current of the stream.

An electric stream always flows spirally toward the gravitative center of the mass, or system, or wave of systems, toward the apex of each of their cones of energy.

Magnetic streams always flow spirally toward the inertial planes of the mass, or system, or wave of systems, toward the bases of their cones of energy.

These two streams pass each other going in opposite directions in the same cones of energy and all mass carried by the streams is conditioned by their motion.

Attraction and repulsion are merely apparent effects of electric action and magnetic reaction.

Attraction and repulsion are the apparent effects of the opposites of motion.

One is an effect of revolution, the other of rotation.

One is an effect of gravitation, the other of radiation.

One is an effect of contraction, the other of expansion.

One is an effect of inhalation, the other of exhalation.

One is an assembling or associating force, an assimilative force of gravity, or growth, which causes mass to draw together, to integrate, to accumulate. The other is a disassembling or dissociating force, and eliminative force of emission, which causes mass to emanate, to separate, to disintegrate.

One is the force of displacement Which generates high pressures as accumulated potential; the other is the force of replacement which releases high pressures and accumulated potential into low pressures and low potential.

In any mass its constant of centripetal force is its constant of power to attract.

In any mass its constant of centrifugal force is its constant of power to repel.

Let us consider these opposite effects of motion separately. First let us consider the contractive pressure of electricity and its effect, which is that of attraction.

Electricity attempts to displace substance by taking it from its expanded position in inertia, setting it in motion and gathering it together in solid masses.

Charging light units draw closer to each other. They appear to attract one another.

They gravitate toward each other.

They revolve around each other and rotate upon themselves.

As they draw closer together they charge each other, thus mutually assisting each other in remaining in their unstable position of displacement.

Each part of every charging light unit or system appears to attract each other part irrespective of its potential. Contraction of volume is the inevitable effect.

Accumulating mass absorbs heat.

Higher electric pressure increases heat.

Heat absorbing light units are raising their potentials through vitalizing inhalation.

They accumulate potential by nature's process of raising low potentials to the low melting points characteristic of low pressures and low potentials and then freezing them into form at the low freezing points characteristic of low pressures and low potentials; and then repeating this process in the higher potentials of each succeeding octave of inhalation.

Light units which are increasing their potentials are endothermic, contracting, generating light units. Generating light units or systems are centripetal.

Their force is in the direction of nucleal centers of closing spirals.

Centripetal, closing spirals pack accumulating mass more closely together into vortices which are ever whirling toward the apices of ever shortening cones.

The whirling vortices of closing spirals of opposing cones become nucleal centers of maximum integration and maximum resistance to integration.

They are the gravitative centers of forming systems.

They are the focusing points toward which all charging light units of increasing potential, and integrating mass "fall," and become absorbed as heat units of potential energy; and away from which all discharging light units of -lowering potential and disintegrating mass "rise" and are radiated as heat emanations.

Centripetal, closing spirals of opposing cones accumulate positive charge and its accompanying heat resistance into restricted areas at their melding apices which form centers of gravitative force.

The apices of spiral cones are the focusing points of the high potential of their systems.

All light units of increasing potential decrease in volume as they approach these focusing points.

Decrease in volume means increase in density. Increase in density is resisted by magnetic reaction and evidenced in heat.

Heat radiates. Radiation expands and expansion cools the surface of the accumulated mass. Cold generates. Generation contracts. Contraction condenses.

By this process, a contracting shell of high pressure is formed around any heated mass to prevent expansion, and the hot center ever increases in density as it cools.

This is nature's method of changing dimensions of motion in order to produce apparently different substances with which to build the forms thought out by Mind.

No better illustration of nature's processes could be found than a comparison with man's processes of transforming iron into the appearance of other substances by exactly the same methods.

Iron, superheated and plunged into icy water, will appear quite another substance than the iron of which it is composed.

The same iron, or an iron alloy, when cooled in molten lead will have other qualities not there when assembled by the metallurgist.

The pressures employed by man in his processes of transformation give to the substances used by man many and varied appearances and forms.

Just so with the pressures employed by nature in her processes of transformation by growth.

Everything constructed by nature "grows."

Growth is an accumulation and assimilation of electric potential caused by endothermic, inhalative genero-activity, followed by eliminative redistribution as the result of exhalative radioactivity.

Nothing in nature evades the law of growth nor knows another process.

Nature assembles all her forms, and transforms her assembled forms, by raising their opposing pressures to high potentials from low potentials.

Nature heats everything which she wishes to transform through growth in high pressure crucibles, and moulds them by high pressure into the desired forms.

Nature then subjects them to sudden or gradual cooling by sudden or gradual release of pressure exactly as man cools his heated metals after moulding them into the forms desired by him.

Nature freezes her growing things at their characteristic low melting points with every exhalation and melts more for accumulation with each sequential inhalation.

Nature, the great engineer, builds a supporting framework of bone, or of wood, or fibre, for all her growing things, out of low octaves of high potentials, upon which she superimposes her flesh assembled from high octaves of low potentials.

The frameworks of nature's structures require the locked potential positions of higher opposing pressures and higher melting points than is required by the flesh superimposed thereon.

This is as true of the growing vegetable as of this growing solar system.

The low temperature of our atmosphere supplies a sufficient furnace to bring the low potentials of the flesh of growing vegetables to their melting points. The low pressure of expansion then freezes them into the densities appropriate to their low pressures.

The high opposing pressures and temperatures of the sun do exactly the same thing. Planets are melted in its furnace and moulded into shape by the opposing pressure walls which trim and prune them into harmonic spheres of dimensions proportionate to their potential positions.

High pressures produce more dense substances of greater strength for the framework of nature's structures whether those structures are vegetables, animals or solar systems.

Increase in density means decrease in axial of speed-time dimension and increase in orbital of power-time.

Expanded substances are described by chemists as "active" and contracted substances as "inactive." Gases, for example, are classed as active, and solids as inactive states of substances.

That is because expanded substances unite more readily in low potential positions where expansion pressure has separated light units to great distances.

They are so expanded that they integrate readily. Their opposing streams join.

Hard substances on the contrary, do not unite so readily in the low pressures of this planet. They require the force of such high opposing pressures as those of our sun to make them unite.

Two gases such as fluorine (501 —) and lithium (501+) will leap together with explosive violence in ordinary atmospheric pressure.

Pour several liquids in the same stream and soon they will all blend if the planes of their atoms are not too far removed.

Can be no increase or decrease in any effect of motion without a balancing increase or decrease in its opposite effect.

Apparent decrease in activity of a dense mass is merely a lessening of the speed of rotation and a balancing increase of the speed of revolution.

There are two speeds, two opposing speeds, which are equal and opposite.

To apply the brake to one is to accelerate the other and vice versa.

Just so with volume.

Expanded volume has less apparent ability to attract. Therefore, there must be relatively less positive charge in expanded than in contracted volume.

The volume of a hydrogen or lithium atom is greater than that of a beryllium atom, and the volume of beryllium is greater than that of boron. The boron atom has greater power to attract and greater power to repel than the beryllium atom.

The power to attract lessens as volume increases.

The power to repel also lessens as volume increases.

This is true in every one of the octaves of the elements, in every element, in every atom of every element and in every planet and light unit of every atom.

Each element has a different volume and mass and each one, in accordance with its potential positionA stream of metal balls would require the pressure force of a very high temperature to expand their particles so that they would blend as one liquid metal stream.

The constant of activity would not in any way be changed by thus changing its dimensions.

The metal would not become more active by expanding it. The expansion would but retard one time dimension and accelerate the other.

It was not less active while it was contracted. What it lacked in activity of rotation is made up for in activity of revolution.

Activity never lessens and inactivity never increases because of any change of dimension.

Every expression of motion has its equal and opposite expression.

There, has a separate and individual ratio of attraction and repulsion power.

In any mass the decrease in volume is in exact proportion to the increase in its potential.

In any mass the decrease in volume is in exact proportion to the increase in positive charge, contraction pressure and temperature.

Mass of less volume is of relatively higher potential, greater positive charge and greater pressure than a similar mass of greater volume.

Mass of less volume is contracted mass, and similar mass of greater volume is expanded mass.

Contracting mass draws away from similar, expanding mass in the opposite direction, forming an eccentric orbit of revolution around the nucleal center of its system.

The orbit of any contracting mass is ever drawing closer to the nucleal center of its system in closing spiral lines.

All mass with a decreasing orbit is ever accelerating its speed of revolution in that orbit.

All of the conditions precedent to the appearance of increasing ability of mass to attract and to repel have eight conspicuous effects in common. These are increasing centripetal preponderance, pressure, temperature, speed of revolution and positive charge, and decreasing volume, area of orbit and speed of rotation.

On the contrary, all of the conditions precedent to the appearance of decreasing ability of mass to attract and to repel have the eight opposite effects in common. These are decreasing centrifugal preponderance, pressure, temperature, speed of revolution and negative discharge, and increasing volume, area of orbit and speed of rotation.

In any mass the greater its speed of revolution, the greater its power to attract and to repel.

In any mass the greater its speed of rotation, the less its power to attract and to repel.

As all mass is constantly changing both of these dimensions, all mass is varying in its ability to attract and to repel.

Revolution is the opposite of rotation.

One exactly balances the other in accordance with the law that there can be no increase or decrease in any effect of motion without a balancing decrease or increase in its opposite effect.

Also, one eventually overtakes the other, in accordance with the universal law of sequential preponderance in all opposite effects of motion.

Revolution is an effect of motion employed by electricity to increase surface tension pressure in order that it may accomplish its desire of converting the universe into solids.

Electricity conquers magnetism in its sequentially preponderant power of generation and regeneration.

Rotation is an effect of motion employed by magnetism to counteract the desire of electricity by dissociating that which electricity has associated.

Magnetism conquers electricity in its sequentially preponderant power of degenerating that which electricity has generated.

All mass is simultaneously electric and magnetic, but preponderantly one or the other cumulatively in endless repeative sequence.

All mass simultaneously revolves and rotates though one effect is always preponderant while the other one is preparing for its right of preponderance.

All opposite effects of motion are simultaneous in the expression of their sex opposition but preponderant in sequence in each sex expression.

Each oscillation of the opposing electric and magnetic forces is simultaneous, but one is greater than the other.

In this universe of more and less, all division into the more and the less occurs simultaneously, but both unequal divisions are cumulative in their inequality. One always overtakes and overbalances the other though both are progressing in opposite directions.

Man's inhalation, for example, is simultaneously accompanied in a less degree by his exhalation, and conversely his exhalation is accompanied in a less degree by his inhalation.

While he is inhaling in preponderance through his nostrils, he is exhaling in a less degree through every pore of his body. Conversely, while he is exhaling in preponderance through his nostrils, he is inhaling in a less degree through his body.

The time will eventually come when the inhalation-exhalation sequences will become preponderant through his pores. He will then gradually lose vitality until disintegration has conquered his ability to integrate sufficiently to hold his body together as a unit.

Degeneration will eventually conquer generation until regeneration again has its turn.

All idea is repeative and no effect of motion once started ever ends.

The end of an octave is but the beginning of another octave.

The end of a cycle is but the beginning of another cycle.

The end of a wave is but the beginning of another wave.

Also, the end of a life is but the beginning of another life.

There is no death.

Man cannot die, nor can motion end, nor can idea evade repeativeness, nor can sex evade its sequential preponderance.

Attraction and repulsion are opposite sex effects.

If the law which states that "all opposite effects of motion are simultaneous in the expression of their sex opposition, but preponderant in sequence in each sex expression" is sound, then all mass which attracts also simultaneously repels. Also, one of these qualities is preponderant in proportion to the preponderance of one or the other states of motion which determines the potential of the mass.

Furthermore, if the law is true, any mass which is preponderant in its power to attract, eventually becomes preponderant in its power to repel.

If this is true, any mass which is increasing its power to attract, must also be increasing its power to repel in excess of the increase of power to attract in order to attain its alternate right of preponderance. Conversely, for the same reason, any mass which is decreasing its power to attract, must also be decreasing its power to repel in excess of the decrease of power to attract.

The excess in each instance is in universal ratio.

If this is true, there must be a point of equilibrium where the preponderance of gravitational power passes to preponderance of radiational power at both ends of the cycle of motion at which points motion is impossible, except that which is continued by impetus, for in such an equilibrium there could be no force to cause motion.

It has been contended that matter could not both attract and repel for the very reason that one would counteract the other and prevent motion.

This would be true if the opposing states of motion were exactly balanced in every mass.

This is true only at the two passing points above referred to, for at all other positions in the wave of energy the opposing charges are unequally balanced.

Sex is the result.

The two passing points where the opposing forces are in equilibrium are the sexless position 0= and the double tone bi-sexual 4^{+}_{+} which marks the limitations of motion in any wave of energy.

The sexless position is chemically registered in the inert gases, herein known as the master tones, and the bi-sexual position is herein known as the carbon line.

Through these two passing points energy can continue only because of impetus.

At these two passing points all effects of motion are reversed.

The orbit of expanding mass is ever drawing away from the apex of the cone of its system in opening spiral lines, following the contour of the cone toward its base. All mass of expanding orbit is ever decelerating its speed of revolution and accelerating its speed of rotation.

Discharging light units or systems separate or draw away from each other, and also draw away from charging light units or systems. They not only appear to repel each other, but also seem to be repellent within themselves.

Each part of every discharging light unit or system appears to repel each other part, irrespective of its potential.

It radiates away from adjoining masses.

It expands from within itself even as does the system of which it is a part.

As light units separate one from another, they discharge each other.

Discharging light units are those which are releasing potential through devitalizing exhalation.

Light units or systems, which are decreasing their potential are exothermal, expanding, radiating light units.

Radiating light units or systems are centrifugal. Their force is in the direction of the expanding orbits of opening spirals.

The purpose of magnetism is to replace that which electricity has displaced; to dissociate, disassemble, diffuse, disintegrate and radiate that which electricity has associated, assembled, integrated and generated.

Centrifugal opening spirals distribute disintegrating mass over more expanded ecliptic areas, and break up the nucleal, gravitative centers by distributing positive charge over proportionately greater areas which are in equilibrium with the greater areas of negative discharge, thus reducing potential by replacement of that which has been displaced.

It has heretofore been written that all motion is spiral and all direction is curved.

All direction is also universal.

All mass follows spiral orbits either northerly toward, or southerly away from gravitative centers of systems.

All mass seeks the ever changing pressure zones of its own ever changing potentials, revolving and rotating always from west toward east, without any exception in any mass throughout the universe of dimension.

Neither the effect of attraction nor the effect of repulsion is due to substance but to centripetal and centrifugal force of motion.

The effect of attraction belongs to positive electric charge, and this, in its turn, to electric domination.

The effect of repulsion belongs to negative electric discharge, and this in its turn to magnetic domination.

One need have no better illustration of this truth than the piece of iron which leaps to one pole of a "magnet" and apparently is repelled by the other pole.

If the attributes of attraction and repulsion belonged to substance, instead of to motion, the iron of the "magnet," would either attract toward any of its parts or repel from them all.

Much of the misunderstanding regarding the effects of the so-called "magnet" is due to a lack of knowledge of electric and magnetic action and the universality of direction.

An electric stream is flowing swiftly toward the apex of every one of the countless opposing spirals within the "magnetic" bar.

Each opposing spiral cone of energy changes its relations in a manner which will later be made clear.

The pressure and velocity of the stream within each cone of the "magnetized" bar increase in inverse ratio to the square of the lessened distance and to the cube of the lessened volume, as the volume is compressed into closer quarters.

The electric excitation of the "magnetized" bar increases the oscillation of the little pumps of which all matter in motion is composed.

The breathing of the light units of the "magnetized" iron is faster than that of the normal iron. The inhalation-exhalation sequences are so vastly increased that a normal piece of iron "falls" toward the direction of the flow exactly as heavy trees are uprooted and sucked into the maelstrom of the spirally swirling cones of a cyclone.

The effects above described are effects of gravitative preponderance, which universally increase in the direction of north, and north is always at the conical apices of two opposed spiral electric streams which meet at gravitative centers.

Substance has no relation to gravitative or to radiative effects.

Neither pole is attracted to or repelled by the other.

One might as reasonably assert that logs which are speeding through the sluice of an open dam are attracted by the dam and then repelled by it, rather than being carried by the movement of the rushing waters.

Or, one might as reasonably assert that houses and trees which are being sucked into the cone of a whirlwind are attracted by the wind rather than by the motion of the wind.

The electro-magnet, which it properly should be called, does to the iron filings exactly what the whirlwind does to the houses and trees.

The accompanying drawing will show clearly how all of our familiar and safe wind pressures are upset when opposing whirlwind cones sweep over the land.

All effects of motion are whirlwinds.

The nearer the gravitative center, the greater the whirlwind.

The solar system is a whirlwind with Mercury swirling swiftly near the gravitative center where the vast pressures whirl it around the sun in eighty-eight days at a speed of about thirty miles each second, against the earth's eighteen miles, Jupiter's eight and Neptune's leisurely three miles per second.

The gravitative center of any mass in motion is the point of greatest density and least speed - of rotation.

The center of any rotating mass is the point of least axial speed.

Motion ceases at the vortex of a whirlpool in the equilibrium of maximum motion-in-opposition.

Magnetic streams flow universally toward the south just as electric, streams flow universally toward the north. Electric streams degenerate into magnetic streams, which find their south at the bases of cones in which the maximum motion is always in the plane of the equator of the rotating mass.

These are the planes of radiation where the maximum radio-active force is near the equator, the hottest part of the surface of any mass. The centers of the bases of the generative cones are at the poles of rotation, the coldest part of any mass.

Mass is disintegrated by a magnetic force exerted equatorially just as it is integrated by an electric force exerted axially.

Just as the phenomenon of attraction is caused by the flow of a centripetal stream whirling spirally, with ever increasing swiftness, toward the vortex in the apex of the cone of its spiral, so is the phenomenon of repulsion caused by the flow of a centrifugal stream whirling spirally, with ever decreasing swiftness, toward the base of the cone of its spiral.

The electric stream displaces substance by accumulating the universal constant, under increasingly higher pressure equilibriums, into relatively solid masses, and the magnetic stream diffuses that solidity into tenuity by releasing those high pressures.

Affinity, in the chemical sense, and attraction in the electrical sense, are analogous.

Both are effects of gravitation.

The attraction of gravitation is but a resultant of centripetal force of which deceleration of the speedtime dimension of the universal constant and acceleration of power-time is the condition precedent.

Unequal valency; in the chemical sense, and repulsion in the magnetic sense, are analogous.

The repulsion of radiation is but a resultant of centrifugal force of which acceleration of speed-time dimension of the universal constant and deceleration of power-time is the condition precedent.

The preponderance of one of the opposites of motion is, therefore, the condition which must be present in mass in order that it may be preponderant in its ability either to attract or to repel.

Substance, then, merely appears to attract or to repel, and that appearance is relative.

Both forces are equal. A preponderance of one is balanced in its opposite by a preponderance of the other. The two, added together, cause an appearance of stability which is maintained, for a time, by motion.

The relative ability of a substance to attract and to repel is in the same ratio as the increase or decrease of the opposing pressures and other dimensions which determine the potential of a charging or discharging system.

In any mass the apparent ability to attract increases with increase of positive charge and decrease of volume; also the apparent ability to repel increases with increase of negative discharge and decrease of volume.

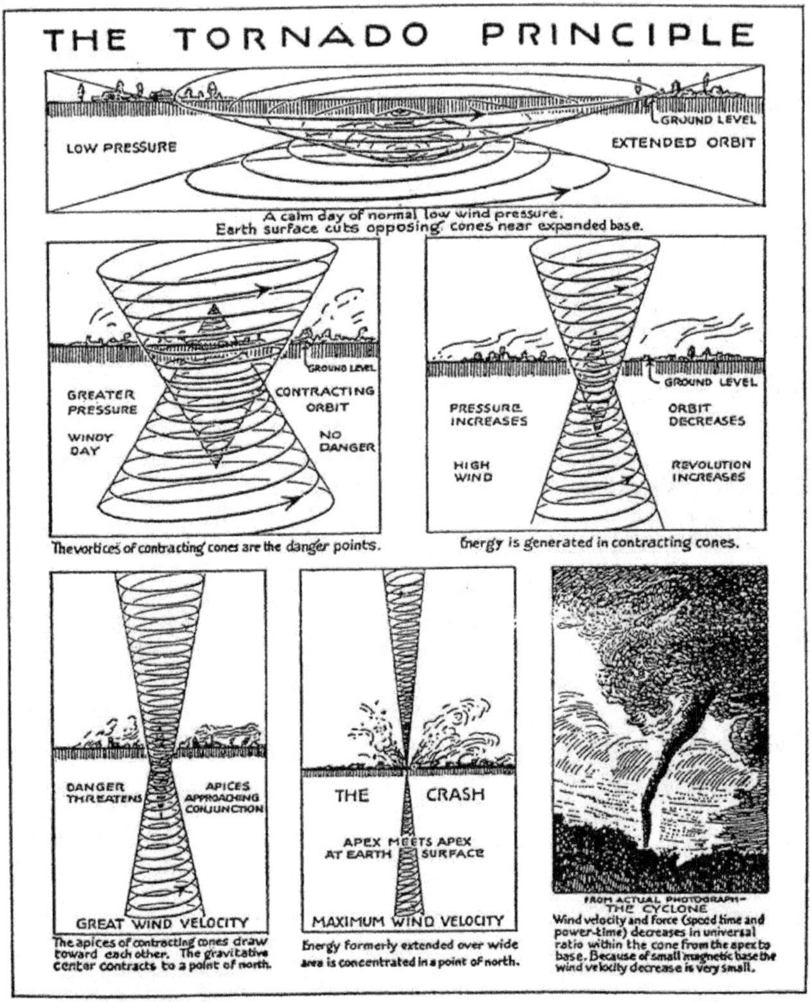

THE DANGER POINT OF A WHIRLWIND IS A STRONG GRAVITATIONAL POINT OF NORTH TOWARD WHICH HEAVY OBJECTS RISE AS NAILS RISE TO A "MAGNET."

In any mass the preponderance of the apparent ability to attract or to repel is proportionate to its preponderance of positive charge or negative discharge.

In any mass increase of positive charge is accompanied by increase of negative discharge in universal ratio until the conductivity of negative discharge exceeds the inductivity of positive charge, in accordance with the universal law of sequential preponderance of all opposite effects of motion.

PERIODICITY OF ATTRACTION.

The relative ability of the elements of matter to appear to attract is in the order of their periodicity, as has been shown in the chart of the periodic table of the elements.

The first gravitational tone is 1+, the lithium line.

The second gravitational tone is 2+, the berylium line.

The third gravitational tone is 3+, the boron line.

There are mid-tonal pressure walls, in the seventh, eighth, ninth and tenth octaves which in their aggregate constitute one tone between 3+ and 4++.

The fourth tone, 4++, is a bisexual tone in which the ability to attract is equal to the ability to repel. This progression is increasingly male in sex and increasingly electropositive in charge.

PERIODICITY OF REPULSION.

The relative ability of the elements to repel is in the same order.

The first radiational tone is 1 — , the fluorine line.

The second radiational tone is 2—, the oxygen line. The third radiational tone is 3 — , the nitrogen line.

The same relatively repellent order regarding mid-tonal pressure walls prevails on the female side of 4++, as on the male side.

The planes of these opposing pressure walls vary from 0° at 0= to 90° at 4++.

1+ and 1— are absolutely parallel to each other, likewise 2 + and 2— , and 3 + and 3 —, in each wave, but in each half of the wave the pressure walls oppose the opposite halves of the adjoining waves.

The plane of the double tone, 4++ in the fifth octave, is at an angle of 90° to the south inertial and secondary vertical planes of their cubes, and is parallel to the primary vertical plane. The other 4* positions approximate these relations.

The relations of the planes of the tonal pressure walls is of vast importance and together they form one of the most important of the dimensions.

If there is such incontrovertible evidence that the ability of mass to appear to attract and to repel mass is but relative because of the variation in states of motion within each mass, is it not better to rewrite the law as it has been suggested at the beginning of this chapter?

Every mass has the apparent relative ability to attract and to repel every other mass, its relative ability depending on its relative potential.

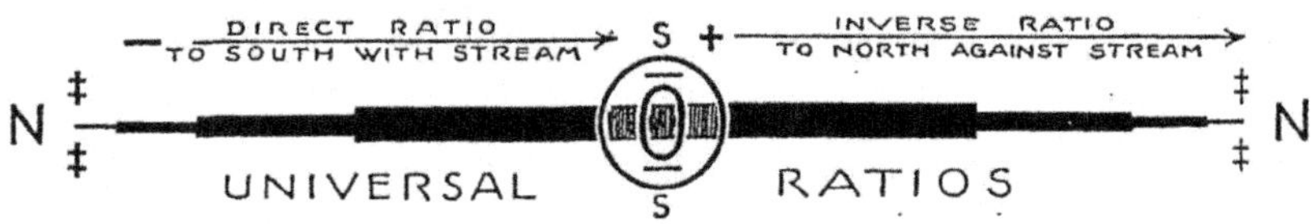

CHAPTER XII

GRAVITATION AND RADIATION

Gravitation is the generative force and radiation is the degenerative force of the universal constant. These are the opposing powers which, within all mass, seek an equilibrium zone of pressure for the potential of that mass.

Gravitation is the generative force of increasing potential and the regenerative force of decreasing potential.

It is the power within the electric force of action to attract the electric force of action.

It is the contractive power within electricity to divert the universal constant of energy into centripetal vortices of closing spirals of increasing speed, thereby attracting similar states of motion into an accumulation of mass the pressure of which increases toward its center.

It is an expression of the power of electricity to accumulate by induction and, by so doing, to force magnetism to increase its resistance to that accumulation.

It is the inductive force.

It is the desire within the electric force of action to integrate into the appearance of form.

It is the power of electricity to associate by displacement.

Radiation is the power of magnetism to dissociate by replacement.

Radiation is the degenerative force of decreasing potential.

It is the power within the magnetic force of reaction to resist the electric force of action.

It is the separative force which repels, spreads, separates, diffuses and redistributes that which has been assembled by the collective force.

It is the conductive force.

The attraction of gravitation and the repulsion of radiation is nature's simple method of distribution and redistribution of all masses, so that each mass will find its proper position.

It is not proper to conceive either of these apparently opposite forces as two forces.

The south wind and the north wind are not two winds. They are the same wind blowing in opposite directions.

It is more correct to say that gravitation and radiation are processes.

The one motive force which directs these processes is equally divided into opposite effects, but these opposite effects are unequally balanced.

The unequal divisions of the two, opposites totalled together constitute an equilibrium.

The One force never subdivides into any minus expression of force without counterbalancing that minus with an equal and opposite plus.

Gravitation is a synthetic process of putting things together, and radiation an analytic one of taking them apart.

The chemist uses these processes in every action and reaction.

Consider for example the reduction of iron oxide at high temperature by passing a jet of hydrogen over it.

What happens?

The hydrogen falls toward the higher potential of the oxygen of the iron which is sufficiently expanded by the high temperature to absorb the hydrogen, and the hot iron is sufficiently expanded to release the oxygen.

This is an effect of gravitation in respect to the oxygen and the hydrogen.

They unite, they mutually integrate, and freeze into amorphous crystals of such extended orbits that they assume the liquid state known as "water."

On the contrary, it is an effect of radiation in respect to the iron and the oxygen.

Both the iron and the oxygen have been brought to such a state of expansion that their ability to hold together is gradually weakened until their pressure preponderance is reversed.

Attraction has changed to repulsion.

The iron expels the oxygen which falls toward the proper pressure zone for so expanded a state of motion.

The oxidation process is an effect of the electric pressure of gravitation. The reduction process is an effect of the magnetic pressure of radiation.

They exactly balance.

The reduction in valence, pressure, temperature and other dimensions of the iron is balanced by an exact increase of the dimensions of the hydrogen oxide.

The plus of gravitation in any mass is always balanced by the minus of radiation in some other mass, in accordance with the pressure laws, "every pressure develops an equal and opposite pressure," and "the degeneration of any mass is exactly balanced by the regeneration of another mass." All mass is constantly in motion.

This is a universe of perpetual motion. The universal constant of energy is expressed by mass in motion.

Every mass is continually changing its dimensions in accordance with its relation to every other mass.

Change in the position of mass causes change of every dimension of that mass.

"All mass is potential out of place, and all mass constantly seeks the proper pressure zone for its changing potential."

All mass constantly runs the entire gamut of every dimension of the wave of energy of which it is a swirling part, until it has run the entire cycle represented by that wave.

No mass can remain fixed in position, not even that which has been apparently arrested in its motion.

The apple, obeying the laws of gravitation falls to the ground to seek the pressures for its relatively high potential, where it is apparently arrested in its motion. In reality it never ceases to fall until it has reached the center of the planet.

It merely changes its dimensions.

The disintegrating apple rises in the air to seek the proper pressures for the relatively low potential left behind by the electric stream which continued to the gravitative center of the planet.

Like all mass, the apple is simultaneously accumulating and distributing its accumulation of energy.

It is both charging and discharging.

The interruption of the apple's fall to the earth's center and subsequent reversal of the charge within the mass of the disintegrating apple, does not alter the opposite directions of motion either for the charge or for the discharge.

The accumulated electric potential continues spirally north by way of east in the electric stream to the planet's center, and the disintegration emanations continue south by way of west, in the magnetic stream of the earth's ecliptic.

The bound energy being released by the disintegrating apple exchanges its power-time preponderance for speed-time preponderance.

The balancing opposite of greater power-time is within the planet.

Consider familiar effects of gravitation and apply that observation to others less readily understood. The apple falls to the ground.

The gas rises into the air.

The planet floats in space.

The apple and the gas are potentials out of place. When released one falls, the other rises. One gravitates and the other radiates toward the pressure zones of their respective accumulations of potential, and they pass each other going in opposite directions.

A planet is potential in place for the moment, ...

as the stone heretofore was removed before being dropped into the water.

If suddenly it were released from out beyond Neptune's orbit, what would happen?

Assuming that it held itself together and did not explode in so low a pressure zone, it would fall with increasing swiftness toward the sun in a line ever slightly curving northeasterly until it reached the orbit from which it had been removed.

Arriving at the plane of its former orbit, it would sink below it toward the sun with decelerating speed, then after oscillating• above and below for a time to lose its impetus and to find the inertial equilibrium position of its potential, it would eventually proceed in approximately the same orbit, as before. It would have been somewhat damaged by expansion and surface ionization. Its potential would be slightly lowered as a consequence of its adventure in lower pressure zones, and therefore its orbit would be slightly farther from the sun than before its removal.

Once more, imagine the giant hand picking up the planet and removing it in the opposite direction, toward the sun instead of away from it.

If suddenly released within Mercury's orbit, for example, what would happen?

For the purpose of analogy, let us forget the fact that its low density in comparison to that of Mercury would cause its surface to become white hot and its oceans to disappear in a tenuous vapor. It would fall away from the sun curving southeasterly towards its orbital plane of pressure at an ever decreasing speed, exactly as an atom of gas would rise from the earth and fall at an ever decreasing speed, in an ever curving southeasterly line toward its proper plane of pressure.

The dimensions of this planet would not permit it to remain in Mercury's 'pressure zone, any more than the density of a wooden ball would allow the ball to remain under water in the pressure suitable to a stone.

It would approximately find its former orbit, but because of the increased potential absorbed during its adventure in higher pressure zones, its orbit would be slightly nearer to the sun' than before its removal.

This universe of motion is one of equilibrium from the beginning of motion to maximum motion, during which progression stability exchanges its reality for an illusion of stability.

There is a true position for every potential.

The true position must be found for the exact dimensions of the universal constant of energy which is stored up as mass.

The desire of mass to find the position appropriate to its changing potential is the cause of all motion of mass.

All mass, seeking the true position for its changing potential, displaces other mass which is also seeking the true position for its changing potential.

All mass displaced must be replaced by its exact equal and opposite.

The present theory that the moon would fall to the earth if it were not sustained by its motion is a mistaken one.

The moon is not sustained in its position because of its motion, but because of its potential which demands its own equilibrium pressure.

The earth and the moon push each other away by their preponderance of expansion pressure with greater violence than they pull each other together by their contraction pressure.

The moon is assisting in the replacement of displaced energy and is ever on its way toward inertia, following its spirally curving path through such aeons of time that its successive orbits appear exactly equal in dimension.

If the moon were detained in one position for a time, it would race to the place where normally it would have been had it not been detained.

Just so with the planets.

The earth would not fall into the sun if motion ceased, any more than a balloon would drop to the earth, or a cork sink in water.

The hydrogen expelled from the sun cannot drop back to the sun. The expansion pressure of the sun's radioactivity will not permit it.

The expulsion of the planets by the sun and the impossibility of their return is based on the same principle. The difference is only one of relative potential.

Mass in motion cannot cease its motion.

Mass is an unstable condition which cannot remain unchanged for one second.

Instability cannot become stabilized.

The motions of the planets and their satellites are not continuations of an original impetus, nor are they continued because of the non-resistance of the ether.

They are revolving in their orbits and rotating upon their axes because they are floating in the flowing streams and whirling vortices of their own particular waves of energy accumulation. They cannot do otherwise than follow the direction of the pressures from behind, and the suction from in front. They are ever seeking a place of rest and never finding it, so long as they are burdened with the form of concept.

Rest from ceaseless motion can only come to them in inertia by total redistribution of their accumulated mass.

Diffusion and disappearance in inertia is the lot of planets as it is of men and of all evolving things.

Slowly changing their dimensions, they are all completing their centrifugal journeys south by way of west to their havens of rest where they await their regeneration.

Slowly expanding, they are drawing away from the sun, assisted by the sun in their recession.

The sun of the system is pushing them all slowly away to cool, and drawing unto itself new light units for its regeneration which will enable it to replace the ejected ,planets and to continue its own potency.

The planets are the finished product of the sun's fashioning and the regenerative light units are the raw product from which the planets are fashioned.

As the sun is preponderantly pushing the planets, so are the planets doing, likewise with their satellites, the grandchildren of the sun.

When the planets left the equatorial plane of the sun they were even then preponderantly radiative masses of such dimensions that their expulsion was imperative.

As the sun's desire to push them farther and farther away exceeds its desire to attract them, their dimensions gradually adjust themselves to this desire.

The nearer a mass is to its sun, the denser the mass, the higher its freezing point, the higher its equilibrium pressure the smaller its volume, the faster its revolution, the slower its rotation, the more nearly parallel its plane of revolution to the solar ecliptic, the greater the positive charge, the greater the eccentricity and the higher the potential, the greater is the ability of mass to attract the positive charge of other mass and to expel its negative discharge.

The farther a mass is from its sun, the more tenuous the mass, the lower its freezing point, the lower its equilibrium pressure wall, the larger its volume, the slower its revolution, the faster its rotation, the greater the angle of its plane of revolution to the solar ecliptic, the less its eccentricity,, the weaker the negative discharge and the lower the potential, the less the ability to attract other mass and to assist its own expulsion from other mass of higher potential.

To expect this planet to fall to the sun if its motion were checked is equivalent to expecting an inflated balloon to drop to earth.

If these statements are demonstrable, then the Newtonian law cannot be true, for every change of dimension whatsoever in any mass alters the ability of that mass to conform to the requirements of that law either by exceeding those requirements or by falling short of them.

Every change of dimension in a mass changes all the dimensions in the mass.

This universe of dimension is divided into pressure compartments of states of motion which vary in orderly ratios. Between the compartments are inertial walls which readjust their positions with every changing dimension of motion in the universe.

A ball falling to the ground simultaneously displaces every atom in the universe and changes its dimensions.

Something must simultaneously rise from this planet toward inertia, to replace the falling ball.

Mass expanded to greater volume must rise to the proper pressure zone for that increased volume. Low potential must rise to replace high potential which has fallen.

The farthermost star must contract or expand to adjust its density to the changed potential thus caused.

All of the planets and satellites of any system owe their positions of the moment to their dimensions and respective relations of the moment.

They are all constantly falling toward the violet of disappearance, in positions appropriate to their expanding dimensions of decreasing potentials.

In the same way, all of the generative light units which are regenerating any system are constantly falling toward the yellow of maximum incandescent appearance, in positions appropriate to their contracting dimensions of increasing potentials.

Dimensions are as relative as the state of motion which they measure.

All dimensions of mass simultaneously contract and expand with its changing potentials.

The inertial planes which lie between any two masses or systems are relatively closer together in dense compact systems than in expanded systems of more widely separated parts.

If opposing dense masses are forced into closer proximity, the four pressure zones which lie between the gravitational centers of the masses and their inertial planes are more restricted.

The more restricted the pressure zones of a system, the more restricted the orbits of all planets and satellites within the four pressure zones of that system.

Restricted orbits demand an orderly acceleration of all masses revolving within them.

Accelerated mass revolving around the nucleus of a system increases the generative power of the vortex of that system, its maximum increase being at the perihelions of the planes of revolution of all the masses of the system.

Accelerated revolution charges. Charging bodies attract.

Accelerated rotation discharges. Discharging bodies repel.

The ability of a mass to attract increases as the speed of revolution increases.

The ability of a mass to repel increases as the speed of rotation decreases.

Increase of generative power of a system means increase of the centripetal force of the system.

Increase of the centripetal force of a system means increase of the potential of a system.

Increase of potential means increase of positive charge.

Increase of positive charge means increase of power to attract.

The ability of one mass to attract another depends upon the relative positive charge of each and its relative position in respect to other masses.

Increase of speed of revolution of the planets of a system means deceleration of rotation of the planets of that system.

Deceleration of rotation of the planets of a system means decrease of the centrifugal force and consequent increase of the centripetal force of that system.

The ability of one mass to repel another depends upon the relative negative discharge of each and its relative position in respect to other masses. Let us repeat the first law of gravitation.

"Every mass has the relative apparent ability to attract and to repel every other mass, its relative ability depending upon its relative potential."

Increased centripetal force due to increased speed of revolution of masses revolving in restricted vortices, together with the lessened centrifugal force caused by retarding the rotation of the masses revolving in such vortices, necessarily raises the potential of a system.

All dimensions of such systems change with the increased ability of the system to generate.

Volume decreases. Orbital areas decrease.

Decrease of volume is exactly balanced by acceleration of revolution. Equal areas must be covered in contracted orbits as in expanded orbits of equal mass:

In a contracted orbit, thirty trillion revolutions per second may be necessary to balance the area covered by an expanded orbit making one revolution in ten years, but an equilibrium of the universal constant must be maintained.

Melting points are higher in contracted orbits. All standard units simultaneously change.

Just so with all other dimensions. Their change would be purely relative and always in balance.

The coefficients of all changes of dimensions of given masses would be in equilibrium at all times as equal totals of the universal constant.

The attraction of gravitation in favoring the generation of energy is enabling electricity to accumulate as mass.

All mass consists of energy accumulated by the attraction of gravitation into the appearance of form.

All form is held together more or less closely by the relative force of gravitation which accompanies mass of various dimensions and relations.

The law for big mass is the same as that for little mass.

The law of gravitation which maps out the orbit of the light unit within the atom is exactly the same as that which maps out the orbit of a planet of a solar system.

In considering the effects of gravitation, it is difficult to project one's mind beyond the confines of this solar system. In fact one's observations and experiences are so purely local that one's mind is rather closely bound to the effects of gravitation upon this planet alone.

It is difficult to realize that this solar system is, on a large scale, but the repeative effect of an atom of iron or manganese.

It is difficult to realize that the planetary masses within the atom of iron have as relatively great a variation of ability to attract and to repel as have the planets of our solar system.

It is also difficult to realize that our whole solar system is subject to the gravitational pull of the north overtone point of the wave of which it is but one atom.

Science considers the attraction of gravitation of the solar system as an entirely different effect from the effect of motion within an atomic system.

Atomic motion is presumed to be non-subject to the laws of gravitation. Science names one "gravitation" and the other an "electrical effect." Both effects are the same.

Also are both effects born of the same conditions.

Within an atom the planets move in the planes of the orbits of their proper and changing pressures in a constant endeavor to find the proper pressures of their changing potentials, exactly as do the planets of a solar system.

Until it is very near the nucleal sun, the charging light unit of a generative atom does not take a short cut across lots through higher pressures to fall crashing into its sun any more than does the charging light units of a solar system.

It contracts gradually as it falls spirally toward the sun, and its potential, equilibrium pressure and melting point constantly rise as it falls.

Nor does the discharging light unit of a degenerative atom take a short cut across lots through lowering pressures to break suddenly and explosively into a tenuous cloud at the inertial plane of disappearance, at the farthermost bounds of its wave cycle.

It leaves its nucleal sun with great force until it finds its proper potential. Then it expands gradually as it falls spirally away from its sun, its potential, equilibrium pressure and melting point constantly lowering as it falls.

If the movements of planets and satellites are effects of gravitation and the same effects in smaller mass are "electrical effects," why do smaller masses exactly follow the laws of the larger masses?

The light units of an atom seem independent of the earth's gravitative center but actually they are not. All are revolving true to the planes of their respective potentials.

The moons of Jupiter do exactly the same thing in respect to the solar gravitative center of this system, yet they are not considered "an electrical effect."

They fall toward the sun and away from it with the same apparent disregard that light units of a system evidence in respect to other masses outside their own systems.

Even their accelerations and decelerations are effected by causes other than by whether they are moving toward the sun or away from it.

A later volume will precisely chart the swirling drift of the so-called "ether of space" within and outside of the solar ecliptic area. This drift carries the planets of the solar system with it as relentlessly as particles are carried in the swirling eddies of a rushing stream.

All effects of gravitation are electric effects, and all effects of radiation are magnetic effects.

All effects of motion are electro-magnetic effects.

All mass has a series of gravitative centers toward which it evidences its allegiance in the order of its potential relation.

As a private in the army takes his orders from an under officer, whose group in turn moves as a unit under command of a higher officer and so on until the entire army is coordinated under the command of one supreme officer, so does low potential obey the gravitational commands of low potential, and various states of accumulated potential obey the gravitational commands of accumulated potential, and so on until the entire mass is coordinated under one supreme gravitative center.

Every wave of energy constructs resisting pressure walls between its south and north planes, and no mass can disregard those pressures.

Within each wave of energy, all mass moves from low to high and back again to low potential as a marble follows a groove, or as a train follows a track, or as a brook finds the sea.

Let us consider each effect, that of falling and rising, as both gravitative and radiative, also electric and magnetic.

An apple falling to the ground is an inductive electrical effect.

It falls to the ground because gravitation attracts it to the ground.

The positive charge of the apple seeks the greater positive charge of the earth.

The falling apple charges the planet by induction, which raises the planet's potential. The greater proximity of the masses also raises the planet's potential.

The induced positive charge of the apple continues centripetally in the generative flow toward the center of the planet.

The resistance to the assimilation of the apple's positive charge by the planet registers itself in the exact amount of heat which left the apple.

The absorption of the apple's heat, contraction pressure, potential and electropositive charge is an electrical effect of discharge of the apple and an added charge to the planet.

It is an exothermic effect in respect to the apple, and an endothermic effect in respect to the planet.

The absorption of the apple's electric potential by the planet is a gravitational effect because the apple and the planet mutually attract each other and it is also an electric effect because of the absorption of the positive charge of one by the other.

Both apple and planet fall toward each other.

If the apple were as large and as dense as the planet, both would move toward each other with equal speed.

The apple is so small and the planet so large that the deviation of the earth's path is negligible.

Not so with a body like the moon, however, which materially affects the earth's orbit as the two unequal partners whirl in their celestial dance.

Returning to the apple and the planet, as the positive charge of the apple continues its centripetal journey toward the centre of the planet, the negative discharge of the apple expands toward disappearance in the opposite direction.

One "falls," the other "rises."

It is the positive charge which "falls" and the negative discharge which "rises."

The positive charge falls toward positive charge expelling negative discharge as radioactive emanations.

If positive charge falls toward positive charge, it is logical to say that the principle which governs positive charge alone has the ability to attract.

The disintegrated apple rises from the ground because radiation repels it and positive charge expels it.

The negative discharge of the apple seeks the greater expanse of low potential.

Its rising is a radiative effect in respect to the planet from which it is centrifugally rising to seek its own potential.

As it rises, it expands until it finds its orbit in the pressure zone of its potential.

It may impact against the inertial plane of another mass toward which it would centripetally fall and become regenerated.

This would be a gravitative effect in respect to the mass toward which it fell.

Its regeneration by impact against the inertial plane of another mass causes it to contract.

It becomes electro-positive.

Its positive charge is attracted by the potential of the mass toward which it falls and by which it is absorbed as nourishment and finally discharged once more as radiative emanations.

This is the manner of assembling and disassembling of every form of idea.

This is the manner of accumulation and distribution of all energy.

This is the manner in which all bodies are nourished and famished.

This is the process of vitalization and de , vitalization.

All effects of motion are gravitational and radiational effects. Also they are electric and magnetic effects just as they are likewise chemical effects.

Let us now consider the various gravitational and radiational expressions one by one.

Fortunate it is that all of these expressions have dimensions and that all dimensions are measurable.

Let us first briefly consider them in their relation to the subject under discussion, which is the apparent power to attract or to repel.

Let us then, consider ways and means of measuring them and see if, by so doing, some of nature's long guarded secrets will not become simple to comprehend and to utilize.

CHAPTER XIII

EXPRESSIONS OF GRAVITATION AND RADIATION

UNIVERSAL DIRECTION

The cycle of a wave is an orderly progression in the universal direction from south to north by the way of east, and back again to south by the way of west.

All masses revolve from the west toward the cast around the nucleal centers of their systems throughout the entire cycle of their waves.

All masses rotate upon axes throughout the entire cycle of their waves from the west toward the east of their masses.

To these laws, there are no exceptions.

Numerous apparent exceptions, such as the retrogression of Neptune and her satellite, the moons of Uranus and the outer moons of Jupiter and Saturn, are thoroughly in accord with the absolute laws of universal direction.

All direction of motion is universal.

Motion implies direction, demands direction in which to move.

In the dimensionless universe of motion, direction is non-existent.

In the universe of the illusion of dimension, direction is one of the necessary illusions which creates the appearance of dimension.

Direction is, therefore, an illusion which we familiarly call an effect of motion.

All effects of motion are expressed in apparent opposites.

It is well to recall the fact that the concept of motion is universally simultaneous and its expression sequential.

The attraction of gravitation and the repulsion of radiation are instantaneous and continuous. Time is not consumed in transferring the concept of any intended expression of energy throughout the dimensionless universe.

The action which is an expression of the intent has dimension and therefore consumes time.

In other words, the concept image of all idea of thinking is universally simultaneous, but the production and reproduction of the form of idea, through motion, is a series of events which are sequential.

All opposite effects are positive and negative, or more and less, or plus and minus.

Like all other effects of motion in the universe of dimension, direction has its opposites.

In this universe of more and less, the opposites of that effect of motion which we call "direction" are north and south.

All direction begins at the pressureless plane of south and ends at the opposed pressures plane of north.

North is the electro-positive plus direction of the more, and south is the electro-negative minus direction of the less.

The plus electric force is always away from the south toward north and the minus magnetic force is always away from the north and back to the south.

North begins at south at the point where energy expresses itself by impact against the inertial plane.

At this point, energy simultaneously measures the intensity of its concept in harmonic circles on inertial planes over areas which become the bases of opposing cones of energy. It also measures the intensity of its concept at the intersection of the primary and secondary vertical inertial planes at altitudes which become the apices of those opposing cones. The axes of those cones then become the charging pole areas of all mass and the line of its forming wave.

Energy simultaneously measures its volume intensity by connecting the circular inertial bases of conceptual cones with their apices.

The harmonic circles which measure the bases of cones are the octave conceptual dimensions of the energy wave of measurable dimension.

The apices of the cones are the overtones of the wave.

The line of increasing force is from the magnetic base following the northerly electric stream to the apex of every cone of energy.

Conversely, the line of decreasing force is from the electric apex following the southerly magnetic stream to the base of every cone of energy.

South is the direction toward stability and the force of non-motion of substance in inertia.

South is the plane of inertia where every expression of energy begins to gather its force from the expanded area of its harmonic circles, with the intent of overcoming the inertia of substance by concentrating it into harmonic spheres at its overtone points of north.

All energy expresses itself in spiral waves. The inertial plane of every wave is its south.

Every direction away from the inertial plane is north.

South is the plane of inertia which apparently divides, as inertia is overcome, into two series of opposing planes of motion, the positive and the negative series.

Each series of opposing planes of motion tilt spirally away from inertia on opposite sides until the harmonic circles which define their areas, have not only attained angles of 90° to it, but have turned half way around. This process can best be visualized by placing two discs together and viewing them edgewise as lines. Then simultaneously tilt and rotate these discs away from each other on opposite edges until they are seen as two circular planes.

South is the birthplace of motion where inertia is overcome and the wheels of the universal machine begin slowly to revolve.

South is the birthplace of all effects of motion where reality ends and illusion begins.

South is the birthplace of idea which becomes more defined in ever increasing solidity as the form of idea contracts toward the north into harmonic spheres which are diffused into tenuity as they expand toward disappearance on the south inertial plane of their birth.

South is the birthplace of time which accelerates all effects of motion in relative ratios as it contracts toward the north, and decelerates them as it expands on its return to south.

South is the aphelion point of all masses moving in orbits around a point of north.

South is the birthplace of all other dimensions of motion which contract all their standard units of measurement as they concentrate in the electric stream flowing north, and expand those same standard units of measurement as they decentrate in the magnetic stream flowing south.

North is the direction of instability and of the force of motion-in-opposition, where the opposites of every expression of energy meet in their maximum of expression.

North is always the vortex of the whirlpool at which every opposite expression of energy meets in bi-sexual union.

North is the point where sex meets sex, where sexes meld as a bi-sexual one sex.

THE CONCEPT OF ALL IDEA MUST PRECEDE ITS EXPRESSION

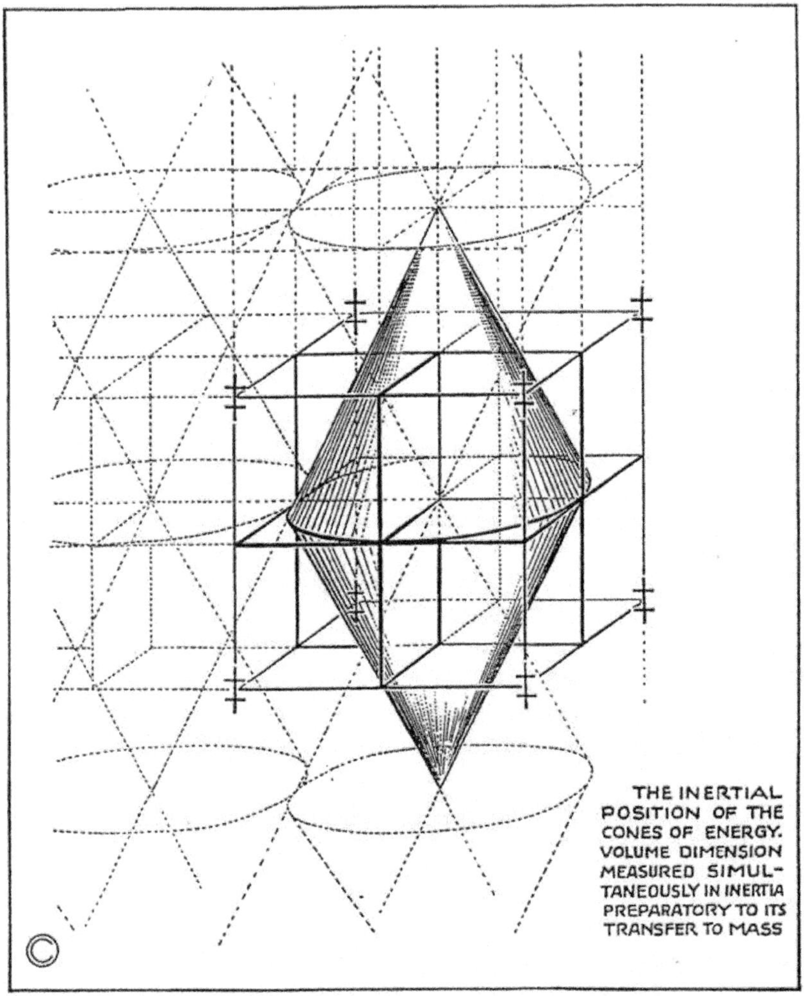

CHART DEFINING POSITION OF CONES OF ENERGY IN CONCEPT IN INERTIA. THE CONCEPT OF ENERGY IS UNIVERSALLY SIMULTANEOUS BUT ITS EXPRESSION IN MOTION IS SEQUENTIAL.

North is the point of self reproduction of the energy of its wave.

North is the perihelion point of all masses moving in orbits around a point of north.

North is the point where generation ends, degeneration begins and reproduction repeats.

Generation is a journey to north from south and degeneration is a return.

Reproduction is a repetition of that journey to mass from plane.

North is the meeting point of all of the positive-negative, plus-minus, male-female pressure walls which have been erected toward both northerly overtone points of every wave, to help sustain the illusion of stability which this universe of motion constantly produces.

Form in motion is a reflection of concept in inertia.

Form is conceived in harmonic plane circles of non - motion, and reflected in harmonic spheres of motion.

North is the point of maximum instability where the maximum gyroscopic motion of the universal machine lends its assistance in supporting the reflection of stability.

The bi-sexual plane of the overtone of every wave is the flywheel of the universal machine, revolving with gyroscopic perfection of balance at an angle of 90° to the inertial plane of concept of its wave of energy.

In this reflected position, its resistance planes are parallel. There are no bevel gears, no precessional motions and no intersecting planes.

Gyroscopic imperfection of motion lies in precessional motion of wheels with bevel gears, and in intersecting planes of resisting pressures.

No better example of gyroscopic imperfection of motion could be found than our own solar system in which all of the planets revolve in planes of some variance to the solar equatorial plane, where resistance pressure walls intersect, and where precessional motion necessitates bevel gears for every wheel.

The overtone plane of gyroscopic perfection is the plane where north meets south and east meets west in bi-sexual unity.

The overtones of gyroscopic perfection are where the electric poles have contracted to a point, and where the ever shortening positive cones of energy turn their outer positive contours to inner negative ones by expanding their bases to the planes of their apices.

The planes of gyroscopic imperfection are the opposing planes of pressure walls ever moving tonally in locked potential positions toward the ultimate north of their waves of energy.

These planes of gyroscopic imperfection are the tonal positions of the elements of matter in which various states of energy are locked within ever contracting pressure compartments of the cones of their waves.

The opposing planes are the positive-negative equal and opposite actions and reactions which constitute the more and the less of positive and negative action and reaction. At these planes, reproduction of motion is only possible through union.

These planes are the planes of sex, male and female, which constitute the division of all effects of motion into the opposites of motion.

North is the direction of the action of effort, as south is the direction of its reaction.

North is the point toward which electricity apparently attempts to gather the universal substance together into one solid inert mass, but failing in this it gathers an illusion of the substance into innumerable separate harmonic spheres through motion of the thinking process.

ALL VORTICES TURN FROM WEST TO EAST
AND THEIR APICES POINT TO NORTH

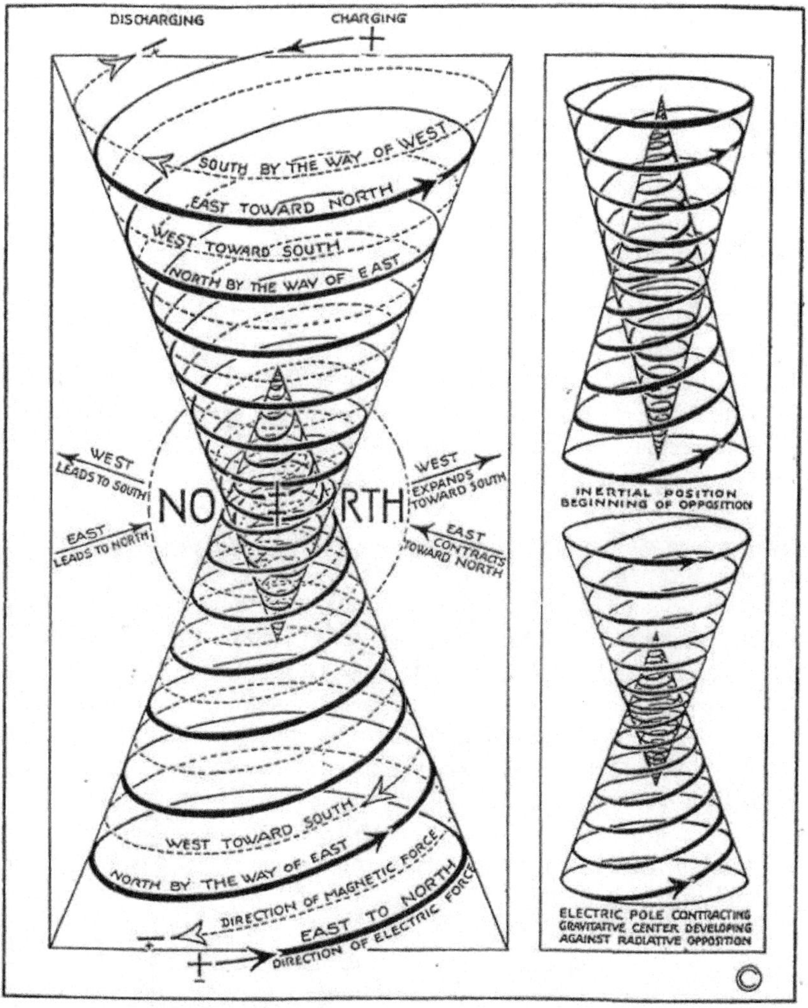

MASS IS ACCUMULATED AROUND A VORTEX. A VORTEX IS FORMED BY THE CONTRACTION OF THE AXES OF TWO OPPOSING CONES OF ENERGY. THE GREATER THE CONTRACTION THE GREATER THE ACCELERATION OF MOTION WITHIN THE VORTEX.

All direction is an effect of gravitation and radiation.

All gravitative effects are electrically dominated.

All gravitative effects are the result of inhalation.

All radiative effects are magnetically dominated.

All radiative effects are the result of exhalation.

Electricity moves always in the direction of north, by the way of east.

Magnetism moves always south, by the way of west.

Nature divides these pressure compartments into octaves, four of which are contracting pressures which she gives to electric control, and the other four are expanding pressures which she gives to magnetic control.

Between the third and the fourth pressure walls in the seventh, eighth, ninth and tenth octaves, the opposing pressures become so great that nature creates mid-tonal pressure compartments where storm centers are much more concentrated and velocity of revolution is multiplied.

Nature accumulates intensity of energy expression in every wave from the southerly inertial line of the inert gases to the northerly carbon line of maximum motion.

The cones of energy, within which all expressions of motion are contained, are ever changing their positions so that their apices are ever moving spirally away from points of concept and returning to those same points.

The accompanying charts of the mechanics of motion will more clearly demonstrate nature's process of energy accumulation and distribution.

The spiral direction of all motion is the cause of the two other opposites of direction known as east and west.

East is a contraction of the inertial south of concept and memory of form toward the north of reflection of concept through motion, and west is north's expansive return toward south.

Motion cannot express itself in the direction of a straight line.

Newton's first law of physics which states that a moving body left to itself moves on forever in a straight line with a uniform velocity, is not in conformity with the laws of motion.

In this universe of varying pressures, all masses floating "in space" constantly move in the direction of their changing potentials. This direction is always spiral.

All motion being spiral, all direction being curved, and all pressure planes being conic sections, electric action can not proceed directly north from south in a straight line, but must progress toward north in a spiral direction.

As electro-positive action proceeds northerly, it contracts.

The direction of contraction is north by the way of east.

East is toward least rotation at the gravitative center of any mass.

The maximum of east is where east meets north following the charging areas of mass. As electro-negative action returns toward south, it expands.

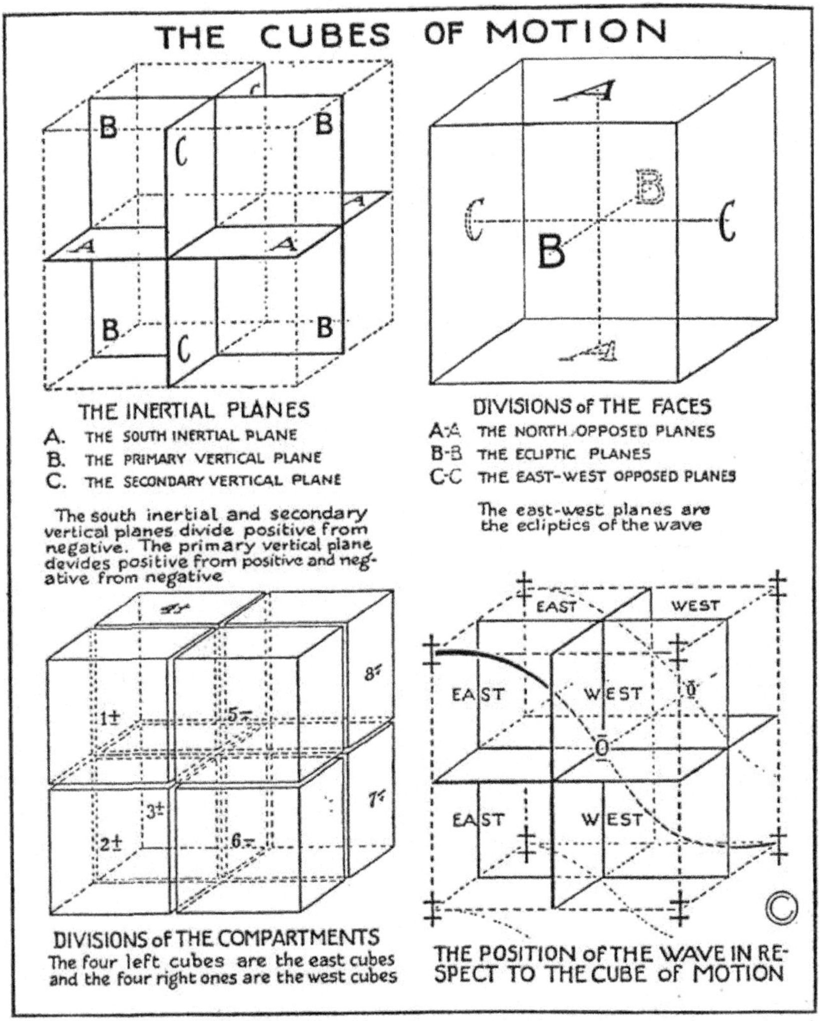

CHART SHOWING DIVISIONS OF THE CUBES OF MOTION
WHICH DEFINE THE LIMITATIONS OF WAVES OF ENERGY.

The direction of expansion is south by the way of west.

West is toward greatest rotation at the surface of any mass.

The maximum of west is where west meets south following the ecliptic plane of any mass.

The minimum exertion of the easterly force of contraction must therefore be in the plane of the equator cf any mass, and its force directed toward the gravitative center of that mass.

In every mass the maximum exertion of the easterly force of contraction is within the charging areas of the generative cones of which the pole of rotation is the axis.

In every mass the maximum exertion of the westerly force of expansion is within the discharging areas of the radiative cones of which the equator is the base.

In every mass north meets east at the pole of rotation, the axis of the generative cones of energy, of which the north easterly electric stream and the south westerly magnetic lines of force are the opposing contours.

It may be well to recall the law of generation: "All mass is generated and regenerated by a contractive pressure exerted in the direction of its gravitative center. Its minimum of generative pressure is exerted from its equatorial plane and its maximum pressure from its pole."

South meets west at the axes of the radiative cones of energy of which the expansion of the equatorial plane of revolution into the isoclinal planes of magnetic force are the contours.

Thus may we repeat the law of radiation of mass: "All mass is radiated and diffused by an expansive pressure exerted in the direction of its surface. Its minimum of radiative pressure is exerted from its pole and its maximum from its equatorial plane."

East contracts toward north and west expands toward south.

Contraction is centripetal and expansion is centrifugal.

The increase of centripetal force of any mass is in the direction of generation, and the increase of centrifugal force is in the direction of radiation.

Centripetal force accumulates and centrifugal force dissipates.

Mass is accumulated in the direction of its generation, and dissipated in the direction of its radiation.

Centripetal force decelerates rotation and accelerates revolution.

Centrifugal force accelerates rotation and decelerates revolution.

The deceleration of rotation is in the direction of generation and deceleration of revolution is in the direction of radiation.

All vortices turn from west to east and their apices point to north.

If the above laws are well founded, the directions of east and north must be related to the attraction of gravitation.

Also, the directions of west and south must be related to the repulsion of radiation.

Also, if deceleration of rotation increases in the centripetal, easterly direction of contraction, decelerated rotation must, in some manner, be related to the attraction of gravitation.

Conversely, if acceleration of rotation increases in the centrifugal, westerly direction of expansion, accelerated rotation must, in some manner, be related to the repulsion of radiation.

Also, if acceleration of revolution increases in the centripetal, easterly direction of contraction, accelerated revolution must, in some manner, be related to the attraction of gravitation.

Conversely, if revolution decreases in the centrifugal, westerly direction of expansion, decelerated revolution must, in some manner, be related to the repulsion of radiation.

THE CREATING UNIVERSE IS A REFLECTION
OF ITS CONCEPT IN INERTIA

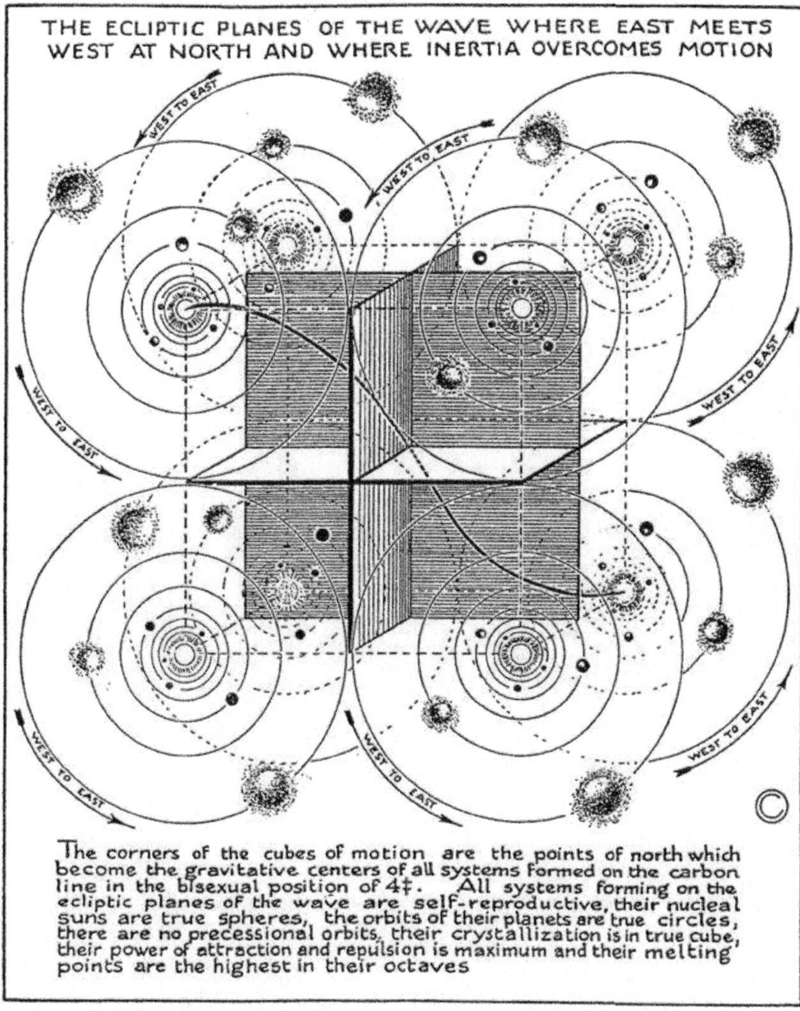

NO "PART" OF THE UNIVERSAL SUBSTANCE PASSES BEYOND THE BOUNDARY OF ITS OWN CUBE OF MOTION. THE INERTIAL PLANES ARE BARRIERS INTO WHICH ALL APPEARANCES DISAPPEAR.

CHAPTER XIV

UNIVERSAL MATHEMATICS—UNIVERSAL RATIOS

Universal mathematics are basically simple dimensions in ratios of equal and opposite tonal actions and reactions of opposite expressions of the One force.

All expression of force is either plus or minus equilibrium of motion-in-inertia.

Universal mathematics are based on the plus and minus relationships of tonal pressures due to the opposition of sex, force and motion.

Opposition means plus and minus.

There can be no expression of force without the evidence of that expression in pressures.

All dimensions are tonal.

All expression of force is tonal. All pressures are tonal.

All effects of motion are tonal. All tones are definite relations.

All definite relations are in accord with the simple formula of the locked potentials.

All direction is either toward the electric force of higher potential which is increasingly resisted or toward the magnetic force of lower potential which is increasingly assisted in the universal ratio.

All directions are pressure directions.

This universe of motion is a universe of varying pressures which cause that motion.

All pressures are either the contraction pressures of charging mass or the expansion pressures of discharging mass.

Let us add to the pressure laws a dimension law.

All dimensions contract in the direction of electric force and expand in the direction of magnetic force in universal ratio.

Equilibrium of motion-in-inertia is represented by zero.

Zero in sex, force and motion means an equilibrium of pressures.

Four means maximum pressure opposition.

The intermediate twos and threes, plus and minus, are the comings and goings between the cold zero of expansion in the violet of inertia and the hot four of contraction in the yellow of opposed motion.

Zero in force does not represent nothingness, nor does plus mean more than nothing nor minus mean less than nothing.

Such a concept of mathematics is not in accord with a universe of the illusion of motion.

The One substance is a tangible substance. It is SOMETHING.

This is not an empty universe. It is not a void. Non-dimension does not mean nothingness.

The universe of the One thinking substance is not one of quantity or dimension.

It is a substance capable of causing an appearance of quantity through the life principle of the substance which we term "energy."

The universal constant of energy is X quantity.

X quantity is apparently divisible.

This divisibility of quantity and its dimensions are relative and measurable.

The relations of its dimensions are in fixed ratios.

These ratios are simple and absolute, but their apparent variability is complex.

The universal constant may be added to or multiplied by, but its accumulation never varies in its relative dimensions.

The dimension X is unimportant for it represents the illusion of a total of apparent motion which disappears in the equilibrium of inertia.

The dimensions of relative ratios are important, for by knowledge of these relations one will be enabled to assemble divided quantities in any desired multiple to produce any desired effect. All dimensions are relative.

All dimensions are either more or less than equilibrium.

This is a universe of more and less.

Every effort of motion which is added to must be equally subtracted from.

Mathematics are bounded by the absolute limits of effects of motion measured by adding to or by subtracting from in universal ratio.

Mathematics cannot transcend universal limitations.

Multiplication and division are but ratios of more and less.

This universe of dimension is limited in its expression to more and less. All units are either plus or minus, therefore all systems other than the double tone unit systems 504t and 100= are either plus or minus in their pressure totals. Every plus pressure total must be balanced by a minus one to maintain a system in equilibrium.

No mathematical conclusion, the product of which does not yield an equilibrium, can be a correct conclusion.

The product of every mathematical conclusion must balance as an equilibrium in order for it to be a correct conclusion.

If correct conclusions regarding effects of motion are mathematically demonstrable, they are also mechanically demonstrable.

Also they are chemically and electrically demonstrable.

Also they are measurable as dimensions in C:heir potential relations of plus X or minus X.

The universal see-saw is ever tilting above and below its balancing point in inertia. Both movements are simultaneous and exactly balanced. The wave is the universal see-saw within which all dimensions are measured.

Many times in these pages it has been stated that a change in any one dimension causes a simultaneous change in all of the other dimensions. A sphere which is doubled in its radius is squared in its plane area in section and cubed in its volume.

A mass, which has expanded to the cube of its former volume, freely floating in space could not have so expanded without changing its potential position to one appropriate to double its former distance from its gravitative center but in its same plane.

In such a position the constant of opposing pressures is one-eighth that of the original position, for the same constant of pressure has been spread over eight times the volume.

In such a position the constant of temperature has also been expanded to cover eight times the volume.

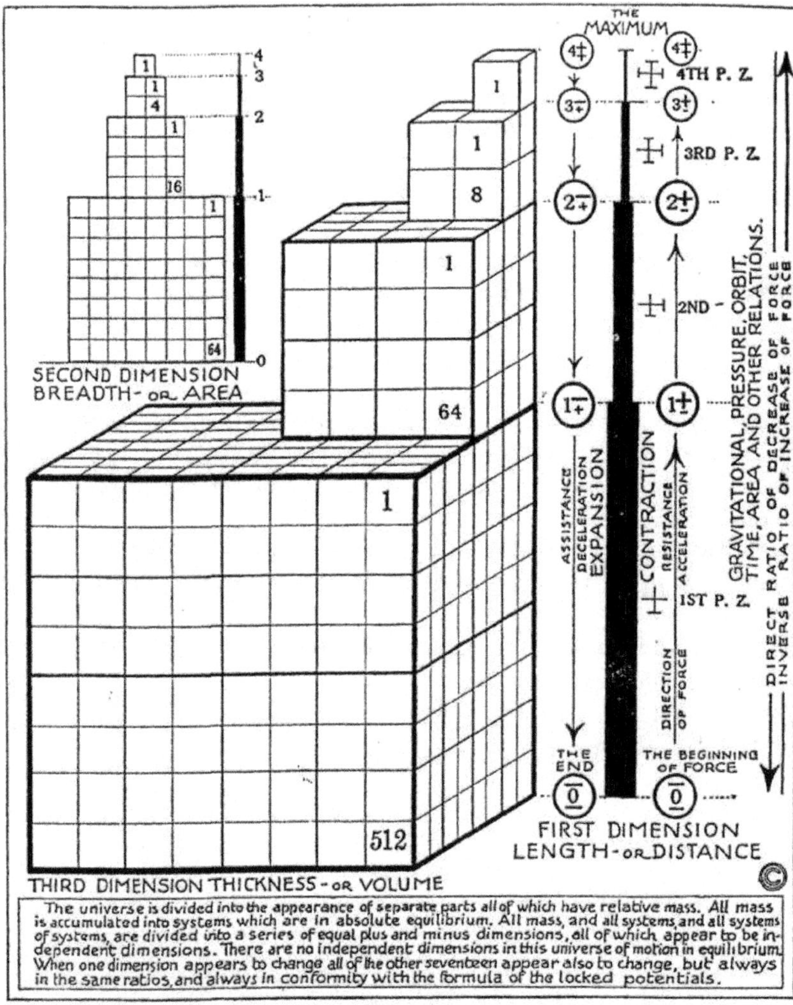

DIMENSION CHART No. 1. DISTANCE AREA AND VOLUME RATIOS IN CONTRACTING AND EXPANDING UNITS OF ALL EXPRESSIONS OF MOTION

All temperature dimensions of expanding mass increase in their expansion dimension, registering greater cold, and decrease in their contraction dimension, registering greater heat.

It must not be forgotten that all effects of motion are expressed in their plus and minus opposites.

All plus effects of motion have been clearly defined as generative, contractive effects, and all minus effects have been defined as radiative, expansive effects.

It must not be forgotten that all mass is either preponderantly charging, or adding to, or it is preponderantly discharging, or subtracting from.

For this reason all effects of motion in mass must be measured in both of their opposite dimensions, their plus and their minus dimension.

The plus dimension shall herein be called "the contraction dimension."

The contraction dimension is the charging dimension of the electro-positive force which winds the cosmic clock.

The minus dimension shall herein be called "the expansion dimension."

The expansion dimension is the discharging dimension of the electro-negative force which unwinds the cosmic clock.

To illustrate, consider an expanded mass at B, of double its diameter at A.

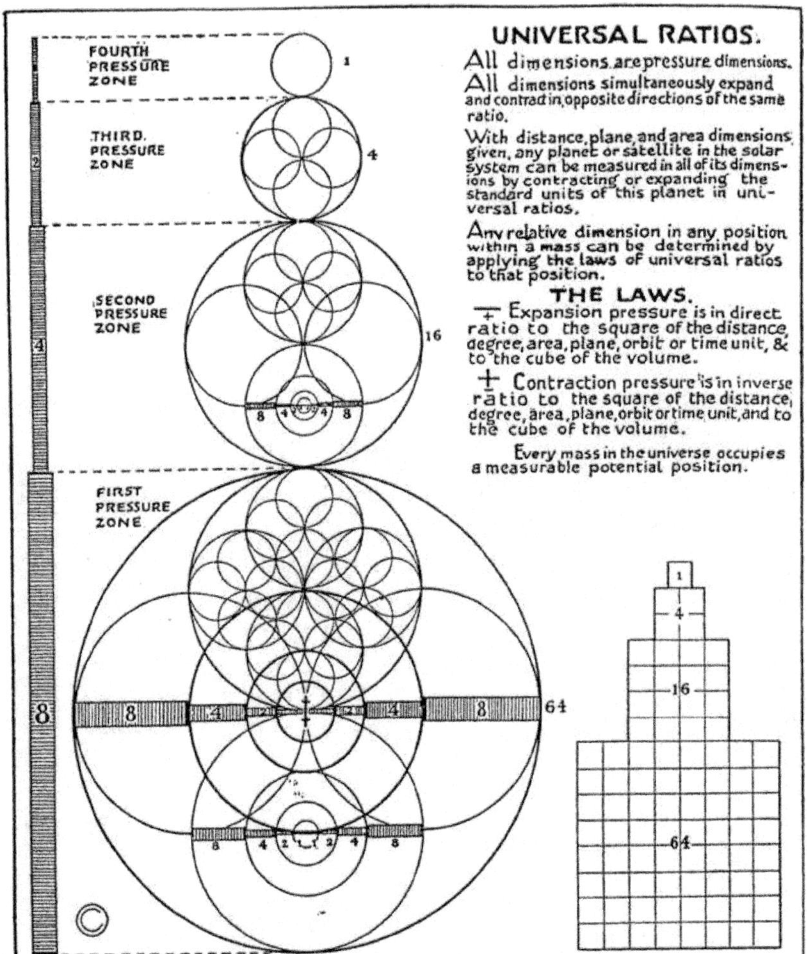

DIMENSION CHART No. 2. NATURE DIVIDES ALL OF HER EXPRESSIONS OF ENERGY INTO OCTAVES AND TONES OF EQUAL CONSTANTS OF UNEQUAL DIMENSIONS. THE DIMENSIONAL RELATIONS OF OCTAVES AND TONES VARY IN RATIOS WHICH ARE ABSOLUTE AND UNIVERSAL

Assume A to be 60,000,000 miles from the sun. At B it would be twice its former distance or 120,000,000 miles.

At B its expansion temperature dimension, as registered in cold, would have increased by eight times just as its volume would have increased by the cube of its former volume.

At B its contraction temperature dimension, as registered in heat, would have decreased to one eighth because the heat units would have become spread over eight times its former space.

At B, rotation, the speed-time expansion dimension would be the square, in direct ratio, of the position at A.

Conversely at B revolution, the speed-time contraction dimension would be the square, in inverse ratio, of the position at A.

Just so with all of its pressure dimensions and effects, from density to ionization, and from ionization to time, sex or crystallization.

The charts herein printed clearly show the tonal relations of all potential positions in the wave.

The seven tones of the universal constant are consecutively removed, one from the other, the square of the distance to the next highest potential. The energy of each of the four units is exactly equal to that of each of the others.

1+, for example, is removed from 2+ by the square of the distance to 3 +, which is the next highest potential.

By a study of the accompanying dimension parts one can readily see that any change in the expansion or contraction dimension of any effect of motion is in either direct ratio or inverse ratio to the square of the distance, area or plane dimensions, or to the cube of the volume dimension.

All dimensions are pressure dimensions.

All dimensions simultaneously expand and contract in opposite directions of the same ratio.

All effects of motion are measurable either in distance, area or volume ratios. Also all are measurable in both the ratios of contraction and of expansion pressure.

The ratios of contraction and of expansion pressure shall herein be termed "The universal ratios."

Expansion pressure is in direct ratio to the square of the distance, area, plane, orbit or time unit, and to the cube of the volume.

Contraction pressure is in inverse ratio to the square of the distance, area, plane, orbit or time unit, and to the cube of the volume.

Every mass in the universe occupies a measurable potential position.

With distance, plane and area dimensions given, any planet or satellite in the solar system can be measured in all of its dimensions by contracting or expanding the standard units of this planet in universal ratios as a comparison.

Let us consider some of these effects. We know the diameter of Jupiter, its plane of orbit and its distance from the sun.

From these we can easily determine its potential position and rotation period.

Let us roughly demonstrate the principle and check the result by our actual knowledge of its rotation period.

For simplicity, let us bring Jupiter back to our known potential position and give it a standard unit of rotation from our knowledge of our own position.

By calculating in inverse universal ratio it is an easy matter to determine that the diameter of Jupiter was about 17,000 miles when it was in the earth's potential position.

With more than twice the earth's circumference and rotating at the speed of the swirling spiral discharging ecliptic area of this particular part of the solar vortex which we occupy, it would take more than twice the time the earth would take to complete its turning. Roughly, its day would be about fifty hours.

That being ascertained, its rotation period, if it were in the earth's plane, would be about eleven hours.

Allowing the difference of about an hour in greater speed for the slight difference in plane, its rotation, if precisely calculated, would check with the known rotation of nine hours and It has heretofore been written that all effects of motion are expressed in seven equal tones of four units.

Fifty-five minutes. In calculating Mar's rotation, its difference of plane would retard rotation so appreciably that its day would be lengthened by about nine hours more than it would be if it were in the earth's plane.

For another example, let us calculate what the rotation of the earth will be when it is 360,000,000 miles from the sun.

Let us assume an even twenty-four hours as its present standard unit, an even 8,000 miles as its diameter, and 90,000,000 miles its distance from the sun, ignoring the fractions and loss by radiation. At 180,000,000 miles its diameter will be 16,000 miles and at 360,000,000 miles it must be 32,000 miles.

At 180,000,000 miles its day must be twelve hours and at 360,000,000 miles it would be six hours.

When in this position its density would be about one sixty-fourth of ours and on its surface iron would melt at about 22°. It is hard ...

If we similarly work the other way toward the sun and calculate the longer periodic day of Mercury, we should find that Mercury, if in our plane, would rotate in about eleven days. Mercury is about 7° removed from us in plane n the direction of higher pressures.

It is, in fact, in about the plane of the maximum expansion pressure opposition of this solar tornado, so by calculating the increasing pressure resistance in that position we find Mercury's day to be approximately 800,800 of our days.

This means that the positive charge of Mercury is so preponderant that its day must be practically a continuous one.

Let us for a moment consider the vast unsuspected range of temperatures and densities, of this solar system.

The temperature of the sun's crust is presumed to be about 6,000°.

In reality, it goes into the inconceivable pressures of hundreds of billions of degrees.

This is easily demonstrated. Consider, for example, the melting point of iron on this planet as 1,500°.

In the higher potential position of half this distance, or 45,000,000 miles, iron would freeze at 12,000°.

At 22,500,000 miles its melting point would jump to 96,000°.

By continuing in the universal ratios for pressures, the figures leap so amazingly fast that it is over 200,000,000,000° when still 187,500 miles away from the sun and 8° away from its plane of high pressure.

Considering this, one need no longer wonder at the tremendous speed of hydrogen expulsion from the sun or be mystified by its corona.

Density, being measured by pressure laws, would place this dimension in the sun at more than a million times the density of this planet instead of less than one-half.

Mass would correspondingly increase into the ...With a few simple facts of position, rotation periods and other dimensions can be easily calculated.

The astronomer of to-day must necessarily find markings to measure the dimensions of rotation. He can find none that are definite on Uranus, Neptune or Mercury. Hence, his conclusions must be conjecture and therefore unreliable.

By the aid of the laws of motion herein con-mined, conjecture is removed from the science of astronomy thus making it now possible for it to live up to its intent as an exact science.

Any relative dimension in any position within a mass can be determined by applying to that position the laws of universal ratios.

UNIVERSAL MATHEMATICS

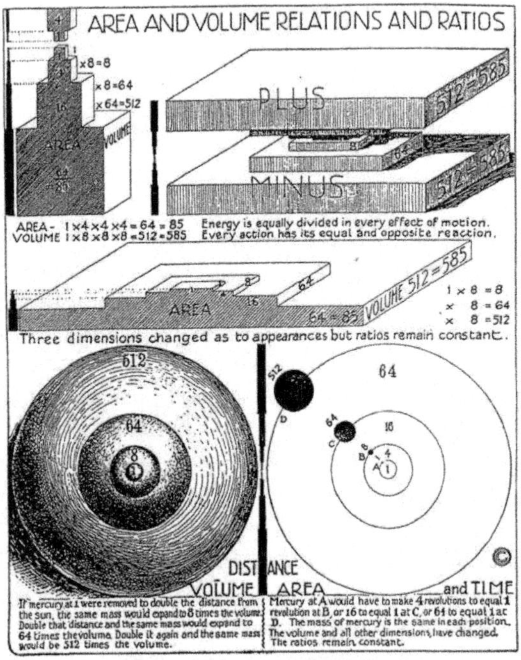

DIMENSION CHART No. 3. THE UNIVERSAL REPRODUCTIVE CONSTANT NEVER VARIES ITS RATIOS NO MATTER WHAT THE WAVE DIMENSION OR THE ACCUMULATION OF POTENTIAL. DIMENSIONS OF MASS CHANGE BUT THE RATIOS AND RELATIONS NEVER CHANGE

CHAPTER XV

EXPRESSIONS OF GRAVITATION AND RADIATION

UNIVERSAL MATHEMATICS

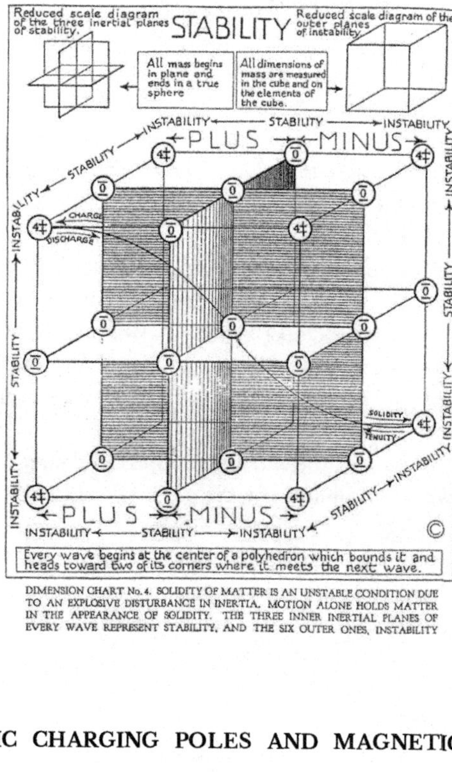

DIMENSION CHART No. 4. SOLIDITY OF MATTER IS AN UNSTABLE CONDITION DUE TO AN EXPLOSIVE DISTURBANCE IN INERTIA. MOTION ALONE HOLDS MATTER IN THE APPEARANCE OF SOLIDITY. THE THREE INNER INERTIAL PLANES OF EVERY WAVE REPRESENT STABILITY, AND THE SIX OUTER ONES, INSTABILITY

THE ELECTRIC CHARGING POLES AND MAGNETIC DISCHARGING BASES

Every particle of matter in this universe is connected with every other particle of matter by electric charging poles which are the controls of opposing electro-magnetic cones of energy.

The apices of these opposing cones meet at the gravitative centers of every particle of matter.

The bases of these opposing cones meet at the inertial planes which lie between any two masses. .

The gravitative center of every particle of matter is the telegraphic center of communication, and the electric poles are the channels of communication. By means of this connection, every particle of matter in the universe is grayitatively and radiatively informed of any change of dimension in any other mass.

All mass simultaneously responds to these communications by a sympathetic contractive or expansive readjustment of its own dimensions. The electric poles are vortices which control the northerly flowing electric stream and determine the southerly flowing magnetic stream.

All energy expresses itself in motion. All motion is expressed in waves.

All waves are sequentially evolved by electric actions into accumulations of mess around minute whirlpool storm centers.

All whirlpool storm centers are formed by resistant magnetic reactions.

All waves, all effects of motion and all dimensions of motion within the wave are measured by the opposition of the electric poles and magnetic bases.

Opposition between electric and magnetic flows begins on the south inertial planes. The two flows pass each other at 180°, and the opposition reaches its maximum at an angle of 90° to the planes. During this progression the 180° of opposition is rigidly maintained.

The electric pole measures the northern opposed distance limitations of the wave at trough and crest in points of wave altitudes which we shall call the overtones.

The magnetic base measures the southern opposed area limitations of the wave which we shall call the harmonic circles.

Thus are distance and area, the first two dimensions of motion, born of inertia.

By connecting the overtones with every point of the harmonic circles, opposing cones are produced.

Thus is volume, the third dimension of motion, born of inertia.

Energy is simultaneously conceived in inertia and sequentially expressed in motion away from inertia.

All dimensions of energy, both gravitational and radiational, are simultaneously marked off in inertia and sequentially transferred in expression to the wave which records sequences of motion.

Thus is time, the fourth dimension of motion, born of inertia.

By the expression of concept in opposing cones of generation and radiation, sex, the fifth dimension is born of inertia.

Within the opposing cones, by reproduction through sex union exerted in sequence, and in opposing pressures and potentials, the sixth and seventh dimensions are born of inertia.

By resistance to the opposing electro-magnetic flow temperature, the eighth dimension, is born of inertia.

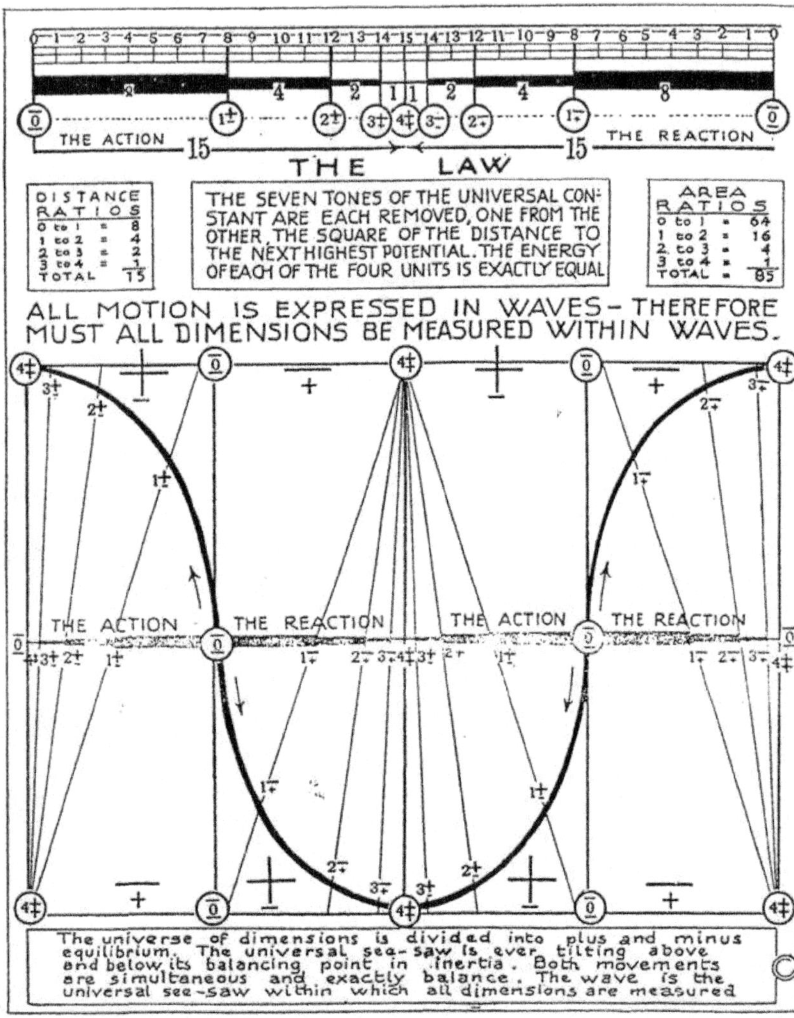

DIMENSION CHART No. 5. DISTANCE DIMENSION OF TONAL RELATIONS. ALL MASS HAS A MEASURABLE TONAL RELATION TO ALL OTHER MASS. ALL POTENTIAL OF ENERGY IS ACTIVE, ORDERLY DISPLACEMENT OF INACTIVE INERTIA, THE RATIOS OF WHICH ARE MEASURABLE IN ALL DIMENSIONS

And so are all the dimensions born of inertia, by overcoming it and expressing their opposition in alternating oscillations. "

And so, also, are all of the opposites of each dimension born of their relative positions in the opposing cones of energy.

The nearer to the axis and to the apex of the cone the greater the density, temperature, pressure, potential, power-time and all effects of electro-positive preponderance.

This is the direction of areas of increasingly high contraction pressure.

The nearer the base of the cone the greater the tenuity, the speed-time and the tendency to ionize, and the lower the temperature, pressure, potential and all effects of electro-negative preponderance.

This is the direction of areas of increasingly low expansion pressure.

The equator of all mass is, therefore, the dividing plane between the opposing plus and minus pressures of the electro-magnetic forces.

It is the plane where expansion pressure is preponderant in the maximum expansion of the mass. It is the plane of least density.

The pole of... maximum density and rigidity.

All electro-positive actions are produced in all mass by contraction of the generative cones of energy toward the high contraction pressures of their poles of rotation.

All electro-negative reactions are produced in all mass by expansion of the radiative cones of energy toward the high expansion pressures of their equators.

This action and reaction of contraction and expansion supplies the electro-magnetic motor force for the construction of the little corpuscular pumps of which all mass is composed and by which its mechanics are coordinated.

In the process of accumulation of little mass into big mass, the little pumps meld into one big pump, each working as a unit but all working for the whole. This is as true in the accumulation of mass into the form of man as into a planet.

Big mass is but a multiplication of the power of little mass.

The desire of electricity is to accumulate mass toward the north.

The desire of magnetism is to dissipate mass toward the south.

Electricity attempts the expression of its desire for action by opposing inertia and ends in non motion of its speed-time dimension at the ultimate gravitative centers of all masses and systems. This effect is counterbalanced however, by its opposite effect of increased speed of revolution in power-time dimension.

Magnetism attempts the expression of its desire to suppress motion through opposing it, and ends in expressing great motion at the equators and ecliptic areas of all masses and systems. This effect is, in its turn, also counterbalanced by its opposite effect of increased speed of revolution in power-time dimension.

Electricity strives to simulate inertia by gyroscopic perfection of motion.

Magnetism, in seeking to suppress motion actually assists it by drawing the harmonic circles of its area dimension gradually into the plane of the electric north, thus creating a new south plane of zero latitude around the point of north at the overtone position of each wave. This plane is reflected at the equator of each mass of each wave.

This new reflected image of the south inertial plane in mass or system will be called the ecliptic plane of mass or system.

The ecliptic plane of mass or system revolves with revolving mass or system.

The ecliptics of all elements between the in ertial harmonic circles and the overtones vary in their expansion and contraction according to their position and the relative expansion and contraction of the opposing cones of energy.

At the overtones, the ecliptic is a plane born of the melding of both contours and bases in the plane of the melded apices of the opposing cones.

From the overtones toward inertia, the ecliptics of all waves, systems and masses expand as the bases of the generative cones expand.

The apparent relative ability of mass to attract and to repel is governed by the contraction of its polar magnetic bases and the expansion of its ecliptic.

The greater the expansion of the ecliptic and the greater the diameters of precessional orbits, the less the ability of a mass to attract and to repel.

The less the expansion of the ecliptic, and the less the diameters of the precessional orbits, the greater the ability of a mass to attract and to repel.

In any mass the diameters of its polar magnetic bases and of its axial precessional orbits increase as the mass recedes from, and decrease as it approaches its nucleal sun's equatorial plane.

In any mass the expansion of its ecliptic, the diameters of its equatorial precessional orbits and of its polar magnetic bases increase as the mass recedes from, and decrease as it approaches its nucleal sun's equatorial plane.

If these laws are well founded, the expansion of the ecliptic, the diameters of polar magnetic bases and the dimensions of precessional orbits must be related to the attraction of gravitation and the repulsion of radiation.

Let us consider some familiar effects of the above principles in relation to this planet and solar system.

Consider the great expansion of the ecliptic plane areas of the outer planets of low potential as compared to those of the inner ones of high potential.

Consider the tenuity of the outer planets where the precessional orbits are extended, as compared to the density of the inner ones where the precessional orbit's are restricted.

Consider the preponderance of centrifugal force which counteracts the gravitative power of the very much decomposed outer planets as compared to the preponderance of centripetal force which assists the inner planets in holding themselves together.

Consider the outer planets' charging poles which are far removed from their poles of rotation, as compared to the inner planets' charging poles which are closer to their axial poles the nearer the planet is to the sun. The charging poles are wrongly termed "magnetic poles."

Consider the slight attraction and repulsion power of the outer planets which float in extremely low pressure zones, as compared to the great attraction and repulsion power of the inner ones which float in high pressure zones. To remain as close to the sun as Mercury requires a potential approaching that of the sun itself.

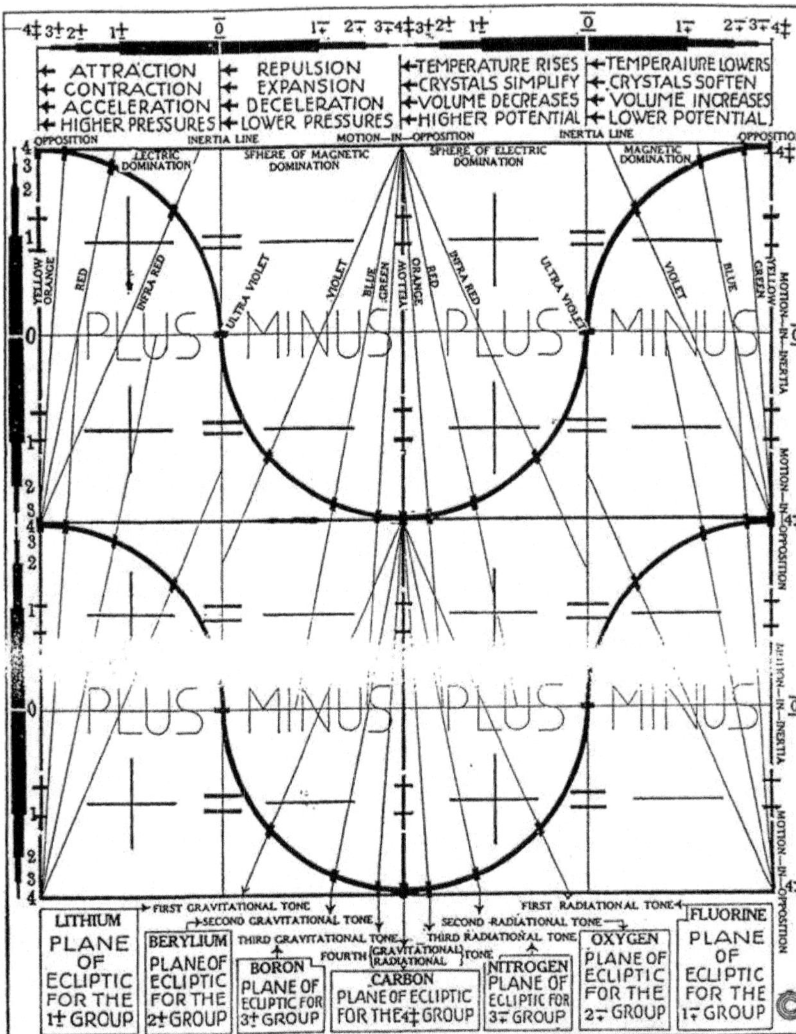

DIMENSION CHART No. 6. DISTANCE DIMENSIONS OF ENERGY OF TONES WITHIN A WAVE. THE FOUR UNIVERSAL REPRODUCTIVE CONSTANTS ARE PLACED IN THEIR TRUE RELATIVE POSITIONS.

Consider the low melting and freezing points of the outer planets where our gases are their solids, as compared to the high melting points of the inner planets. To remain frozen as close to the sun as Mercury requires a pressure equilibrium approaching that of the sun itself.

Let us now consider the charging poles in respect to their apparent relative ability to attract.

It is commonly supposed that the north pole of a magnet is the positive pole, which attracts, and the south pole of a magnet is its negative pole, which repels.

The apparent ability of the positive pole of a magnet to attract the negative, and the negative to attract the positive, has been one of the evidences which has built up the theory that opposite charges attract and like charges repel.

Further deceptive evidence in support of this theory lies in the fact that the north positive pole of a "magnetized" bar of iron will appear to repel the north positive pole of a compass needle, and, on the contrary, the south negative pole of a "magnetized" bar of iron will appear to attract the north positive pole of a compass needle.

The evidence that like charges repel is as convincing as that the moon keeps pace with moving man, or that the earth is flat. It is evidence that one can really see, like other illusions of motion.

The truth is that north is the apex of a cone into which a super-normal electric stream is spirally flowing, due to electric excitation.

The reason that the south pole of the bar of iron appears to attract the north pole of the compass needle is that the electric stream is flowing through both the iron and the needle in the same direction, from south to north.

To expect them to do otherwise would be equivalent to expecting two water pipes, through which streams are flowing, to continue their flow as one stream if the water pipes were joined together in such a way that the streams were flowing in opposite directions.

Just as the two separate streams of water would apparently repel each other if the pipes were so joined, so would they appear to attract each other and flow as one stream if the pipes were joined so that their streams were flowing in the same direction.

One may demonstrate the truth of this by cutting a "magnetized" bar of iron anywhere between its opposite poles. It will then be seen that a new north and south pole will appear on each of the two separate bars. This process may be repeated indefinitely, always with the same result.

The so-called "magnetized" bar of iron is one in which a strong electric inductive current has so greatly contracted the generative, and expanded the radiative cones of energy of the atoms of iron that their polar magnetic bases and their ecliptic expansions have been vastly reduced, and the speeds of their generative and radiative flows correspondingly increased. Atoms of iron not so treated, leap toward these faster flowing streams.

The term "magnetized" was given to iron so treated because iron exposed to the magnetic field of a generative coil always causes this effect.

The magnetic field of a generative coil is the radio-active emanation, or discharge, of an overcharged coil.

It is the degeneration of a generating charge when it leaves the generative coil.

In other words, it is the leakage or overflow from an overfilled receptacle.

Not so however, when it impacts against the iron.

It then becomes regenerated.

The negative discharge becomes a positive charge.

The iron bar becomes electrified, not magnetized.

The bar of iron, and the so-called magnetic poles of a revolving rotating mass, such as this planet, are two different effects.

Every mass, such as this planet, is supposed to be a "magnet."

It is, but not like the "magnetized" bar of iron, or the compass needle. It is a double "magnet."

Its two charging poles meet head on at the gravitative center of the planet and the oppositely flowing electric streams meet there exactly as oppositely flowing streams of water would meet if water pipes were opposed as above described.

In any mass when these two streams meet they oppose and spread against each other's force in the direction of the ecliptic plane area of the mass.

It is commonly supposed that the "magnetic" pole of this planet is analogous to a bar magnet," being one continuous bar extending from the negative antarctic south to the positive arctic north.

A compass needle, nearing the south "magnetic" pole, dips so violently that it seems desirous of plunging arrow-head-first directly into the sea.

This apparently supports the theory that opposite poles attract, for here the north attrac tive positive pole of the compass is attracted to its south supposedly repellent negative pole.

Carry this experiment farther and approach the north "magnetic" pole with the compass.

Upon nearing it, the same effect is produced as that at the south pole.

The magnetic needle seems to desire to dive vertically into the sea.

This appears to be the opposite effect from that cited in the magnet bar and compass experiment.

The north attractive positive pole of the planet appears to attract the north attractive positive pole of the compass, and the south repellent negative pole of the planet appears to attract the north attractive positive pole of the compass.

The explanation lies in the fact that the one north direction of attraction in the bar of iron and compass is continuous, while the two north directions of attraction in the planet are opposed. They meet at the center of the earth at the apices of two opposing cones.

The magnetic bases of these two cones are respectively in the arctic and antarctic regions. As mass generates the magnetic bases disappear...

The diameters of the bases extend from the known major charging poles through the poles of rotation to the unknown minor charging poles situated at equal distances on the opposite sides of the poles of rotation.

It has previously been explained that the north of any mass is its gravitative center.

The direction of north is along the electric axes of the contracting cones of generation from their bases to their apices.

North is always in the direction of genero-activity, high pressure and high potential.

In any mass, north is the gravitative-radiative center where the apparent ability to attract and to repel is at its maximum.

On the contrary, south is always in the direction of radio-activity, low pressure and low potential.

South is an extension of the equatorial plane which divides any mass. It is that part of mass where radiative emanations are at their maximum.

It is the plane of disappearance of the contours of the expanding cones of radiation.

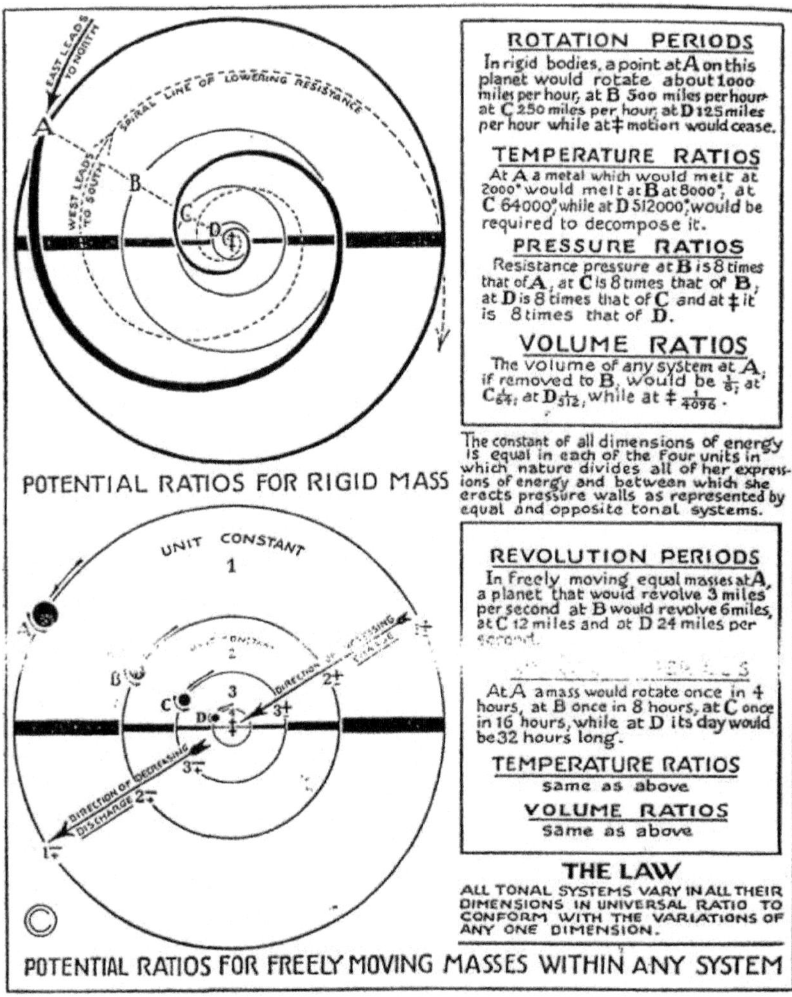

DIMENSION CHART No. 8. ROTATION PERIOD OF ANY UNMARKED PLANET CAN BE CALCULATED FROM KNOWN POSITION AND REVOLUTION. MASS AND OTHER DIMENSIONS CAN BE CALCULATED FROM KNOWN POSITION AND ROTATION

It must continually be borne in mind that electricity contracts and attracts from within, and that magnetism expands and repels also from within.

Consider the isoclinal lines which girdle this planet approximately parallel to its equator, according to very careful surveys for terrestrial magnetic charts, at every ten degrees of latitude between the equator and the poles.

If that portion of the planet between any of these isoclinal lines and either of the poles were lifted out, one would be looking into one of the gripping cone clutches of the universal machine, or one of the slipping disc clutches, the apex of which reaches somewhere near the equatorial plane of the planet.

The contour of the cone thus exposed would give the direction of the magnetic lines of force which emanate from the planet and seek their regeneration at the pole of the ..... hemisphere from which they emanate.

This same effect of magnetic lines of force may be produced by the well known experiment of causing iron filings to find magnetic lines of force by placing them on a piece of paper which is vibrated rapidly over a "magnetic" bar of iron. Some will always follow the direction of the outward flowing magnetic stream, and some will find the direction of the inward flowing electro-regenerative stream.

The current within a bar of iron flowing from south to north is an electric flow and the current is an induced current.

The discharged current which flows outside the bar of iron is a magnetic flow which is conducted by the more expanded surrounding medium to a lower potential, or is deflected and regenerated by the resistance of the surrounding connecting medium. When so deflected, it is again attracted to the south pole of the bar of iron, where it re-enters as an electric flow.

Science describes this effect as magnetic induction.

Magnetic induction is impossible.

Induction is an evidence of regeneration through sufficient resistance to degenerative conduction. Induction is an effect of generation or regeneration.

Induction is centripetal. Its flow is northerly. Conduction is an effect of degeneration. Conduction is centrifugal. Its direction is southerly.

If this is true, then induction must be related to the attraction of gravitation and conduction to the repulsion of radiation.

If it is true that these are so related, it must necessarily follow that a strong inductive effect is always simultaneously accompanied by a strong conductive effect.

If this latter is true it must necessarily follow that increasing induction, which means increasing positive charge, must be accompanied by an increasing power to attract.

It must also be accompanied by an increasing negative discharge and an increasing power to repel. It is easy to test these statements by applying them to any known inductive and conductive effects.

Consider the storage battery, for example.

Increase its charge and its discharge also increases. Electric bulbs connected with its conductive outlet will brighten.

Consider the sun. Its ability to radiate and to repel is great because of its great ability to generate and to attract.

Consider each planet in the order of its potential position in its system.

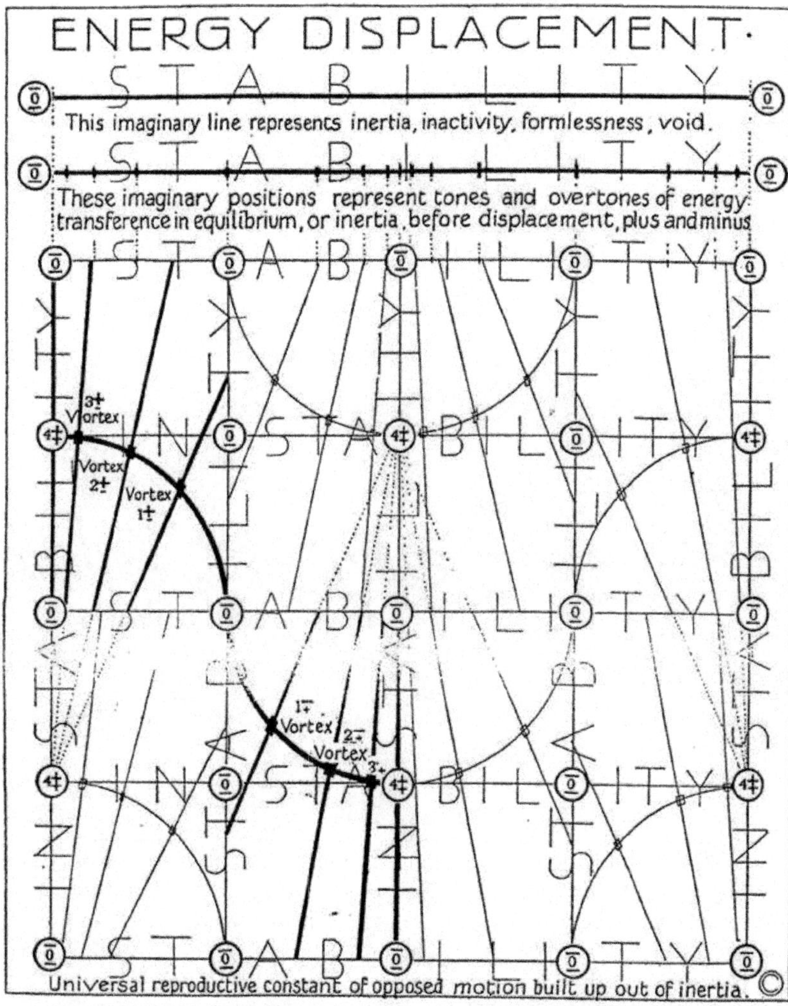

DIMENSION CHART No. 7. STABILITY IS THE INACTIVITY OF A STATE OF EQUILIBRIUM. MOTION IS ACTIVE AND OPPOSED TO EQUILIBRIUM. ALL MOTION IS RELATIVELY UNSTABLE. STABILITY OF MATTER IN MOTION MAY ONLY BE SIMULATED BY THE UNION OF EXACTLY EQUAL AND OPPOSITE PLUS AND MINUS DIMENSIONS.

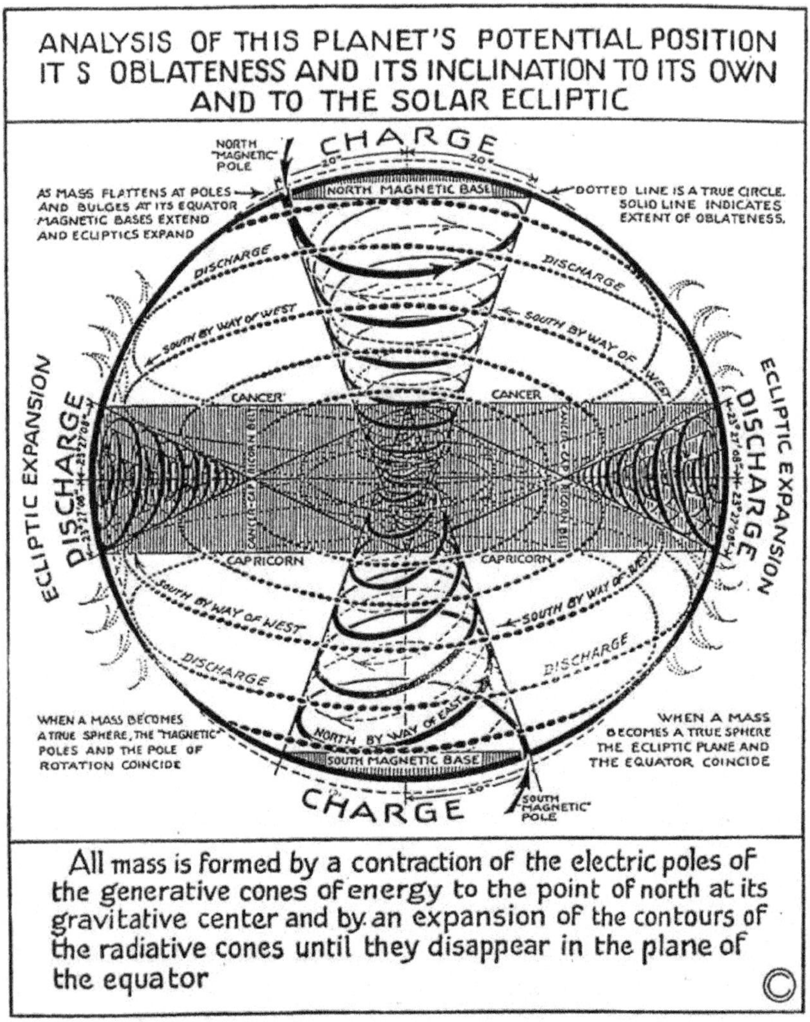

AS MAGNETIC BASES CONTRACT TOWARD THE POLE OF ROTATION, THE CANCER CAPRICORN BELT, WHICH REPRESENTS THE ECLIPTIC AREA, ALSO CONTRACTS TOWARD DISAPPEARANCE IN THE PLANE OF THE EQUATOR

The ability of each to discharge and to repel lessens with the lowering of its potential position in its system.

Just so with all mass. As its potential is lowered, which means that its polar magnetic bases are enlarged, and its ecliptic expansion is increased, its ability to generate, charge, attract, radiate, discharge and repel is also increased.

When a bar of iron is "magnetized" it is in reality electrified.

The magnetic bases of the iron atoms have been contracted.

Let us now imagine the charging poles of this planet as two immense bar "magnets" turned positive end to positive end, and placed so that they meet at its gravitative-radiative, attractive-repellent, charging-discharging, genero-radiative center.

Let us see what is the potential position of the earth and what relation the positions of its so-called "magnetic" poles and the expansion of the Cancer-Capricorn belt have to its ability to charge, attract, discharge and repel.

Let us see why its orbit is inclined over 7° to the solar equator and why the space allotted to it is defined as a distance of 92,900,000 miles, beyond which it cannot go without increasing its polar bases and ecliptic expansions and within which it cannot trespass without decreasing them.

Up above Hudson Bay, on this planet, is a shifting point known as the "north magnetic pole." This is the planet's point of maximum electric charge.

This, and a corresponding shifting point near the south pole, are the two points of maximum generation.

At these two points of our nameless planet the universal force connects its charging wires to this storage battery which we call the earth.

These points shall therefore be termed the "charging poles."

The charging poles are practically 20° away from the pole of rotation. A circle drawn through them would define the polar magnetic base of this planet.

North of the. equator, 23°27' 08", is a line indicating the northerly limit of the intersection of this planet's ecliptic plane with itself.

South of the equator, at the same distance, is the southerly limit of intersection.

If the planet were a perfectly true sphere, the charging poles and the axis of rotation would coincide. There would be no magnetic base.

There would also be no Cancer-Capricorn belt, for the plane of the ecliptic and of the equator would coincide.

Furthermore, the plane of the earth's ecliptic and its equator would coincide with the plane of the solar equator.

This planet's ecliptic is inclined over 7° to the plane of the solar equator and its equator is inclined 23° 27' 08" to the plane of its ecliptic.

This results in a very low potential as compared to Mercury or to Venus and a high one in respect to the outer planets.

It also results in a low freezing point and a rigidity that would be impossible in a position ten million miles nearer to the sun or in a plane 2° nearer to that of the solar equator.

The potential position of this planet necessitates a small percentage of oblateness, or flattening of the poles.

The oblateness of the planet accounts for the difference of about 3° in the extension of the polar magnetic bases and the ecliptic expansion. To flatness at the poles is ascribed 1 1-2° and to the bulging at the equator is ascribed the other 1 1-2.°

As a planet finds a lower potential position for its relative mass its oblateness increases, and so also do the polar magnetic bases and Cancer-Capricorn belts move their positions toward each other.

As Cancer-Capricorn belts and polar magnetic bases expand, the power of the mass to attract and to repel lessens.

Oblateness also increases as centrifugal force causes its equator to bulge suggestive of the beginning of the return journey from mass to plane.

In any mass the area *of its ecliptic expansion, the areas of its „polar* magnetic bases, and the positions of its charging poles are governed by the oblateness of the mass.

In any mass as oblateness decreases, polar magnetic bases and ecliptic expansion decrease their areas, and charging poles draw closer to its pole of rotation.

If the position of the charging electric poles and the Cancer-Capricorn belt in mass conditions the ability of mass to attract and to repel, and these positions are governed by the potential position of the mass itself, it must necessarily follow that the pressures which determine that potential position must be related to gravitation and radiation.

NATURE'S METHOD OF STORING ENERGY IN MASS

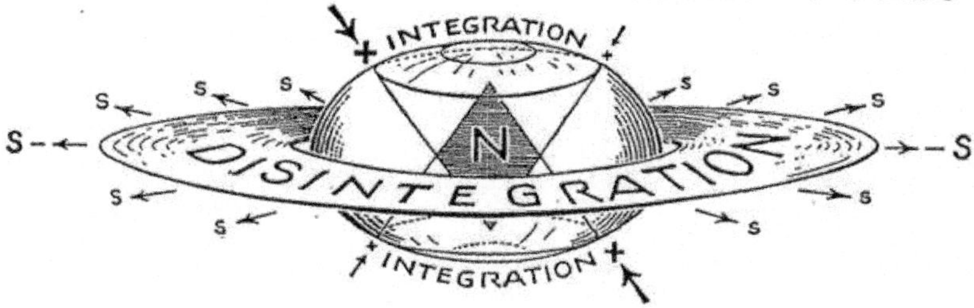

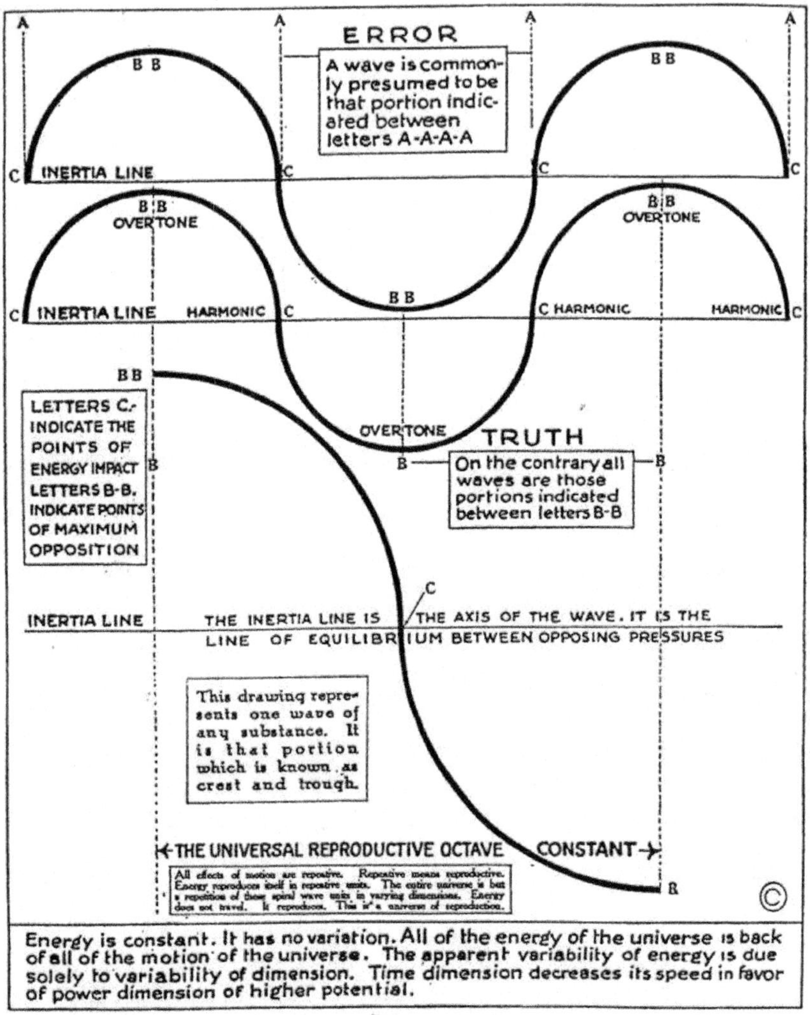

ALL ENERGY IS EXPRESSED IN MOTION. THE ENERGY OF THINKING MIND "CREATES" A UNIVERSE OF MOTION. ALL MOTION IS EXPRESSED IN WAVES

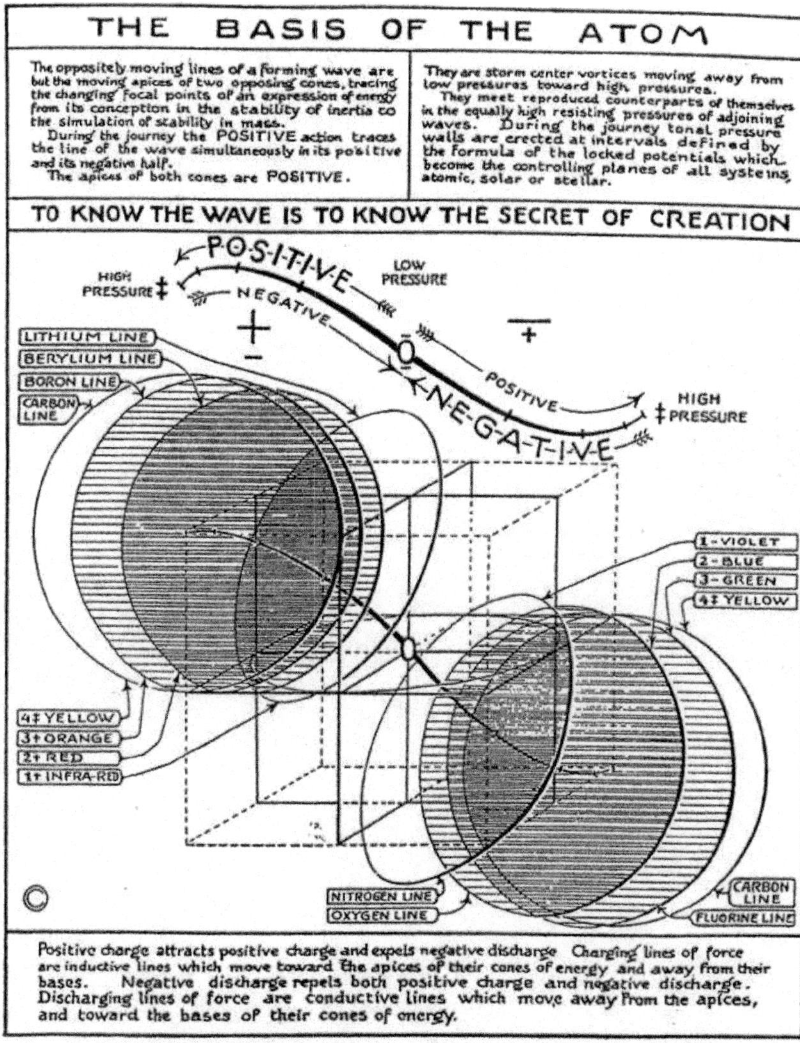

THE PRESSURE WALLS OF ANY WAVE SHOWN IN THEIR LOCKED POTENTIAL POSITIONS. THESE PRESSURE WALLS ARE THE BASES OF THE ELEMENTS AND THE CONTROLLING PLANES OF ALL SYSTEMS.

CHAPTER XVI

THE WAVE

EXPRESSIONS OF GRAVITATION AND RADIATION

To know the wave is to know the secret of creation.

The wave is nature's method of transferring the dimensionless concept of form in inertia to dimensional form in mass in motion by an impact of the energy of the concept against the inertial plane.

All waves are the expression of force, a record of the universal constant or its multiples in accumulated energy.

The dimensions of any wave are the dimensions of the multiples, in universal ratios, of the energy constant represented by that wave.

Waves are not undulations such as those produced by the shaking of a rope up and down. They are actions and reactions beginning at and growing from harmonic points of impact upon the inertial plane of the wave.

Nor are waves continuations of motion beginning at one source and transferred in sequence.

Waves are simultaneously generated from inertia at intervals which are sequential, and in dimensions which are opposed and sequential.

Sequential intervals of the expression of force in motion are simultaneously recorded on the inertial planes of equilibrium of each consecutive octave of motion.

Within each consecutive octave every expression of motion is sequentially produced and reproduced in every atom of every element until it is finally recorded in the inertial planes.

All of the energy of the universal constant is existent in inertia and all of its variations in accumulation are stored in the sequential inertial planes of equilibrium which have their chemical representation in the inert gases, from which they borrow their appearance of existence of mass in motion.

The inert gases are the storehouses of all of the states of motion contained within the mass of the wave.

The purpose of the wave is to transfer states of motion from one potential to another.

This is nature's method of accumulating the energy constant from low potential to high potential, octave by octave, in a series of progressive steps until maximum motion has been reached.

Every state of motion is the result of a concept of that state.

The purpose of motion is to contract concept into form and then to expand it into the memory of form.

All concepts are but recollections of eternal ideas.

All forms are but the regenerated memories of universal Mind.

Each action of motion is recorded by a reaction in the master-tone inert gas of each octave.

Any expression of motion whether of gravitation or radiation, or whether the tossing of a marble or the revolving of a planet, is simultaneously recorded by impact against the inertial plane of every octave of recorded motion in the universe of dimension, and from there produced and reproduced sequentially in waves of mass in motion.

The sequences of a wave are tonal and its tonal intervals have an appearance of existence in masses of relative dimensions.

Let us repeat the definition of a wave: "The wave is nature's method of transferring the dimensionless concept of form in inertia to dimensional form in mass in motion by an impact of the energy of the concept against the inertial plane."

All motion appears in mass and disappears in plane.

This is the process of evolution and devolution in its utmost simplicity.

The appearance of motion in mass is by way of the positive tones of the wave and its disappearance into plane is by way of the negative tones of the wave.

An impact of a stone upon the surface of the water transfers both its positive, gravitative actions and its negative, radiative reactions simultaneously upon the entire surface of the water.

Near the point of impact small harmonic circles become the contracted bases of opposing cones of high altitudes.

Near the point of impact short high waves of power-time dimension simultaneously pile themselves up in sequential stages.

Ten miles or a thousand miles away harmonic circles of increasingly larger bases, which become the expanded bases of cones of low altitudes, are simultaneously marked off on the inertial plane of the water's surface.

These are the expanding radiative cones of lessening generative energy which are dissipating the energy of the impact into its equivalent in speed.

These opposing forces simultaneously proceed in opposite directions from the harmonic reproductions of the impact on the water's surface.

The generative cones are ever seeking contracted gravitational centers to continue their appearance as form, and the radiative cones are ever seeking the expansion of equilibrium in inertia to dissipate their appearance as form, into plane from which all form is evolved.

Each wave is, therefore, built up simultaneously in sequential stages in sequential preponderance of opposite dimensions.

Waves are not those parts which are either wholly above or wholly below their axes.

One wave of any dimension is that portion of the sequence which is bounded by the turning point of one crest and the next trough.

The inertial plane of the wave coincides with the line of axis of the wave.

A wave begins at the inertial plane and extends in both directions from the inertial plane to its repeative point at trough and crest.

The popular concept that light travels along undulating waves is not in conformity with the laws of motion. Waves are constructed in sequential stages until they meet at their overtone positions in trough and crest.

No state of motion travels beyond the boundaries of its own wave mass. It is reproduced by union with its opposite effect at every inertial plane which divides masses in motion in the universe of dimension.

Neither is the wave in one plane. The wave is a spiral.

The wave is not simply a curved line. The line of the wave is the moving vortex line of the maximum high pressure of the opposed cones of the wave.

The axis of the wave is in the inertial plane of birth of the wave.

A wave is not a single unit. It is a series of two opposed units.

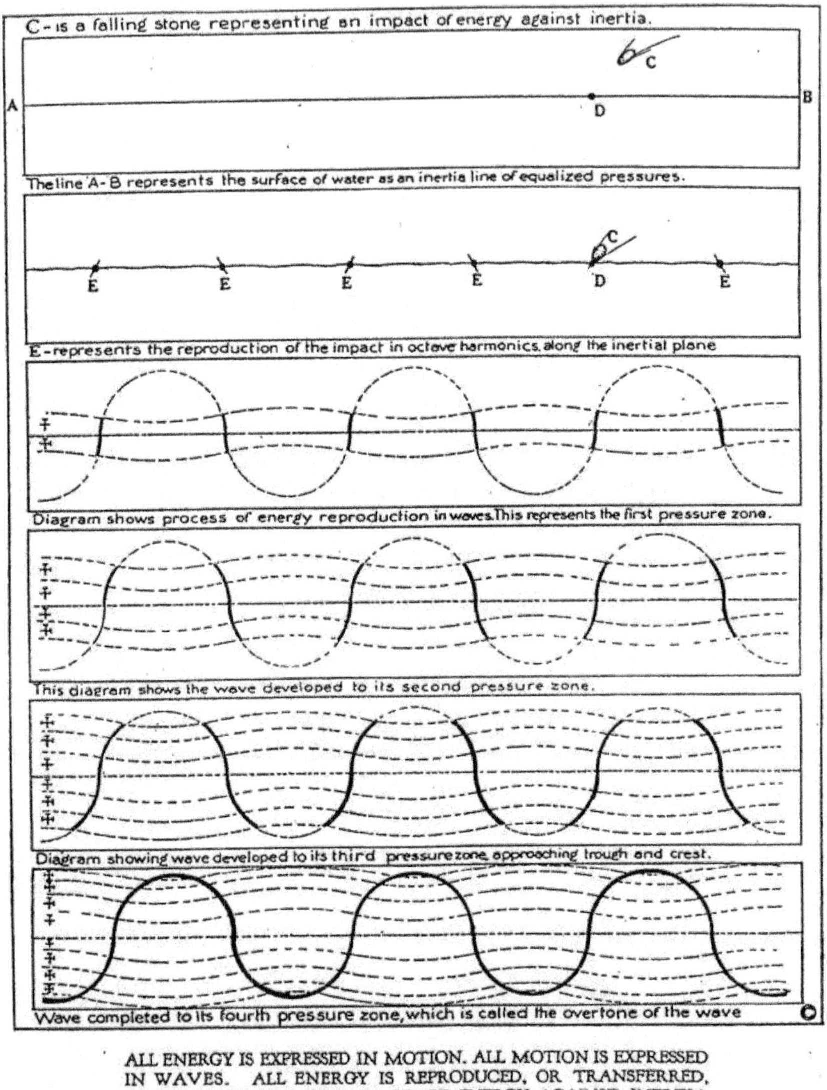

ALL ENERGY IS EXPRESSED IN MOTION. ALL MOTION IS EXPRESSED IN WAVES. ALL ENERGY IS REPRODUCED, OR TRANSFERRED, OR TRANSMITTED, BY IMPACT OF ENERGY AGAINST INERTIA

A wave is not simply a line. A wave is mass in opposition.

The wave is a series of two opposed volumes, the forms of which are cones.

The moving line of the wave is a spiral record of the variable instability of motion.

The wave is too complex a subject to more than touch upon in this volume. In the second volume it will be charted in all of its complexities while considering the structure of the atom.

A study of the various wave charts will assist in visualizing the structure of the wave and its changing planes.

A mass is an effect of resistance to the formation of wave series.

A mass is a simultaneously evolving and devolving harmonic sphere in volume transformed by motion from harmonic circles in plane.

All mass of perfectly balanced motion is spherical.

A true sphere is only possible at the exact point of north at the overtone of the wave.

The evolution of mass from plane to sphere and its diffusion back to plane are by the way of the cone.

The sphere is the perfection of form, and the perfection of the illusion of stability in motion.

All generating mass is aiming for spherical perfection of form by means of gyroscopic perfection of motion.

The dimensions of a mass are the dimensions of the resistance exerted against the formation of the wave.

The resistance to the formation of the wave is greatest at the apex of the cone and least at its inertial base.

Therefore, the power dimensions of mass are increasingly great along the pressure line toward north of the wave, and maximum in its ultimate north.

The high pressure line of the wave is at the electric pole of all mass just as the low pressure plane is at the equator. The bases of the isoclinal cones mark varying stages of increased pressure as they near the poles and depart from the equator.

Harmonic spheres are formed in the vortices of the contracted north from the expanded nebulae of the south.

Therefore, north is the direction of that attribute of motion which is termed the attraction of gravitation, and south is the direction of the repulsion of radiation.

The duration of the wave is the interval during which motion can be continued in the wave.

No matter whether the duration of a wave is one ten-thousandth of a second or ten thousand billion years, every stage of its evolution is exactly the same. Its volume must be transferred to mass in whirling spheres which, in turn, are dissipated into plane.

Motion diffuses away from the north line of the wave toward the south plane of inertia.

Harmonic spheres expand from the north of their contracted forms to the south harmonic circles of their expanded concept.

All expression of energy is a concentration into harmonic spheres in motion of expanded concept in inertial plane.

Form disappears into south by diffusion from north.

Therefore south is the direction of that attribute of motion which is termed the repulsion of radiation.

North is the direction of electro-positive charge. Therefore positive charge attracts.

South is the direction of electro-negative discharge. Therefore negative discharge repels.

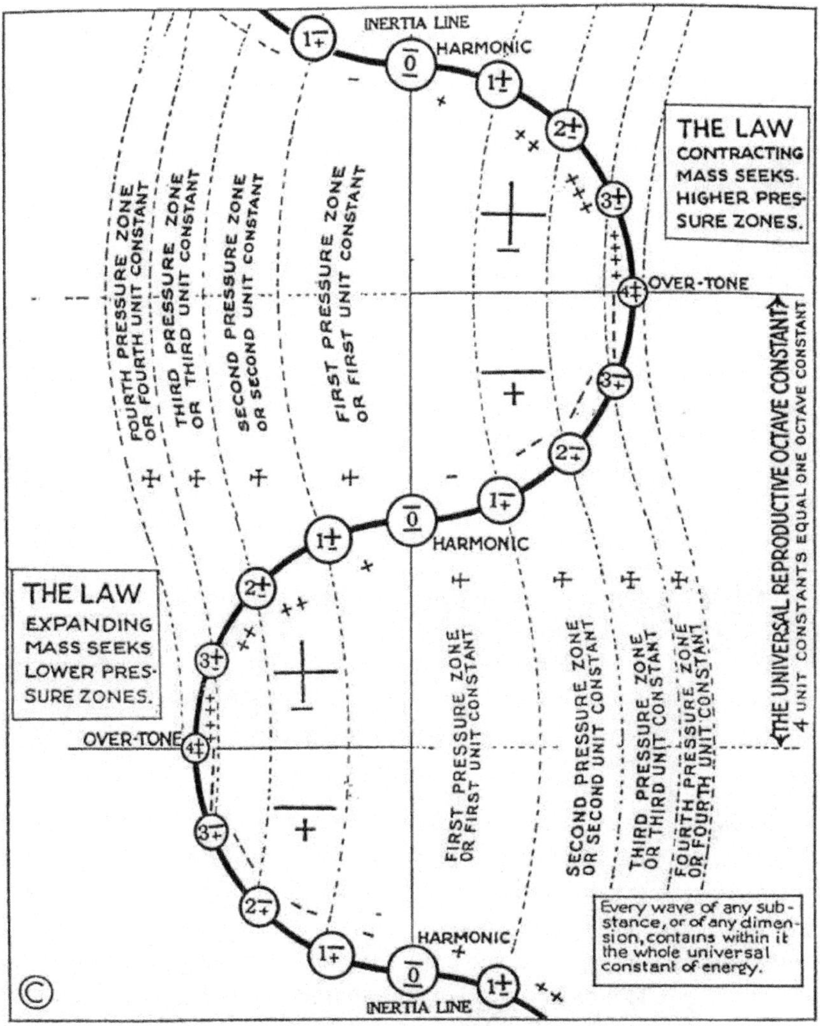

PRESSURE ZONE DIAGRAM. THE UNIVERSAL OCTAVE CONSTANT DIVIDES ITSELF INTO FOUR UNITS OF SEVEN TONES. EACH UNIT OF TWO TONES IS DIVIDED BY PRESSURE ZONES, WHICH CAUSE ALL MASS TO ROTATE AND TO REVOLVE IN SPIRAL ORBITS.

If these statements are true then positive charge cannot possibly attract negative discharge.

North is the direction of the generative action of displacement.

South is the direction of the radiative reaction of replacement.

It will be recalled that the concept and expression of all energy is simultaneously universal and its preponderance of opposition is sequential.

Waves are the expression in motion of the concept of energy.

Energy expresses itself by an apparent division of its force into equal opposites of more and less.

Therefore, each wave is divided into opposites.

Also the entire sequence of waves of any expression of energy is divided into equal opposites of changing dimensions of an unchanging constant.

In order to comprehend more fully the spiral construction of *a wave, it would be well to imagine the universe of dimension within which all energy is expressed as being divided into a series of cubes.

We will call these the cubes of motion.

Sub-divide each of these cubes by three median planes, each one of which is parallel to two of its six faces.

We will call these the planes of inertia.

Let us call the horizontal one of these three planes the south inertial plane of concept. The visible vertical plane will be called the prime vertical and the receding plane the secondary vertical.

It will be observed that these three planes sub-divide the cube into eight cubic compartments of equal dimensions.

Let us bear in mind that the cubes of motion are each sub-divided into eight cubic compartments of equal dimensions ; the inner faces of which constitute the three inertial planes.

Of these eight cubes, the left four are the cubes of positive force and electric domination, while the right four are the cubes of negative force and magnetic domination.

For purposes of convenience, these cubes of motion will be numbered in accordance with the diagram on page 155 as 1 +, 2 +, 3 +, 4+ and 5 —, 6 — , 7— and 8 — .

The point of intersection of the three inertial planes at the center of each cube of motion is the point of beginning of the line of the wave.

From this point, the line of the wave extends spirally in both directions to the corners of the cube.

Let us call the spiral line of the wave the electric pole of the wave.

Let us call the vertical line of intersection of the three inertial planes the electric pole of concept.

Let us call the corners of the cube the north points, or overtones of the wave.

From the harmonic circles of the horizontal planes the contour of the opposing cones which bound the mass of the wave is developed.

We have now left unnamed and undisposed of the six outer faces of the cube, or twenty-four faces of the sub-divided cube.

We shall call the two vertical faces which parallel the primary vertical inertial plane the ecliptics of the wave, the two faces which parallel the secondary vertical plane the east-west planes, and the two horizontal faces the north opposed planes.

All motion begins on the south inertial plane as more fully described in the preceding and following chapters and expresses itself in motion by expansion in both directions from the south inertial plane toward contraction at two points in the diagonal north corners of the cube.

By a study of the chart on page 155 it will be observed that the horizontal and the secondary inertial planes divide positive charge from negative discharge. These planes divide the opposing tone series of each wave.

The primary vertical plane, however, divides the entire wave progression from another wave progression.

It divides the positive series from the positive, and the negative series from the negative.

Every wave of energy of any kind or of any dimension is recorded in series of opposing tones.

Tones are storm centers formed by resistance to the electric action which constitutes the be ginning of motion.

Tonal vortices are the centers of revolving and rotating masses which build equal and opposite tonal pressure walls within the opposed tonal wave of energy to stabilize the motion within the compartments thus divided.

Tonal pressure walls are contractions of the south inertial planes toward the ecliptic of the wave.

Tonal pressure walls are the ecliptic planes of their systems.

Tonal pressure walls are reflected in every mass in every element to measure the potential of that mass in reference to its system, just as the tonal pressure wall of an entire system measures the potential and defines the potential position of that system in its wave.

The principal tonal pressure walls by means of which the potential position of a mass can be measured are the more or less expanded Cancer-Capricorn belts which define the limitations of its equatorial precessional orbits, and the polar magnetic bases limited by their charging poles, which define the polar precessional orbits.

By these two pressure walls any mass can be most accurately measured and many otherwise unanswerable questions can by this means be answered.

The position of the polar magnetic base of any mass can be calculated with precision with the knowledge of its equatorial inclination to its own orbit and its oblateness.

Both of these positions can be calculated in any mass by finding its true potential position in its system and applying the laws of universal ratios to that position in comparison with the standard units of any other known position.

The tonal pressure walls erected within the opposing cones are those various states of motion which we call the elements of matter.

Tonal pressure walls are erected in orderly mathematical relations and divide the energy of each wave into equal parts of the same constant.

Mid-tonal pressure walls are erected between tonal pressure walls, and their total dimensions equal the constant of a whole tone.

It will now be well to consider the process of overcoming inertia by force which gives us the various states of motion of the One substance.

CHAPTER XVII

EXPRESSIONS OF GRAVITATION AND RADIATION

TIME-THE FOURTH DIMENSION

Time is the measure of universal repeativeness.

All phenomena of nature are repeative. All repetition is sequential.

Time is the interval between the sequences of events.

Were there no events, time would not be. If nothing "happened" in the universe, there would be no intervals.

Intervals of time are illusions which give birth to other illusions known as relations.

Without intervals of time, relations would not be.

Without relations, dimensions would not be. All dimensions are relative.

Time is a dimension.

Time is therefore relative.

Time dimension marks the periodicities of all phenomena of motion.

Time belongs essentially to motion, and is not an attribute of substance.

In inertia time, like all other dimensions, does not exist.

In opposition, time appears to exist.

In opposition, there are apparent intervals which create that illusion of motion which we call speed.

Speed is the time consumed in relation to the distance covered.

In the highest perceptible octave, the speed of reproduction of the accumulated universal constant is 186,330 miles per second.

This speed of 186,330 miles is the speed with which energy overcomes inertia and sets it in motion in the highest octave of the lowest potential of matter perceptible on this planet.

This is the speed of reproduction of all pressures in the fourth octave only. Higher octaves have increasingly greater speeds.

As energy accumulates the universal constant into multiples, the intervals of production and reproduction are lengthened in universal ratio to correspond with those multiples.

Each succeeding octave has its own time limit for reproducing the image of concept.

Each wave of accumulating energy consumes more time but the constant is not changed.

The intervals of electric accumulation gradually lengthen and their speeds of reproduction correspondingly lengthen.

Intervals lengthen in proportion to energy accumulation.

The greater the complexity of any state of motion, the greater the interval of reproduction of that state of motion.

The wave of great energy of which our solar system is a part consumes countless billions of years in completing its intervals and in reproducing itself, while a wave of low potential within it consumes but an incalculably small fraction of time.

If the constants of all the waves of low potential that appeared and disappeared ,in one hour were calculated, the total would' be exactly the same as the constant of one wave of one hour's duration.

Within each consecutive octave, the speed of the previous octave is accumulated in the universal ratio into multiples of that speed.

As each octave wave of energy is but a variation of the dimension of the universal constant and the multiples of the universal constant are repeated within each larger wave, so are the various speeds repeated within each wave.

The reproductive speed of genero-active light decreases in lowering octaves in inverse universal ratio, and radio-active speed increases in lowering octaves in direct ratio. The lower the potential, the greater the speed of reproduction.

Every effect of motion in any octave is repeated in sequence in the various speeds of every other octave.

Every effect of motion is cumulative and repeative within its accumulation.

For clarifying the meaning of these laws, one needs no better example than the sound of the human voice reproducing itself in the fifth octave, the "air."

Through the air sound reproduces slowly, but the expanded sound reproduces at the various speeds of each consecutive octave both lower and higher, through which it passes.

The sound of the human voice very slowly reproduces itself against the cliff side a mile away on the other side of the valley and returns as an echo.

The expanded sound of the voice in the highest octave, however, will girdle the globe many times before the last echo has returned from across the valley.

The sound of a pistol shot may be heard and reproduced by radio a thousand miles away from the scene of the action before the sound can be heard a half mile from the place of the action.

That illusion of motion which gives us the idea that light travels at various speeds is due to the greater and less intervals which greater and less potentials require to overcome inertia.

The concept of energy of low potential overcomes the inertia of a lower potential position more easily and more quickly than the energy of high potential overcomes the inertia of a relatively lower potential. The equilibrium pressure walls of high potential positions require relatively greater intervals of time to overcome their inertia.

In a universe of equilibrium this is necessary, otherwise the universal constant would be upset.

Light appears to travel and this illusion of motion gives us the universal yard stick known as the "speed of light."

The "speed of light" of the fourth octave is the expression of desire of electricity for action.

The "speed of light" is the universal genero-active speed of the highest octave of lowest perceptible potential.

One of the outstanding characteristics of opposed forces is the ultimate ability possessed by each to conquer the other. Each accomplishes this by assuming the preponderance of the other through a simulation of its attributes.

It is a conspicuous fact that the universal, relatively slow, genero-active speed which resistance has decelerated to 186,330 miles per second at the fourth octave of its journey from plane toward mass, is gradually appropriated by magnetism and applied to the radio-active speed from mass toward plane.

The speed of perceptible radio-active helium ejections from radium (1002 +) exactly equals the genero-active absorptions of ethlogen (402 +).

From actinium (1003 +) on the ejection speed increases until, in tomium (1004 $^{+}_{+}$) it is exactly 186,330 miles per second.

As genero-active force decelerates its power-time because of the work performed in mass accumulation, radio-active force accelerates its speed-time to balance by dissipation.

Reactions must keep pace with actions.

All down the octaves the battle between the two opposite forces continues, electricity ever losing speed as it works to gain power, and magnetism ever absorbing the lost speed for the very purpose of dissipating the accumulated power by increasingly forceful explosive ejections.

In accumulated mass, when the tenth octave is reached, magnetism has developed a power to repel radio-active emanations from mass toward plane at the universal speed of 186,330 miles per second.

When radioactive emanations from mass reach the universal speed equalling the speed of perceptible light, mass has reached the limit of its ability to accumulate opposing pressures into high potential.

The universal radio-active speed of high potential is the ending of the cyclic exhalation, just as the universal genero-active "speed of light" is the beginning of the cyclic inhalation.

Thus, during the entire battle between the two opposing forces, the universal equilibrium between the opposing power and speed pressures is preserved down through the octaves from inertia to inertia.

It is because of the continuous battle between the two opposing forces that mass is constantly changing its potential. Because of this fact, it is also constantly out of place in respect to the potential position of the next moment.

In moving from the potential position of this moment to that of the next moment mass is condemned to walk the treadmill of perpetual motion.

All potential out of place must be simultaneously balanced throughout the universe by a repetition of displacement in each changing dimension, and a replacement in an exactly opposed dimension.

Displacement and replacement are universally simultaneous.

An action calculated to displace is simultaneously accompanied by a reaction to replace.

All gravitational and radiational expressions are simultaneous in their opposition.

The universal see-saw must go down in unison with its going up.

Action and reaction are not sequential events. They are simultaneous oscillations, but the repetition of the actions and reactions are events separated by sequential intervals.

All effects of motion are simultaneously opposed, but their repeative acts are sequential.

That which man calls "energy" is the displacement of stability and its sequential replacement.

That which man calls "potential energy" is a locked state of energy displacement balanced by its equal replacement.

That which man calls "kinetic energy" is the ability of the opposing forces to perform "work" during the sequential intervals between displacement and replacement.

That which man calls "sex" is the degree of displacement, which is male, or replacement, which is female.

That which man calls "voltage" is the increasing displacement. It is heading northeasterly, against resistance, in the centripetal direction of all charging systems.

That which man calls "amperage" is the increasing replacement. It is heading southwesterly, with assistance, in the centrifugal direction of all discharging systems.

Force is continuous. It is not sequential. It does not consume time. It is universal. It is life. Consider, for example, the attraction of gravitation as force.

The attraction of one mass for another does not consume time. Force is continuous. The expression of the force of gravitation in drawing two masses together, however, does consume time.

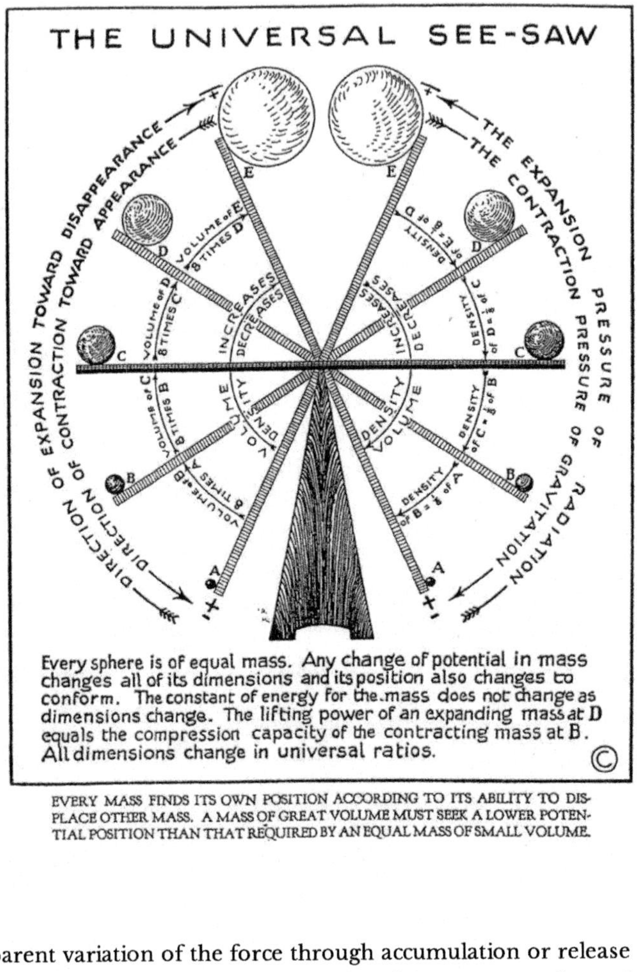

EVERY MASS FINDS ITS OWN POSITION ACCORDING TO ITS ABILITY TO DISPLACE OTHER MASS. A MASS OF GREAT VOLUME MUST SEEK A LOWER POTENTIAL POSITION THAN THAT REQUIRED BY AN EQUAL MASS OF SMALL VOLUME.

An apparent variation of the force through accumulation or release of potential constitutes an event which is reproduced in sequence from the inertial planes which separate all masses.

The force of the universal constant must not be confused with its opposite expressions.

One is unchanging and dimensionless.

The other is constantly changing and has varying and opposite dimensions.

In motion, force has the illusion of existence. In inertia force exists as a potentiality without the illusion of motion.

When an event takes place "anywhere" in the universe the concept of that event is simultaneously measured in inertia "throughout" the universe of non-dimension.

This is the first step toward the production and the reproduction of an event.

The second step is the sequential and universal reproduction of the concept of that event in plus and equal minus potential.

Simultaneity is essential to the maintenance of an equilibrium.

The dimensionless universe of inertia, the apparently "nothing," has taken on the dimensions of the apparently "something."

The illusion of space, time and motion has appeared.

Duration has also appeared.

Like all effects and dimensions of motion, time has its opposite expressions, both in effects and dimensions.

The opposites of time are power-time and speed-time.

Power-time is genero-active and therefore accumulative. It belongs to electricity. It begins with incredible speed of rotation and no speed of revolution and ends with no speed of either opposite pressure. The effect is rigidity.

Speed-time is radio-active and therefore dissipative. It belongs to magnetism. It begins with incredible speed of revolution and no speed of rotation and ends with no speed of either opposite pressure. Its effect is tenuity.

The greater the accumulation of electric energy and the slower the generative speed, the greater the speed-time of radio-active emanations from that accumulation.

The greater the attraction of cohesion in stored energy of the high potential of rigid bodies, the greater the deceleration.

That which man calls "mass" is changing potential out of place constantly seeking place because of its changing potential.

By "place" we mean equilibrium.

The constant search for an equilibrium position by all mass is the reason for its constant motion.

Accumulation of displaced energy from low equilibrium pressure walls to high equilibrium pressure walls, its storage as potential in various compartments bounded by those pressure walls, its redistribution into place by discharge and its reproduction throughout the universe, are sequential events in time dimension.

Time in intervals of seconds, minutes, hours, days, months, centuries, periods or cycles is a dimension measuring the sequential displacement and replacement of potential, accumulated from inertia and redistributed into inertia.

The intervals of time on this planet are standard units born of this planet's potential which alone determines those intervals.

As the potential changes the standard units must change.

The long year of our planet's low potential position in motion grew out of the shorter one of the high potential position held at birth, because of the deceleration of its revolution.

Our short day similarly appeared because of the acceleration of rotation as the planet's potential was lowered by increased distance from the sun.

Our year is now lengthening. It is continually expanding toward disappearance with the deceleration of our revolution, and our day with all of its sub-divisions is gradually shortening. It is continually contracting toward disappearance with the acceleration of our rotation.

The power-time dimension of each mass of a system expresses itself by deceleration of rotation speed-time which, thus retarded, expresses its equal and opposite reaction in accelerated revolution. They exchange attributes.

Power is accumulated from time by the resistance of revolution to the speed of rotation by the application of its power brake to the fast rotating wheels at the cost of losing its own power and absorbing the lowered speed.

This process lengthens days and shortens years. It is a charging effect. It transforms time into power by storing energy into mass, the universal storage battery.

Just as mass contracts itself into appearance, so does it expand itself into disappearance.

Just as the time intervals of this process contract, so do they necessarily expand.

Potential appears because of preponderant charge.

Potential disappears because of preponderant discharge.

Jupiter's year is nearly twelve of our years, and its day less than one-half of our day. It is expanding its years into disappearance by decelerating its revolution and is contracting its days into disappearance by accelerating its rotation.

Contracting, generating bodies decelerate the speed of rotation of inner planets by proximity.

The closer the planets of a system, the more the relative speed of rotation of inner planets is retarded by proximity. Each acts as a brake upon the wheels Of the other until they gradually meld in rigidity.

In melded rigid bodies the speed of rotation of inner parts is less than that of outer parts.

Deceleration of rotation of the planets of a system increases the surface tension pressure of a system.

If this law is well founded, then deceleration of speed of rotation must be related to the attraction of gravitation.

Increase of surface tension pressure is nature's process of effecting cohesion through composition.

The greater the deceleration of rotation, the greater the centripetal force of contraction pressure.

Expanding, emanated bodies separate because of their accelerated rotation.

The farther apart the planets of a system, the more their speed is accelerated by the release of the brakes upon the wheels of each.

Acceleration of rotation of the planets of a system decreases the surface tension pressure Of a System.

If this law is well founded, then acceleration of speed of rotation must be related to the repulsion of radiation.

Decrease of surface tension pressure by acceleration is nature's process of distributing assembled substances through decomposition.

Our standard units of time, or of any other dimensions are not a proper basis for calculation of the dimensions of any other potential.

Relative time dimensions of different planets are very easy to determine however, and through them, with such other relative dimensions which we can as easily determine, such as distance, relative areas, intervals of revolution and rotation, of plane and other comparative dimensions, it is possible for us to compute those relative dimensions which we cannot otherwise determine such as density, temperature and pressures.

We measure the mass and density of the sun and planets of our systems by our own standard units of gravitational intensity just as we do their time dimensions.

We arrive at wrong conclusions because our premises are wrong.

Though it has been calculated to be only twenty-five per cent as dense, the sun is, in reality, inconceivably more dense than this planet.

The sun's mass is vastly more than 332,000 times that of the earth. Mercury is very much more than 1.21 of the earth's mass, and Jupiter is not 317 times the mass of the earth, as calculated.

As a matter of fact Jupiter's huge volume is approximately only eight times the volume that our earth will be when in Jupiter's potential position.

Jupiter is, roughly, only double the mass of the earth, and Mercury's mass actually exceeds that of the earth.

When our planet has reached Jupiter's potential position its diameter will be approximately 40,000 miles, which is nearly equal to the radius of Jupiter.

Doubling the radius is equivalent to cubing the volume in direct ratio according to the universal law respecting all expansion pressure dimensions.

Consider the opposite effect.

When our planet was in Mercury's potential position its diameter was approximately 2,500 miles, or less than that of Mercury.

A time interval of a planet of an atomic system is as relatively long as the same time interval of the planet of a solar system. More than that, every planet of every atom has its own relative standard units of dimension which are as appropriate to it as are those of any planet of our solar system.

With the appearance of the intervals of duration comes the appearance of variation of the more and less of duration which we call faster and slower, or acceleration and deceleration.

Appearance of variation is as characteristic of time as of any other effect of gravitation and radiation.

There is but one "speed" by which all motion is measurable, the speed of the universal constant.

Less speed is but an accumulation of the speed-time constant transformed into power.

More speed is but a release of that accumulation.

Deceleration is but a contraction of time, and acceleration its expansion.

All dimensions are relative and the ratios of all dimensions are universal.

If time is the interval between events, and events are effects of motion, time must therefore be as relative as the standard units of the events it records.

Time on this planet is merely a relative dimension which measures intervals in the sequential expression of motion which belong to this planet.

Time must expand and contract in the universal ratios common to all dimensions of motion when applied to planets in other potential positions.

Minutes must shorten as expanding mass rotates faster, and lengthen with contracting mass.

Years must balance by lengthening as expanding mass revolves more slowly, and shorten as revolution increases.

A year is one periodic revolution of a mass around its sun.

A day is one periodic rotation.

All planets vary in both of these periods in opposite directions of the universal ratios and this variation of time is characteristic of all opposites of dimension in all mass.

The opposites of all effects of motion vary in the opposites of their several dimensions in the direct and the inverse of the universal ratios.

If these premises are right, then time dimension must be taken into account in the writing of the law of gravitation and radiation.

If variation of time dimension of a mass changes the ability of the mass to appear to attract or repel, then the law which takes into consideration but two of the dimensions of the mass, ignoring all others, cannot be complete.

Time and power appear by lengthening the day and shortening the year, and disappear by reversing these effects.

CHAPTER XVIII

EXPRESSIONS OF GRAVITATION AND RADIATION

TEMPERATURE-THE EIGHTH DIMENSION

This universe of more or less is a universe of varying pressures.

Temperature is a dimension of relative and opposing pressures as expressed in its opposites, heat and cold.

The popular concept that temperature measures only the degree of heat is not in conformity with the laws of motion.

Heat is improperly presumed to be an effect of motion which is operative in both directions.

In other words, that which we call cold is assumed to be less heat.

This idea must be eliminated from man's thinking. Heat and cold are as much the opposites of temperature dimension as positive and negative electricity, contraction pressure and expansion pressure are opposites of other dimensions.

Every dimension must have its opposite expressions which persist in their opposition. Each of these are not relatively less or more of the other.

Deceleration is not less acceleration. It is the result of the expression of one force just as acceleration is the result of the expression of its opposite.

Neither is negative electricity less positive electricity. Neither is the blue end of the spectrum less of the red end of the spectrum. It is as inaccurate to describe cold as less heat as to describe blue as less red, or to describe negative discharge as less positive charge.

Cold, expansion pressure, radiation, the blue half of the spectrum and negative electricity are the evidences of the domination of one of the two opposing forces, every expression of which is in an opposite direction from that in which heat, contraction pressure, generation, the red half of the spectrum and positive electricity are expressed.

The greater the contraction of charging bodies the more heat a body will register from generation, and conversely, the greater the expansion of discharging bodies, the more cold a body will register from radiation.

Like the pressure gage on the boiler which indicates the pressure developed within, or the voltmeter on the dynamo which indicates the resistance to induction developed by the charging of the generator, or the ammeter which registers the discharge conducted from that accumulated voltage, heat measures the resistance which magnetism sets up against integration by compression into smaller volume, and cold measures its disintegration by expansion into larger volume.

Contraction of volume by integration of the same mass into lesser space is resisted by expansion pressure.

Resistance to contraction heats by the opposition of the opposing forces.

Heating bodies approach each other and recede from cooling bodies.

If this law of motion is well founded, then heating bodies and the attraction of gravitation must be related.

Expansion of volume by disintegration into greater space is assisted by the expulsive force of contraction pressure.

Expanding bodies recede from expanding and from contracting bodies.

If this law of motion is well founded then cooling bodies, expanding bodies and the repulsion of radiation must be related.

Expanding bodies cool. Expansion of volume repels.

Cooling bodies recede from cooling and from heating bodies.

Expanding bodies seek lower pressure equilibriums. Cooling bodies contract.

Contracting bodies attract.

Contracting bodies seek higher pressure equilibriums.

To the process of contraction is due the illusion of attraction.

Contraction of volume is nature's process of integration.

Approaching bodies mutually heat.

Heating bodies charge. Charging bodies raise potential.

If this law is well founded then heat, charging bodies and the attraction of gravitation must be related. Also positive charge must attract positive charge.

Heating bodies radiate. Radiating bodies repel all other bodies.

Receding bodies mutually cool.

Radiation cools the radiating body and the emanated body.

Cooling bodies discharge. Discharging bodies lower potential.

If this law is well founded then cold, discharging bodies and the repulsion of radiation must be related. Also negative discharge must repel both negative discharge and positive charge. bodies Dooms contract and contracting bodies heat.

The re-heating of degenerating bodies by contraction is nature's process of regeneration.

Heat is ejected from heated bodies. Radiation lowers pressure and potential of radiating and ejected bodies.

Radiating and radiated bodies seek equilibrium positions in lower pressure zones appropriate to their lowered potentials.

Radiation of heat is nature's process of solidifying integrated substances of cooling bodies into locked potential positions.

Radiation expands and the consequential regeneration freezes the emanations expelled from radiating bodies. It also cools the radiating body, thus regenerating it also.

Expansion disintegrates the emanating body.

Disintegration is nature's process of redistribution.

Disintegration freezes radiating and radiated bodies.

Cooling is nature's process of effecting rigidity in radiating bodies and beginning the repetition of the same process in emanated bodies.

Radiation is discharge.

Discharging and discharged bodies cool. Cooling bodies generate.

Generating bodies draw closer to each other. They attract.

Generation heats.

Heating under pressure is nature's method of assembling mass.

Heating is nature's process of moulding form.

Cooling is nature's process of complexing form.

All form is simplified by heating.

All form becomes complex by cooling.

The sun of a system shapes her melted planets into spheres, the simplest of forms, puts them out to cool and thus begins their complexing.

The complexities of nature's multitudinous forms in those effects which we call "living" matter, begin with cooling.

The closer the planets of a system, the more retarded the speed-time dimension and the higher the melting points of the system.

It takes great contraction pressure to force bodies into close proximity

The greater the contraction pressure, the greater the resisting pressure.

The greater the resistance of opposing pressures, the higher the melting point of a mass.

If this law is well founded, then high melting point, high pressure equilibrium and the attraction of gravitation are related.

Bodies in close proximity will not remain in close proximity if the contraction pressure force which keeps them there is released by the counter pressure of expansion.

The less the resistance of opposing pressures, the lower the melting point of a Mass.

If this law is well founded, then low melting point, low pressure equilibrium, and the repulsion of radiation are related.

Thus it may be seen that preponderance of one opposite effect of motion is the condition precedent for the appearance of the other.

Thus it may be seen that heat and cold, like all other effects of motion, take their respective positions on the universal see-saw and tilt up and down simultaneously but alternate in their sequential preponderance of opposition.

Thus it may also be seen that temperature is but an effect of motion, an illusion of dimension, born of motion only. It is in no way an attribute of substance.

The One substance cannot be heated nor can it be cooled.

Like all opposites heat and cold are born with and of each other.

Let us consider whether or not the following commonly accepted temperature cycle is correct and complete.

"Cold contracts, contraction heats, heat expands and expansion cools."

Is not the cycle incomplete. because of the omission of that which makes of this universe a creating or evolving one?

Cold does not contract. Cold generates electric force.

Electricity is the attractive force and it is electric generation which contracts. It is proper to say that expanding bodies cool and that cooling Lodies contract, but not that cold contracts.

Conversely, heat does not expand. Heat radiates magnetic force.

Magnetism is the separative force and it is the separative force of radiation which expands.

It is proper to say that contracting bodies heat and that heating bodies expand, but not that heat expands.

The complete temperature cycle is as follows :

Thus is nature repetitive in all her states of motion by her method of conducting all her opposing dimensions in cycles.

The temperature of the universe is constant. Any variation of the constant is but a multiplication or division of that constant in direct or inverse universal ratios common to the variations of all dimensions according to whether the dimension is an expansion or a contraction pressure dimension.

The idea conveyed by the word "heat developed," or "energy developed" or "energy generated" wherein a heretofore presumably non-existent heat, or energy, is supposed to be developed is not in accord with the laws of motion.

Accelerated motion, being simply due to the decreased volume of a changed potential position, does not alter the constant of energy which produced that motion.

The higher temperature of a decreased volume does not mean more heat than the lower temperature of the larger volume, of an equal mass.

It means that the same constant of heat has readjusted itself to the changed potential position in accordance with the nineteenth law of motion.

The constant of heat energy is the same for both volumes and both masses.

Any force of the universe of dimension is an opposing pressure force.

The pressure force which compresses great volume into little volume and registers the intensity of that compression in heat is the male, electropositive, genero-active, electric force of inhalation.

Inhalation is an endothermic force. That means that it is heat absorbing in the commonly accepted scientific sense. "Heat absorbing" in the true sense means gathering together the potential of resistance from a large area and compacting it into a small area of the same constant.

The state of motion which produces incandescence is one in which the directions of the opposing forces are directly south and north across the pressure zones which define the orbits of floating bodies.

A meteorite, for example, when attracted by this planet from its proper potential position where it floats in space, "cuts across lots" into the higher pressure zones of this planet, becoming luminous from the resistance to so disorderly an invasion of zones of higher pressure.

The temperature of a meteorite increases in inverse universal ratio as it approaches the planet toward which it is falling.

Increase of temperature is a contraction pressure dimension.

A falling meteorite is an effect of gravitation which produces incandescence because of the rapid change of its potential position.

A comet falling to the sun is almost analogous to a falling meteorite. Its potential position is such that its path evades the sun and gives it a continuous orbit which eventually ends by a plunge into high pressures near the sun, exactly as a meteorite is worn away and disappears into incandescence by the resistance of the earth's high pressures.

A comet falling to its perihelion is an effect of gravitative preponderance, and one rising to its aphelion is an effect of radiative preponderance.

High potential gathered together in small focus in a searchlight, for example, will cut a visible luminous streak through the low potential of the air, an incandescent path against the night sky. This streak of light reverses the negative low potential of the illuminated area, increasing its positive charge.

The temperature of the path of light decreases in direct universal ratio, as the distance from its source increases.

Decrease of temperature is an expansion pressure dimension.

The radio-active emanations leaping violently from the sun with the explosive force due to great pressure from behind, develop incandescent streaks of light for millions of miles. These streaks of light form what is known as the corona of the sun. The violence with which they rise directly away from the sun produces a state of incandescence which disappears only when the radio-active emanations find the equilibrium pressure of their potentials and float in west to east orbits around the sun.

The temperature of the corona "rays" decreases in universal ratio as their distance from the sun increases.

The corona ray and hydrogen flame rising from the sun are effects of radiation, the exact opposite of that of a meteorite falling to the earth, but the reason for their incandescence is the same.

Every element has its own equilibrium pressure. Therefore, every element has its own melting point. More than this, every planet of every atom has its own equilibrium pressure and, there- here- fore, also has its own melting point for its mass and for each one of its elements.

The active force which compresses great volume into little volume and registers the intensity of that compression in heat is the male, electro-positive genero-active force of inhalation.

The reaction force which expands little volume into large volume and registers the intensity of that expansion in cold is the female, electro-negative, radio-active, magnetic force of exhalation.

Exhalation is an exothermic force. That means that it is heat releasing in the commonly accepted scientific sense. "Heat releasing" in the true sense means the redistribution of accumulation of heat over a large area, the constant being unchanged.

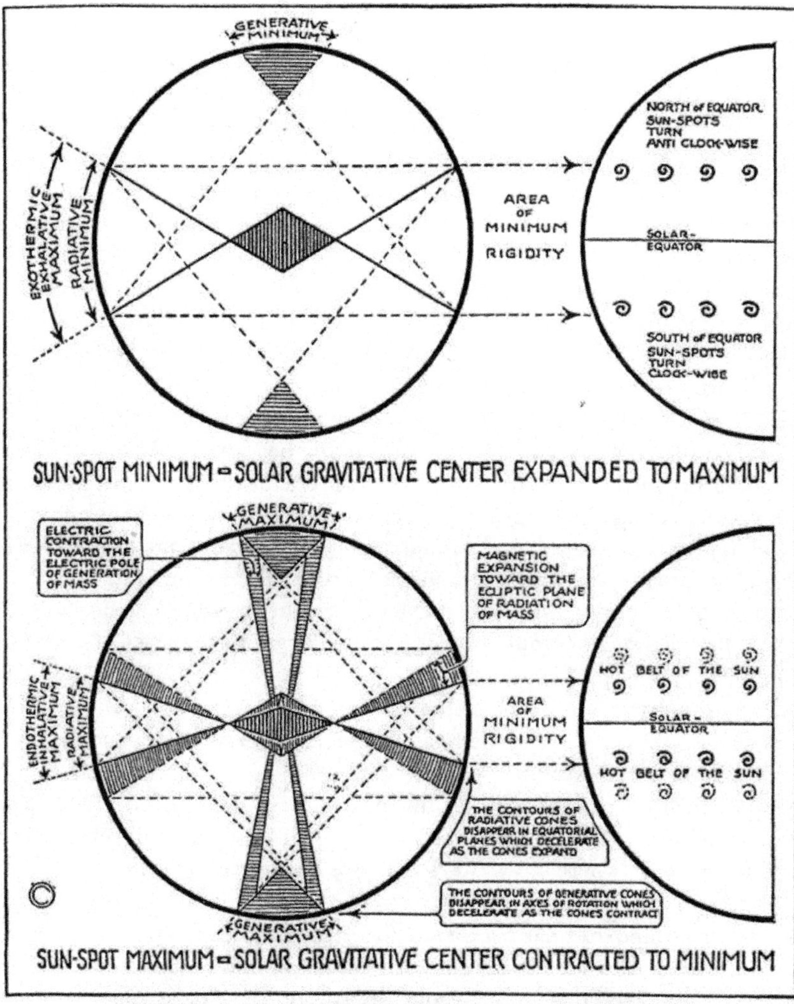

CHART No. 1. THE BREATHING OF THE SUN. EXPLAINING THE PERIODIC SHIFTING OF SUN-SPOTS IN CONFORMITY WITH THE CHANGING MAGNETIC BASES AND ECLIPTIC PLANE OF THE SUN

When heat gathered from a large area has been compacted into a sufficiently small area to cause a violent impact of opposite pressures seeking equilibrium, a state of motion is produced known as luminosity or incandescence.

The nearer the equalition of increasing pressures, the greater the luminosity.

The vortex of any system is always luminous. It matters not whether the system is of low potential and pressure opposition or of high potential and pressure opposition, there is always a sufficient pressure opposition at the vortex to cause a state of incandescence.

It must be remembered that the melting point of low potential is correspondingly low and that melting points rise as opposing pressures increase.

The state of violent motion which produces incandescence at the nucleus of the hydrogen atom is as relatively violent as the state of motion which produces incandescence in the sun of the carbon atom or the sun of our solar system.

The law for little mass being the same as for big mass, it follows that each planet in this solar system must have its own melting point as a mass, and its own relative standard unit melting points for every sub-division of its mass.

The opposing pressures which would melt a mass of zinc into a liquid, for example, would not even affect the rigidity of a mass of carborundum.

It can readily be seen, therefore, that a temperature which would be extremely hot to the mass of zinc would be but a warm breath to the mass of carborundum.

It is these relative temperatures, densities and pressures which lead us to form wrong conclusions regarding the relative temperatures, densities and pressures of the planets of this system.

The relatively expanded mass of this planet could not stand the heat of the pressure zone in which Mercury floats. This planet would become a molten ball in Mercury's orbit whereas Mercury's rigidity is hardly affected by it.

On each planet of this system, the degrees of heat and cold measured in their own relative standard units are so varying that one cannot judge of conditions on any other body when measured by standards common to this body.

On Mars we see polar ice caps and we assume that the temperature must drop below the 32° to which we are accustomed as the freezing point of water, in order that the ice caps could be possible. As a matter of fact water on Mars would not freeze at 32°. It would require a very much lower temperature. An atmosphere which would be too cold for us to survive would be comfortably warm for Martians.

We see the red fire spots of Jupiter and assume by our standard units of heat that Jupiter must be very hot whereas on the contrary, it is relatively very cold.

The heat of a flame at the surface of Jupiter would be below the freezing point of water on this planet.

The rings of Saturn, judged by our standard units of density, are presumed to be composed of solid substances like what are commonly known to us as boulders.

The rings of Saturn are composed of solid masses but the solidity of Saturn's rings would be as a heavy smoky vapor to us.

The outermost planets of this system and the nebulae beyond them are of so much lower pressure equilibriums that states of incandescence which would be extremely hot for their potentials would be colder than liquid air to us.

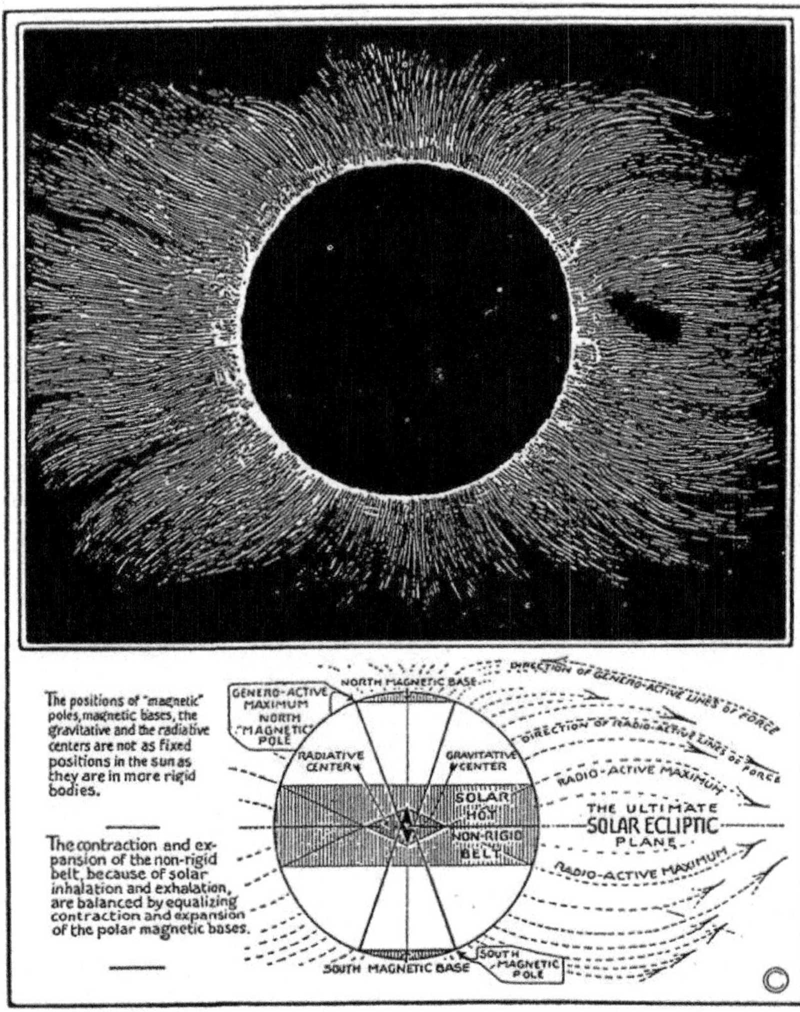

CHART No. 2. THE BREATHING OF THE SUN. EXPLAINING THE PERIODIC VARIATION OF THE SOLAR CORONA IN CONFORMITY WITH THE CHANGING MAGNETIC BASES AND ECLIPTIC PLANE OF THE SUN

It does not require much imagination to visualize a condition of relative heat on the planet Neptune when one considers that hydrogen freezes into a rigid solid in the ordinary temperature of Neptune whereas on this planet its freezing point is —250° C.

It is perhaps. difficult to realize that substances sufficiently solid to be used as building materials on one planet would be liquids and vapors on another. The very bricks and iron beams we use in our structures would be but liquids to the inhabitants of Mercury.

Conversely, frail substances to us would become the staunchest of building materials to the possible inhabitants of Saturn or Uranus.

On this planet we should not dream of building our houses of ice below the arctic circle. We fail to realize, however, that our staunch houses of stone and iron are but the ices of those substances, the only difference being that the melting points of the ices with which we build are so much higher than the normal temperature of this planet, that they are to us as dependable solids as the ice of water is to the eskimo.

All of our dependable solids are but the ices of various substances of varying states of dependability, their dependability being conditioned by their own separate locked potential positions.

By a study of the table of the elements in Chapter VI. one will see that the melting point of the inert gas at the beginning of the fifth octave is — 271° C. whereas the melting point of the substance in the first tone is +186° C., that of the second tone +1280 ° C., the third +2350 ° C. and the double tone +3600° C. Going back down the negative side of the scale, the melting point of the substance in the third tone is —210° C., that of the second —218° C., the first — 223° C. and the master tone — 271 ° C.

In every octave, the melting points rise and fall in an orderly manner as pressures increase in their opposition and relax from that opposition.

In the mid-tones alone are there any irregularities in the orderliness of increase and decrease, but mid-tones are characteristically irregular in all of their dimensions.

This does not mean that mid-tonal irregularities are exceptions to the law. It simply means that midtones are split-tones and the totals of all dimensions of all the split-tones in any octave are the constant of the double tone of that octave.

In temperature, as in all other dimensions, the variation of heat which gives us what we call higher temperature is merely a preponderance of heat at the expense of its opposite dimension, cold.

The constant of energy in all of its expressions is equal in every tone of every octave, the mid-tones between each tone counting as one tone.

All variations of temperature are, therefore, but variations of the opposites of dimension.

All variations of dimension are orderly, and in universal ratios.

The relative temperatures of the planets of this solar system are as much in conformity With the universal ratios upon which the formula of the locked potentials is based, as the temperatures of the various elements are in conformity with their law.

Without the variation of temperature in systems and the masses of systems, nature could not produce her effects of form, but she makes no variation in one opposite of any system without balancing that variation in the opposite dimension of an opposite system.

With all of the conditions governing the variation of temperature, standard units of temperature, like all other dimensions, are purely relative and must change to suit every changed condition.

One cannot, for example, give the melting point of aluminum as 659° C. as fixed and unchanging under all conditions.

A pressure of 1,000 pounds surrounding the metal would so change conditions that it would still remain frozen at a much higher point than 659° C.

Conversely, by heating it in a vacuum, it would melt at a very much lower point.

We, therefore, cannot set our standard units of temperature to conditions prevailing in the sun or any of the planets and the only way to find the true temperatures existing upon the various masses of this solar system, is to calculate them by universal ratios and set them down as a table of standard units of temperature for each separate mass.

If variation of temperature varies the apparent ability of mass to attract and to repel then the temperature dimension should be taken into consideration in writing the laws of gravitation and radiation.

S
TEMPERATURE
TEMPERATURE
N
DECREASES
INCREASES
S

CHAPTER XIX

EXPRESSIONS OF GRAVITATION AND RADIATION
COLOR-THE FIFTEENTH DIMENSION

Every effect of motion is recorded by nature in as substantial a manner as a business man records his inventory and without chance of human error.

As man records his facts with pen and ink in ledger volumes, so does nature record her effects of motion with light in octave volumes.

Every effect of motion differs from every other - effect of motion and is recorded with a preponderance of one or the other of the many colors of light.

Light is the universal language.

The colors of light are the letters of the alphabet.

Combinations of the letters of light are the words of the language of light.

Simple effects of motion are simple words of few letters.

Complex effects of motion are complex sentences and paragraphs with long words of many letters.

Every effect of motion is cumulative and repeative within its accumulation.

Every effect of motion in any octave is repeated in sequence in the various speeds of every other octave. A simple effect of motion, such as hydrogen, is written in the language of light in simple words of simple letters, for its history is brief. Hydrogen (401+) has within it the short• history of its accumulation of only three preceding octaves.

The spectrum of hydrogen is preponderantly red and that preponderance is recorded dominantly in one bright line of red, and less conspicuously in three other lines of red which indicate similar positions (301 +, 201+ and 101 +) of lower potential through which it passed in preceding octaves.

On the contrary, the spectrum of a complex state of motion such as iron is written in the language of light in complex paragraphs, of long, involved and complex sentences, words and phrases.

The spectrum of iron is preponderantly orange-yellow. That preponderance is recorded dominantly in its octave line and less conspicuously in six other lines of orange-yellow which indicate similar positions of lower potential through which it passed in preceding octaves.

The history of hydrogen as compared to that of iron is like the history of a three year old child as compared with that of a Napoleon.

All effects of motion absorb light and give forth light.

To absorb light is to decelerate its reproductive speed.

To decelerate light is to generate it by lengthening its reproductive intervals.

To generate light is to draw it closer to its gravitative center.

The ability to draw light closer to its gravitative center is the measure of its ability to attract.

To give forth light is to accelerate its reproductive speed.

To accelerate light is to radiate it by shortening its reproductive intervals.

To radiate light is to expel it from its radiative center.

The ability to expel light from its radiative center is the measure of its ability to repel.

All states of motion which are preponderant in their ability to attract record their preponderance on the red side of the spectrum.

All states of motion which are preponderant in their ability to repel record their preponderance on the blue side of the spectrum.

If these premises are well founded it must necessarily follow that the record of states of motion in color must be related to the attraction of gravitation and to the repulsion of radiation.

All light is a complexity of all colors.

That most remarkable of instruments known as the spectroscope separates light into its various colors.

The spectroscope also separates different effects of motion into their separate colors.

When man invented the spectroscope, he made the greatest stride toward solving the mysteries of nature by thus being able to write down her language in letters of light.

The effects of motion revealed by the spectroscope, show the cumulative history of each separate state of motion written within itself.

There should be no difficulty in writing a complete history of states of motion which will lead clearly to the .very door of the Holy of Holies.

The unseen universe of the first three octaves and the greater part of the fourth is clearly written in hydrogen and helium. It is quite clearly recorded in the discharging elements, nickel, mercury and tungsten. It is more clearly recorded in manganese, iron, molybdenum, rhodium, ruthenium, titanium, vanadium, zirconium and other predominantly male charging elements in which the resistance to integration assists man in writing down their history in the language of light.

It will require a volume in itself to rewrite a spectrum analysis in the universal language of light. Suffice it for this volume of first principles merely to suggest perhaps a more logical and workable electro-magnetic basis for this physical universe of dimension.

As each and every element is not a separate substance but a variation of the One substance, so is it also not an apparent separate state of motion but a variation of many states of motion.

All of the states of motion which go to make up any element are within that element.

Octave waves of low potential of which the elements are tones are within octave waves of high potential.

Within helium is the history of its growth.

Helium is a master-tone and helium itself is therefore devoid of spectrum lines of its own.

The three red lines of helium are the antecedents of hydrogen in octaves of the "unseen" universe, and other prominent lines tell the story of the six empty spaces which follow hydrogen.

Consider the spectrum analysis of iron, for example.

One can see at a glance the lines which belong to iron and those which tell its recent and remote history.

More important still, one can tell by their positions whether they represent the relative ability of the iron atom to charge or to discharge. Any other attribute of the states of motion which are assembled into that state of motion which we designate as iron is as clearly recorded in its spectrum as the words on this page.

One would have no difficulty whatsoever in recognizing the line of wave length 7817.2 as belonging to iron and 7392.3 as recent history and 6944.8 as extremely remote history. To facilitate the better reading of the language of light, herein follows a partial list of lines whose wave lengths belong to iron or to its immediate raid-tone associates, and also other lists indicating its recent and its more remote history.

BELONGING TO IRON	RECENT HISTORY	REMOTE HISTORY
7181.8	6916.8	6944.8
6495.1	6827.8	6678.1
6380.9	6335.4	6270.4
5905.8*	6230.9	6232.8
5862.5	6157.9	6137.8
5859.8	6102.3	6027.2
5816.5	6003.2	6024.2
5658.9	5930.2	5983.1
5555.0*	5701.7	5934.8
5041.9*	5686.6	5662.7
5041.2*	5497.5	5476.8
4920.6	5455.8	5415.4
4919.1	5455.2	5367.6
4859.9**	5324.3	5328.2
4789.7**	5227.3	5269.6
4736.9	5191.6	5233.1
4592.8*	5002.0	5192.5
4548.0	4982.7	5151.0
4260.7	4957.4	5110.5
4171.1	4938.9	5068.9
4057.9	3669.7	4443.3
3682.3	3606.8	4309.5
3605.6	3570.3	3622.2

*Dominant. **Conspicuously dominant.

The division of the visible spectrum into several thousand lines, each one of which is different in its shade of color and in its plane from every other, and of the invisible spectrum into thousands of other lines, tells in its own convincing manner that this universe of varying motion is a universe of varying pressures. By the "visible" spectrum, we mean that portion of the spectrum which can be detected by the evidence of human sight.

Great portions of the heretofore "invisible" spectrum are now detected by the bolometer and by the photograph negative.

Every state of motion is indicated by its own particular color line, exactly as it is indicated by its own degrees of temperature, plane and pressure.

Color is one of the great dimensions by means of which we will be enabled to measure the potential positions of states of motion which man will soon need to reproduce for the continuance of his very existence.

The spectrum begins at the 0= position of the inertial plane with an absence of color.

The beginning of resistance to integration is indicated in both directions by ultra-violet.

On the positive side of the wave, as genera active pressures increase, the violet merges into an infra red, then quickly into red, orange-red, orange and the yellow of north.

On the negative side of the wave, as radioactive pressures increase, the ultra violet merges into violet, then slowly into blue, greenish blue, green and the yellow of north.

Yellow is the meeting point of highest pressures, temperatures, densities and potentials of the wave.

From yellow the 4 position in the wave pressure walls are tonally erected back through the color pressure positions to the disappearance of color in the inertial plane.

Color therefore, like temperature, is an indicator of a state of motion and has no existence other than an appearance of existence.

As the condition and potential position of all mass can be determined by such dimensions as its plane, pressure and temperature, so also can its condition be determined by the colors which it is able to generate and radiate.

All mass is both generative and radiative. All mass indicates its ability to generate by the color pressures indicated by genero-active lines on the red side of the spectrum, and its ability to radiate by radio-active lines on the blue side of the spectrum.

The preponderance of color lines of a mass is indicative of its potential position in its wave.

A preponderance of red or orange indicates that a mass is on the outward journey toward the north, and a preponderance of green or blue indicates that a mass is on the return journey to plane.

Charging systems; therefore, are preponderantly recorded in the red end of the spectrum and discharging systems are preponderantly recorded in the blue end.

There are many evidences which seem to contradict this law in the spectrum lines of some of the positive elements but this contradiction is an illusion, similar to the illusion of perspective, and easily comprehensible.

The most outstanding of these apparent contradictions is the characteristic yellow D line of sodium.

If sodium were perfectly consistent with the law, its red line should be prominent and its yellow line weak, instead of which they are the reverse. The explanation is simple.

Sodium (601 +) is the first positive tone of the sixth octave.

At the fifth octave the super-inhalation of the cycle ends with its maximum of pressure.

In sodium, therefore, at the beginning of the super-exhalation, the intense accumulated pressures of inhalation cause so great a storm of contraction that sodium registers her overtone in preponderance to her true tone.

One may more easily understand this situation by drawing in a full breath, holding it in suspense for a moment and then releasing it. The pressure at the moment of release is great.

A perfect analogy is that of the old-fashioned church organ in which the controls are not sufficiently adjusted to prevent a pipe from sounding its overtone instead of its true tone when the boy who pumps the bellows suddenly becomes over vigorous.

This plus effect in sodium is counterbalanced, as all effects of motion are always counterbalanced, by exactly opposite minus effects in the corresponding positions 701+, 801+ and 901+ of the following three octaves.

In potassium (701+), even though the proper red preponderance is recorded, sodium's -off- setting discharge sweeps down through the blue side of the spectrum in a wave of increasing and decreasing intensity, ending suddenly in an intense line far down toward the violet.

In rubidium (801+), even though its own red preponderance and the history of its evolution is well recorded, sodium's offsetting discharge sweeps less far down through the blue side of the spectrum. Its wave of increasing and decreasing intensity ends in two blue lines of vigorous discharge, one of which belongs to rubidium itself, the other of which is history.

In caesium (901 +) sodium's offsetting discharge becomes equalized.

The spectrum of any element can only be obtained when that element is in a state of incandescence, which necessitates an increase of radiative, expansive pressure. This fact has much also to do with the recording of the overtone of sodium instead of the true tone.

In the sun, for example, sodium is under tremendously high pressure but upon this planet it is under low pressure. By subjecting it to a state of incandescence, its pressures become super-normal.

There is a great difference of opinion as to the direction in which evolution is proceeding, whether from the direction of white stars into the orange and red stages, or whether the colored stars are younger and will become white with increasing age.

The red stars are the younger. They evolve through orange and yellow to their white of maturity in the north apices of their cones. White in maximum motion is a reflection of white in inertia.

When degeneration begins, first green and then blue predominate. They are ageing.

It must be constantly borne in mind that standard units of pressures, and other dimensions in a potential position such as that of the sun, expand and contract to fit the standard units of measurements on this planet.

Therefore all pressure color lines that are visible in the high pressures of the sun expand in the same ratios when recorded in our planet's lower pressures, so that when so recorded they maintain their same relative positions.

Also it must be constantly borne in mind that increasing pressures are recorded nearer to the yellow, so that lines of consecutive octaves of increasingly higher potential record themselves in the direction of yellow.

If, therefore, yellow by the way of red is in the generative direction of north by the way of east, and violet by the way of blue is in the radiative direction of south by the way of west, pressure color lines must, in some manner, be related to the attraction of gravitation and the repulsion of radiation.

If the red side of the spectrum indicates a contracting state of genero-active preponder' ance, it must necessarily follow that all masses which record the red side in preponderance are electro-positive and preponderantly attractive.

Their preponderant dimensions are plus.

If the blue side of the spectrum indicates an expanding state of radioactive preponderance, it must necessarily follow that all masses which record the blue side in preponderance are electro-negative and preponderantly repellent.

Their preponderant dimensions are minus.

Every photographer is familiar with the effect of the absorption of light by red, orange and yellow, for these colors always translate their values darker than their constants.

Conversely, green, blue and violet, which are preponderantly light emitting always translate their values lighter than their constants.

If the red side is contractive, generative and attractive then red systems must be adolescent.

If the blue side is expansive, radiative and repellent, then blue systems must be senescent.

If the above premises are well founded and the color of a state of motion indicates the condition or potential of that state of motion, then color is as dependable a dimension as miles, feet and inches, or degrees of temperature and plane.

If color is as dependable a dimension as distance, temperature and other dependable dimensions, color should therefore be considered in the writing of the law of gravitation and radiation.

CHAPTER XX

EXPRESSIONS OF GRAVITATION AND RADIATION
UNIVERSAL MECHANICS-ROTATION-REVOLUTION MASS-PLANE
THE TWELFTH, THIRTEENTH, FOURTEENTH AND SIXTEENTH DIMENSIONS

In considering and comparing man's methods with nature's, let us first be reminded of the fact that the process of thinking out all idea is universal.

Man has no other manner of thinking out his idea than has the universal One.

The inner Mind is not another kind of Mind. Mind is universal. Therefore, there can be no two manners or methods or processes of thinking.

Exactly as there can be no two separate ways of thinking, one for man and one for God, so also can there be no two separate sets of principles or methods of constructing the ideas evolved by man and God in thinking.

The mechanics of the universal One are the mechanics of man.

The universal One is the great architect and engineer. Man can not transcend His principles nor discover new ones unknown to Him.

Man, the architect, designs supposedly new plan of effecting this purpose and the mechanical processes adopted by her in transforming her concepts of form into their appearances of reality in motion.

Nature's processes are clearly visualized in the various simple effects and periodicities with which we are perfectly familiar. It is only necessary to co-ordinate these effects in their orderly sequences by putting them together part by part, in order to clearly comprehend this vast but simple plan.

We are too prone to take various effects singly without coordinating them, or, if we take effects in groups, we are too prone to stop there without attempting to trace them back to their common beginning and ahead to their common ending.

Take for example, the orbits of our planets. We measure them and study them as orbits, but there we stop.

The most careful study and charting of orbits alone accomplishes nothing. We must trace back to the beginning and follow on to the ending every stage of the journey to and from mass of which these orbits are but a part.

By thus going back and charting the states of motion of this solar system as indicative of relative positions in their common journey, these orbits and their eccentricities will have a different meaning for us.

The purpose of nature is to produce and to reproduce the ideas thought out by the image making faculty of universal Mind.

Mind creates that which Mind thinks.

To produce and to reproduce idea in form, or in other words to quicken the concept with what we call "life," motion must be given to the universal Mind substance, out of which the form of all idea is born.

Inertia overcome by the energy Of motion always ends in mass.

Mass is the pigment with which nature paints all of her pictures with their illusions of dimension, upon the cosmic canvas of the inertial plane.

From the concept of form to the perfection of form as represented in the sphere, the perfection of orbit as represented in the true circle, the perfection of plane of motion as represented in the angle of 90° to the inertial planes, is a progressive cycle through imperfection in all of these effects.

Let us then begin this magic and ecstatic journey of creating things.

Let us trace the evolution of true circles through the ellipses.

Let us trace the evolution of the sphere from the shapeless ovoid through the whirling stages of oblateness to the perfection of true sphere.

Let us trace the evolution of volume from the plane of no dimension into mass.

Let us trace the evolution of plane itself through wide angles of ecliptic expansion to the one plane of perfect gyroscopic motion.

Let us trace the evolution of opposing dimensions of increasing and decreasing temperatures, volumes, densities, and all other sex expressions from the beginning of sex opposition in the wide expanse of south to the melding sex in the bi-sexual contracted point of no and back again.

Let us not forget that this universe of form is but a contraction of the concept of idea into the form of the idea. Form eventually expands into disappearance but is eternally continuous as idea.

All effects of motion are sequential contractions of centripetal, generative force which' compose mass by attracting it, and expansion' of centrifugal radiative force which decompose mass by repelling it.

Let us draw a mental picture of a "quantity" of energy representing the constant of the vase? wave of which the solar system is a part and: let us mark off the harmonic circle of this wave on the south inertial planes of the cubes of motion.

It will be remembered that the volume of the constant is represented by two opposed cones, the altitudes of which have been marked off by the electric pole at the intersection of the three inertial planes of the cubes of motion. These marked off altitudes represent the limitations of expansion of the wave.

The center of each harmonic base is also the apex of the opposing cone.

Imagine, then, the two opposing cones for each wave intersecting so that each apex meets the apex of another cone at the centre of the magnetic base of its opposite.

This is the position of the cones of energy in concept as simultaneously marked off throughout the universe.

This is the position of the opposing male-female, positive-negative cones of energy at the beginning and at the ending of every effect of motion as expressed in the wave before inertia has been overcome by motion and after motion has been conquered by inertia.

This is the position of the opposing cones of energy in the dimensionless universe of inertia.

This is the birth of energy in man's "spiritual" universe.

The transition to man's "physical" universe of solids of matter can now be easily visualized by imagining the gradual contraction of each electric pole to the points of north at the overtones of each wave.

ENERGY IS CONCEIVED IN INERTIA, STORED IN MASS AND RECORDED IN PLANE

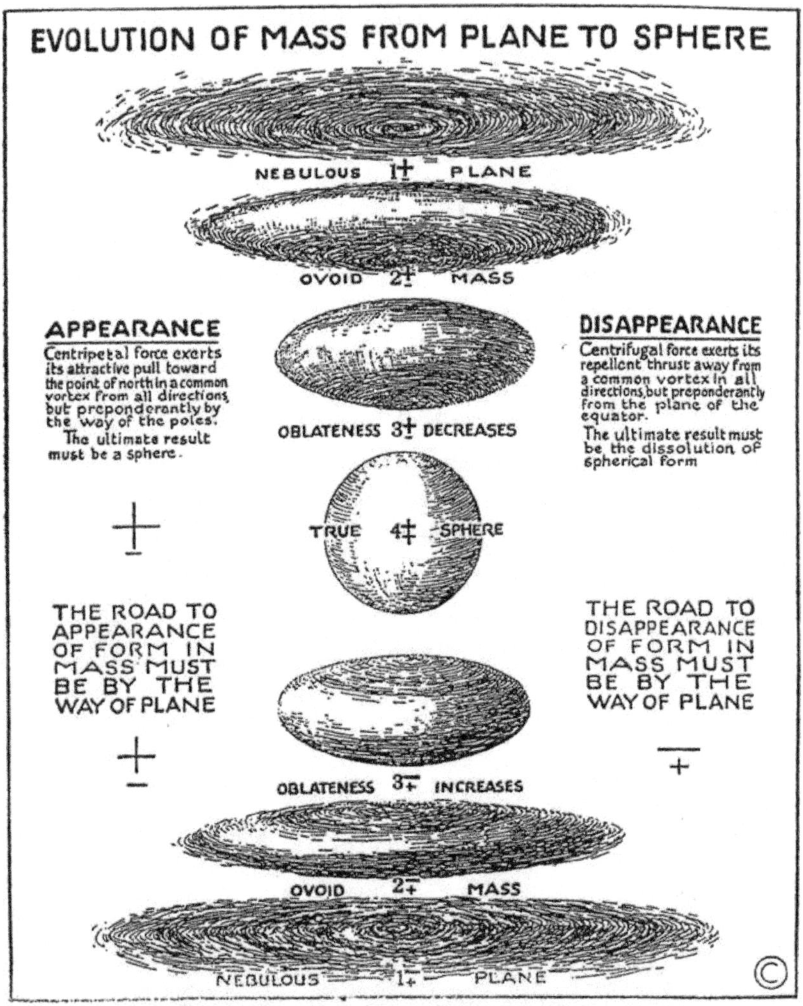

MASS IS GENERATED INTO THE APPEARANCE OF FORM BY THE ATTRACTION OF GRAVITATION AND IS RADIATED INTO THE DISAPPEARANCE OF FORM BY THE REPULSION OF RADIATION

Visualize this transition and note its happenings.

The constant of dimensions of the magnetic bases cannot change with changing dimensions for they mark the extension of the wave. There fore, as the axes of the cones contract and the contours of the cones sequentially expand until they disappear into the one plane of their bases, the planes of the magnetic bases are transferred to the equators of forming masses, which, added together, equal the constant of the-whole.

The constant of dimensions of the electric poles cannot change with changing dimensions for they mark - the volume, or expansion dimensions of the wave. Therefore, as the axes of the cones contract, the altitudes of the contracting cones are transferred to the poles of rotation of forming masses which, added together, equal the constant of the whale.

Observe then that energy in concept inertia is expressed by magnetic base of cone meeting magnetic base, and apex of cone meeting apex at the south inertial plane of the cubes of motion.

Observe also that energy in motion is expressed by the disappearance of cones, by apex and base melding with apex and base at the ecliptic planes of the cubes of motion through the contraction of the electric poles.

The entire gamut of all effects of motion is run during this process of the contraction of the opposing electric poles to a point of disappearance in mass, and the expansion of the magnetic bases from the inertial planes of non-motion to the ecliptic planes of maximum motion and the consequent disappearance of cones in mass.

During this process the point of north draws the design of the wave in a spiral line from the centers to the corners of the cubes of motion.

Through contraction of the electric poles, centripetal force is born in the inertial plane and is increased in force in whirling masses which are contracting with the contraction of the poles of the opposing cones of motion as they near the apices of those cones on their outward journey to mass, and is decreased in force as they return to plane.

Through contraction of the electric poles, centrifugal force is born in the inertial plane and is increased in force until that plane has gyrated unsteadily to its overtone position of maximum contraction at the point of north of the cubes of motion on its outward journey to mass and is decreased in force as it returns to plane.

Although centripetal force is preponderant on the outward journey to mass from 0= to 4^{+}_{+} in the positive half of the wave, centrifugal force increases in excess of centripetal force until the former overtakes and counterbalances the latter at the overtone of the wave.

This is in conformity with the fact that negative discharge increases as positive charge increases until the former overtakes the latter and the power of disintegration exceeds that of integration, causing dissipation of accumulated energy.

This is also in conformity with the fact that the force of radiation increases as the force of gravitation increases until the former overtakes the latter and dominates the wave.

Conversely, although centrifugal force is preponderant on the return journey to plane from 4t to 0= in the negative half of the wave, centrifugal force decreases in excess of centripetal force until the latter overtakes the former at the harmonic of the wave.

This is in conformity with the fact that negative discharge decreases as positive charge decreases until the latter overtakes the former and integration again exceeds disintegration, causing the wave to repeat itself.

MASS AND PLANE IN OPPOSITION

Saturn is the one outstanding example in our solar system of the battle for supremacy between electric centripetal force which desires to retain the spherical appearance of form in mass, and magnetic centrifugal force which desires its disappearance.

The greatly accelerated rotation of the equatorial belt of this expanding sphere of relatively low potential tends to counteract the effect of gravitation and is expressed by throwing off rings from portions of Saturn's surface. The rings are in the plane of Saturn's maximum radiation. Radiative preponderance is struggling to retain its expression in plane, while the subordinate generative force of the rings is attempting to re-express itself in mass. This they will eventually do. The rings will become satellites of Saturn when the swing of the poles sufficiently increases its angle. This is what has occurred in the case of Uranus. Jupiter is even now preparing to throw off a series of concentric rings which will also regenerate into new satellites.

EXPLAINING THE RINGS OF SATURN AS THE NECESSARY EFFECT OF ITS POSITION DURING THE RETURN JOURNEY FROM MASS TO PLANE

This is also in conformity with the fact that the force of radiation decreases as the force of gravitation decreases until the latter overtakes the former and supplies the impetus for overcoming inertia in the repetition of the expression of the same constant of energy in a new wave.

This is the process of formation of mass, its dissolution and its repetition by means of the wave, for every expression of energy.

This is the genero-active process of production and reproduction, or creation, of any of the ideas of Mind, and the radio-active process of their dissipation or dissolution into but the memory of those ideas.

The effect in relation to plane has been a gradual contraction and the building up of opposing pressure walls of increasing potential in ever shortening cones.

Another effect in relation to plane has been to overcome its inertia and set it in motion.

The force of motion toward plane is always toward south by way of west and is therefore centrifugal.

The effect in relation to volume of the cones has been a division into separately, whirling masses.

The effect in regard to the cones of energy has been their transference to mass, within which they continue their office of opposing and of alternating conquest on the journey from plane to mass and back again to plane.

When apex meets apex at the center of the magnetic bases within masses, then the outward journey is completed.

At this point, sex meets sex in a bi-sexual union at the true point of north where both revolution and rotation disappear.

The force of motion away from plane is always toward north by the way of east and is therefore centripetal.

When apex meets apex at the center of the magnetic bases of south inertial planes then is the return journey completed.

The contraction of the generative cones ends at the electric poles and is the effect of centripetal force.

The expansion of the radiative cones ends at the ecliptic plane and is the effect of centrifugal force.

The gradual contraction of the two opposing and intersecting cones into their disappearance in one plane causes all substance forced in the direction of the two vortices to whirl in the ever shortening spiral orbits and ever increasing pressures of the electric stream.

The same cause forces all substance expelled from the contracted north to whirl in the ever lengthening spiral orbits and lessening pressures of the magnetic stream.

The contracting electric centripetal stream is the condition of motion necessary to produce that effect of motion which we call the attraction of gravitation.

The expanding, magnetic, centrifugal stream is the condition of motion necessary to produce that effect of motion which we call the repulsion of radiation.

The electric stream and the magnetic stream are one. They are but travelling in different directions.

The electric stream is travelling toward the apex of a cone in the ever contracting direction of the outward journey to mass, and the magnetic stream is travelling toward the base of a cone in the ever expanding direction of the return journey to plane.

Each stream is forever passing and following the other as the degeneration or regeneration of it.

The electric stream of contraction is the plus force which ends in mass.

The magnetic stream of expansion is the minus force which ends in plane.

Both forces, intensify toward north and build unstable and opposing tonal pressure walls which become stable and reproductive by their union at the point of north.

Both forces meet in reproductive union in equal high intensities in the double tone at the bisexual plane of north.

There remains but one more effect of which to make careful note in order to completely visualize the mechanics of motion of both the outward journey from plane to mass and the return journey to plane.

As the axes of the opposing cones of energy contract and their contours expand, the apices of the cones of energy bend gradually away from the inertial junctions to the corners of the cubes of motion.

Thus spiral Waves are formed and all spiral motion is born.

Thus is eccentricity of orbit a necessary stage in the evolution of perfection of orbit.

Thus is the ellipse a necessary stake in the evolution of the circle.

Thus is the unsteady gyration of precessional motion of expanded plane in all mass a necessary stage in the evolution of perfection of gyroscopic motion in one plane.

Thus is the amorphous and irregular crystal a necessary stage in the evolution of the perfect cubic crystal.

Thus are the polar surfaces of all masses the regions of transference of the inertial cold of nonmotion, and the equators the regions of transference of the resistant heat of maximum motion.

Thus is the concept of energy in the one point of north in inertia divided into its opposites of expression in sex in the appearance of two points of north at the overtones of every wave in order that the dimensionless universe of simultaneity in inertia may become a universe of dimension with sequential intervals of reproduction of its productions.

Thus does the sexlessness of inertia become bisexual in its reflection in motion.

It will be remembered that the harmonic circle of a wave is its magnetic base which when transferred to mass, is the ecliptic of the wave and of every sub-division of the wave.

It will be remembered that when the electric pole of a wave is reflected in accumulated mass, it ends in the gravitative center of the mass and of every sub-division of the mass.

There is but one electric pole and one magnetic base of unchanging constants to the volume of every wave.

When the entire volume of a wave as measured out by pole and plane is transferred to separate masses through motion, the electric pole and magnetic base is reflected in every whirling sub-division of that volume.

In every wave the constant of its cone volume in inertia is the constant of the volume of all masses in motion within the wave.

The position of the charging poles represents the increase of electric force. This increase is in the direction of north at the overtone of the wave, and toward the reflections of north at the gravitative centers of all masses of the wave.

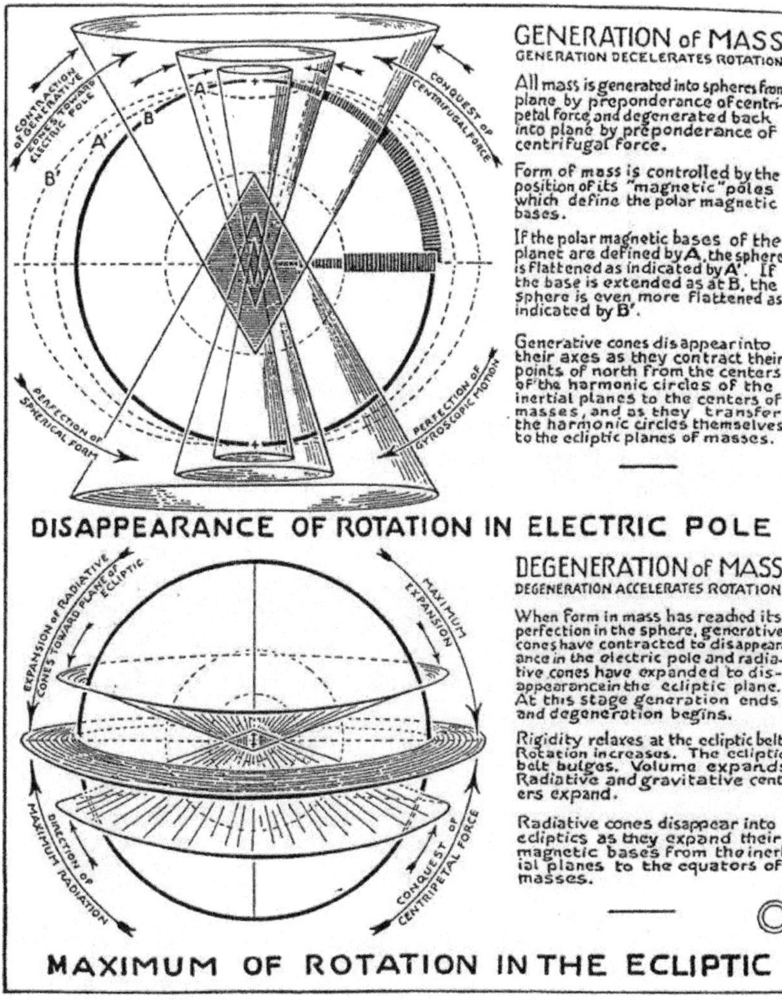

EVOLUTION OF MASS. ELECTRICITY EVOLVES MASS INTO THE FORM OF A TRUE SPHERE AND MAGNETISM DEVOLVES IT INTO PLANE. THE PROCESS IS ORDERLY AND PERIODIC

The expansion of the magnetic base represents the increase of magnetic force. This increase is in the direction of south at the harmonic plane of the wave, and toward the reflection of that harmonic plane in the ecliptic areas of all masses of the wave.

The contraction of the charging poles represents the generative force which expresses its conquest over the magnetic force by the contraction of area of orbit, by deceleration of rotation and acceleration of revolution of individual masses.

The expansion of the magnetic base represents the degenerative force which expresses its conquest over the electric force by expansion of orbital area, by acceleration of rotation and by deceleration of revolution of individual masses.

The electric pole of generation gathers separately moving masses together into the bound energy of rigid bodies by the mutual force of attraction of charging bodies and gives to each mass of the wave a portion of itself.

Electricity then expresses its ultimate conquest of magnetism by a reversal in mass of its original desire for action through motion and simulates the desire of magnetism for non-motion.

The magnetic base of degeneration expresses its ultimate conquest of electricity by actively asserting its repellent force. It more vigorously pries apart the bound energy stored in mass by its preponderance of centrifugal force.

Magnetism then expresses its ultimate conquest of electricity by a reversal in mass of its original desire for inaction and simulates the desire of electricity for motion.

Electricity starts the outward journey from non-motion to mass with intense motion, ends with non-motion and then transfers its energy to assist magnetism on the return journey.

Conversely, magnetism starts the outward journey from non-motion to mass with intense opposition to motion, ends with non-motion and begins the return journey with intense does this universe of more and less alternate between the more and the less, by exchange of the balances of power and speed from one to the other.

Thus is all motion characterized by oscillation.

Thus is all oscillation decelerated from the trillions per second in small mass to the one in centuries in big mass.

Thus does power-time conquer speed-time by absorbing its speed, and speed-time conquer powertime by dissipating its power.

Thus does the preponderantly male accumulate the female in each oscillation until eventually the female is preponderant.

Thus does the preponderantly red end of the spectrum accumulate the blue, until the blue end is preponderant in violet.

Thus do all effects of motion alternate in preponderance as each opposite force conquers the other by yielding to its desire.

For a concrete example of one of these effects, let us consider the four inner planets of our solar system which are sufficiently expanded in relation to each other to revolve and rotate freely, in accordance with the rule that bodies moving in inner orbits revolve faster and rotate slower than do those of outer orbits.

If these four planets had been heated together and set out to cool as one solid mass, each mass forming concentric rings or shells one around the other, their power-time conditions in revolution would motion.

Magnetism is overtaken on the return journey to plane by the intense speed of low potential, the impetus of which causes its regeneration on the positive side of the inertial plane.

The speed-time dimension of the magnetic return exactly equals the power-time dimension of the electric start.

Each of the opposing forces conquers the other by simulating the desire of the other. Thus be reversed in rotation.

Mercury revolves at about twenty-nine miles per second and circles the sun four times to the earth's once.

Venus moves about twenty-two miles per second and circles the sun more than twice to the earth's once.

The earth revolves about eighteen miles each second.

Mars slows down to fifteen miles and takes nearly two years to complete one circuit of the sun.

The process of generation of mass reverses this order in rotation.

Consider for example, the earth as a contracted complex rigid solid.

A mass on its surface at the equator rotates about one thousand miles per hour.

A mass one thousand miles below the surface rotates about seven hundred and fifty miles per hour.

A thousand miles deeper and the speed is but five hundred miles.

Three thousand miles down the speed reduces to two hundred and fifty miles per hour and at four thousand miles practically ceases.

In any mass the speed of rotation of bound energy increases in the direct universal ratio from the gravitative center of force.

In any system the speed of revolution of separated equal masses of bound energy revolving in the same plane, decreases in the inverse universal ratio from the center of force.

In any system accelerated revolution increases power-time dimension and accelerated rotation increases speed-time dimension.

In any mass decelerated rotation increases power-time dimension and decelerated revolution increases speed-time dimension.

In any mass or system the decrease in rotation or revolution is in inverse universal ratio and is balanced by a corresponding increase of the opposite effect in direct ratio.

When opposing forces conquer each other by simulating each other's attributes in motion they also simulate each other's mathematical ratios of increase and decrease.

There is but one force and when each apparent opposite exchanges attributes of motion, it exchanges ratios in conformity with these changes.

The difference is only a difference in the appearance of form in mass due to contraction or expansion, and in time dimension due to a reversal of ratios.

Never for one moment does the appearance of form in mass escape from the governing plane of the reality of form in concept in inertia.

Plane follows mass, governs mass and effects its evolution.

Plane eventually dominates mass and controls it till its dissolution.

Mass is stored energy, bound into form as potential energy.

To be stored, energy must be frozen into a dense, rigid solid.

Mass, in freezing, must radiate its heat.

Radiation cools.

Radiation is preponderant where expanding magnetic bases meet at the ecliptic planes of masses.

Where magnetic bases meet each other in mass the speed of rotation is at its maximum. Cooling mass contracts.

Contraction is preponderant where charging poles intersect ecliptic planes at the gravitative centers of all masses.

At gravitative centers, the speed of rotation disappears and revolution increases. Both of these effects of motion are expressions of power-time, increasing positive charge and increasing potential.

Generation expresses its conquest over radiation through resistance to the magnetic force as expressed in decelerated rotation and accelerated revolution.

Radiation expresses its conquest over generation through resistance to the electric forces as expressed in accelerated rotation and decelerated revolution.

The final conquest of electricity is at the true point of north where both accelerated revolution and decelerated rotation end in non-motion at the end of the outward journey to mass.

At this point the charging poles equalize preparatory to their reversal.

In this bi-sexual position the appearance of stability in motion-in-opposition has reached its maximum.

The final conquest of magnetism is at the inertial plane of south where both decelerated revolution and accelerated rotation end in non-motion at the end of the return journey to plane.

It will be remembered that electricity desires the accumulation of energy into rigid bodies of non-motion, and expresses that desire through resistance to a force established by itself and opposed by magnetism.

It will be remembered that magnetism opposes motion but is forced to react equally to every electric action of induced motion.

It will, therefore, be seen that the composition and decomposition of mass is but a series of alternate electric conquests over magnetism, followed by magnetic conquests over electricity.

Electric conquest, through motion which ends in a simulation of non-motion, results in the appearance of rigid bodies.

Electricity winds the cosmic clock to its ultimate binding point at the point of north where force unites with force to create a dead center of non-force.

Magnetic conquest, through motion which ends in a simulation of non-motion, results in the disappearance of rigid bodies.

Magnetism unwinds the cosmic clock to its ultimate releasing point at the plane of south where force departs from force to create a dead center of non-force.

Through motion electricity simulates the stability of inertia and also through motion magnetism reattains the real stability of inertia.

Rigid bodies are relatively cool contracted bodies.

Rigid masses of stored energy are accumulations of expanded masses into contracted masses, the decrease of rotation of which has been transformed to a corresponding increase in revolution.

Nebulous masses of discharging potential are released accumulations which reverse the order of their revolution and rotation as they expand and separate into more simple masses of lower potential.

Charging bodies are those which are transferring the constant of their speed-time in revolution to power-time in rotation.

Discharging bodies are those which are exchanging the constant of their power-time in rotation to speed time in revolution.

If the foregoing premises are correct in principle, then the four dimensions, rotation, revolution, mass and plane must be related to the attraction or gravitation and the repulsion of radiation.

Let us now consider each of these dimensions separately, ever bearing in mind that all mass is formed from within itself and that, as a consequence, the increase in any gravitative effect is accompanied by an increase in a radiative effect in opposite directions of the same ratio.

More positive charge in a mass does not mean less negative discharge.

Greater ability to attract does not mean less ability to repel.

Each opposite effect simultaneously increases and decreases its preponderance until one overtakes the other and assumes the preponderance of the other 'in passing. This is the basic principle of mass formation and deformation.

The formless universe of thinking Mind is an inert universe of the real stability of non-motion imbued with a desire to overcome inertia through motion.

The universe of form in mass is the gyroscopic expression of the desire of thinking Mind to give form to the ideas of Mind; and to overcome motion by inertia in order to regain its lost stability.

When motion overcomes inertia it stimulates the stability of inertia in the gyroscopic, gravitational points of north which are developed in every creating form of thinking Mind.

When inertia overcomes motion it simulates form by recording it in inertia.

The record of the idea of Mind in inertia is the eternal soul of that idea.

Idea is forever recorded in soul in inertia and repeated in form of mass in motion. No idea of Mind ever began or ever ended.

CHAPTER XXI

EXPRESSIONS OF GRAVITATION AND RADIATION

ROTATION—THE TWELFTH DIMENSION

Many theories have been advanced regarding the cause of rotation of mass. It is generally assumed that mass has been given an original impetus which keeps it in motion.

The cause of rotation is extremely simple and not shrouded in mystery. All mass is constantly changing its potential. It, therefore, must change its position as its potential is changed, for every potential has its own place or position in this universe of dimension.

Let us recall a basic law : "That which is generated must be radiated." Planets generate in preponderance north and south of their Cancer-Capricorn belts on their day light hemispheres.

Planets preponderantly radiate in preponderance at the boundaries of their ecliptic expansions and on their dark hemispheres.

To generate means to contract from within.

The generative portion of a planet pulls against the spiral lines of force and thus retards motion in that direction.

To radiate means to expand, expel or repel from within.

The radiative portion of a planet pushes against the spiral lines of force and thus accelerates rotation.

In a high potential position, the opposed pressures which caused that high potential are more equally distributed over the entire surface of the mass.

At the overtone of the wave, where all planets are true spheres, the ability to generate and to radiate is equally distributed over the entire area of each planet. As the potential of a mass diminishes, the ability to generate confines its activity more closely to the area surrounding its charging poles and decreases in intensity in the direction of its equator.

When our sun, for example, has reached its overtone position at the north point of the wave, its radioactivity will have overtaken its genero-activity.

The corona of the sun will then be as prominent at the poles as at the equator. The charging poles will then coincide with the pole of rotation.

Conversely, the genero-activity of the sun will be as great at the equator as at the poles. The ecliptic will then coincide with the equator. There will be no ecliptic expansion.

The equatorial belt of the sun will then be as rigid as the polar regions, and sun spots will be confined to the plane of the equator until they entirely disappear.

The generative position of a - planet is the charging portion.

It is regenerative.

It is endothermic, or heat absorbing.

The radiative portion of a planet is the discharging portion. It is degenerative.

It is exothermic or heat releasing.

That which is being drawn into a planet from within is an opposing force. Its effect is opposite to the effect of the force of that which is being expelled from a planet.

Celestial mechanics employ these two forces to keep the wheels of nature revolving. Nature sets these two forces one against the other in a manner which man would do well to more closely emulate.

Nature always directs her force against a tangent and continues it without a break.

Nature accumulates her power to its high explosive, high pressure, high temperature and high potential position and then regenerates it over and over again until every last particle of it has performed work on its way to dissolution.

Consider the solar system, for an example of universal economy.

The sun represents the accumulation of generated energy which runs the wheels of this particular atom of the universal machine.

The sun is the storage battery of this solar system.

The explosive radio-active emanations from the sun are regenerated in a continuous stream by impact against the inertial plane of her nearest planet. From the inertial plane its motion is continued by a regenerative positive force pulling from within the planet in a spiral, tangential direction.

Mercury uses what it needs of this power and passes it on by expelling it from within in a greater tangential direction.

One after the other the intake of each planet absorbs the regenerated exhaust of the previous one and passes it on from planet to planet in an ever increasing tangential direction, until all the power of the primary explosion has been utilized to perform the work of giving form to the idea of universal thinking.

No power is wasted.

All of the exhaust energy of the sun passes along the lines of its ecliptic expansion as bound energy confined within pressure walls, as truly as the exhaust energy of an explosion in - a. cylinder head passes within the walls of the cylinder of man's machine.

The radiation of the sun does not pass into space in a casual manner. It is directed toward the south by the way of west and within the limits of its own ecliptic area which is approximately 16°.

Consider the mechanics of man as a comparison to those of the solar system.

In man's motor engines the force of each explosion performs a small proportion of the work which that amount of stored potential is capable of performing.

The larger portion of energy is wasted in the exhaust.

Man must learn to regenerate the heat which has not performed work.

He must also learn to direct his pulsations of accumulated force in a continuous stream tangentially toward the direction of least resistance if he desires to transmit accumulated energy into speed.

Conversely, if he desires to transmit power, he must learn to direct his pulsations of accumulated force less tangentially, and more directly in the direction of greater resistance.

The greater the resistance the greater the generation of power and the less its dissipation in speed.

The less the resistance the less the generation of power and the greater its dissipation in speed.

Universal mechanical principles are perfect. They are perpetual in their source of supply and , they are not wasteful. Every particle of energy is used before its final dissipation.

Man's supply of energy is as inexhaustible as the universe from which that supply is drawn.

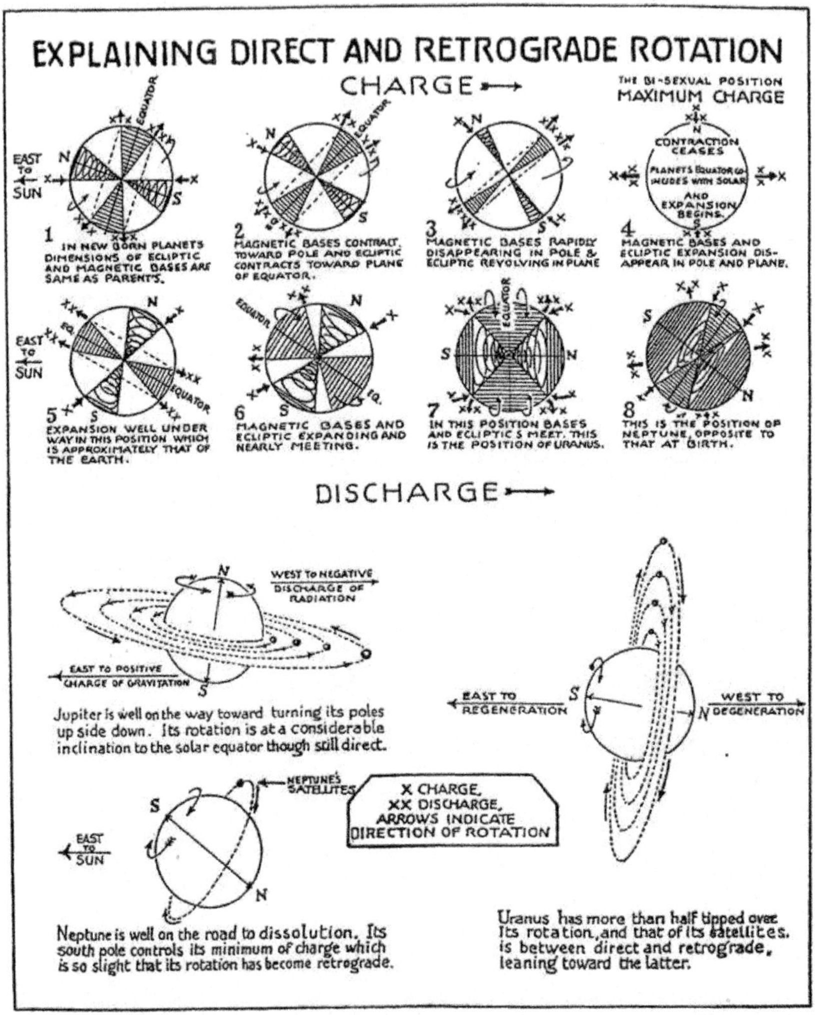

ALL MASSES ROTATE ON THEIR AXES AND REVOLVE AROUND THEIR GRAVITATIVE CENTERS IN THE SAME DIRECTION. THE APPARENT CONTRARY EFFECT IS DUE TO CHANGE OF POSITION ONLY

Man can so perfect his mechanical principles that he can have as continuous a supply of power to perform his work as this planet has to continue its rotation.

Perpetual motion for man need be limited only to the wear and tear of the parts of his machines. The driving power for those machines is inexhaustible.

All mass rotates from its local west toward its local east, just as all mass revolves from its local west toward its local east.

The local west is a surface direction. It is in the direction in which the sun appears to set.

The local east is a surface direction. It is in the direction in which the sun appears to rise.

The universal west is the expansion of north which is ever away from the sun of any system.

It is the centrifugal direction of negative discharge.

It is the direction in which all planets are spirally threading their way on their return journey from mass to plane.

The universal east is the contraction of south which is ever toward the sun.

It is the centripetal direction of positive charge.

It is the direction in which all generating light units are spirally threading their way on their outward journey toward the melting pot.

Universal power accumulating mechanical principles are as perfect as are universal power distributing principles.

Low potential runs the gamut of all the intermediary potentials, with a preponderance of regenerative over degenerative power until it has found the highest potential position in its wave.

It then returns by the reverse of the same principles in easy stages of lessening regeneration and preponderant degeneration.

Let us recall that north by the way of east is the direction of generation, and south by the way of west is the direction of degeneration.

Imagine the degenerative solar emanations following the centrifugal lines of force of the corona until they become regenerated by following the centripetal lines of force which attract them to this planet as positive charge.

It cannot be too often repeated that the radio-active force is the degenerative force and is centrifugal.

Conversely, the genero-active force is the generative force and is centripetal.

In a low potential position, where the ratio of genero-active preponderance is very materially reduced, the balance of radio-active centrifugal force is materially greater in proportion. The pinwheel-like effect of rotation due to centrifugal preponderance gradually gains control.

In such a position force is exerted in tangential directions of gradually lessening resistance from planet to planet, which gradually results in dissipation of power, as expressed in revolution, through speed as expressed in rotation.

A study of the accompanying chart on page 272 will make this more clear. On studying the chart, one must bear in mind that the contractive force of attraction is exerted from within, consequently retarding rotation. It is as though the planet were pulling at a rope wound spirally around itself,

It must be recalled that the expansive force of repulsion is also exerted from within, consequently accelerating rotation. It is as though the planet were rotating with the aid of a propeller with its shaft turned toward the local west.

The direction of rotation of a planet gradually changes in reference to its local direction but never changes its universal direction.

Its local direction of morning at birth is not its local direction of evening when it has aged.

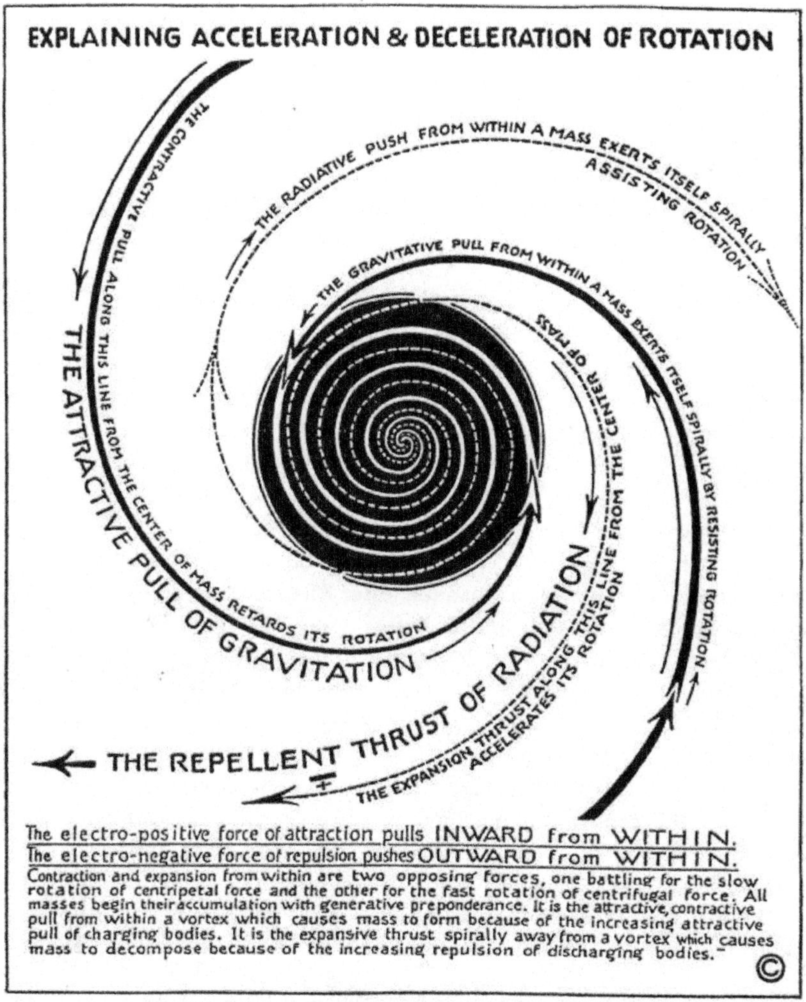

ILLUSTRATING THE OPPOSING FORCES OF GRAVITATION AND RADIATION CONQUERING AND BEING CONQUERED BY SEQUENTIALLY COMPOSING AND DECOMPOSING MASS

In the morning of a planet's life the sun dominates it through its north charging pole. Its local east and west are therefore those with which we are familiar on this planet. And the direction of rotation of the sun is counter-clockwise in reference to an observer located north of the solar system.

At the planet's noon of maturity the sun rises and sets in the plane of the planet's equator. Its local east and west are therefore in the plane of the sun's rising and its setting.

In the planet's evening the poles reverse their position. Its local east and west are therefore the reverse of those at birth and the direction of rotation is clockwise in reference to an observer similarly located.

During its entire period it never rotates or revolves in any other direction than the expanding direction of centrifugal force which ever draws away from north in the direction of north's- expansion, the west which leads to south.

The rotation of a planet in space might well be likened to the rotation of a ball when rolled upon the floor.

The greater friction of the high potential of the floor causes a greater resistance to the motion of the ball than the lesser friction of the low potential of the air, which impacts against the upper surface of the ball.

The planet rolling along the floors of space is resisted in exactly the same manner by the difference in friction between the higher pressures impacting against its inner surface and the lower pressures impacting against its outer surface.

The equator of a ball rolling across the floor propelled by a dead center blow, will always be in contact with the floor and the pole of rotation of the ball will always be parallel to the floor. This is because the conditions of resistance remain constant.

Resistance pressures which cause the rotation of a planet are not analogous to that of the floor and the ball when propelled under such conditions. The resistance not only is greater against the surface of the planet which is toward the sun but also against that hemisphere of the planet which is toward the ecliptic plane of the sun.

Conversely, the resistance is less against the hemisphere which is away from the sun and also that one which is away from the ecliptic plane of the sun.

The former state is preponderantly inductive and the latter is preponderantly conductive.

The greater the resistance to an action of force the greater the genero-activity.

The greater the genero-activity the greater the power of mass to absorb heat.

The less the resistance to the reaction of force, the greater the radio-activity.

The greater the radio-activity the greater the power of mass to give out its heat.

A planet or satellite can only rotate true when its equator is exactly in the plane of the solar or planetary ecliptic.

In this position, it is exactly analogous to the rolling of a billiard ball which has been projected without any "english."

In this position, its pole of rotation is at an angle of 90° to the plane of the equator of its primary.

When in this position, a planet's polar magnetic base has contracted into disappearance so that its electric pole and its pole of rotation coincide.

Also the equatorial planes of primary and planet coincide.

When in this position, its gravitative center of north is a point of no dimension and its radiative center is in a plane which measures the diameter of the mass.

When in this position, the diameter at the equator is equal to the diameter at the poles.

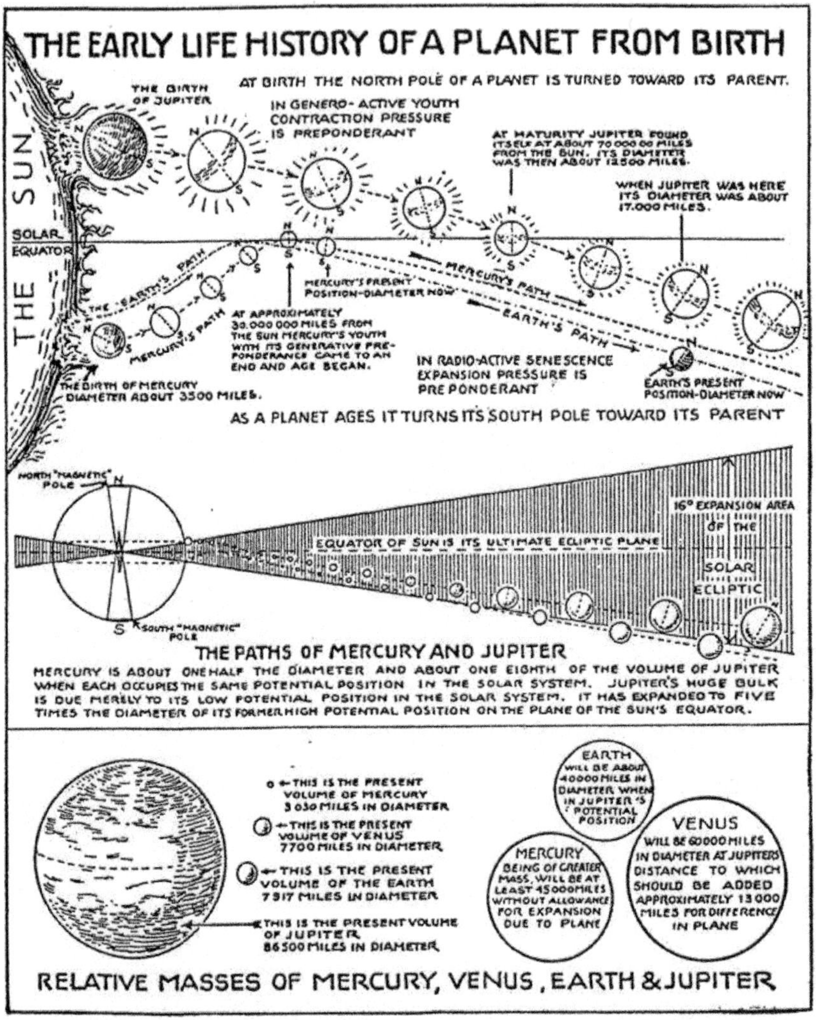

PLANETS ARE BORN, GROW TO MATURITY THROUGH GENERATIVE PREPONDERANCE, THEN FADE AND "DIE" THROUGH RADIATIVE PREPONDERANCE. ALL FORM APPEARS AND DISAPPEARS BY THE SAME PROCESS

This position is only possible at the ecliptic of the wave where generation ends and degeneration begins, and for new planets and satellites at the ecliptic focus of a system for their mass, where their youth ends and their age begins.

All mass rolls along the floors of space upon that part of its surface where radiation is at a maximum.

The blow which gives the impetus to the planet is struck from within exactly in the plane of its ecliptic, the plane of maximum discharge.

The resistance to that blow is greatest at the charging poles, the points of maximum charge.

As the plane of maximum discharge and the points of maximum charge change constantly during a planet's life period so must the planet therefore constantly change its position in relation to its primary.

As the ecliptic area expands and its charging poles draw away from its poles of rotation a planet gradually turns upside down. It then appears to rotate in the opposite direction.

Suns give birth to planets and planets to satellites until just before they have perfected their spherical form.

Planets are born from sun spots which are located some degrees from the solar equator. After birth they continue to generate during their brief youth.

During this period, they draw ever closer to the focussing point for their particular mass in the solar ecliptic area until the equatorial plane of the mass coincides with the solar equatorial plane.

For any matured mass the focussing point in the solar ecliptic area is always in the plane of the solar equator, its distance from its center of force depending upon its relative mass.

This position marks the end of the young planet's preponderantly generative period and the beginning of its preponderantly radiative period.

From this position the new planet gradually recedes as it gradually expands, and tilts its poles as a consequence of its expansion toward its parent and then away from it until it has reversed it natal position. Reference to the charts on pages 221 and 223 will make this statement more clear.

One rotation of a planet is one day of a planet. It is the standard unit from which the hours, minutes and seconds are derived.

After determination of the relation of a planet to that of the earth as a standard unit, the day of any planet may be determined by a calculation in universal ratios.

With the knowledge of the potential position of any planet as indicated by its relative distance, plane and revolution period, its-rotation period can be as easily calculated as its relative mass.

Distance, plane and revolution periods are easily determinable. Other dimensions are very often impossible to ascertain.

At present, we can determine the periodic day of a planet by observing the return of markings visible on its surface.

The days of Mercury, Venus, Uranus and Neptune would be forever beyond our exact knowledge without the ability to calculate potential positions and without the law of universal ratios, for there are no visible dependable markings on these planets.

The period of rotation of smaller planets, such as Ceres and Eros would also be hopelessly indeterminable without the aid of this law.

The rotation period of either a planet or satellite when near its gravitative-radiative center is so long that such a mass always keeps the same surface toward that center.

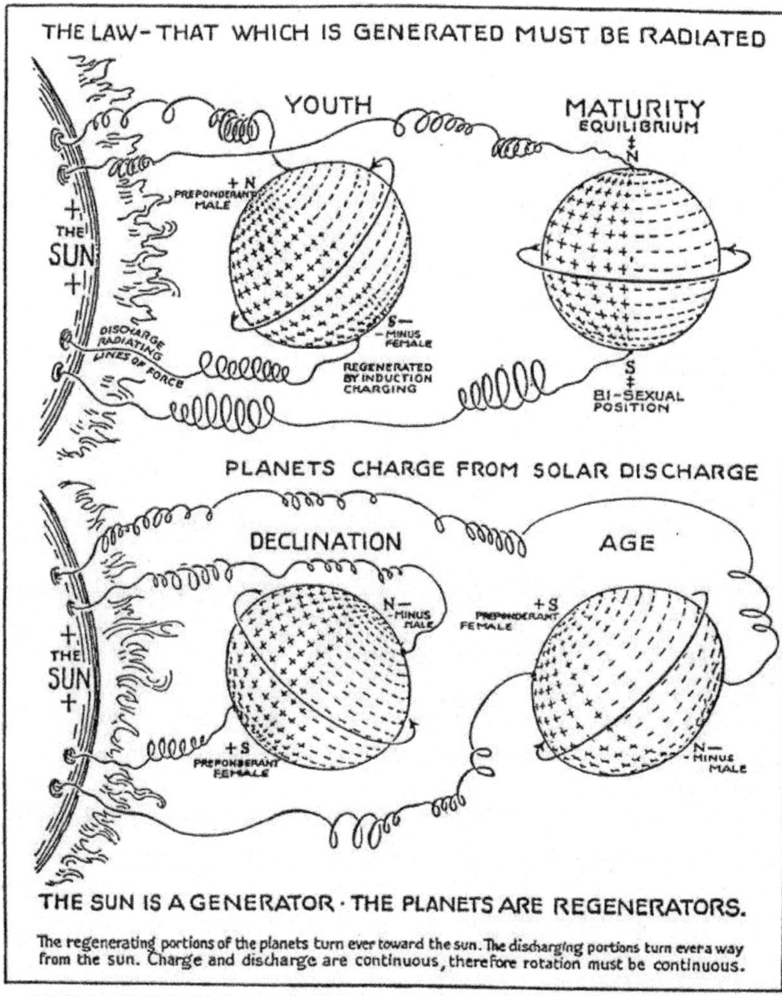

DURING THE YOUTH OF A PLANET ITS GENERO-ACTIVE, CENTRIPETAL PREPONDERANCE CAUSES IT TO CONTRACT. IT THEN CHARGES. AFTER MATURITY ITS RADIO-ACTIVE PREPONDERANCE CAUSES IT TO EXPAND. IT THEN DISCHARGES

Mercury, for example, is so embedded in the dense high potential pressures of such close proximity, not alone to the sun but also to the focus of its ecliptic area in the plane of the solar equator, that it cannot turn faster than the contracted ecliptic area pressure of the sun, in that position, will allow it.

Venus has not only journeyed into the much lower pressures of twice the distance from the sun but has also broken well away from its close relation to the very high pressures of the solar equatorial plane.

As a consequence, Venus is rotating sufficiently fast to periodically expose her entire surface to the sun.

The earth's satellite, and in all probability two to four of Jupiter's, are still so bound to the high pressure zones of their gravitative centers that they are obliged to keep their same faces constantly toward their parents.

The reason for the accelerated rotation of the outer planets of a system and the decelerated rotation of the inner ones is very simple.

Outer planets are farther south in their systems and inner ones are farther north.

Magnetic acceleration of rotation is toward the south and toward increasing oblateness which leads to plane.

Electric deceleration of rotation is toward the north and toward decreasing oblateness which leads to mass.

In a high potential position ; the contraction of genero-activity from within is sufficiently great to retard the pin-wheel-like impetus developed by its radio-active expulsion from within.

In a low potential position, where the ratio of genero-active force is very materially reduced, the balance of radio-active force is materially greater in proportion. The pin-wheel-like effect of rotation due to centrifugal preponderance gradually gains control with a resultant acceleration.

It must be recalled that acceleration of any one dimension must be balanced by deceleration of another.

What a planet gains or loses in power-time must be balanced by a gain or loss in speed-time.

Neptune, the outer planet, her satellite, and some of the outer satellites of Jupiter and Saturn appear to rotate in the opposite direction to that of the other planets. This is termed the "retrograde direction."

Planets never cease turning in the same direction. They but change their positions in relation to us as observers.

If one looks down on the north pole of a mass which is turning from west to east it will appear to turn counter clock-wise, as though the hands of a clock turned backwards.

Conversely, if one looks up on the south pole of a mass which is turning from west to east it will appear to turn clock-wise.

We are not permitted to change our positions in space to so observe the various planets, but the various planets have changed their relative potential positions so that we see the poles tilting in sufficiently different angles to produce the same effect as though we had changed our position.

We look almost directly at the south pole of Uranus and as a consequence it turns quite clock-wise, its four moons revolving retrogressively and always in view. In this .position they transcribe full circles instead of foreshortened ones.

We see Neptune with its north pole tilting upside down.

Naturally Neptune will appear to rotate in quite the opposite direction, and her satellite s will also appear to revolve in the opposite direction to that of our planet.

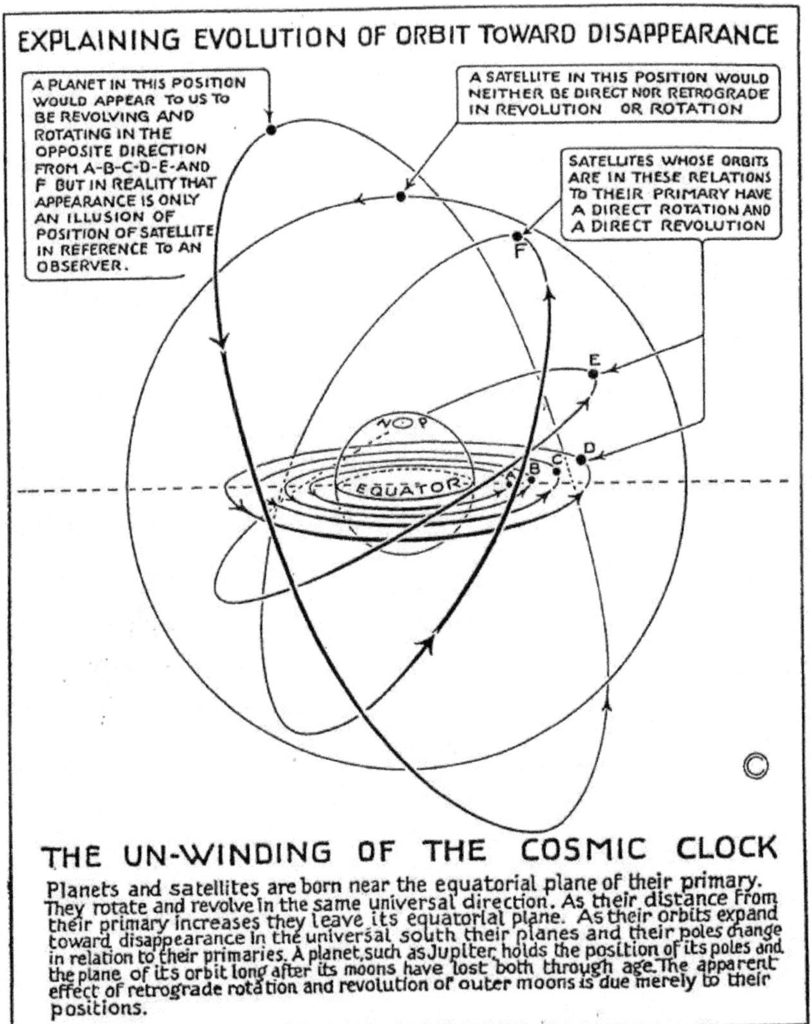

THE COSMIC CLOCK WINDS ITSELF TOWARD SOLIDITY INTO THE APPEARANCE OF FORM, AND UNWINDS ITSELF TOWARD NEBULOSITY INTO THE DISAPPEARANCE OF FORM. THE PROCESS IS ORDERLY AND PERIODIC

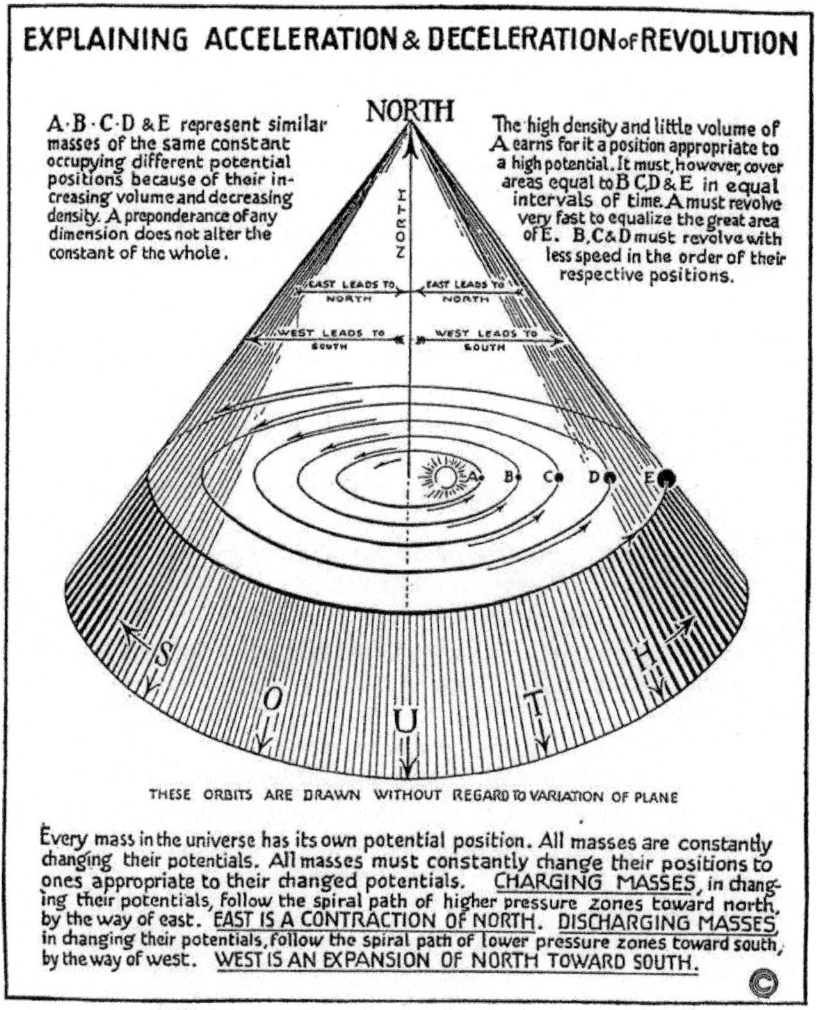

ACCELERATION AND DECELERATION ARE ADJUSTMENTS OF TIME UNITS TO HARMONIZE WITH CHANGED POTENTIAL POSITIONS. TIME MUST EXPAND AND CONTRACT WITH EXPANSION OR CONTRACTION OF MASS

Just so with the outer satellites of Jupiter and Saturn. These two planets have not turned upside down, but the satellites which rotate and revolve in a retrograde direction have broken so far away from the ecliptic control of their primaries that the effect is the same as though they were still close to their primaries and their primaries had turned upside down.

The chart on page 227 representing the evolution of the orbits of planets' moons, will clearly illustrate this happening.

These outer satellites of Jupiter and Saturn which revolve in retrograde directions to us as observers, will continue to break still farther away from the control of their primaries until they become comets which have two controls instead of one.

Let us recall another basic law which reads: "All mass simultaneously expresses both opposite effects of motion, and each opposite effect is cumulatively preponderant in repeative sequences." Consider the effect of this law upon the rotation of a mass.

A new born planet is increasingly generative for a time. Being a small mass as compared to the sun, it matures more quickly.

During the contractive period it rotates in such a position that its equator is at an angle of nearly 90 degrees to the solar equator.

As radiative oscillations accumulate toward the equilibrium - of maturity, the equator dually settles down to a plane of coincidence with the solar equator, the pole of rotation tilts to an upright position and the charging poles creep towards the pole of rotation.

As radiative oscillations accumulate to a negative preponderance for the mass, the equator slips below the solar equatorial plane, the poles of rotation tip farther toward a reversal of their natal positions and the charging poles creep down and up the planet's contour toward its equator.

Negative preponderance in its sequence turns the planet upside down as its potential position lowers.

Its discharging surface becomes very much greater than its charging surface. When this position has been reached, the planet appears to rotate the other way, the opposite from direct, which is termed the retrograde direction.

If these statements are true and the rotation of a mass varies in speed and power according to its potential position, then the twelfth as well as the first dimension, should be taken into consideration in the writing of the law of gravitation.

If these statements are true, slow rotation must be related to the attraction of gravitation which accumulates mass through the power of genero-active energy expressed inductively as positive charge, and fast rotation to the repulsion of radiation which redistributes mass through the power of radioactive energy expressed conductively as negative discharge.

CHAPTER XXII

EXPRESSIONS OF GRAVITATION AND RADIATION
REVOLUTION-THE THIRTEENTH DIMENSION

All mass revolves around a nucleal center which becomes the gravitative-radiative center of that mass.

All shapeless, amorphous mass revolving spirally in the electric stream of centripetal force around a vortex becomes rotating spherical mass when sufficiently accumulated.

Fast revolution is nature's method. of generating energy into an accumulation in mass, and slow rotation is her method of storing that accumulation.

Fast rotation is nature's method of dissipating stored accumulations of energy in mass.

When fast revolving mass becomes fad rotating mass the ratios of its separate parts reverse their dimension attributes.

Rotation gives its speed to revolution and takes power from revolution in equal exchange.

Rotation is an effect which is born of revolution.

All revolving mass is either heading toward a vortex, thus increasing both charge and discharge, or away from a vortex, thus decreasing both charge and discharge.

The revolution of mass begins in the maximum tenuity of the inertial plane and ends in the maximum rigidity of the point of north at the overtone of the wave.

The outward journey begins with a preponderance of positive charge and of increasing speed, and ends at the point of cessation of speed.

The return journey begins with a preponderance of negative discharge and maximum speed from the accumulation of mass at the point of north and ends with cessation of speed at the inertial plane.

Whether planet or light unit, all mass, discharged from the sun, rises away from the sun until it finds its potential position and then revolves around it in slowly expanding spirals until each discharged mass has expanded into disappearance.

This volume is necessarily too brief to enter into all of the complexities of the systems of lower potential, such as those of the lithium, berylium, boron, nitrogen, oxygen and fluorine lines.

For purposes of analogy, it would be more simple to confine this brief explanation to the potential position of our own solar system with which we are most familiar.

Our solar system occupies a high potential position in its wave, a position corresponding, in all probability, to the position of the element manganese.

Our solar system is a mid-tonal pressure wall erected near the apex of the positive cone of the wave, very close to the 4++ position of the carbon line.

A later volume will contain a series of drawings which will define the approximate position of the solar system in its wave.

By a study of these drawings it will be seen that the zodiacal expansion of the solar ecliptic area indicates with unerring precision the exact relation of this solar system to its point of ultimate north.

The sun of this system is speeding through space at an inconceivable speed, ever tilting its pole of rotation toward its ultimate point of north and ever contracting its polar magnetic base as it nears its destination.

The solar ecliptic is ever tilting and contracting its base toward and into the ecliptic planes of the cubes of motion and contracting its area to a plane which will coincide with the solar equator.

As our sun speeds spirally toward the point of north, it carries with it all of the planets which it has discharged. These planets with all of the sun's radiative emanations are swirling about the sun as one of the pressure walls of the cone of the wave of which our solar system is a part.

If the cone of the wave were not an ever bending one the planets would all revolve in the same plane and there would be no zodiacal expansion of approximately 16°.

When the exact position of this solar system is calculated in reference to its ultimate destination at the overtone of its wave, the orbit of Neptune will be one of its important measuring units.

With the orbit of Neptune as a magnetic base and the center of the orbit as the end of a plumb line dropped from an assumed altitude as an apex, the position of the sun in relation to this point will tell us a marvelous story.

When this operation is repeated with all of the planets, always being certain that the same assumed altitude is used in each case, the direction of the bending line of our wave can undoubtedly be closely approximated.

If revolution of mass began at the south inertial plane and continued its outward journey in unbending cones, the laws of motion which govern orbital variation would be very simple to write and to comprehend.

The ever changing cones of the wave, their ever changing axes and their ever changing magnetic bases, reflecting themselves in tonal inertial pressure walls and equatorial planes of evolving masses, give to the masses in motion all of their complexities of precessional orbits and variation of ecliptic planes.

We are accustomed to think of the orbit of a planet as a continuous and repeative one of the same dimensions, instead of as a slowly expanding spiral the repeative revolutions of which so closely coincide that periods of thousands of years must elapse to mark a noticeable change.

If the plane of this system were located as far toward the south in the cone of the wave as the 2+ potential position, orbital extension would be very noticeable in short spaces of time.

Located as our solar system is, however, close to the apex of the positive cone of the wave, where the sun's speed is increasing in the universal ratio as it hurries into ever increasing pressures toward its point of north, the increased pressures of the ever increasing higher potential position, toward which the sun is dragging the whole system, practically offsets the extension of planetary orbits.

The consequent gradual decrease of the zodiacal expansion also helps to offset orbital extension of planets.

If revolution of mass is spiral all orbits must be conic sections.

If the pressures within the cones of the wave were evenly distributed in horizontal directions, even though unevenly distributed in vertical directions, all orbits would be practically true circles.

The bending of the cones of the wave results in such unequal horizontal distribution of pressures that the conic sections in which orbits lie are in planes which conform to the variation of pressures.

The reason for the decelerated revolution of the outer planets of a system and the accelerated revolution of the inner ones is very simple.

Outer planets revolve in orbits farther south and inner planets revolve in orbits farther north.

Magnetic deceleration of revolution is toward the south magnetic bases of the cones of waves.

Electric acceleration of revolution is toward the north apices of the cones of waves.

In a high potential position an orbit is very much restricted, a mass is very much contracted, and its weight, specific gravity and density are very high.

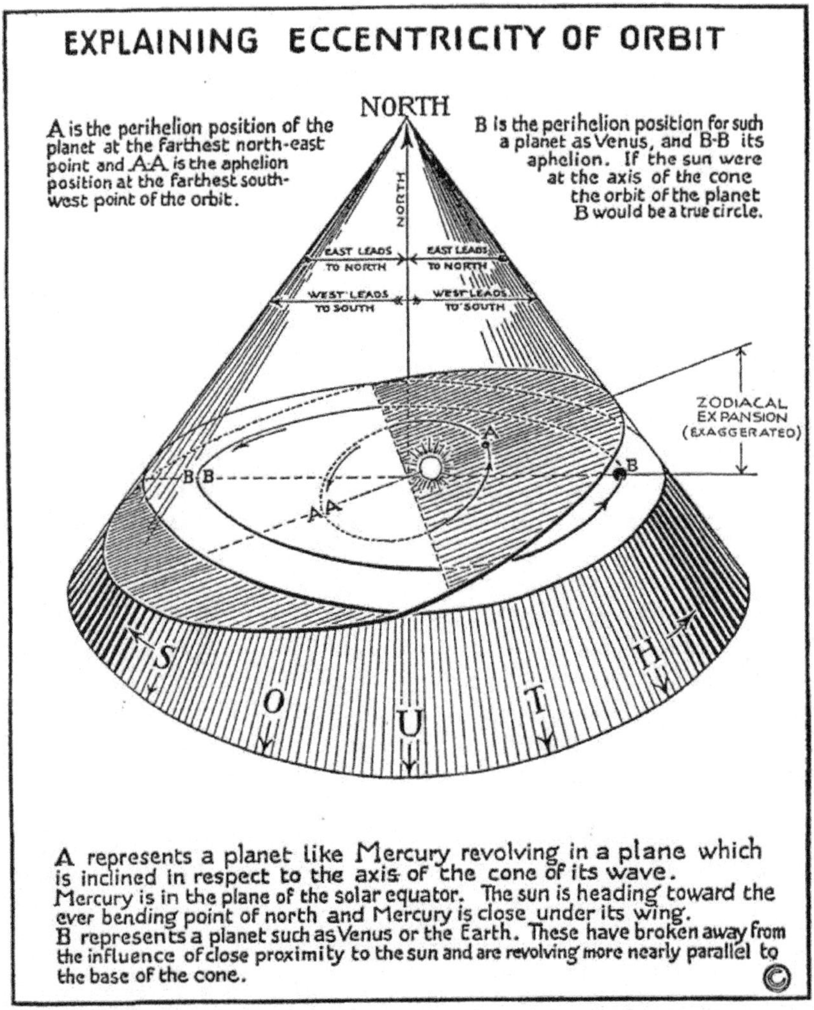

THE APPOSING PRESSURES ARE GREATER IN THE HIGH POTENTIAL POSITIONS OF PERIHELIA THAN IN THE LOWER POTENTIAL POSITIONS OF APHELIA

In this potential condition it occupies a position very close to the gravitative-radiative center of its system.

A mass in a high potential position must cover an equal orbital area in the same amount of time as would the same mass in the same plane expanded to a low potential position.

The high potential must therefore circle its sun four times to the one revolution of an equal mass in the same plane but twice the distance from its sun.

The accelerated or decelerated revolution of any part of an orbit is due to its eccentricity.

Every equal area of the orbit of any mass must be covered in an equal interval of time.

Kepler's well known second law of motion reads as follows: "The radius vector of each planet describes equal areas in equal times," or "the straight line joining a planet to the sun sweeps out equal areas in equal intervals of time."

The orbit of Mercury is the most eccentric of the system. Consequently, there is a greater relative acceleration as the planet approaches its perihelion and greater relative deceleration as it approaches its aphelion than of any other planet in this system.

Among the comets where eccentricity is very great, the acceleration of the comet as it approaches the sun and its aphelion position of maximum deceleration might be likened unto the speed of the antelope as compared with that of the tortoise.

ECCENTRICITY OF ORBIT

Why Mercury should swing around the sun in so great an ellipse, why the orbit of Venus is so nearly perfect a circle and why there should be a variation of eccentricity among the planets can be easily explained.

It will be remembered that all mass moving on the outward journey to north is generative, and that all generative mass is accelerative in its orbit.

All orbits are conic sections.

A conic section which is parallel to its base is a circle.

A conic section which is slightly inclined to its base is an ellipse of very little eccentricity.

The greater the inclination of any conic section to the base of the cone, the greater the eccentricity of an orbit.

It will be remembered that the apex of the cone of energy is the point of north.

An elliptical conic section has upon its surface two points, one of which is nearest to north and the other of which is farthest from north.

The point nearest to north is not only nearer to the moving apex of the cone of energy, which is also the line of the wave, but it is also nearer to the bending axis of the cone.

The point nearest to south is not only farther away from the moving apex of the cone of energy but it is also farther away from the bending axis of the cone.

That section of an eccentric orbit which lies above a circular conic section is the north-east section of an orbit.

Conversely, that section which lies below a circular conic section is the south-west section.

If the north-east section of an eccentric orbit is that part of the orbit in which the perihelion is located and if acceleration of an orbit always increases toward its perihelion, then the northeast section of the orbit and its perihelion must in some manner be related to the relative ability of a mass to appear to attract.

If the south-west section of an eccentric orbit is that part of the orbit in which the aphelion is located, and if deceleration of an orbit always increases toward its aphelion, then the south-west section of the orbit and its aphelion must in some' manner be related to the relative ability of a mass to appear to repel.

The acceleration of attraction is always toward the perihelion of an orbit and the deceleratio n of repulsion is always toward its aphelion.

In any mass the aphelion of every orbit is the point of maximum exhalation and the beginning of inhalation.

In any mass the perihelion of every orbit is the point of maximum inhalation and the beginning of exhalation.

The interval of time between one exhalation-inhalation of any mass is the standard unit year of that mass.

The inhalation impulse of any mass is endothermic, generative, and centripetal.

The exhalation impulse of any mass is exothermic, radiative and centrifugal.

If the perihelion of an eccentric orbit is that part which is preponderantly heat absorbing and generative, it must necessarily follow that the mass which is travelling toward the perihelion of its orbit is increasingly electropositive.

If the aphelion of an eccentric orbit is that part which is heat discharging and radiative, it must necessarily follow that the mass which is travelling toward the aphelion of its orbit is increasingly electronegative.

If the charging and discharging of the northeast section of an orbit is in excess of that of the south-west section, it must necessarily follow that the variation in plane which makes an eccentric orbit possible is related to the attraction of gravitation and the repulsion of radiation.

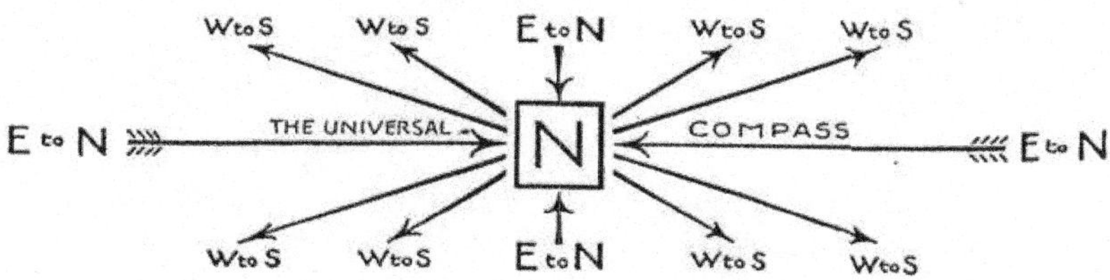

The science of crystallography is today without the basic foundation of a fundamental law. It is today but an organized collation of known effects of unknown causes. It is today beyond the power of man to determine in advance the exact crystallization of any element, compound, mixture or alloy. Nor can cleavage, twinning or other effects of crystallization be determined in advance of experiment or observation.

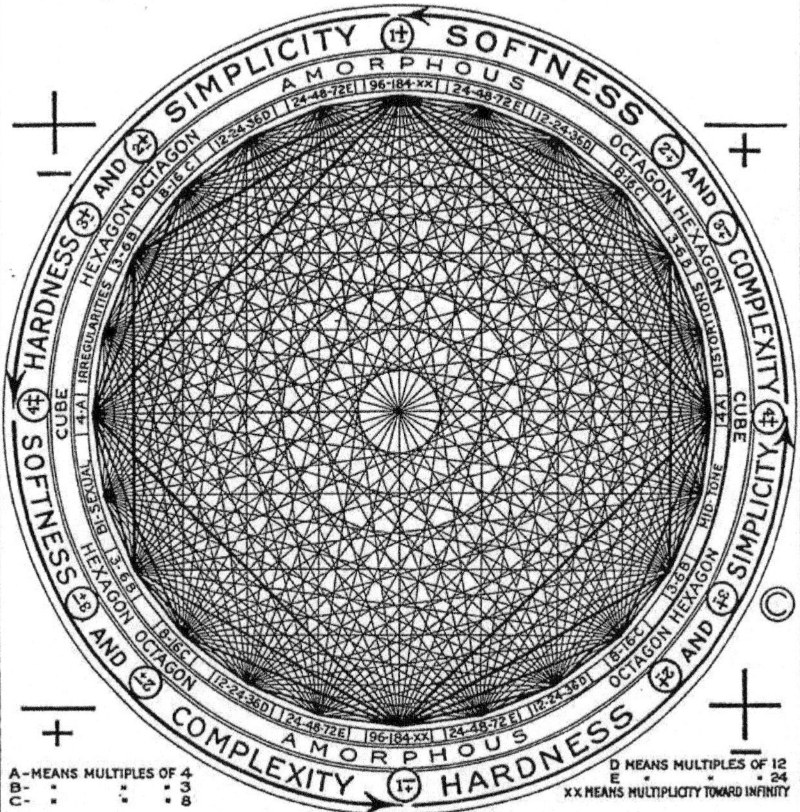

By this series of charts, however, of which this is the basic principle, it will be no longer necessary for the chemist or metallurgist to waste precious effort in experimentation. By the application of these simple laws all effects can be worked out on paper, even to those amorphous effects which cannot be determined by experiment. An application of this series of drawings to the following series, which ties crystallography to chemistry and electricity as a higher chemistry and electro-chemistry, will greatly simplify the labors of the research chemist.

CRYSTALLIZATION CHART No. 1. BASIC PRINCIPLE OF CRYSTALLIZATION IN ACCORD WITH THE FORMULA OF LOCKED POTENTIALS 4.3.2.1.0.1.2.3.4.

CHAPTER XXIII

EXPRESSIONS OF GRAVITATION AND RADIATION
CRYSTALLIZATION-THE TENTH DIMENSION

All matter is crystallic. Crystals are the record in form of the state of motion of the potential which produced that form.

Solids of matter are but accumulated potential, so therefore all mass is an accumulation of crystals of varying forms. The variation of crystallic form is due to the variation of potential.

As matter is but light transformed from speed-time dimension in plane to power-time dimension in mass against resistance which is registered in heat, so are crystals the reaction record of that transformation which is registered in cold.

As light accumulates the one substance by the attraction of its generative motion and melts it into the idea of form according to the dimension of its potential position, so does the reaction of that action freeze it into the appearance of the form which belongs to its potential position.

Crystals are records in form of potential position attained by the action of generation.

Generative action melts. Radiative reaction freezes.

The melting point of any element depends upon its potential position, its pressure environment.

Nature, in her economy of energy, prevents waste of her effort of generation by freezing that effort into the record of the position it has attained.

Crystals are the frozen records in form of the genero-active effort of accumulating potential.

All potential positions are tonal. All form is tonal.

All crystallic forms are records of tonal periodicities.

As all accumulating mass is aiming toward perfection in the simple form of the sphere, so the separate tones which constitute accumulating mass are aiming toward perfection in the simple form of the cube.

True cubic crystallization can only take place at the overtone position of the wave in the cubes of motion.

The journey from plane to mass is recorded by the locking of the successive efforts of energy developed in the attempt to reach that position into the formation of crystals.

As the journey from plane to mass is in the direction of resistance which is indicated endothermically in temperature dimension by greater heat absorption, so is the resistance to mass formation indicated by crystals in a tonal periodicity ranging from softness to hardness.

So also this resistance to mass integration is registered crystallically in a tonal periodicity of form ranging from amorphous complexity to cube simplicity.

So also the return journey to plane is registered by a reversal of these tonal. periodicities.

As the resistance to mass formation is registered in each of the eighteen dimensions by equal and opposite positive and negative plus and minus tonal matter, and as crystalli7ption is one of those eighteen dimensions, it therefore follows that variation of density of crystallic form is as complex as variation of potential is complex.

A volume for this subject alone is necessary. These chapters must necessarily be limited to the emphasizing of the one purpose for which these groups of chapters have been written, namely, of demonstrating that the power of mass to attract is as variable as its power to generate light pulsations into appearance as accumulated potential; also that the power of mass to repel is as variable as its power to degenerate light pulsations into disappearance as discharged potential.

The journey from the soft, amorphous, complex crystal to the hard simple one is a centripetal one in which the intended accumulation starts toward its ultimate vortex from many directions and in many planes which register the amorphous violet of red-blue in color, and ends in one direction and one plane which registers yellow in color.

The return journey back to, softness from hardness starts from the bisexuality of a one plane position, arrives at the base of the female cone of energy divided in many directions and registers in the violet of blue-red in color.

If it is true that the attraction of gravitation and the repulsion of radiation are sufficiently variable to cause great differences in hardness of crystallization and also great differences in form, according to the potential position of the crystallizing mass, the tenth dimension must be taken into account in writing the laws of gravitation and radiation.

CHAPTER XXIV

EXPRESSIONS OF GRAVITATION AND RADIATION

PLANE AND ECLIPTIC—THE SIXTEENTH AND EIGHTEENTH DIMENSIONS

Plane and ecliptic are two of the most important dimensions. Each is worthy of a volume in itself.

This chapter, therefore, will deal briefly with these dimensions, as this series of chapters is written primarily for the purpose of showing the relation of all dimension of mass to the phenomena of gravitation and radiation.

The outward journey from plane to mass and back again to plane is a journey into appearance from inertia of non-dimension to the inertial bi-sexual position of formed mass at 4t and back again to disappearance in inertia of non-dimension.

The dimensionless universe knows neither plane nor mass.

The universe of dimension knows infinite variety of both plane and mass.

In the evolution of mass from the inertial plane of the concept of mass, plane evolves in orderly periodicity as mass evolves.

It has heretofore been written that the conquest of either opposite in any expression of force by the other is always accomplished by a simulation of the attributes of the one conquered.

Mass overcomes the concept of plane in the non-dimensional universe of inertia, by simulating plane in an objective universe of motion.

When motion begins the process of overcoming inertia, the plane of forming mass is infinitely complex.

When motion has completely overcome inertia to the full extent of the energy of any particular action, the plane of formed mass is infinitely simple.

It is then in one plane, the plane of the equator of each mass in a system. (See page 141.)

During the evolution of plane from the complexity of many directions to the simplicity of one, the forming corpuscles of systems revolve in many orbits but change their positions until they eventually revolve in one plane.

When the one plane is reached in formed mass the genero-active action has reached its maximum.

Radio-active reaction then preponderates.

It has been heretofore written that mass attains an appearance of stability through motion and retains that appearance only by a continuation of motion.

All expressions of energy are represented by varying stages of evolution each of which is registered in each dimension.

When the maximum of any expression of energy is reached at the overtone position of the wave, the one simple unstable plane of motion begins its complexing into many planes.

The open complex condition of forming mass in the nebulous, shapeless state is that in which the area of variation in plane approximates 90 degrees to the equatorial plane of maximum motion, at which position mass appears and disappears as form.

The closed and simple condition of formed mass in the solid, spherical state is that in which there is no area of variation in the ecliptic or equatorial plane-which marks the limitations of the expression of energy which fathered any particular mass.

It has elsewhere been explained that the opposing cones of energy disappear by expansion into equatorial planes and by contraction into poles of rotation.

As these cones contract and expand, all parts of each system revolve around a forming nucleus in the gradually lessening and increasing expansion of plane area.

This expansion which differs in all systems in orderly periodicities, is exemplified in our solar system in that effect which we call the zodiacal area.

In our solar system the area of plane expansion of the ecliptic for major masses within the system is approximately eight degrees -on either side of the solar equatorial plane.

All major masses within our system must continue their journeys within this area.

Beyond this area only those very much smaller masses, such as asteroids and comets are permitted to extend their ecliptic planes, and expand their plane areas, toward their disappearance.

These smaller masses and comets might be likened to the insignificant leakage of rare gases through even well fitting piston rings in an engine.

Their potential is too low to keep them within the defined area and the comets are so lacking in density that their ability to regenerate and contract from hundreds of thousands of miles in diameter at their aphelions, to an hundred miles at their perihelions makes of them nomad wanderers throughout great expanses of our swirling solar, hurricane.

In their continued search for true potential positions for the rapidly changing potentials of these expanded masses their alternate inhalations and exhalations are like the gaspings of a dying man.

Generative inhalations greatly contract the volumes of highly expanded mass of low potentials and radiative exhalations greatly expand them.

This accounts for the tremendously eccentric orbits of the comets and the expanded ecliptic areas of such small masses as the asteroids.

All mass is but a reflection of its concept.

Mass is conceived in inertia and reflected as the matured image of its concept at an angle of 90 degrees to the plane of concept.

The immatured or "growing" image of concept is recorded in plane at angles which vary from the beginning of mass formation in the inertial plane of non-dimension in concept, to the completion of mass formation in the inertial plane of maximum dimension in mass which is at the equator of mass.

Just as the idea of man is reflected as the image of man on the plane of the water's surface at a 90 degree angle from the object reflected, so are the matured concepts of universal idea reflected in the universe of maximum dimension which lies at an angle of 90 degrees to the universe of non-dimension.

Growth is idea evolving in transit to its maturing point in a reflecting plane at the equator of mass and devolving back again to inertia.

All mass is a reflection of the concept of that mass.

The greater the angle of the reflecting plane of forming mass to the plane of concept in inertia, the greater the positive charge and negative discharge of that mass and consequently the greater its ability to appear to attract and to repel.

Preponderance of power of mass to appear to attract increases as the reflecting plane progresses through the tonal positions of 1 + 2 + and 3 + to its maximum at 4++.

Preponderance of power of mass to appear to repel increases as the reflecting plane progresses through the tonal "positions of 1 — 2 — and 3 — to its maximum at 4++.

The elements of matter and all expressions of energy in combination are states of motion of varying potentials which represent various stages of progress toward and beyond maturity, the reflection of concept.

Each potential has its own evolving, evolved or devolving plane position in its wave.

Each plane is but a registration in wave position of a potential, just as a tone, color, temperature or any other dimension is a registration of a state of motion.

Just as locked potentials of high positive charge and high melting points, in which the dominating spectrum lines are in the orange and yellow, have a greater power to attract than locked potentials of lower positive charge and lower melting points, in which the dominating spectrum lines are in the infra red and red, so have locked potentials of 70° + to 90 ° ++ in plane greater power to attract than those which register 1° + to 70° +.

Conversely, just as locked potentials of high negative discharge and high melting points, in which the dominating spectrum lines are in the green and green-blue, have a greater power to repel than the elements of lower negative discharge and lower melting points, in which the dominating spectrum lines are in the ultra violet and blue, so have locked potentials of 70° — to 90° ++ greater power to repel than those which register 1° — to 70° —

If elements of great angle of plane and little expansion of plane area in their octave waves have a greater power to appear to attract or repel than elements of little angle of plane and great expansion of plane area, then it must necessarily follow that the power of mass to attract or repel is partly conditioned by the relation of the plane position of the mass, and not alone by distance and the product of attracting masses.

If this is true, then plane of increasing angle and lessening expansion of plane area in the positive half of the wave must in some manner be related to the power of mass to appear to attract.

Conversely, plane of increasing angle and lessening expansion of plane area in the negative half of the wave must in some manner be related to the power of mass to appear to repel.

If these premises are well founded the sixteenth dimension must be considered in the writing of the laws of gravitation and radiation.

The greater the expansion of the ecliptic plane area of forming mass the less the positive charge and negative discharge of that mass and consequently the less its ability to appear to attract and repel.

Preponderance of power of mass to appear to attract and to repel increases as expansion of ecliptic plane area decreases.

As the ecliptic plane area contracts to a spiral in one plane in the direction of the carbon line on the positive half of the wave, the elements within that half of the wave have an ever increasing power to appear to attract:

Conversely, as expansion of the ecliptic plane area increases from the carbon line to the line of the inert gases, the power of the elements within this negative half of the wave to appear to repel decreases.

The more restricted the expansion of the ecliptic plane area, the higher the potential.

Conversely, the greater the expansion of the ecliptic plane area, the lower the potential.

Time is necessary for registering the evolution and devolution of plane as it journeys from its conceptual stage in the universal white light of Mind substance to its matured reflection in the simulated white light of the simulated substance, and beyond to the melding point of simulation and reality in the white light of universal Mind in inertia.

Comprehension of this process will clarify the mystery of growth from infancy to maturity and beyond to "death" where life eternal is and begins again in endless repeative sequences in time, space and motion.

If these premises are true then elements of contracting ecliptic plane areas which belong to the charging positive half of their respective octave waves must in some manner be related to the power of mass to appear to attract.

Conversely, the elements of expanding ecliptic plane areas which belong to the discharging negative half of their respective octave waves must in some manner be related to the power of mass to appear to repel.

If these premises are well founded the eighteenth dimension must be considered in the writing of the laws of gravitation and radiation.

CHAPTER XXV

EXPRESSIONS OF GRAVITATION AND RADIATION IONIZATION—THE NINTH DIMENSION

All mass is an aggregation of light units assembled into systems and into systems of systems.

All mass is held together by internal surface tension pressure generated by itself.

Any mass of high pressure and ,potential which is brought into a zone of low. pressure and potential will rapidly lose the light units of which it is composed.

An environment of extreme low pressure and potential surrounding a mass of high pressure and potential will reduce the ability of that mass to generate internal surface tension pressure.

Under such conditions a mass of high potential will expand, thus separating its particles. They will fly away from their mass with more or less violence according to the consequential reduction in internal surface tension pressure.

This effect is the attempt of nature to maintain an equilibrium.

High potential out of place must adjust itself to the place in which it finds itself.

This separation of particles is the radiative process due to the electro-magnetic power of repulsion.

It will be recalled that bodies receding from each other discharge each other.

It will be recalled that discharging bodies discharge their high potential into lower potential and thus redistribute accumulated mass. It must not be forgotten, however, that a discharging body is merely preponderant in its ability to discharge. It is also a charging body in a lesser degree.

Discharging bodies while discharging their high potential are simultaneously accumulating high potential from lower potential by the centripetal force of generation.

Any mass of low pressure and potential which is brought into a zone of high pressure and potential will lose the light units of which it is composed more slowly in its new potential position.

The mass will contract, thus drawing its light units and systems closer together.

This contraction of particles is the generative process of attraction.

It will be recalled that bodies approaching each other charge each other.

Charging bodies of higher potential regenerate discharging bodies of lower potential. This is the process of accumulation of mass.

Accumulating mass being preponderantly gravitative increases its internal surface tension pressure as it accumulates and thus loses less of its particles.

This universe of dimension expressed by motion is a corpuscular universe of varying pressures.

The corpuscles which constitute the appearance of form are little pumps which pump themselves into closer proximity to other corpuscles when they are generatively strong and pump themselves away from other corpuscles when their generative ability relaxes.

When generative corpuscles pump themselves together in a cohesive mass they retain that position by the high pressures which their many pumps have generated.

All of the corpuscles of the One substance pump themselves into the various states of potential which we call the elements of matter.

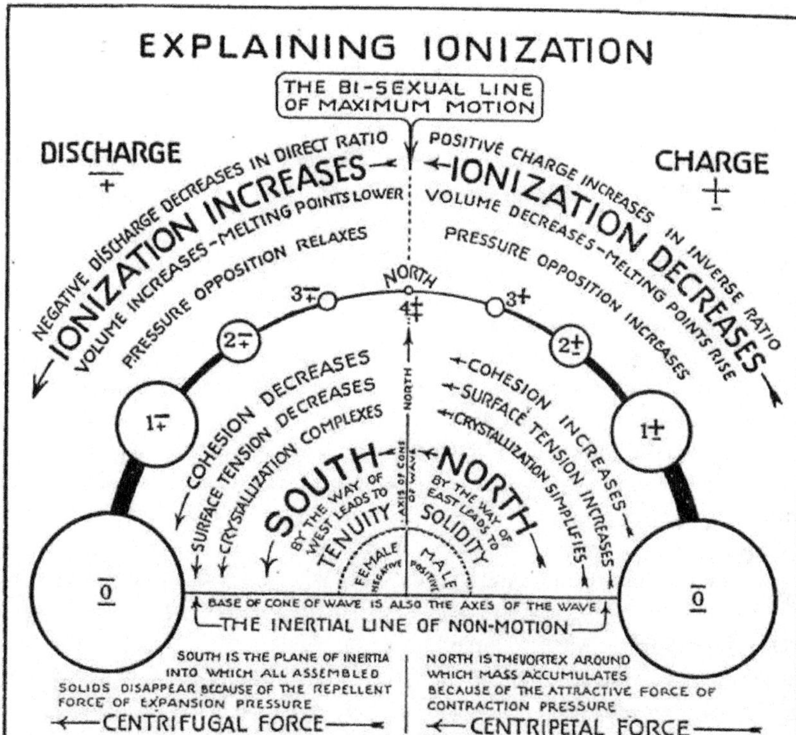

The universe of dimension is a corpuscular universe. Solids of matter are composed of corpuscules called IONS. Ions are integrated into solids of matter by high contraction pressure, against great resistance. The process of integration is a generative, contractive process. Solids of matter are disintegrated into nebulosity by high expansion pressure. IONIZATION IS THE PROCESS OF DISINTEGRATION. Ionization is the taking apart of solids, corpuscle by corpuscle. High potentials require high contraction pressures to compress ions into small volume. Low potentials violently ionize high potentials. Solidity is an effect of motion in which the electric stream accumulates ions centripetally around a vortex. Nebulosity is an effect of motion in which the magnetic stream dissipates ions centrifugally away from a vortex. All chemical elements, compounded as solids, ionize in universal ratios in accordance with the formula of the locked potentials and the following pressure laws:

PRESSURE LAWS

1. THE GREATER THE POSITIVE CHARGE, THE GREATER THE PRESSURE OF CONTRACTION.
2. THE GREATER THE PRESSURE OF CONTRACTION, THE LESS THE VOLUME.
3. THE GREATER THE NEGATIVE DISCHARGE, THE GREATER THE PRESSURE OF EXPANSION.
4. THE GREATER THE PRESSURE OF EXPANSION, THE LESS THE VOLUME.

MASS IS HELD TOGETHER BY THE PRESSURES OF ITS POTENTIAL POSITION. A DENSE MASS WILL BREAK UP INTO ITS UNITS WHEN PLACED IN A LOW PRESSURE ENVIRONMENT. THIS PROCESS IS CALLED IONIZATION

Chemists call these little corpuscular pumps ions.

When chemists subject any substance to the strain of a potential so far removed from the correct potential position that its surface ions cannot stand the suction, the surface ions lose their hold and fly away.

Chemists call this effect "ionization."

Let us assume for example that a piece of silver (803 — D) is subjected to the suction of a very low potential such as nitric acid.

The piece of silver would gradually disappear.

Its surface ions would fly away with explosive violence, thus raising the lower surrounding potential.

As the nitric acid charges by impact with and absorption of the silver ionic discharge, the process of ionization diminishes.

If there is enough nitric acid to completely ionize the silver the silver ions will expand into disappearance as a cohesive solid.

In this event the generative ability of the mass of silver has been entirely overcome by the unwinding power of centrifugal force which has thus been placed in control.

If a piece of any metal which is of a lower potential than silver, copper for example, is inserted into this solution, the silver will reappear and the copper will disappear.

The reason for this is very simple.

Copper ions, being of lower potential than silver ions, have less ability than silver to hold themselves in the position of a cohesive solid.

They therefore succumb more easily to the expanding power of the lower potential.

The strain of resistance against the unwinding power of centrifugal force is thus removed from the silver ions and allows them to reform into their crystallic position, but not as a solid lump of silver.

A solid substance when ionized by being subjected to a lower potential position, even if regenerated, will not come together again as a solid while in a lower potential position.

To reform as a solid mass of silver with the same internal surface pressure and the same power of cohesion, the crystals would have to be resubjected to the pressure of the high potential which caused the original density.

This could only be done by bringing the crystals to their melting point and allowing them to reintegrate their systems under such a pressure.

A metal of low potential, such as sodium, will ionize with violence in water, but a metal of high potential, such as aluminum or nickel, will hardly be affected by water.

Ionization is a disintegration process just as radioactivity is a disintegration process.

Both of these effects of motion are the attempts of nature to redistribute accumulated high potential into lower potential.

This planet, for example, while generating energy from the sun and the inner planets Mercury and Venus, is also discharging radioactive emanations in the direction of the planet Mars along the increasingly tangential pressure lanes of the system.

It is proper to define this discharge of potential from the planet which is approximately in its proper potential position as a radioactive effect, for it is normally discharging that which it is normally generating.

If, however, some giant hand should remove the earth far away from its potential position into the low pressure position occupied by Saturn, for example, the earth (assuming for the moment that it did not explode) would discharge its potential so furiously that the process would then be termed "ionization." It would be losing its particles in such clouds that it would be quite analogous to that of a piece of soft metal suspended in a strong acid solution.

A good example of what would take place under such conditions is seen in the comets which leave vast trails of ionized Material in their wake or push them ahead of them according to whether their direction is toward or away from the sun.

The trail of the emanations from a comet cannot properly be called radio-active Radio-activity on the other hand is a normal replacement of that which electricity is genero-actively displacing.

All substance is radio-active. All substance is emitting ions.

A normal outflow of radio-active emanations in accordance with a normal ability to generate ions could be termed a radio-active effect.

A piece of radium for example, is generating higher pressures by pumping the ions of lower potential into its centripetal vortices.

In a lesser degree it is ejecting ions, centrifugally hurling them away from its vortices at a speed approximating 180,000 miles per second.

It is possible for radium to generate and emit its generated ions in the form of incandescent projectiles of inert gases in the potential position occupied by it on this planet. If this piece of radium were in the position occupied by Venus or

Mercury, both its genero-activity and its radio-activity would be increased a thousand fold bemuse of the environment of its high potential position.

On the contrary, if this piece of radium were in the position occupied by Neptune it would disintegrate by ionization to such an expanded volume that both its genera-active and radioactive powers would be correspondingly reduced.

The accompanying chart explains the relative ability of mass to hold itself together through cohesion and to tear itself apart through the release of surface tension pressure according to the law of the formula of the locked potentials.

As in all forming mass ionization decreases in the inverse of the universal ratio and in the order of the formula of the locked potentials as ....>>>>>>>missing words<<<< in direct ratio as the mass expands toward south.

All effects of ionization, all genero-active and all radio-active effects are governed by the four pressure laws here repeated:

The greater the positive charge the greater the pressure of contraction.

The greater the pressure of contraction the less the volume.

The greater the negative discharge the greater the pressure of expansion.

The greater the pressure of expansion the less the volume.

If substance disintegrates through the process of ionization and radio-active emanations, then these two processes used by nature for the replacement of material collected for the building of her ideas, must in some manner be related to the power of repulsion.

Emanations because the process is more nearly analogous to the chemical reaction which we call ionization.

Ionization, therefore, can be understood as that process in which a high potential is placed in an environment of very much lower potential and thus more quickly subjected to disintegration.

The process of ionization is a quick and abnormal return to disappearance in plane in the return journey to the southerly zone of expansion.

Ionization is an abnormal replacement of that which electricity has displaced.

If separate substances under differing conditions have a relative power of disintegration through ionization or radio-active emanations, then the power of repulsion must be relative.

If the power of repulsion is relative and according to the potential of the substance and its potential position, then must these effects of the ninth dimension of motion be taken into consideration in the writing of the laws of gravitation and radiation.

IONIZATION PERCENTAGES

AN EXAMPLE

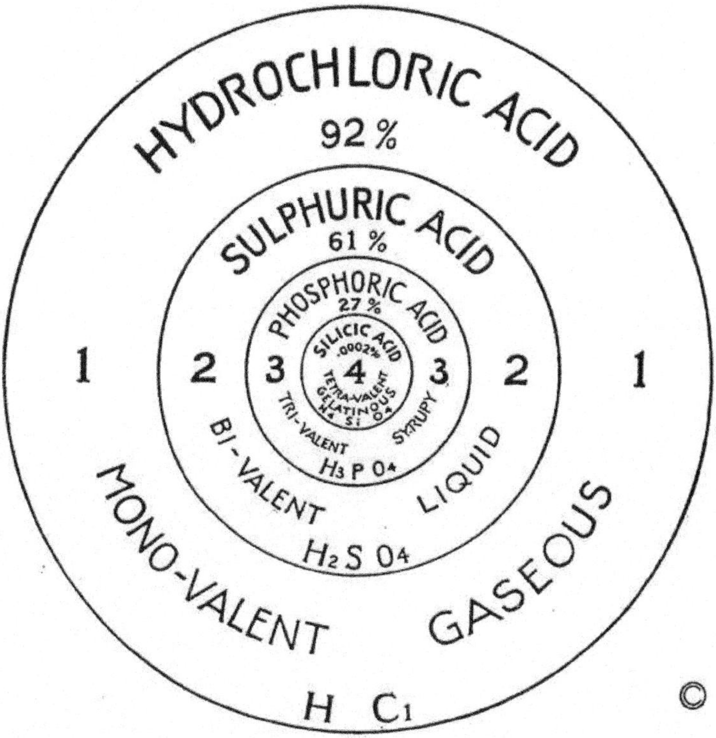

Ionization decreases as positive charge increases. Positive charge, centripetal force, genero-activity and contraction are attributes of mass appearance. Ionization is an attribute of mass disappearance. Ionization therefore increases as negative discharge, centrifugal force, radio-activity and expansion increases.

ALL EFFECTS OF MOTION OBEY THE ORDERLINESS OF THE FORMULA OF THE LOCKED POTENTIALS. IONIZATION IS A DISINTEGRATION EFFECT OF MOTION AND THE RATIOS OF DISINTEGRATION ARE IN THE DIRECT OF THE UNIVERSAL AS THOSE OF INTEGRATION ARE IN THE INVERSE.

CHAPTER XXVI

EXPRESSIONS OF GRAVITATION AND RADIATION

VALENCY—THE ELEVENTH DIMENSION

Valency is one of the great dimensions by means of which states of motion can be measured in their relative tonal pressure intensities.

The term "valence" is a standard unit of tonal relations just as a day is a standard unit of the periods of rotation, or as a year is a standard unit of the periods of revolution.

Valency is a measurement employed by chemists to classify the various elemental tones in relation to their relative willingness, or unwillingness, to unite with each other.

Chemists have found that some of the elements will consent to unite with some other elements only with persuasion while they are very desirous of uniting with certain others.

They have found, for example, that one sodium atom (1+) will unite willingly with one chlorine atom (1—). The valency of these two elements, the first being a positive action and the second being an equal negative reaction, are both said to have a valency of one.

A sodium atom (1+) will unite less willingly with a sulphur atom (2 —) which has a valency of two. An increasing unwillingness to unite with sodium is found in the phosphorous atom (3 —) which has a valency of three.

Carbon (4++) has to be forced under great pressure to unite with any element of a valency of one and in each case the number of atoms have to be equalized to correspond to the valency. Carbon (4++), for example, demands four atoms of hydrogen (1+) and the high temperature It is an accepted fact that any positive and negative elements of equal valence will unite much more readily than either of these elements will unite with an element of higher valency.

If this is true then the present accepted laws of gravitation cannot be true.

It will be observed that the valency of all of the elements is in accordance with the formula of the locked potentials. The inert gases have zero valency for they will not unite with any other element, although they will unite very readily with each other, not as compounds, but as interlocking substances.

The inert gases of lower potentials integrate within the inert gases of higher potentials.

All elements of the lithium line have a positive valence of one. Their preponderance of power to attract is in the relation of one-eighth of the energy of their respective octave waves.

All elements of the berilium line have a valence of two. Their preponderance of power to attract is in the relation of two-eighths of the energy of their respective octave waves.

All elements of the boron line have a positive valence of three. Their preponderance of power to attract is in the relation of three-eighths of the energy of their respective octave waves.

Pressure of the arc light, to induce union.

It is self-evident, therefore, from the chemist's practical experience that the elements have not equal powers of attraction for each other, mass for mass, or volume for volume.

If the laws of gravitation as at present understood were faultless, valency in the elements would be inconceivable.

If the ability of one mass to attract another were conditioned only by relative distance and the product of their masses, then equal masses of hydrogen (1+) and oxygen (2 —) would attract each other as readily as an equal mass of hydrogen (1+) and fluorine (1.—).

This is not the case, however, for a double quantity of hydrogen and an abnormal pressure must be used to induce union with oxygen.

On the contrary, hydrogen and fluorine will leap together with explosive violence in ordinary temperatures.

All elements of the carbon line have a positive-negative, or bisexual valence of four: Their approximately equal power to attract and to repel is in the relation of four to three, four to two and four to one of the energy of the other elements in their respective octave waves.

All elements in the nitrogen line have a negative valence of three. Their preponderance of power to repel is in the relation of three-eighths of the energy of their respective octave waves.

All elements in the oxygen line have a negative valence of two. Their preponderance of power to repel is in the relation of two-eighths of the energy of their respective octave 'Waves.

The elements in the fluorine line have a negative valence of one. Their preponderance of power to repel is in the relation of one-eighth of the energy of their respective octave waves.

The mid-tones have a fluctuating valence but it must be borne in mind that the mid-tones are split tones and the greater the number of mid-tones and the greater their total of valence, the more the overtone of their wave is affected by subtraction Of positive charge and negative discharge.

Carbon is the only over-tone of truly equal positive and negative valence. All other elements in the carbon line are either negatively or positively preponderant.

In adopting standard units of valency measurements, the physicists have based their calculations from the element hydrogen as the unit of one. This is akin to adopting one note on the keyboard of a piano as a key the for every octave scale whether it is for the key of one flat, three flats or five sharps. As in musical tones each octave has its keynote which is a definite tonal relation to the entire octave, so in chemistry each octave of the elements has its own keynote.

Hydrogen (401 -1-) should be adopted as the unit of valency measurement of the fourth octave only.

Lithium (501 +) for the fifth octave, sodium (601 -I-) for the sixth octave, potassium (701-1-) for the seventh octave, rubidium (801 +) for the eighth octave, caesium (901-1-) for the ninth octave and the unknown element (1001+) preceding radium for the tenth octave.

When the standard units of valency measurements are changed to conform with true tonal relations valency can be more accurately calculated, but while one element is forced to stand as a unit constant or keynote for all of the tones of every octave the miscalculations of valency will be as disproportionate as similar tonal calculations on a keyboard would be inharmonious.

If it is true that elements of different valencies have a different power to appear to attract and to repel, then valency, the eleventh dimension, must be taken into consideration in the writing of the laws of gravitation and radiation.

CHAPTER XXVII

EXPRESSIONS OF GRAVITATION AND RADIATION

TONE—THE SEVENTEENTH DIMENSION

Tone, in the sense in which we understand the meaning of the word sound, is one of the great dimensions.

Tone is registered in sound as it is in color, plane, temperature and other dimensions.

Every expression of energy has its own particular tonal sound just as it has its own color plane or degree of temperature.

Sound is generally conceived to be the result of a concussion taking place in the air. The "ether of space" is generally conceived to be soundless. This concept is not in accord with the laws of motion.

Sound is from the beginning and from the very first octave.

It matters not how low or how high the potential, every active and reactive oscillation is accompanied by sound.

Sound increases in resonance as potential accumulates. Both effects of motion are due to the same cause, the generation of accumulated energy from the first to the tenth octaves and its radiation into inertia.

All states of motion register themselves tonally in the opposites of sound in the same periodicity as they register themselves in the other dimensions.

All sound is caused by potential impacting against potential or separating from potential.

All sound is the result of explosions of accumulating or redistributing energy.

Every generative action and every radiative reaction is an explosion.

All explosions are either genero-active or radio-active.

Genero-active explosions are those in which two opposing potentials seek each other with violence. Such explosions are gravitative. They are born of centripetal force and they are due to the power of matter to appear to attract.

Genero-active explosions draw corpuscles into forming mass. These are the explosions by means of which mass is accumulated.

Genero-active explosions are endothermic or heat absorbing.

Radio-active explosions are those in which high potential discharges into lower potential with violence. Such explosions are radiative. They are born of centrifugal force and they are due to the power of matter to appear to repel.

Radio-active explosions eject corpuscular emanations from mass. These are the explosions of expanding mass by means of which accumulated mass is redistributed.

Radio-active explosions are exothermic or heat expelling.

Genero-active explosions are caused by the desire of positive charge to accumulate as mass.

Radioactive explosions are caused by the desire of negative discharge to redistribute accumulated masses of stored energy into a state of inertia.

Genero-active and radio-active explosions in sequence are analogous to the intake and exhaust of a pump.

The preponderance of one or the other is the condition precedent to mass formation or mass dissolution.

The alternating explosive oscillations which simultaneously integrate and disintegrate evolving and devolving mass cause sounds of greater or less intensity according to the potential position of the actions and reactions which cause those sounds.

Just as all motion is expressed in waves so are all waves registered in their various dimensions. All states of motion are measurable as dimensions.

Sound is a dimension.

Sound being a dimension is, therefore, measurable.

Explosions in the low potential position of the first six octaves are registered in the elements as full tones. Each full tone of sound is a whirlpool formed around a central nucleus, or vortex, toward which the generative energy induced by the effect of the explosion rushes with increasing violence, and away from which the reaction to that explosion rushes with decreasing violence.

When energy accumulates to the high potential positions of the sixth and seventh octaves, the tonal explosions take place as full tones from the 0 = position in inertia to the 3 + and 3 — positions in their octave waves.

At these points the accumulation- of genera active and radio-active force is so great that five midtonal vortices are formed between those positions and the over-tone of the wave. These mid-tonal vortices are the bases for ten new elements to each octave, five of which are positive and the other five negative.

In the still higher potential positions of the eighth, ninth, and tenth octaves many mo re mid-tonal vortices appear which form the bases of many more elements, half of which in each octave are positive and half negative.

Sound emanates from the explosions of every potential no matter how low or how high. More than this, the sound from either genero-active or radio-active explosions, register themselves in every octave both higher and lower than the octave of source.

For a familiar example let us consider the sound of the human voice which is a genero-active explosion because of the fact that it is a higher potential generated out of a lower.

The series of explosions which give birth to this sound becomes radio-active in the lower octaves and redistributes that accumulated energy into the lower potentials against which it impacts in that state of potential which we would term the air. The sound radiates slowly but its discharge into the potential of the lower octaves will travel around the planet several times while the same sound travels across the valley through the air.

On the contrary, its impact against a cliff will retard its progress in the higher potentials of higher octaves but the sound continues to the end of the cycle. The cliff side undergoes an increase in positive charge because of the impact of energy against it.

Just as we can hear the explosions of genero-active energy through the senses of hearing by impact of that energy against our ear drums, so can the explosions of low potential be reproduced with delicate instruments so that their regeneration into higher octaves would make them discernible to our sense of hearing.

The bombardment of radio-active emanations can even now be amplified so that they can be heard. Master mechanics must devise instruments so delicate that low potential explosions. may be amplified and measured with as great accuracy as they have devised instruments for recording even a millionth degree of temperature.

It must be remembered that all explosions travel both ways, up and down the octaves, for there can be no action without a corresponding reaction nor can there be a reaction of an action without a repetition of both.

This is a universe of reproduction and any effect of motion runs the entire gamut of all effects of motion. The force of that which is running away from inertia is equal to the speed of that which is returning to inertia. The speed of one is very great and its force very little. On the contrary the force of the other is very great and its speed very little.

For the purposes of comparing the variable relation of tone to the attraction of gravitation and the repulsion of radiation it is only necessary to point out the different speeds at which any sound reproduces itself according to the potential in which the sound finds itself.

Just as high potential discharges into low with ever increasing speed of reproduction, so does sound raise its tone and increase its reproductive speed. It also decreases its wave dimensions as potential powers.

Just as nature's mechanical principles do not permit a waste of energy by allowing the discharge of any accumulated energy to be used without repeated regeneration, so must that gradual and sequential discharge and recharge be registered in ever lessening sound intensity and with ever increasing speed as power diminishes.

In any mass the lower the octave the higher the potential and the slower the speed of reproduction of any effect of motion.

In any mass the higher the octave the lower the potential and the greater the speed of reproduction of any effect of motion.

In any mass the lower the octave the greater the wave dimension and the lower its tonal registration in sound.

In any mass the higher the octave the smaller the wave dimension and the higher its tonal registration in sound.

Low potential radio-active explosions can be amplified and regenerated to genero-active ones of electropositive force.

When measurements of tonal positions are made possible and correlated to plane, color, temperature and other dimensions, a higher and more complex chemical analysis than that of to-day will be made possible.

The simple, modern chemical analysis of a grain of wheat will not allow a synthesis which will enable one to produce the same substance. The more complex chemical analysis of all of the dimensions which enter into that grain of wheat will make it possible to reproduce exactly that substance even to the retaining all of its attributes.

If the premises above stated are sound and the facts are true, it must necessarily follow that the states of motion which produce genero-active and radio-active explosions must in some manner be related to the power of matter to appear to attract and repel.

If varying potentials have varying power to appear to attract or repel, the force which we call repulsion must necessarily be a variable and relative force. The variability and relativity of this force must be dependable upon the relative potential position of that force.

If these premises are well founded then the seventeenth dimension must be taken into consideration in the writing of the laws of gravitation and radiation.

It must necessarily follow that the attributes of attraction and repulsion which seem to belong to matter are merely illusions in respect to matter for they belong to motion only.

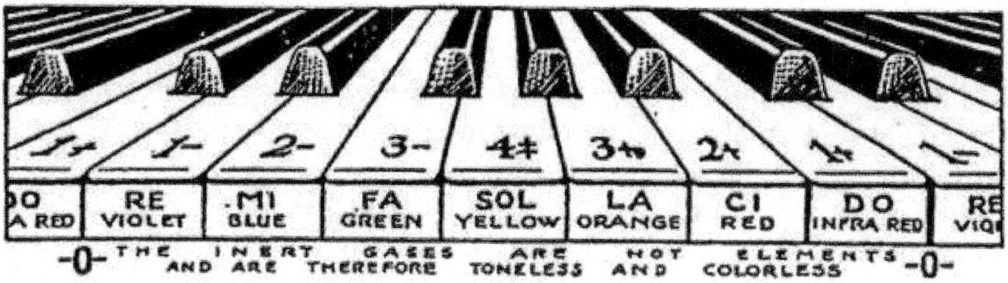

CHAPTER XXVIII

CONCLUSION

The purport of these writings is to illumine the road leading to eternal life by knowledge of the journey through illusion and back again to reality, taken by man in his repeated adventures in time, space and motion.

In order to illumine the way it is first necessary to trace the simulations, reflections and illusions of the apparently many substances, forms and things back to their base in the reality of the One thing.

In attempting to do so it has been possible in this one volume to touch the very fundamentals but lightly in order to correct existing misconcepts.

Even though later volumes will consider the very many effects of motion in great detail, the basic principle of the one cause of the many effects will not be enlarged upon.

It cannot be enlarged upon.

This brief concluding chapter is written to draw from all that has heretofore been written the one lesson that all that man calls "the created universe" is but an illusion of the forms of ideas thought out by Mind.

Ideas, and their expression in form have no existences whatsoever. They are unreal. They are but images conjured up by the image making faculty of Mind in the ecstasy of thinking.

Their appearance of existence is due solely to motion and limited to the effects of motion.

Increase motion-in-opposition and every effect of the illusion intensifies to its limitation in the simulation in non-motion-in-opposition of the universal white light of Mind.

Decrease motion-in-opposition and every effect of the illusion nebulizes and eventually disappears into the white light of non-motion-in-inertia.

Every idea is constantly changing.

Every effect of motion is constantly changing. Changing things can have no existence.

On the contrary, all that man calls the undependable unreality of the unseen universe, is in fact the only reality.

Mind is the only real thing in the universe and Mind is all that is.

Mind is the only substance in the universe. There is no other substance.

Thinking Mind is the only living thing in the universe. The thinking of Mind is the life principle of the One substance.

Thinking Mind evolves ideas and registers them in form through motion.

Man's physical universe of solids of matter is an aggregation of the forms of ideas thought out by Mind and held in suspense for a time.

If these premises are well founded one can more intelligently answer the supreme question "What is God?"

If there is but One substance, One Being, One Mind, One force, and that One is the only existing reality, must not that One be that which we term God?

If all that which we know as form is but the changing illusion of the image making faculty of thinking Mind, then God must be formless and unchanging.

If there is but One Mind and man is admittedly Mind, then is not the form of man unreal and the real man formless?

If the real man is formless and the image of man is but an illusion of his thinking, is not that illusion of man self creating?

And is man not also God?

And are not all things also God?

Are not all things the One thing, thinking out the several ideas of the One real thing in the appearance of many unreal things?

Is not that which we call "heaven" but an image of man's thinking.

If the statement herein made that form has no existence, and that nothing in this universe has time, place or position, is in accord with the laws of motion herein formulated then it must follow that man's "heaven" and "hell" must be illusions.

If such places exist they must be somewhere IN the universe. They cannot be extraneous to it.

If they exist within the universe their existence must have dimension.

If they are dimensionable they must be subject to the laws of changing things.

There is no "part" of the universe which enjoys the special privilege of immunity from the laws of gravitation and radiation.

Man's "heaven" and "hell" are but illogical concepts of the outer mind. The inner Mind rejects such unwholesome imaginings.

They are traditions, inherited from an age of superstition, of ignorance of nature's laws, of fear, of belief in an avenging God, and of an attitude of mind which demanded the miraculous as a deific qualification.

Man is self creative as all idea of Mind is self creative.

That which we call "self" is but the changing form of idea thought out by the unchanging formless One. Individuality, therefore, is non-existent except as it appears to exist in things of changing form.

If individuality is only an effect of more or less sustained motion and ceases with cessation of motion then individuality disappears with form at the passing point of absolute inertia in the cycle of motion.

If individuality and form is an idea only and sustained in the appearance of existence by the electromagnetic force of thinking, then that which man calls God cannot have form nor can the attribute of individuality be attributed to Him.

God must be, can only be, universal.

If God is universal then all else is universal.

If God is omnipresent, omnipotent and omniscient then all the universe is omnipresent, omnipotent and omniscient.

When man learns that God is Mind, that Mind is the One living, pulsing, thinking force, and that HE is that force, then man will have arrived at another stage in his evolution.

When man learns that true thinking is an equilibrium of action and reaction, and that untrue thinking is unequal and opposed action and reaction, and when he further learns that he must suffer the consequences of his unequal actions by paying the penalty through the reaction in accordance with the absolute law from which there is no appeal to God or man, he will then think true.

When man learns that all his thinking is electro-chemically recorded in the heavy master- I tones which constitute a record of the evolving idea of his self creating soul, and when he finds that a badly opposed record will keep him centuries behind more equally opposed ones, he will then have a thought as to the kind of a soul he is creating.

When man learns that this universe of solid things is but a reflection of the ideas of those things, and that he is but a simulation of the idea of himself being thought out in eternity by himself, then he will know the ecstasy of inner thinking.

Age and "death" are but sequences alternating with youth and life.

These two opposing effects of motion are born together but each travels a different direction along the wave of life. They pass each other at maturity where generation of one sequential life ends and its degeneration begins, only to meet again at the inertial plane of eternal life where degeneration ends and regeneration begins in another change of preponderance for another journey through time, space and motion.

There is no "death."

There is no darkness.

There is only life in this universe of light. God is life.

God is light.

God is all that is.

Just so long as man looks for the God-force outside of nature and outside of himself, just so long as he bows in fear to the personal deity of his early inheritance, he will be the slave of his own imaginings.

To know that the universal force is Mind, and that man and all else that is is Mind, is to inspire man with the ecstasy of inner thinking.

The God-force speaks to inspired man of inner thinking in the universal language of light which all may understand when they but desire to understand.

Few there have been but countless numbers there will be who will know the light of inner thinking. Gautama, the Buddha, knew it faintly as Mohammed later knew it.

Abraham dimly visioned it.

Jacob knew the light less vaguely. The symbol of the Shekinah was his ecstatic visioning.

Moses knew the ecstasy of inner thinking in greater clarity.

Abraham lived again in Jacob, and in Moses, and again in David.

David and the prophets of his primitive day knew the light more clearly still and left a symbol of the seven lights so that others to come might know that they knew tonal laws of evolving and devolving things.

David lived again in Jesus.

Jesus, the Nazarene, knew the universal language of light in all its fullness.

He knew the ecstasy of inner thinking as no man has ever known it.

He knew the structure of the atom as no one before or since has known it.

Jesus knew the universality of all things, the One-ness of all things. He gave that knowledge to the then dull witted, brutal, lustful, loveless world in His much needed message of brotherly love. He lived again in John, and Paul, and Plotinus, and all those messengers who knew the light of universal thinking.

In Jesus day man was not ready for the fullness of His mighty teachings.

Man was still new. He was still in the ferment of his intellectual brewing, still searching for the avenging god of tradition to whom he could appeal for preferential rulings.

Jesus gave to man the One great message of all time. He taught the universality of all things in the white light of the universal One of impartial love from Whose rulings there is no appeal. But only a few could faintly understand.

Today the world is ready and eagerly awaits the completion of His message.

When Jesus said: "I have yet many things to say unto you, but ye cannot bear them now," he referred to His complete knowledge of the universal force.

When he further promised, as recorded in the 16th Chapter of John, that the Spirit of truth will again come to "guide you into all truth" and "he will show you things to come," He prophesied the completion from time to time of His unfinished message as evolving man is able to "bear" (comprehend) that message.

The illumination of the immaculate light was complete in Jesus.

Those messengers of the light who will complete His message to man will comprehend the fullness of His annointing in the light from His words: "All things that the Father bath are mine: therefore said I, that he shall take of mine, and shall skew it unto you."

Jesus gave to man sufficient unto his day and wisely withheld that which should be for another day.

That which is herein translated from the light and that which is yet to come, will be for the day of man now dawning.

All who desire to know the light of universal thinking can know it when they can but comprehend effects of cause sufficiently well to recollect from within their inner Minds the light of cause.

When that day comes to man he will then know that:

Everything that is must be of everything else that is.

Nothing can be of itself alone.

There can be no two of anything in the universe, two substances, two Minds or two beings. All things are universal. ONE.

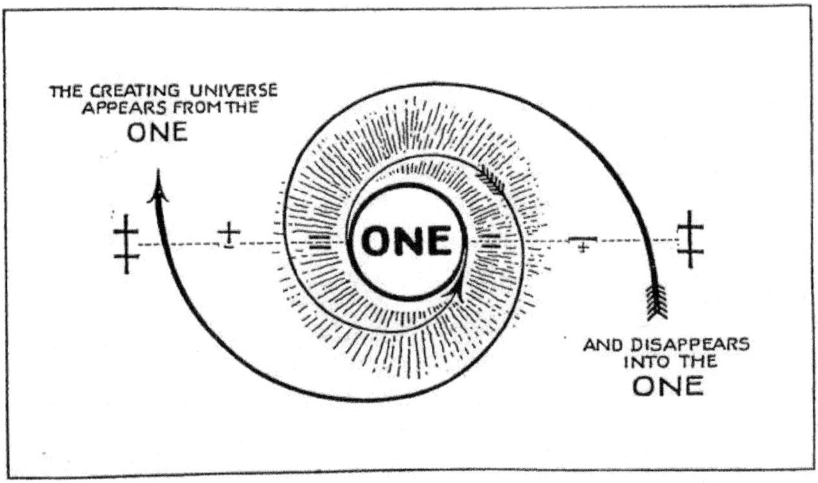

And now it will be well to pause for a time in the ecstatic work of translating the immaculate light of universal thinking into words for which man has made no words, to the end that man may assimilate that which is herein written down and thus prepare himself for further revelations of the light.

Consider well these words for by knowledge of universal cause alone can man hope to comprehend universal effect.

Faith and belief will in no wise open the doors of heaven to man. They but point out the path which leads to them. Through comprehension alone can man hope to know the language of light. And when that day comes to waiting man then will he know that truth, beauty and love, in equilibrium, are the very foundations of universal existence.

When he acquires the stability of perfect balance in his thinking, then will he be ready for the light; and for the ecstasy of universal thinking in the knowledge of all things; and for all-power within universal limitations; and for all-presence in unity with the One.

NEW LAWS AND PRINCIPLES

1. The material substance of Mind cannot evade its materialization into the form desired by Mind.
2. The whole idea of all things is in the seed of all things.
3. All thinking is creating that which it is thinking.
4. All idea, and all forms of idea are the result of union between equal or unequal opposite actions and reactions of force.
5. Unions of opposed actions and reactions are possible only within certain limitations. When union does not take place there can be no reproduction
6. Equal and opposite actions and reactions, when united, are satisfied in their unions and will remain united. . .
7. Stable unions will always reproduce true to species.
8. Unequal and opposite actions and reactions, when united, are unsatisfied in their unions and will always seek their true tonal mates .
9. Unstable unions never reproduce true to species.
10. Unstable unions tend to return to their separate tonal states. . .
11. If either mate in an unstable union finds a more equal mate, it will always leave the former and go to the latter.
12. No idea of Mind has place or position in time or space. All idea is universal.
13. All mass is regenerated by absorption of the impacting radio-active energy of all other mass.
14. All mass is degenerated by its own radiation.
15. All mass is generated by accumulation of the universal constant of energy into higher potential. . . .
16. That which is generated must be radiated.
17. All opposite effects of motion are simultaneous in their expression. . .

18. The coefficient of cold for an expanded volume of mass of low pressure and potential becomes the coefficient of heat for the same mass in a contracted volume of higher pressure and higher potential.

19. In any wave the induction current seeks the high pressure at the apex of its cone of energy and the conductive current seeks the low pressure at its base.

20. Everything that is, is of everything else that is. Nothing is of itself alone. All created things are indissolubly united.

21. There are no unconditioned facts of matter in a universe of motion. There are but appearances of facts...

22. The greater the pressure the higher the freezing point.

23. The lesser the pressure the lower the freezing point. 24. No state of motion ever began or ever ended.

24. All mass is both electric and magnetic.

25. All mass simultaneously expresses both opposites of all effects of motion, and each opposite is cumulatively preponderant in sequence.

26. All electromagnetic mass forms into systems of units which revolve in spiral orbits both centripetally toward and centrifugally away from nucleal centers.

27. All preponderantly charging systems are positive systems

28. All preponderantly discharging systems are negative systems. . .

29. All preponderantly contracting systems are positive systems.

30. All preponderantly expanding systems are negative systems. . .

31. All systems whose spirals are preponderantly closing spirals are positive systems.

32. All systems whose spirals are preponderantly opening spirals are negative systems.

33. All systems of preponderantly lessening volume are positive systems. . .

34. All systems of preponderantly increasing volume are negative systems.

35. All systems of preponderantly increasing potential are positive systems.

36. All systems of preponderantly lowering potential are negative systems. .

37. All preponderantly integrating systems are positive systems.

38. All preponderantly disintegrating systems are negative systems. . .

39. All preponderantly generating systems are positive systems.

40. All preponderantly radiating systems are negative systems. All preponderantly heating systems are positive systems 43. All preponderantly cooling systems are negative systems.

41. Electricity attracts, magnetism repels.

42. Electricity and magnetism move in opposite directions, their departure from each other being at 180°...

43. Electric lines of force approach each other at 180°

44. Magnetic lines of force depart from the line of direction of electric force and also of magnetic force at 180°.

45. Electric energy reproduces itself by induction and dissipates itself by conduction, at an angle of 90° to the lines of direction of induction and conduction. . .

46. All mass is potential out of place, and all mass constantly seeks the proper pressure zone for its constantly changing potential

47. Positive charge attracts positive charge and expels negative discharge.. . .

48. Negative discharge repels both negative discharge and positive charge. .

49. The union of an action with its reaction is always followed by the reproduction of separate actions and reactions...

50. All mass is generated and regenerated by a contractive pressure exerted in the direction of its gravitative center. Its minimum of generative pressure is exerted from its equatorial plane and its maximum pressure from its pole.

51. All mass is radiated and diffused by an expansive pressure exerted in the direction of its surface. Its minimum of radiative pressure is exerted from its pole and its maximum from its equatorial plane.

52. The generation of all energy is accomplished only through the resistance exerted against the direction of the force of any established motion. . .

53. X in power-time dimension is the square root of X in speed-time distance-area dimension and its cube root in volúme.

54. The radiation of all energy is accomplished only by the assistance, exerted in the direction of the force, of any established motion.

55. High potential is generated from low potential against an accumulating pressure resistance equal, in inverse ratio, to the cube of the equilibrium pressure of the low potential, and is degenerated with equal pressure assistance in direct ratio

56. All motion begins in the plus, contractive, endothermic impulse of thinking, and ends in the succeeding minus, expansive, exothermic impulse.. .

.

57. In any mass a change in temperature is in inverse ratio to a change in volume.

58. The greater the positive charge, the greater the pressure of contraction. .

59. The greater the pressure of contraction, the less the volume.

60. The greater the negative discharge, the greater the pressure of expansion.

61. The greater the pressure of expansion, the less the volume.

62. Every pressure develops an exactly equal and opposite resisting pressure.

63. In every mass, the attraction of the accumulating pressure and the repulsion of the distributing pressure exert their forces in opposite directions.

64. In any mass the lifting capacity, in relation to high potential, is equal to the compression capacity in relation to low potential.

65. The degeneration of any mass is exactly balanced by the regeneration of another mass.

66. Every mass has the relative apparent ability to attract and to repel every other mass, its relative ability depending on its relative potential...

67. Every ody attracts and repels every other body with a force which increases and decreases in the universal ratios in accordance with its potential position and according to whether the direction of the mass is toward the north pr toward the south. .

68. Any compound mass of varying, plane will eventually separate into its constituents, each of which will find its true position in its own plane and pressure zone.

69. In any mass its constant of centripetal force is its constant of power to attract.

70. In any mass its constant of centrifugal force is its constant of power to repel.

71. Increase in density means decrease in axial of speed-time dimension and increase in orbital of power-time...

72. Activity never lessens and inactivity never increases because of any change of dimension.

73. Every expression of motion has its equal and opposite expression...

74. There can be no increase or decrease in any effect of motion without a balancing increase or decrease in its opposite effect.

75. The power to attract lessens as volume increases.

76. The power to repel also lessens as volume increases.

77. In any mass the decrease in volume is in exact proportion to the increase in its potential.

78. In any mass the decrease in volume is in exact proportion to the increase in positive charge, contraction pressure and temperature.

79. In any mass the greater its speed of revolution, the greater its power to attract and to repel.

80. In any mass the greater its speed of rotation, the less its power to attract and to repel.

81. All mass is simultaneously electric and magnetic, but preponderantly one or the other cumulatively in endless repeative sequence.

82. All mass simultaneously revolves and rotates though one effect is always preponderant while the other one is preparing for its right of preponderance.

83. All opposite effects of motion are simultaneous in the expression of their sex opposition but preponderant in sequence in each sex expression.

84. All idea is repeative and no effect of motion once started ever ends...

85. The relative ability of a substance to attract and to repel is in the same ratio as the increase or decrease of the opposing pressures and other di-

mensions which determine the potential of a charging or discharging system. . .

86. In any mass the apparent ability to attract increases with increase of positive charge and decrease of volume; also the apparent ability to repel increases with increase of negative discharge and decrease of volume...

87. In any mass the preponderance of the apparent ability to attract or to repel is proportionate to its preponderance of positive charge or negative discharge.

88. In any mass increase of positive charge is accompanied by increase of negative discharge in universal ratio until the conductivity of negative discharge exceeds the inductivity of positive charge, in accordance with the universal law of sequential preponderance of all opposite effects of motion.

89. All mass constantly runs the entire gamut of every dimension of the wave of energy of which it is a swirling part, until it has run the entire cycle represented by that wave. . .

90. No mass can remain fixed in position, not even that which has been apparently arrested in its motion. . .

91. There is a true position for every potential.

92. Every change of dimension in a mass changes all the dimensions in the mass.

93. Accelerated revolution charges. Charging bodies attract.

94. Accelerated rotation discharges. Discharging bodies repel.

95. The ability of one mass to attract another depends upon the relative positive charge of each and its relative position in respect to other masses. .

96. The ability of one mass to repel another depends upon the relative negative discharge of each and its relative position in respect to other masses. .

97. The cycle of a wave is an orderly progression in the universal direction from south to north by the way of east, and back again to south by the way of west.

98. All masses revolve from the west toward the east around the nucleal centers of their systems throughout the entire cycle of their waves..

99. All masses rotate upon axes throughout the entire cycle of their waves from the west toward the east of their masses.

100. Form in motion is a reflection of concept in inertia

101. All direction is an effect of gravitation and radiation.

102. All gravitative effects are electrically dominated.

103. All gravitative effects are the result of inhalation.

104. All radiative effects are magnetically dominated.

105. All radiative effects are the result of exhalation...

106. Electricity moves always in the direction of north, by the way of east.

107. Magnetism moves always south, by the way of west

108. In every mass the maximum exertion of the easterly force of contraction is within the charging areas of the generative cones of which the pole of rotation is the axis.

109. In every mass the maximum exertion of the westerly force of expansion is within the discharging areas of the radiative cones of which the equator is the base.

110. Contraction is centripetal and expansion is centrifugal.

111. The increase of centripetal force of any mass is in the direction of generation, and the increase of centrifugal force is in the direction of radiation.

112. Centripetal force accumulates and centrifugal force dissipates. . .

113. Mass is accumulated in the direction of its generation, and dissipated in the direction of its radiation...

114. Centripetal force decelerates rotation and accelerates revolution. . .

115. Centrifugal force accelerates rotation and decelerates revolution...

116. The deceleration of rotation is in the direction of generation and deceleration of revolution is in the direction of radiation

117. All vortices turn from west to east and their apices point to north...

118. All dimensions contract in the direction of electric force and expand in the direction of magnetic force in universal ratio

119. Every effort of motion which is added to must be equally subtracted from

120. Every plus pressure total must be balanced by a minus one to maintain a system in equilibrium.

121. All temperature dimensions of expanding mass increase in their expansion dimension, registering greater cold, and decrease in their contraction dimension, registering greater heat.

122. The seven tones of the universal constant are consecutively removed, one from the other, the square of the distance to the next highest potential. The energy of each of the four units is exactly equal to that of each of the others.

123. All dimensions are pressure dimensions.

124. All dimensions simultaneously expand and contract in opposite directions of the same ratio.

125. Expansion pressure is in direct ratio to the square of the distance, area, plane, orbit or time unit, and to the cube of the volume.

126. Contraction pressure is in inverse ratio to the square of the distance, area, plane, orbit or time unit, and to the cube of the volume.

127. Every mass in the universe occupies a measurable potential position. . .

128. Every particle of matter in this universe is connected with every other particle of matter by electric charging poles which are the controls of opposing electromagnetic cones of energy.

129. The nearer to the axis and to the apex of the cone the greater the density, temperature, pressure, potential, power-time and all effects of electropositive preponderance. . .

130. The nearer the base of the cone the greater the tenuity, the speed-time and the tendency to ionize, and the lower the temperature, pressure, potential and all effects of electronegative preponderance.

131. The apparent relative ability of mass to attract and to repel is governed by the contraction of its polar magnetic bases and the expansion of its ecliptic.

132. The greater the expansion of the ecliptic and the greater the diameters of precessional orbits, the less the ability of a mass to attract and to re-

pel.

133. The less the expansion of the ecliptic, and the less the diameters of the precessional orbits, the greater the ability of a mass to attract and to repel.

134. In any mass the diameters of its polar magnetic bases and of its axial precessional orbits increase as the mass recedes from, and decrease as it approaches its nucleal sun's equatorial plane.

135. In any mass the expansion of its ecliptic, the diameters of its equatorial precessional orbits and of its polar magnetic bases increase as the mass recedes from, and decrease as it approaches its nucleal sun's equatorial plane.

136. In any mass, north is the gravitative-radiative center where the apparent ability to attract and to repel is at its maximum

137. South is an extension of the equatorial plane which divides any mass. It is that part of mass where radiative emanations are at their maximum.

138. In any mass the area of its ecliptic expansion, the areas of its polar magnetic bases, and the positions of its charging poles are governed by the oblateness of the mass...

139. In any mass as oblateness decreases, polar magnetic bases and ecliptic expansion decrease their areas, and charging poles draw closer to its pole of rotation.

140. All motion appears in mass and disappears in plane.

141. The evolution of mass from plane to sphere and its diffusion back to plane are by the way of the cone...

142. The greater the complexity of any state of motion, the greater the interval of reproduction of that state of motion.

143. The reproductive speed of genero-active light decreases in lowering octaves in inverse universal ratio, and radio-active speed increases in lowering octaves in direct ratio...

144. The lower the potential, the greater the speed of reproduction.

145. Every effect of motion in any octave is repeated in sequence in the various speeds of every other octave...

146. Every effect of motion is cumulative and repeative within its accumulation.

147. Displacement and replacement are universally simultaneous. . .

148. An action calculated to displace is simultaneously accompanied by a reaction to replace. All gravitational and radiational expressions are simultaneous in their opposition.

149. All effects of motion are simultaneously opposed, but their repeative acts are sequential.

150. Contracting, generating bodies decelerate the speed of rotation of inner planets by proximity. . .

151. Deceleration of rotation of the planets of a system increases the surface tension pressure of a system. . .

152. The greater the deceleration of rotation, the greater the centripetal force of contraction pressure...

153. Acceleration of rotation of the planets of a system decreases the surface tension pressure of a system. . .

154. The opposites of all effects of motion vary in the opposites of their several dimensions in the direct and the inverse of the universal ratios. . .

155. Time and power appear by lengthening the day and shortening the year, and disappear by reversing these effects...

156. Heating bodies approach each other and recede from cooling bodies..

157. Expanding bodies recede from expanding and from contracting bodies.

158. Cooling bodies recede from cooling and from heating bodies.

159. Expanding bodies seek lower pressure equilibriums. 164. Contracting bodies seek higher pressure equilibriums.

160. Heating bodies charge. Charging bodies raise potential.

161. Cooling bodies discharge. Discharging bodies lower potential.

162. Radiating and radiated bodies seek equilibrium positions in lower pressure zones appropriate to their lowered potentials.

163. The greater the resistance of opposing pressures, the higher the melting point of a mass. The less the resistance of opposing pressures, the lower the melting point of a mass.

164. Every effect of motion is cumulative and repeative within its accumulation.

165. Every effect of motion in any octave is repeated in sequence in the various speeds of every other octave. .

166. In every wave the constant of its cone volume in inertia is the constant of the volume of all masses in motion within the wave.

167. In any mass the speed of rotation of bound energy increases in the direct universal ratio from the gravitative center of force.

168. In any system the speed of revolution of separated equal masses of bound energy revolving in the same plane, decreases in the inverse universal ratio from the center of force.

169. In any system accelerated revolution increases power-time dimension and accelerated rotation increases speed-time dimension.

170. In any mass decelerated rotation increases power-time dimension and decelerated revolution increases speed-time dimension.

171. In any mass or system the decrease in rotation or revolution is in inverse universal ratio and is balanced by a corresponding increase of the opposite effect in direct ratio.

172. The greater the resistance the greater the generation of power and the less its dissipation in speed.

173. The less the resistance the less the generation of power and the greater its dissipation in spud.

174. The greater the resistance to an action of force the greater the genero-activity

175. The greater the genero-activity the greater the power of mass to absorb heat.

176. The less the resistance to the reaction of force, the greater the radioactivity

177. The greater the radio-activity the greater the power of mass to give out its heat

178. All mass rolls along the floors of space upon that part of its surface where radiation is at a maximum. . .

179. Every equal area of the orbit of any mass must be covered in an equal interval of time.

180. The greater the inclination of any conic section to the base of the cone, the greater the eccentricity of an orbit

181. The acceleration of attraction is always toward the perihelion of an orbit and the deceleration of repulsion is always toward its aphelion. . .

182. In any mass the aphelion of every orbit is the point of maximum exhalation and the beginning of inhalation.

183. In any mass the perihelion of every orbit is the point of maximum inhalation an d the beginning of exhalation.

184. The interval of time between one exhalation-inhalation of any mass is the standard unit year of that mass.

185. The greater the angle of the reflecting plane of forming mass to the plane of concept in inertia, the greater the positive charge and negative discharge of that mass and consequently the greater its ability to appear to attract and to repel. . .

186. Preponderance of power of mass to appear to attract increases as the reflecting plane progresses through the tonal positions of 1+ 2+ and 3+ to its maximum at 4++.

187. Preponderance of power of mass to appear to repel increases as the reflecting plane progresses through the tonal positions of 1— 2— and 3 — to its maximum at 4++.

188. The greater the expansion of the ecliptic plane area of forming mass the less the positive charge and negative discharge of that mass and consequently the less its to appear to attract and repel...

189. Preponderance of power of mass to appear to attract and to repel increases as expansion of ecliptic plane area decreases

190. In any mass the lower the octave the higher the potential and the slower the speed of reproduction of any effect of motion.

191. In any mass the higher the octave the lower the potential and the greater the speed of reproduction of any effect of motion.

192. In any mass the lower the octave the greater the wave dimension and the lower its tonal registration in sound.

193. In any mass the higher the octave the smaller the wave dimension and the higher its tonal registration in sound.

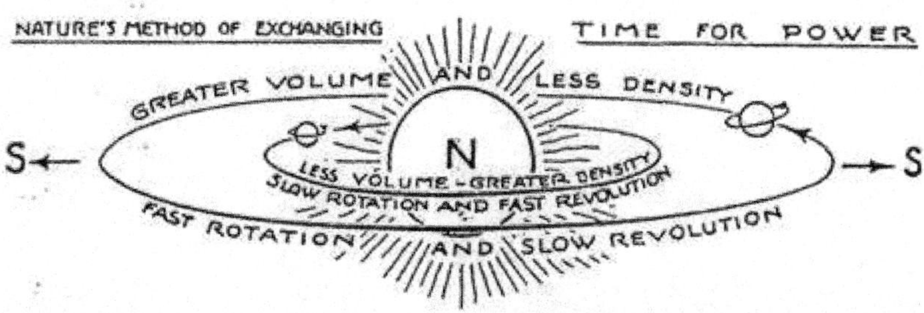

Swannanoa—Headquarters of The University of Science and Philosophy

Sculpture Gardens of the Works of Walter and Lao Russell

Printed in Dunstable, United Kingdom

73140019R00248